THE THIRD WORLD BEYOND THE COLD WAR

The Third World beyond the Cold War
Continuity and Change

LOUISE FAWCETT

and

YEZID SAYIGH

OXFORD
UNIVERSITY PRESS

OXFORD

UNIVERSITY PRESS

Great Clarendon Street, Oxford OX2 6DP

Oxford University Press is a department of the University of Oxford
It furthers the University's objective of excellence in research, scholarship,
and education by publishing worldwide in

Oxford New York

Athens Auckland Bangkok Bogotá Buenos Aires Calcutta
Cape Town Chennai Dar es Salaam Delhi Florence Hong Kong Istanbul
Karachi Kuala Lumpur Madrid Melbourne Mexico City Mumbai
Nairobi Paris São Paulo Shanghai Singapore Taipei Tokyo Toronto Warsaw

with associated companies in Berlin Ibadan

Oxford is a registered trade mark of Oxford University Press
in the UK and in certain other countries

Published in the United States
by Oxford University Press Inc., New York

British Library Cataloguing in Publication Data

Data available

Library of Congress Cataloging in Publication Data

The Third World beyond the Cold War: continuity and change / [edited
by] Louise Fawcett and Yezid Sayigh.
1. Developing countries—Politics and government.   2. Developing
countries—Social conditions.   I. Fawcett, Louise L'Estrange.
II. Ṣāyigh, Yazīd
D883.T45   1999   306'.091734—dc21   98–49341
ISBN 0–19–829550–2
ISBN 0–19–829551–0 (pbk)

1 3 5 7 9 10 8 6 4 2

Typeset by Hope Services (Abingdon) Ltd.
Printed in Great Britain
on acid-free paper by
Biddles Ltd.,
Guildford & King's Lynn

ACKNOWLEDGEMENTS

This book forms part of the output of the Research Programme on 'Developing States in a Changing World Order' supported by the John D. and Catherine T. MacArthur Foundation and based at the Centre for International Studies, Oxford. We would like to thank the MacArthur Foundation for its support. Institutional support, hospitality, and secretarial assistance were also provided by Exeter College and St Catherine's College. Louise Fawcett is grateful to Robert O'Neill and Adam Roberts for their advice and encouragement, to St Catherine's College Fellows' Secretary, Aby Bidwell, for her valuable assistance, and to Eduardo Posada for supplying helpful comments and suggestions.

CONTENTS

NOTE ON CONTRIBUTORS

AMITAV ACHARYA is Associate Professor at the Department of Political Science, York University, Toronto, Canada.

ROLAND DANNREUTHER is Lecturer in International Relations in the Department of Politics at the University of Edinburgh

LOUISE FAWCETT is the Wilfrid Knapp Fellow and Tutor in Politics at St Catherine's College, Oxford.

JORGE HEINE is ambassador at the Chilean Embassy in Pretoria.

P. R. KUMARASWAMY is Research Fellow at the Harry S. Truman Institute, The Hebrew University, Jerusalem, Israel.

S. NEIL MACFARLANE is the Lester B. Pearson Professor in International Relations at the University of Oxford.

YEZID SAYIGH is Assistant Director of the Centre of International Studies at Cambridge University.

GAUTAM SEN is Lecturer and Course Tutor in the Politics of the World Economy at the Department of International Relations, London School of Economics.

KEITH SOMERVILLE is Executive Producer, BBC News and Current Affairs at the BBC World Service.

RICHARD STUBBS is Professor and Chair at Department of Political Science, McMaster University, Canada.

Introduction

LOUISE FAWCETT AND YEZID SAYIGH

Unravelling the different strands of change since the end of the old bipolar order continues to present a far more complex and protracted task than many imagined. Not surprisingly, a number of assumptions about putative new world orders have already been challenged. After the cold war, not unreasonably, expectations about the prospects for greater peace and security were high. So, perhaps less reasonably, were expectations about the universal acceptance of prevailing Western political and economic values. Victory in the cold war and globalization, now unfettered, lent substance to such hopes and seemed to point the way to an international reality where—as different scholars predicted—history, geography, and ideology would become things of the past, subsumed in a new, highly interpenetrated and interconnected international order. This admittedly utopian vision had parallels in idealist thinking after the First and Second World Wars: the end of a major war, even a 'cold' one, not unnaturally gives rise to hopes for the evolution of a just, peaceful, and prosperous international order.[1]

The post-cold war order, like those that followed the two world wars, has not of course conformed in entirety to this utopian picture, arguably least of all where parts of the Third World—the subject of this book—are concerned.[2] To be sure, some very real progress has been made: it would be wrong to make hasty judgements based on the experience of a mere decade or so, or to overlook the real benefits that the end of the cold war has brought. First and foremost of these, the end of the rivalry between the United States and the Soviet Union has had a major impact on international security.[3] The threat of a nuclear conflagration, along with other types of conflict of lower intensity, has been substantially reduced and so has military expenditure in many countries. Indeed, some major cold war-related conflicts have been successfully brought to an end. Intervention may not be a thing of the past—witness the recent examples of Somalia, Haiti, and former Yugoslavia—but its uses are clearly different and more highly circumscribed.[4] International trade has greatly expanded into areas previously placed off limits by the cold war, giving new meaning to the notion of economic interdependence. The joint effect of the breakdown of ideological and technological barriers has greatly enhanced the prospects for international cooperation and communication at all levels—between states, groups, and individuals. At the level of international organization, the United Nations and regional agencies enjoy new authority and legitimacy. Finally, moves toward the establishment and consolidation of democratic forms of governance have been made in a growing list of countries from Eastern Europe to Latin America and Africa.[5]

There is of course a down side. First, the real benefits that the end of the cold war has brought have been very unevenly distributed; and second, they have been accompanied by some unpleasant side effects. The admittedly powerful forces of integration at work in the international system—present, but less intense before the close of the 1980s—have gone hand in hand with the perhaps less powerful, but none the less highly destabilizing forces of disintegration.[6] Take security, for example. The reduction in interstate conflict has often been matched with an acceleration and intensification of sub-state level conflicts. In states with long-standing ethnic, religious, linguistic, or cultural divides, the end of the cold war has helped unleash and aggravate old rivalries and tensions. Where such newer types of conflict have replaced the older, more familiar disputes that characterized the post-1945 period, the post-cold war peace dividend is hard to perceive. Similarly for some states, growing economic interdependence and globalization *without* the mitigating effects of the cold war has further widened the gap between them and the advanced industrialized countries, producing a dangerous marginalization and tendency towards introspection. The prospects for improved cooperation between states that are weak, poor, and marginalized are not good, while entry to the rich men's clubs is still barred to all but the privileged few. So again for some groups of states, the promise of a new dawn for international institutions has been slow to arrive. So has democratization. In parts of the world democracy's 'Third Wave' has passed by almost unnoticed. In others, and the African subcontinent provides perhaps the best example,[7] it remains a fragile and even reversible process.

No one can deny the massive centripetal pull that the successful Western model exercises over the rest of the world. Yet if we consider the export of the whole package that comprises Western capitalism and liberal democracy, we find a highly problematic and differentiated picture. It is not merely that some states have been unable to engage with the forces of economic and political liberalization. They have also been unwilling, for reasons that some have described as cultural or civilizational. Without embracing the broader Huntington thesis, one can see that one of his key arguments—that the primary distinctions between peoples today are not political, ideological, or economic but cultural—has certain resonance.[8] Conversely it can be argued that it is precisely because of differences in cultural values, and consequently in the political institutions that purport to defend them, that it is economic attributes that are most widely shared and most easily transmitted globally.[9]

How then are we to understand the end of the cold war a decade after its demise? Was it a turning or 'punctuation' point in history comparable to the end of the First or Second World Wars?[10] Has it given birth to a radical new international landscape, and if so what are its principal contours and features? How successfully have a new generation of scholars explained the changed reality of world politics? This book addresses these questions from the perspective of that group of countries which in the cold war came to be known collectively as the 'Third World'.[11]

Turning to the specificities of the Third World case, the end of the cold war produced profound if often very varied consequences. At the very least it has demanded of developing states a reconsideration, if not a fundamental reform, of domestic and external policy. After the initial mixture of expectation and apprehension, the adaptation of policy to meet the exigencies of the changed international environment has been a relatively smooth process for some, an uphill struggle for others. Indeed as this volume shows, different developing countries slip into both the two post-cold war scenarios outlined above (with many falling somewhere between the two). There are the 'successes' or partial successes located principally, though not exclusively, among Pacific Rim and Latin American countries, and the 'failures', albeit with some striking exceptions, located notably in Africa, the Middle East, and South Asia. Why have some states fared so much better than others? State capacity would appear to be an essential ingredient for successful engagement with the international system, but what determines state capacity? Why do some states repeatedly underachieve?[12]

Christopher Clapham has suggested that the most significant recent development for Third World countries, surpassing even the end of the cold war in importance, has been the 'dramatic divergence in economic growth rates between different regions'.[13] One could go further. The end of the cold war has had the effect of exaggerating this divergence, further widening the gap between the haves and the have-nots. The new self-confidence and assertiveness of some developing countries has been matched by a growing sense of neglect, isolation, and vulnerability among others. Weak, poor, and unstable states have been deprived of any strategic leverage they once enjoyed and often, in the face of stiff competition from the emerging states of East and Central Europe and the former

Soviet Union, of aid and development assistance also. Certainly for a number of the developing countries discussed in this book, the end of the cold war would appear to have created as many problems as it has solved, or merely superimposed a new set of problems over old unsolved ones.

A few examples illustrate this point. Debt, poverty, and insecurity remain endemic in parts of the Third World and have not been signifi-cantly relieved by the end of the cold war.[14] Globalization has often exag-gerated inequality, exposing sharp distinctions in the capacities of weak and strong states.[15] It has given rise, among other things, to vertically inte-grated regional divisions of labour and horizontally diversified corporate strategies that limit state autonomy and undermine old notions of sover-eignty. An important consequence for the domestic level is the threat to democracy and human rights, as it is arguably national political institu-tions, rather than globalizing economic forces, that protect individual rights. This does not always reduce the pressure coming from above and below on states to democratize, but the irony is that where the challenge from below takes the form of resurgent ethnic, religious, or nationalist groups, with their concomitant demands for greater representation or autonomy, state legitimacy and integrity come under challenge.[16] This is so severe a challenge, indeed, as to give rise to the notion of 'failed states' in some cases and to prompt calls for the reconsideration of conventional conceptions of statehood and sovereignty.[17]

Conflict, intervention, and war are not things of the past, although their origins are increasingly internal rather than external to states. This may be a positive sign as far as international order is concerned, but the unman-ageability of present civil conflicts and their dangerous spillover effects leave little room for complacency. Not surprisingly, the desire to accumu-late weaponry of all kinds, to meet real or imaginary threats, has not diminished. Nuclear proliferation remains a very real threat, as the May 1998 test explosions in India and Pakistan demonstrated. Nor has the interest diminished on the part of the major arms suppliers (the five per-manent members of the United Nations Security Council) to continue supplying arms to potentially vulnerable states, constrained only by the decreasing ability of buyers to pay (due, for example, to declining oil rev-enues in the Gulf or to the financial crisis of 1997–8 in Asia).

Internationally, developing countries remain prey to the designs of the great powers but lack the comfort and relative stability that the cold war and its alliance systems offered. Admittedly those designs have changed: promoting regional security in a cold war context has at times given way to promoting good government and democratic practices, economic liber-alization and participation in regional and global institutions. All this may be entirely positive, but Western (in this case specifically US) zeal in promoting 'good practices' in Third World countries can have negative consequences when a country like Colombia is 'decertified' for failing to meet US expectations on anti-drugs policies, or Iran and Iraq are lumped together in a policy of 'dual containment'. Particularly worrying is the way in which the end of the cold war, in which old enemies tumbled, has encouraged Western countries to look for new enemies, new scapegoats.[18] The Third World is an obvious target, identified as it is with a plethora of new age woes, ranging from terrorism to refugees, environmental degradation, drugs trafficking, and human rights abuses, to name but the most prominent.

Of the list of accumulated problems that the Third World faces, many are hardly new and have little to do with the end of the cold war; others have been positively exacerbated by its consequences. Indeed there are those who argue that the impact of the end of the cold war on developing countries has been less than is often supposed, and that Third World politics are characterized as much by continuity as change.[19] One's perspective—as the content of this book shows—depends very much on one's vantage point as an observer. This book aims to disentangle some of these divergent views and reflect on the developments of recent years and on their implications for Third World countries.

A number of questions inform this volume. What has really changed in the Third World and what are the major explanations of change? How important is the end of the cold war? Have the changes brought about rendered necessary a redefinition of the Third World in terms of either its parameters or its key characteristics? There are, of course, no easy answers to these questions but this volume aims to provide a general framework within which change in the Third World might be understood and explained.

A central problem is one of definition. What does the Third World consist of and has its membership changed? In the long years of the cold war the Third World became a household term. Even if its boundaries were fluid and shifting and its meaning contested, the Third World was, in the eyes of most beholders, a tangible if 'imagined' community, standing in clear distinction to the First and the Second World.[20] Characterized by a common struggle, in Hedley Bull's words, 'to challenge the established dominance of the West and to secure their emergence as independent sovereign states',[21] the developing countries were united in their vulnerability, and increasingly in their frustration at existing world power structures.[22] Desire for change, to level the playing field, brought unity. There were other commonalities too. Inevitably drawn into the East–West conflict, the Third World also came to share a common security predicament, while becoming the principal locale for conflict in an international system conditioned by nuclear deterrence. For many, the answer lay in non-alignment.

The passage of time however, saw the weakening rather than the strengthening of the ties that bind developing countries, or perhaps revealed how fragile and transient the concept of a Third World identity had always been. After the decade of the 1970s which provided at least the temporary illusion of Third World solidarity in forums as diverse as OPEC (Organization of Petroleum Exporting Countries) and UNCTAD (United Nations' Conference on Trade and Development) the cutting edge of the Third World movement was blunted. Pointing to the growing diversity of developing countries in terms of wealth and power, Robert Gilpin claimed in the latter half of the 1980s that 'only the rhetoric of Third World unity remains'.[23] The end of the cold war, as noted, has aggravated the divisions further.

Certainly, at the present juncture of international politics the continued use of the term Third World needs explaining and defending. Indeed, there are those who dispute that it ever existed, except as a set of assumptions derived through contrast with the model offered by the industrialized nations of the 'First World'.[24] Beyond the cold war there is no longer a Second World, and there is considerable fluidity and movement between the former categories. If we measure the Third World in terms of economic criteria alone, it is still easy to identify the bottom of the pile, represented by states such as those identified by the World Bank as HIPCs (highly indebted poor countries). Yet it is also clear that a number of Third (and Second) World countries have risen, or are rising, into the once exclusive preserve of the First Worlders. A perhaps greater number of Second Worlders have meanwhile slipped in the opposite direction.[25] Nevertheless, the Asian economic crisis of 1997–8 may have highlighted the vulnerability of the NICs (newly industrializing countries) during the transition to OECD levels, but it can by no means be said to have returned them to the ranks of the Third World.

But are economic criteria the best or the only criteria to employ? One ambitious attempt to move beyond crude GDP figures is the Human Development Index, published by the United Nations Development Programme. This attempt to construct a broad index of human welfare, based on GDP, average life expectancy, and educational attainment, is not without its problems. While economic factors remain significant,[26] in the post-cold war era definitions that focus on indicators such as state-society relations or political culture, rather than poverty or superpower bipolarity, may come closer to the mark.[27] Certainly, old definitions and explanations seem less appropriate or at least are open to challenge. The once 'newly independent' states are now middle aged, their struggle with the West has become muted, and their security is no longer defined in East–West terms. Small wonder that the term 'Third World' is widely contested.

A definitional debate need not detain us here: it is a question raised by different contributors and one to which we will return in the conclusion. This book proceeds from the assumption, in line with conventional wisdom, that there *was* an identifiable Third World during the cold war. It is argued here that sufficient, if loose and fluid, commonalities did exist in the thirty or so years between the emergence of the Third World and the end of the cold war to justify the use of the collective term. And although there are new contenders for Third World or 'peripheral' status, just as there are members of the Third World who may no longer view themselves as belonging to this category, there is a general reluctance to drop the term altogether. The contributors to this volume seem to share the view that, while problematic, the term is still a useful one, if only as a starting-point from which to question old assumptions and seek new criteria appropriate to the post-cold war world.[28] The ambiguities surrounding the use of the term notwithstanding, the task of charting the progress of the 'old' Third World into the post-cold war era is valid and interesting. Indeed, given the amount of attention to which the Third World was subject in the cold war period, and the quantity of ink spent in trying not only to describe and explain its condition but also to question its very existence, it makes obvious sense to try to assess the progress of the concept 'beyond the cold war'.

This volume then attempts an overview of the changes brought about in Third World countries since the end of the cold war. It does this in two ways: using themes in order to highlight major areas of change in the Third World (Part I), and using geographical studies as a means of isolating changes specific to certain regions (Part II). The attempt to flag key thematic issues, before turning to look at specific regions, helps to provide some unity to what might otherwise be a very diverse picture. No Third World country has escaped the winds of change, although different countries and regions have been affected in very different ways. Combining a thematic and empirical approach is designed to overcome the high degree of generality implied in the former and the high degree of specificity implied in the latter. The book aims to cater for a variety of constituencies: those who seek the 'big picture' in understanding the Third World in International Relations; those who look for general patterns, explanations, and trends in Third World politics, and those who seek up-to-date information and analysis on the progress of different regions.

The themes chosen (economics, politics, and security) are not, of course, exhaustive, but are broadly interpreted so as to encompass the major areas of change among Third World countries. Without wishing to prejudge our conclusions, it might be argued that among these three themes there is still enough glue to hold together the developing countries as a category and to exclude a number of newer pretenders. Yet it is important to note, and we shall return to this in the conclusion, that the characteristics that today might be held to delineate a Third World may be very different from those prevailing when the term first came into use.

Part I starts with an introductory chapter by Neil MacFarlane that reworks some of the definitional and methodological issues touched on above and goes on to compare expectations with reality: to what extent has the end of the cold war done what we thought it would do, and what have been its less predictable consequences? One important conclusion is that experiences across the Third World are tremendously varied and that these variations have increased over time. This conclusion is shared to a lesser or greater extent by the three following chapters dealing with the three broad themes: economics, politics, and security.

In his chapter on the impact of economic liberalization and globalization, Gautam Sen contrasts the experiences of Chile and the Asian tigers to that of other Third World countries. He suggests that it was the combination of both specific local factors and underlying changes in the international political economy that accounts for the advance and variable speed of market reforms in different parts of the developing world. Thus the end of communism becomes not an explanation for liberalization, but rather an 'important background variable, apparently vindicating and propelling market forces world-wide'. He suggests that a more useful way of differentiating among developed and developing countries is the extent to which each is a price-maker or price-taker in various categories of international trade.

It was market forces and the freeing of economic systems in much of the Third World—a process that well predated the end of the cold war—that was to give rise to more persistent and strident demands for democracy. But economic liberalization is not necessarily accompanied by, nor leads inevitably to, political liberalization, a point made by both Sen and Roland Dannreuther. As highlighted in his chapter, the process of 'political liberalization' remains far from complete, despite widespread disillusionment with authoritarianism and the visible and at times dramatic impact of events in the Eastern bloc. Again the picture is very varied: in many countries where the internal preconditions for political liberalization simply do not exist, any commitment to democracy is weak at best. Further, the Western-oriented value system with which liberal democracy is identified is simply rejected as inappropriate by a number of ruling elites in Third World countries who posit alternative 'world'—notably Asian or Islamic—views.

Differing world views also affect the post-cold war security equation, the subject of the third thematic chapter by Amitav Acharya. The West's attempt to extend democracy in the Third World, like the North's attempt to impose an environmental regime on the South, may be seen as a subtle form of imperialism, demanding new vigilance by Third World countries. One solution tested more successfully by some developing countries than others is the building or strengthening of indigenous institutions enshrining regional values and mores.[29] More generally the removal of superpower 'overlay' and the reduced risk of conflicts becoming internationalized has strengthened local actors and allowed them greater autonomy. This, at least in the short term, has not promoted greater stability, especially in those Third World countries where security problems have multiplied as a result of the 'decompression effect' of the end of the cold war. Again, the source of insecurity here may be domestic rather than external.

A common concern of all authors in Part I has been to identify and describe major changes in the post-cold war landscape and to isolate, as far as possible, the extent to which the end of the cold war was an agent of change. Another concern has been to unearth the sources of change. This brings us to the heart of the so-called 'levels of analysis' problem which so tantalizes international relations scholars. Can change in the Third World be best understood by employing 'top down' or 'bottom up' models?[30] That is, does change at the level of the international system explain all, or should we be looking more closely at domestic forces as an important motor of that change? While in the past 'systemic' analyses were popular (and this was particularly true in the Third World context) now, in the post-cold war era, they seem less adequate. It is state capacity, as many contributors to this book argue, that is vital to understanding the different performance of developing countries in the international system.

This levels-of-analysis thread is carried over into the discussions of different regions in Part II, although again, contributors have their own views on the primacy of different levels, just as they have their own differing views of the impact of the end of the cold war on their region. Here the diversity and complexity so frequently alluded to in Part I is richly displayed: whether discussing economics, politics, or security, experiences vary tremendously from region to region (and often within regions themselves). Indeed it is worth noting here that any attempt to divide up the Third World into regions is perforce somewhat arbitrary and selective—perhaps more so than during the cold war, when the overlay of superpower rivalry emphasized the division of the Third World into distinct 'security complexes'[31]—but we have taken an expansive approach including all major regions where developing countries featured prominently in the cold war era: Latin America, Asia Pacific, Middle East, Africa, and South Asia. In these chapters the themes introduced in the first section are contemplated and discussed, as contributors have concerned themselves with painting the regional landscape before and after the cold war, again isolating the major sources of change.

Optimism is the keynote of Jorge Heine's chapter on Latin America. The region may not yet have 'turned the corner', but the end of the cold war has placed it in a strong international position. Liberalization, democratization, and high levels of interdependence characterize much of the continent. He dismisses the perception of a continent marginalized, and argues that the challenges of globalization and regionalization have been successfully met. Regional integration schemes have flourished and expanded, as the MERCOSUR experience in particular shows.

Is Latin America an exceptional case, or the exception that proves the rule? Other contributors to Part II are as cautious in their optimism, as they are in attributing change to the end of the cold war. The Asia Pacific, as Amitav Acharya and Richard Stubbs point out, is also in some ways exceptional, locating, as it does, some of the most successful economies of the developing world. Yet it has some important implications for developing countries. There economic growth has not gone hand in hand with political liberalization and enhanced regional security. In much of the Asia Pacific, democracy is contested and a potential source of instability to add to the insecurities attendant on continuing great power rivalries in the region.

Optimism is in even shorter supply in Keith Somerville's chapter on Africa. There post-cold war hopes for overnight transformation were quickly dashed and he finds, outside southern Africa at least, few enduring changes to the basic political, economic, and social structure, and little chance for the continent to make an exit from its peripheral status. For Africa, furthermore, there has been no 'peace dividend', as the Rwandan tragedy amply demonstrates. Indeed the post-cold war world is an inhospitable place where Africa has been deprived of any international role or influence that it once enjoyed. Only in the long term does the removal of foreign intervention, an increased commitment to more equitable and participatory economic and political systems, and to workable regional structures, point to a possible way forward.

The drying up of key sources of external support has had a far greater impact on the Indian subcontinent, as P. R. Kumaraswamy demonstrates in his chapter. For India in particular, the loss of Soviet patronage has conditioned economic and security policy in the post-cold war era. But Pakistan has also been downgraded as a United States ally. The strategic policies of both countries, and in particular the arms build-up in the region, was of intense interest to Washington even before the South Asian nuclear tests of May 1998, which showed how developments in individual regions of the Third World can impact on global security. More generally the thesis of marginalization may be also said to apply here as the region finds itself isolated from major military and economic blocs.

In the case of the Middle East, the subject of Yezid Sayigh's chapter, the Gulf War and the rapid progress of the Arab–Israeli peace process revealed the extent to which the end of the cold war fundamentally altered strategic realities. The relationship between structural changes at the regional level and those within individual states since then is less obvious, however. The loss of external support and the decline of oil revenues have deepened the predicament of most governments, yet moves towards political and economic liberalization remain halting and contested. The slow pace of economic reform reveals that difficult, socially painful decisions are being postponed, and suggests a lack either of political will or political capacity by higher echelons of states. This is accompanied by authoritarian reassertion in some cases, and by two-track democracy or polyarchy at best in others, confirming the view that it is not the combination of liberal economics and politics that determines the outcome, but rather the interaction between the two. The challenges to the state as it tackles the task of reform and consolidation mean that the Middle East is undergoing its most protracted transformation since the decolonization.

The very different experience of these regions throws up some interesting and often divergent ideas about the impact of the East–West conflict and its demise. The concluding chapter, by Louise Fawcett, draws together the threads of the thematic and regional chapters, and attempts to describe and explain the key elements of continuity and change in the Third World in the post-cold war era. It assesses the broader implications of change not only in the context of the Third World itself, but also in the context of the Third World's interaction with the international system. And it considers some of the explanations that have been offered to provide a guide to understanding change and development in the developing countries. Finally, in attempting to identify the key characteristics of what today might be said to constitute the Third World, the concluding chapter also returns to the elusive question posed earlier in this introduction and one which by implication recurs throughout the book: is there a Third World beyond the cold war?

PART I

1

Taking Stock

The Third World and the End of the Cold War

S. NEIL MACFARLANE

I. INTRODUCTION

Many of those writing about the cold war and Third World security expected the end of the former to make a substantial difference to the latter. In the decades since the fall of the Berlin Wall and the revolutions in Eastern Europe, it has become increasingly clear that the end of the cold war made less difference to Third World security than anticipated. Moreover, the difference that it did make was somewhat different from that which was expected.

In this introductory chapter, I address a number of definitional and methodological issues related to the subject. This is followed by an examination of expectations regarding the impact of the end of the cold war on the Third World expressed at the end of the 1980s and early 1990s. I then compare these expectations with the progression of events in the Third World since 1989, and discuss the reasons for the discrepancy between expectation and reality. I conclude with a number of observations on salient issues of Third World politics and security that were underemphasized or misconstrued in the cold war era and that receive a fuller airing in subsequent thematic and regional chapters. In particular, I question the extent to which a literature in security studies and international relations that emphasizes the centrality of the state and the explanatory value of systemic structure can adequately explain the evolution of politics in the Third World subsequent to the cold war.

The author is grateful for the support of the Centre for International Relations at Queen's University and the Military and Strategic Studies Program of the Department of National Defence of Canada.

II. CONCEPTUAL AND METHODOLOGICAL ISSUES

Collective discussion of the impact of the end of the cold war on the Third World presumes a shared view of the terms of reference, or at least an understanding of differences in definition, as well as awareness of the analytical implications of definitional choices.

The cold war

Definition of the cold war is reasonably uncontroversial. The cold war—in its Third World manifestation—was a proxy conflict between the West and the Soviet bloc (or between the USA and the USSR) for influence and strategic position in the regions outside Europe and North America. The principal instruments deployed in this struggle were diplomacy, economic assistance, ideology, and, more importantly, arms transfers and various forms of direct and indirect intervention.

Several implications associated with the centrality of the cold war to this analysis should be stressed. First, discussion of the implications of the cold war pushes the analysis towards a systemic approach. Bipolarity and cold war between the two poles are structural factors. Asking what difference the end of the cold war makes is asking a question about the impact of change in the structural environment of Third World states and societies.

This is a legitimate question, but answering it would hardly provide a comprehensive account of the evolution of Third World politics since 1989. The limitations of such an approach should not be ignored. There are other potentially promising structural variables one might choose to emphasize in an analysis of this type. For example, the structure of the international economy might be more important than that of international security in accounting for outcomes in Third World politics and political economy.[1] And there are levels of analysis other than that of global structure relevant to the evolution of international relations in the Third World.[2] At an intermediate level, there may be explanatory value in regional structures of power, transactions flows and institutions of co-operation.

Finally, the characteristics of the units themselves may be of greater significance as explanatory variables than those of the system in which they interact. Structural analysis tends to ignore the character of and diversity within and among units.[3] The basic argument of this chapter, however, is that an emphasis on the structural level of analysis in the assessment of the impact of the end of the cold war in the Third World has produced hypotheses for the most part unsupported, or only partially supported, by the empirical evidence. This suggests that structural (cold war) analysis is not determining. One reason for this is that the states in question are not homogeneous or monolithic. Many of the failures of prediction in early post-cold war analysis of the impact of the end of the cold war on the Third World result from an excessive emphasis on the *state* as principal unit and on the *system of states* as principal structure of analysis. I return to this point in the conclusion.

Analysis of the end of the cold war implies a second methodological choice. Although the cold war had economic and ideological dimensions, it was primarily about security or perceptions of security. As such, this chapter is largely about security issues. Such a focus is perhaps controversial, but it is justifiable even if one adopts a narrow and traditional definition of the concept that focuses on the presence or absence of military threats to states. Security may be seen as a precondition for other desired ends such as growth, democratization, and social justice. As Hedley Bull put it: 'Order in social life is desirable because it is the condition of the realisation of other values. Unless there is a pattern of human activities that sustains elementary, primary and universal goals of social life, it will not be possible to achieve or preserve objectives that are advanced, secondary, or the special goals of particular societies.'[4]

Second, an emphasis on security is not as constraining as it might first appear or as this definition might imply. Security at its core involves an absence of threat to core values.[5] The referent of security can be the individual, the group, the state, or the regional or global system. Concerning the meaning of 'threat', the current understanding of national security goes well beyond external military threats to include both *internal* social (e.g. class structure), economic (e.g. the distribution of wealth), cultural (e.g. ethnic heterogeneity), and political (e.g. legitimacy) and *external* political and economic (e.g. access to resources) issues that are related to the stability and survival of the unit in question, not to mention the array of issues associated with the concept of environmental security.[6] The content of national security may vary with the attributes of the unit under consideration. Taking the state as an example, Barry Buzan once argued that: 'for strong states, national security can be viewed primarily in terms of protecting the components of the state from outside threat and interference. Where the state is weak . . . it is probably more appropriate to view security . . . in terms of the contending groups, organizations, and individuals as the prime objects of security.'[7] In short, a focus on security does not preclude the analysis of social, economic, political, and cultural factors that are relevant to the threat assessments of decision-makers at international, national, and subnational levels of analysis. Indeed, the problem with the current discussion of security may be that it is too broad rather than too narrow.

The Third World

The second concept, the Third World, is also problematic. Definition of the concept has always been controversial. Some have argued that—either prior to or as a result of the end of the cold war—the concept has lost its relevance as a category useful in the examination of political and economic processes outside North America and Europe.[8] Others have gone further to maintain that the concept itself disempowers those states and societies to which it is applied, that it is part of a discourse of dominance and oppression, disenfranchizing and peripheralizing these entities.[9]

The recent literature proposes numerous alternative terms to describe this group of states, among them the 'South', in a North–South dichotomy,[10] the 'Periphery' in a 'Core–Periphery' juxtaposition,[11] and, the 'Developing States' in a 'Developed–Developing' dyad.[12] A number of the authors in this collection believe that the category 'Third World' retains analytical utility. Others do not.

Here it suffices to note the wide array of meanings associated with the concept as it has been traditionally used. In some instances, it had a geographical meaning. The Third World included those areas outside Europe and North America: Asia, Africa, and Latin America. The principal deficiencies with the geographical definition are that it included areas such as Japan that by other measures would be counted as part of the 'West', and that it had no apparent substantive content.

In others, it was related to the processes of colonization and decolonization. One problem here was that the process of colonization was never complete (note Thailand, Ethiopia, and Liberia), and yet one would want to include these non-colonized areas within the category. Moreover, some Western states (e.g. Australia, New Zealand, Canada, and the United States) were themselves colonies at one stage or another in their history, while one would not normally consider them part of the Third World. Finally, as the history of Latin America since the beginning of the nineteenth century arguably demonstrates, formal denial of sovereignty was not a necessary condition for the exploitation that many associate with the concept of the Third World.

Subordinate status, or peripherality, in the world capitalist economy consequently offers another basis for a definition of the Third World.[13] The problems here are at least twofold. First, some Third World societies appear to be exiting the periphery and joining the core. This creates a boundary problem. Examination of this volume's chapter on the Asia

Pacific, when contrasted with that on Africa, eloquently illustrates the difficulty of identifying an economic basis for the category.

Moreover, there exist reasonably well-defined 'peripheries' within many Western states (e.g. the Scottish Highlands, the Canadian Maritimes, Appalachia, and southern Italy, not to mention the decaying urban peripheries of many American and European cities). This exacerbates the boundary problem by rendering it difficult to define core and periphery in terms of collections of states or regions.

A fourth cut at the question relates to the state. Here, the principal defining quality of 'Third Worldness' has to do with the strength of the state and the nature and content of the relationship between state and society. Third World states are characterized by their weakness: their lack of control over their territory and activities occurring within it, their illegitimacy in the eyes of their citizens, the fragility of the rule of law, and the weakness of a shared idea of national community in ethnically heterogeneous and fractious societies.[14] Thomas Weiss and James Blight clearly spelt out the relationship of the weakness of states to regional security: 'In endeavouring to put forward a single explanation for the regional conflicts, the weaknesses and non-viability of many Third World states is probably closest to the truth.'[15]

The problem here is that states in the regions of the Third World vary considerably along all of the axes just mentioned. At one extreme, in the early 1990s, the Somali state not only ceased to function, but ceased to exist. At the other extreme, there are strong states such as Singapore. Turning to democratic legitimacy, they vary from cases where the idea simply does not exist in any meaningful sense as an attribute of the state (e.g. former Zaire) to ones with a long and healthy democratic tradition and an absence of significant internal opposition denying the legitimacy of the constitutional system (e.g. Costa Rica). There are, finally, states in the traditional Third World characterized by great heterogeneity and considerable weakness of the national idea (e.g. Nigeria or Sri Lanka), states that are more or less homogeneous and in which the national idea is reasonably strong (e.g. Argentina), states in which society is heterogeneous but the national idea is strong (e.g. Singapore), and, finally, relatively homogeneous societies where the national idea is weak (e.g. Turkmenistan).

My own approach to this problem was predominantly psychological.[16] Here, membership in the Third World is conceived first and foremost to be a matter of perception, although this perception was (or is) based in important respects on historical and often contemporary socio-political and economic realities. The Third World is an identity based on a perception of peripheralization and victimization. It has to do with a sense of being outside the mainstream, the latter defined in terms of power in international relations and in terms of wealth—a perception both on the part of those inside and those outside. Associated with this is a sense by people in such areas of being exploited, either historically or actually.

This approach to definition, however, falls prey to criticisms similar to those mentioned above. The perception of peripheralization is not limited to states outside the developed West, but is common within them. Moreover, although this construct may have been valid for the regions of the Third World in general at some point in the past, it is less obviously the case now for those areas experiencing rapid economic development and integration into the OECD world. Many Latin Americans, for example, do not see themselves as part of a marginalized Third World, but instead see themselves as being or becoming 'Western'. Meanwhile, many in East and Southeast Asia see themselves not as part of the periphery of the world economy, but as part of its newly emerging centre (the Pacific Rim).

One particular aspect of the perception of marginalization and objectification that deserves elaboration here concerns the cold war itself. Julius Nyerere's oft-cited comment that when the elephants fight the grass suffers, points to a widespread sense in the Third World that it was united in providing the terrain upon which the two superpowers exercised their global rivalry. One of the principal Third World identities—the Non-Aligned Movement—was constructed largely with this threat in mind, and in the hope that joint action on the part of the Third World states would reduce their vulnerability to the bipolar policies of the USSR and the USA.

The problem with this view as well is that the cold war had a widely varying impact on the states of the Third World. Arguably, cold war competition had crucial effects on southern Africa, for example, while it had little if any effect on Central and West Africa. The same contrast exists between Central America and the Southern Cone. Moreover, to the extent that the cold war competition provided a cement binding the states of the Third World together, one might infer that the end of the cold war removed one of the essential underpinnings of Third World identity (see below).

There are, of course, two sides to the perceptual approach. Identity is not only self-defined, but is defined by those outside the group. Whether or not there were 'objective' attributes to the Third World, and whether or not those residing outside the West conceived themselves as comprising a distinct identity, if relevant élites and publics in the West conceived of them in such terms and acted in part upon such conceptions, there would be a meaningful Third World identity.

Certainly there is in Western culture a long history of perceptual marginalization, if not denigration, of areas and peoples outside Europe and its racial extensions.[17] Arguably, this marginalization has served as an ideological basis for the disenfranchisement and exploitation of Third World states and societies. The long bibliography of Western works about the 'Third World' from the 1950s to the 1990s suggests that this history extended into the modern era.

Here, too, however, this monolithic perception of the states and peoples of the Third World has eroded considerably with the passage of time. Even during the cold war era, it was common to encounter an analytical division between a Third World that was arguably 'salvageable', and a 'Fourth World' of the least developed, the 'basket cases'. The emergence of an economically powerful bloc of oil producers fostered another line of perceptual differentiation in the West.

This erosion appears to be accelerating since the end of the cold war. The collapse of the USSR, the increasingly obscure quality of the US strategic interest in Europe, the exclusionary trading policies of the European Union, and the rapid growth of trade with the countries of the Pacific Basin have fostered in the United States (and Canada) a conception of Pacific identity that brings together states of the First and Third Worlds in the region.

The widespread perception of regionalization in international trade, moreover, has encouraged the spread in the northern half of the Americas of a notion of north–south *hemispheric solidarity* that conflicts with traditional eurocentric or 'North-centric' orientations in foreign and foreign economic policy. Many in Japan, meanwhile, see their future to lie in the development of stronger ties with other rapidly developing states along the Western rim of the Pacific Basin. The point here is that traditional international identities are considerably more fluid in the post-cold war context, and that newly evolving conceptions of identity in the North transcend conventional North–South divisions. The cold war and the competition between East and West provided a unifying strategic overlay and as such was one of the principal underpinnings of the Western perception of these regions as a meaningful unity. This is gone.

The basic problem underlying all of these approaches to the 'Third World' is the increasing differentiation both in the subject-matter itself and in the perception of it. The Third World, like any category in social science, was an heuristic simplification. The category at its inception obscured specificity in its quest for generalizability. The ending of the cold war strengthens the tendency towards differentiation in these areas. The deepening differences between Third World states and societies and the weakening of the perception of the Third World identity both within and outside the Third World raise the question whether the category may not now be more of an impediment than an aid to analysis.

At this stage of the study, a firm position on the relevance of the category is unnecessary. The foregoing suggests that it should be abandoned in favour of more regionally specific analytical tools. However, its utility is something to be demonstrated by empirical analysis rather than asserted a priori in an introductory chapter. Among the contributions that this volume may make is the elucidation of the extent to which it makes sense to treat those countries and regions traditionally included in the category as a single object of study. This is one of the principal reasons for including the regional cases in Part II. To the extent that they cannot be so considered, this draws into question the utility of the concept, and invites a more differentiated analysis of the subject-matter.

The impact of the cold war

A further problem of definition deserves mention. Defining the impact of the end of the cold war assumes a settled understanding of what the impact of the cold war was. Differences concerning what the impact of the cold war was will produce differences in interpretation of the consequences of its demise.

One early conventional wisdom implied in the Nyerere aphorism cited above was that the cold war increased the incidence of, and exacerbated conflict in, the Third World as the superpowers diverted their systemic competition from more dangerous to less dangerous theatres.[18] The problem, however, was not merely one of increased incidence of conflict. The interventions of both superpowers into the domestic affairs of Third World states impeded democratic development and encouraged the systematic violation of human rights. The superpowers fostered dependent and sympathetic authoritarian regimes and frequently sustained them in the face of popular and élite opposition, sacrificing ideological nicety to the geopolitical dictates of their competition.[19]

The link between the cold war and the incidence of conflict is difficult to demonstrate empirically, since it is impossible to know what the level of conflict in the Third World would have been in the absence of the cold war. Many of the principal identifiable causes of conflict—weak states, divided societies, economic deprivation, and social discrimination, the poor fit between identity and territoriality—had little to do with the cold war, and might well have produced high levels of conflict in the absence of the superpower competition.[20]

For many years, there was in the literature a different, if not opposing current, focusing on the constraints on superpower competition in the Third World as well.[21] Although both superpowers had an interest in pursuing their competition in the Third World, they sought to avoid serious escalation that might draw them into direct confrontation, as well as being restricted by resource limitation and domestic political considerations.

Some went further to maintain that the structural overlay of the cold war constrained conflict and enhanced stability in the Third World. Since both superpowers sought influence with established states, and since ruling regimes had an interest in the territorial status quo, superpower diplomacy also tended to sustain the latter.[22] In a more general sense, since each engaged in balancing behaviour, they tended to support opposite sides in regional conflicts, contributing to stability, if not to democracy and justice.[23]

A third position maintained that the cold war really did not make that much difference. Although the cold war had an impact, emphasis on the role of superpower competition in the security affairs of the Third World 'ignored what is certainly the most important source of Third World instability, namely insufferable poverty coupled with fundamental domestic roots of conflict'.[24] The simple problem with this line of analysis is that the existence of a phenomenon *prior* to the cold war is not sufficient to conclude that the bipolar competition was irrelevant to its expression during the cold war, since the latter may have acted as a constraining, permissive, or proactive condition. For example, the remarks cited just above concerning the propensity of the superpowers to strengthen their clients suggest that their competition may have mitigated (temporarily) the consequences of the weakness of states.[25] On the other hand, the arms transfer aspect of superpower competition may have increased the incidence of conflict by increasing the availability of the instruments of conflict.

III. EXPECTATIONS CONCERNING THE IMPACT OF THE END OF THE COLD WAR

At the risk of oversimplification, the literature addressing the impact of systemic change on the Third World in the first years after the end of the cold war may be broken down into at least two categories: post-cold war optimism and post-cold war pessimism. The conclusions of both groups on the end of the cold war are largely derived from their assumptions regarding the impact of the cold war itself on the Third World.

First, as already noted, one prevalent view concerning the impact of the cold war on Third World security maintained that the cold war promoted conflict and insecurity in these regions. It followed that the end of the cold war would conduce to greater security and less conflict, as the competitive force of superpower politics was removed from the equation.[26] More strongly, the new cooperativeness between the USA and the USSR not merely removed a source of instability, but actively promoted security, either in the form of condominium and/or through the institutions of the United Nations. The latter had been prevented from properly fulfilling their role in the promotion of security by the cold war-induced impasse within the Security Council. The end of the cold war permitted more decisive action by the organization in response to threats to international peace and security. This expectation was embodied in UN Secretary-General Boutros Boutros Ghali's 'Agenda for Peace'.[27] Such possibilities went well beyond traditional peacekeeping and mediation activities to embrace forceful humanitarian intervention and the involvement of the organization in democratic institution building.[28]

Both of these propositions appeared to be confirmed by rapid movement towards a settlement of the Angola War and the Central American crisis, among others. These involved both a substantial degree of bilateral Soviet-American cooperation in the arrangement of military and political settlements and a prominent role for the United Nations in the implementation of the accords that resulted. Similar mechanisms facilitated a Soviet withdrawal from Afghanistan in 1989. The role of UNTAC in Cambodia was an even more striking indication of what was possible in the new climate.

This felicitous effect had a number of expected spinoffs. On the one hand, the diminution of cold war-related conflict would allow states in affected regions and their patrons to turn their attention from defence to economic and political development. Many anticipated, consequently, a trend of falling defence expenditure, the proceeds from which could be turned to more productive tasks. Likewise, the reduced threat perceived by developed states would produce a peace dividend there as well. This in turn, by stimulating growth, would expand markets for Third World goods, while freeing up a larger share of global GNP for development. Finally, freed of the threat of Soviet or Cuban-inspired destabilization, the Western states could abandon their past policies of support for right-wing authoritarian regimes and turn their attention more fully to the tasks of political development and democratization through such mechanisms as political conditionality.[29] The purported democratizing trend[30] would be sustained also by the delegitimizing effect of the collapse of communism in Eastern Europe on socialist-oriented one-party regimes in areas such as Africa and Central America.[31]

Although, given the rapid decay and subsequent collapse of the Soviet Union, the discussion of superpower cooperation as a means to removing the oxymoronic quality of the phrase 'Third World security' faded rather rapidly, this did little to dampen the optimism characteristic of discussion of the topic in the early 1990s. In an analysis partly informed by hegemonic stability theory, and partly by the hubris of the victor, many American analysts and policy-makers came to the view that the United

States would, in the post-bipolar environment, lead the world towards a more peaceful, prosperous, and democratic future. Hence, George Bush's new world order and Charles Krauthammer's unipolar moment.[32] These expectations appeared to be confirmed by the UN-sanctioned coalition response to Iraq's invasion of Kuwait in 1990–1, and by the humanitarian intervention in Somalia in late 1991.

Turning towards more pessimistic analyses, I have already noted the opposing view that the cold war may have been stabilizing in much of the Third World. The logical corollary regarding the end of the cold war is that its effects were likely to be destabilizing. The demise of superpower competition cleared the way for ambitious regional powers to enhance their influence at the expense of their weaker neighbours. The Iraqi effort to absorb Kuwait is perhaps a case in point. To the extent that flows of resources from the superpowers allowed established client regimes to control internal processes of disintegration, the end of the cold war was likely to result in increasing disorder in such states, as was arguably the case in Zaire, Somalia, and Ethiopia. These factors—in conjunction with others—would produce an increasing incidence of both internal and inter-state conflict.[33] Such expectations were strengthened by the obvious increase in violence associated with the collapse of cold war structures in Europe, and, moreover, by the collapse of post-colonial state structures in the Horn of Africa, and were apparently confirmed by the collapse of Rwanda into anarchy and genocide in 1994, and by the disintegration of former Zaire starting in 1996.

A second variant of structural pessimism was also evident. Some, operating from the dependency or Marxist positions, had taken the view either that bipolar competition preserved a degree of autonomy for otherwise weak Third World states, or, more strongly, that the assistance of the Soviet bloc states actually defended revolutionary movements and states in the Third World against global imperialism. They consequently expected that the demise of the defender would result in a dramatic increase of American and other pressure on progressive states, citing Panama and also Iraq in this context. In a sense, they too subscribed to the new world order thesis, but attributed rather different content to this construct. As André Gunder Frank put it:

The Gulf War was a *Third World War* by the North against the South . . . [T]he allies, led by the USA, clearly signalled their threat to build a new world order with repeated recourse to this same military force and annihilation against any recalcitrant country or peoples—as long as they are poor, weak, and in the Third World South. With the conclusion of the cold war, the Third World (hot) War is not to be fought between East and West, or West and West, but between the North and the South.[34]

In Gunder Frank's view, the Gulf War was a precedent for 'repeated resort to similar wars in the future'.[35]

In a third variant of post-cold war pessimism, some argued that the involvement of major powers in the Third World rested essentially on perceived threat and interest, and that, certainly on the part of the United States and with the exception of certain zones of unavoidable economic importance (e.g. the Gulf), the major threat and interest construct revolved around the cold war. The Angolas of this world were important because the Soviet Union and Cuba were there. Once the USSR and Cuba departed, these states were no longer of significance to the interests of the remaining superpower. In those specific cases where great power interest was involved, the end of the cold war removed an important constraint on intervention by the remaining superpower. In those areas where no vital interest was engaged, it removed the principal incentive to become involved. The result in these instances is a 'decoupling of the core state security structure from the peripheral security structures'.[36] This explained, perhaps, the unwillingness of the Security Council to deploy sufficient peacekeepers to Angola at the end of the cold war to ensure a transition from civil war to internal peace. This in turn contributed to the resumption of civil war in the early 1990s.

This decoupling, it is argued, extends into political economy. In some instances (e.g. South Korea and Taiwan), Third World states obtained substantial economic concessions from the West and considerable flows of assistance as a result of their strategic significance in the struggle against communism. Some took the view that in the post-cold war context, there was little reason to expect similar largesse.

In a more radical variant, some analysts have long argued that the cold war in the Third World was a side show, a distraction from more profound processes in North–South relations—and notably the progressive marginalization of the Third World.[37] To the extent that its ending was important, it was in that it accelerated this marginalization through diminishing the strategic interest of key Western powers and through the probable diversion of flows of private capital and public sector assistance to the newly opening Eastern Europe.[38]

IV. THE END OF THE COLD WAR AND THIRD WORLD SECURITY

It is fair to say that all of these expectations were disappointed in one way or another in the period following the end of the cold war. In the first place, the drying up of competition between the USSR and the USA did decrease the incidence of conflict in specific instances. In the early period of incipient condominium, the two superpowers did co-operate to terminate specific conflicts in which their interests were implicated. For example, American and Soviet cooperation was a critical (though far from the only) factor conducing to a settlement to the war of liberation in Namibia. This settlement, so far, has proven durable.

One might go further in this region and argue that the disappearance of competition between the superpowers was a factor contributing to the achievement of political reform and enfranchisement of the majority in South Africa. The end to Soviet assistance to Nicaragua removed any residual capacity that the Sandinista government might have had to evade the Esquipulas II settlement process. The cancelling of the Soviet blank cheque to Syria had a constructive impact on the Middle East settlement process.

Moreover, in some of the instances in which superpower cooperation produced political settlements, subsequent events suggest that their impact was less than intended. As already noted, the Angola settlement fell apart after an election the results of which UNITA did not like. The Cambodia settlement excluded the Khmer Rouge and this produced a continuation of war at a lower level. The withdrawal of the USSR from Afghanistan appears to have produced an intensification, rather than a diminution of the level of conflict there, as the victors fought over the spoils and were then challenged by the Taleban. Where results appear more durable, as in Central America, those involved in the peace process grew increasingly worried that the winding up of the UN involvement in the region, coupled with the pressure of economic adjustment, might produce a renewal of violence, as those left out before by and large remain left out.[39]

Before addressing expectations regarding democratization and economic development, it is appropriate to examine the competing pessimistic hypothesis relating to the incidence of conflict. Perhaps the best case for arguing that structural change has produced conflict is that of sub-Saharan Africa, as is suggested by the gradual unravelling of the territorial *status quo* in East Central Africa. However, the conclusion is hardly universal even in this region. For example, one would have to exclude much of southern Africa from the generalization. As already noted, evidence from most other regions would suggest that the end of the cold war has either enhanced stability or has had no obvious effect on intra- and inter-state incidence of conflict.[40]

For the Third World in aggregate, it is not clear that the incidence of conflict has increased (or decreased) since the end of the cold war. With regard to ethnic conflict, for example, T. R. Gurr recently argued:

Some observers have drawn a causal connection between the end of the cold war and the escalation of ethno-political conflict. The Minorities at Risk data shows [sic] that ethno-political conflicts were relatively common, and increased steadily, throughout the cold war . . . [T]he greatest absolute and proportional increase in numbers of groups involved in serious ethno-political conflicts occurred between the 1960s and the 1970s, from 36 groups to 55. From the 1980s to the early 1990s the tally increased only by eight, from 62 to 70. Moreover, ongoing ethno-political conflicts that began after 1987 are not appreciably more intense than those that began earlier.[41]

Similar problems arise with democratization and the peace dividend. The peace dividend has been very unevenly experienced. By and large, the defence procurement decisions of states are driven by leadership percep-tions of threat. In some areas, the end of the cold war has diminished threat perceptions (e.g. in Central America). This has resulted in substan-tial declines in military expenditure. To judge from the statistics provided in the IISS *Military Balance*, Guatemala was spending roughly half in 1995 than it was in 1986 on defence. The same is true of Honduras, and this is before adjusting for inflation. In some areas, these perceptions have been aggravated, as in Southeast Asia. Here, we see Singapore spending almost four times as much in 1996 as in 1986, Indonesia almost twice as much, and Malaysia around three times as much.[42] These figures are also nominal rather than real, but still suggest a substantial increase in the level of resources committed to defence spending.

Turning to democratization, yet again the process varies by region. The clearest progress has been made in Latin America as Jorge Heine's chap-ter demonstrates. Very little has in fact been made in Africa, with the exception of South Africa, despite optimistic expectations to the contrary. In a limited number of instances (e.g. Nigeria), retrogression accompanied the end of the cold war. In areas such as Latin America where progress has been made, the combination of democracy with economic liberalism has done little for both rural and urban majorities. It remains legitimate, there-fore, to question whether what we are seeing is not simply another periodic episode of the demilitarization of politics that will be followed by the instability and a remilitarization. If this is so, then we are dealing more with a product of domestic political cycles than one of systemic change.

With regard to the new world order, initial optimism concerning the capacity of the UN to adopt a more ambitious global role in the manage-ment of security has weakened. The ability of the Security Council to agree on common action in the face of crises in the Third World and else-where was dramatically enhanced by the end of the cold war, to judge from the flood of relevant resolutions since 1990. However, other substantial constraints on UN activities (e.g. the lack of a standing force and the dependence of the UN on state contributions of military personnel and financial resources) remained. The result has been a considerable over-stretch of institutional resources.

Moreover, the failure or ambiguous results of a number of substantial UN involvements in regional crises (Iraq, Somalia, Yugoslavia), the open-ended quality of UN commitments, and the increasingly hazardous nature of activities loosely grouped under the rubric of peacekeeping has damp-ened donor enthusiasm for underwriting or providing personnel for such ventures. Perhaps the most poignant image of the down side of post-cold war UN activism was the withdrawal of UN forces from Somalia by the end of 1995, because of lack of progress towards a political reconciliation in that country, and their request for cover from an international rapid reaction force while they pulled out—raising the prospect that they might not have been able to leave on their own without substantial loss of life. A recent study of the Security Council concluded with the observation that—in the context of all of these problems—the real danger of the moment was not overextension, but underutilization of the resources at the Council's disposal.[43]

Turning to unipolar visions of a new world order based on hegemonic stability theory, the 'promise' of the Gulf and Somalia has been largely unfulfilled. American policy since the change of administrations in 1992 (namely, towards Haiti and Bosnia-Herzegovina) suggested considerable reluctance to take a leadership role where this involved potentially sub-stantial commitments of military and other resources and where the task at hand was not obviously related to widely shared perceptions of US vital interest. To judge from the impact of the spring 1992 losses of American servicemen in Somalia on American deliberations concerning Haiti, those celebrating the 'unipolar moment' overestimated American willingness to accept losses in its exercise of a leadership role. The dependence of American leadership on the commitment of financial resources by other states, evident in the Gulf, moreover, suggested that such exercise depends on a degree of solidarity among America's friends that is often difficult to obtain. The extremely difficult and attenuated internal debate over deploy-ment to Haiti, moreover, underlined the dimensions of domestic political constraint on US activism in the Third World.[44] This would appear to be confirmed in doctrine by the Clinton administration's embrace of Presidential Decision Directive (PDD) 25 on the use of US forces in peace-related opertions and in practice by the halfhearted US response to the crisis in Rwanda in 1994, and the reluctance to commit US forces in the follow-on crisis in the region in 1996.

This also puts paid to the neo-Marxist conception of imperialism newly unleashed. The problem with such hypotheses as applied to the Third

World as a whole is that their conceptions of 'north' and 'south', or of 'centre' and 'periphery', are insufficiently differentiated. From the point of view of economic interest, much of the Third World does not really matter. Those entertaining such expectations share the undervaluation of domestic constraint characteristic of those espousing unipolarity. They also overestimate the monolithic character of northern polities and the role of economic factors in determining their policies.

Arguments positing a dissociation between the 'North' and the 'South' in the post-cold war era, though arriving at a conclusion opposite to the one just discussed, evince the same methodological error: insufficient attention to diversity of interest. There are areas of the Third World that have 'enjoyed' enduring and profound importance to the West and continue to do so. Such arguments also attribute to Western interests a static quality that ignores substantial change in the policy agenda of northern states in response to evolving social and economic realities. As the military-political ('high policy') content of Western policy in the Third World declines in some areas of the Third World, other issues outside the traditional realm of security have frequently grown in salience. Several notable examples suggest themselves. An American perception of a threatening trend towards regionalism in the global economy, in the context of waning American pre-eminence, recast American policy-makers' image of their relations with Latin America, culminating in the successful conclusion, and planned expansion of, NAFTA.[45] A growing involvement in, rather than dissociation from, the hemisphere's south was dictated in this instance by trends in the global political economy. Similar patterns may be evident in Japan's trade and investment behaviour in its hemisphere's south.

Indeed, there is a tendency in some instances for 'low policy' issues traditionally placed outside the security agenda to intrude increasingly upon the latter.[46] One reason for the EU southern-tier states' pressure on the union to balance flows of assistance to Eastern Europe with similar flows to the North African littoral was their concern about the impact of instability in and migration from these states on their own security, and in particular about the impact of 'fundamentalist Islam.'

Likewise, in the American context, concern over the flow of migrants and drugs from Latin America and the Caribbean has arguably crossed the line from being a law enforcement issue to being one of security.[47] It has resulted in a deepening integration of hemispheric law enforcement activities, and has produced a further security-related concern in the United States to stimulate economic development among its southern neighbours.

V. CONCLUSION

The discussion thus far has a number of important methodological and theoretical implications. Recalling the points on levels of analysis at the outset, at the risk of belabouring the obvious, efforts to develop generalizations about the 'Third World' and, in this instance, about the impact there of structural change (namely, the end of the cold war) tend to produce as many exceptions as they do evidence consistent with the generalization. Arguments to the effect that the cold war's end is likely to reduce the incidence of conflict in the Third World suit the data in South Africa or Central America, but fly in its face in the Persian Gulf and much of the rest of sub-Saharan Africa. The opposite line of argument suits the latter data but not the former.

Still in the realm of security, Middle Eastern data might suggest that hypotheses positing greater intrusiveness on the part of the North have merit. Those from Africa or East and Southeast Asia suggest the opposite. In the area of political economy, data from sub-Saharan Africa might indicate greater marginalization. Those from Latin America and East Asia suggest deepening integration between North and South.

What all of this suggests is that broad systemic generalizations concerning the impact of the end of the cold war on the Third World are unlikely to have much merit. The real problem was suggested in the first substantial section of this paper. The Third World was a category that always masked considerable variation both from state to state and from region to region. Variation within the category (however defined) has been increasing over time. Indeed, perhaps the most promising generalization that might be attempted here is that the end of the cold war has accelerated secular processes of differentiation by removing a central unifying conceptual overlay affecting the perceptions of both North and South. The end of the cold war allows northern states to approach issues in the Third World, be they political, economic, or security, in their own differentiated terms.

Moving to a second level of analysis, a further general point that emerges from the analysis is that, since so much of the subject-matter discussed above seems to vary along regional lines, it appears that—to the extent that aggregation is useful—a more appropriate focus for analysis may be the regional one. To put it another way, analysis of the end of the cold war has tended to overemphasize the significance of general systemic and structural factors. What may be more useful is to assess the impact of global structural change in terms of the specific nature of the linkages between regions and the international system as a whole, and the character of the regions and the units making them up.

S. Neil MacFarlane

The final level of analysis to mention is that of the unit itself—the state and its relationship to society. In the area of civil conflict, the persistence of conflicts previously related to the cold war even where the two previous cold war adversaries attempted to resolve them (as in Angola, the Horn of Africa, and Afghanistan), the continuation of conflicts that had persisted during the cold war but largely independent of it (as in Cambodia and Sudan), and the sudden exacerbation of conflict in areas where the superpowers had eschewed involvement (as in Rwanda) again suggests that analysts of Third World security have overestimated the global systemic determinants of security and insecurity in the Third World. Analysis of the cold war and its ending may suggest that the impact of this systemic factor varied in relation not only to the perceived strategic significance, but also to the internal characteristics of the subject states in question.

One promising generalization here may be that the superpower competition tended to have a greater impact on states that were weak. The contrast between a Singapore and an Angola illustrates the point. Most of the civil conflicts in the Third World that troubled analysts and policy-makers during the cold war grew not so much out of the competition between the USA and the USSR, but out of local conditions, such as income disparity and the unrepresentative quality of government, or, more strongly, the incongruity between political and social process, and between state and other forms of political identity. They reflected, moreover, the weakness of the state's penetration of society and the lack of means for important social forces (class and/or ethnic) to involve themselves in political life. Often underlying this was the poorly integrated character of national community, or, to put it another way, the lack of fit between the nation-state and élite and popular perceptions of identity. In short, analysis of outcomes during and after the cold war encourages a degree of scepticism with regard not just to global systemic determinants, but to the state as the principal unit of analysis.

This leads me to a final point. The cold war literature concerning the Third World reflected the narrowly politico-military focus of much analysis in international relations and particularly in strategic studies. This favoured inattention or inadequate attention to ongoing processes not directly linked to security as traditionally conceived, but which none the less had and have important security implications. If one examines current comment on critical issues of Third World security and their implications for the West, one finds that the focus has shifted to such issues as migration, environmental threat, and economic issues and their implications for political stability, as well as the strength or weakness of the state and the degree of integration of the communities it serves. Underlying many of them is the problem of population growth.

Most of these issues have been around for a long time. During the cold war, they were largely eclipsed by the issue of Soviet–American and East–West relations in the Third World. Underemphasis on them reflected also the unfamiliarity of the issues for analysts of regional security. Finally, since they were for the most part transnational issues, the discipline's fascination with the state and the system of states as fundamental units of international relations discouraged their investigation.

In this respect, the problems that we face in the analysis of Third World politics and security are part and parcel of the more profound difficulty of problematizing the role of the state in international relations in a period where its centrality to much of what we need to know about is subject to growing debate. From the point of view of international relations scholarship, perhaps the most salutary impact of the end of the cold war is that it weakens this constricting and distortive methodological effect.

Taking stock of the evolution of the Third World since the end of the cold war encourages a broadening of analysis beyond interstate relations and the contest for state power within states to a wider range of questions pertaining to both the units and the system that they form. Despite Gurr's conclusion cited earlier, one set of issues concerns the viability of many states governing diverse and troubled communities where the claim to substate self-determination has grown in force. This in turn suggests that the stable post-colonial territorial settlement in parts of the Third World may in fact be coming apart, as indicated by 1996 events in eastern Zaire.

This is closely related to a second concern—the evolution of structures of regional order that might replace the stabilizing role of cold war competition and balancing. In conditions of diminishing external involvement and the increasingly obvious deficiencies of the United Nations as a provider of the public good of order, can the regions of the Third World themselves generate compensatory structures?[48]

A third is just what the meaning of security should be construed to be in conditions where unconventional issues such as refugee movements, economic migration, population growth, economic stagnation, and environmental decay pose increasing threats to the safety of states or regimes, and where the rights of the individual or group within societies have come to be seen to be a matter of legitimate international concern—not only intrinsically, but in that their systematic denial may be interpreted as a threat to international peace and security. The emerging focus on human security and on its inescapable connection to issues of environmentally sustainable development and to legitimizing political reform reflect this increasingly evident interpenetration of purportedly distinct areas of enquiry.

2

The Political Dimension
Authoritarianism and Democratization

ROLAND DANNREUTHER

I. INTRODUCTION

The ideological framework of the cold war provided the developing states of the Third World with two opposing models for socio-economic and political development. The capitalist, pro-Western model posited an explicit link between the promotion of capitalism, the securing of economic growth, and the development of democratic forms of governance. Modernization theory, with its roots in post-war American social sciences, provided the intellectual and theoretical framework for this favoured developmental path. In contrast, the opposing socialist critique assumed the inherent structural injustice of the international capitalist system and that developing countries could only overcome such structural constraints by promoting state-controlled, inward-orientated economic policies. It was only then, it was argued, that genuine social and political equity could be attained. Emerging as much from the Third as from the First or Second Worlds, the many varieties of structuralist and dependency theory provided intellectual coherence to these radical and socialist critiques.[1]

The democratic ideal, being the desired political objective of both these models, became a battleground for the ensuing ideological confrontation. In the early years of decolonization in the 1950s, modernization theorists were quietly confident that developing countries would make a swift transition to modernity and that democracy would be the political outcome. It was expected that the old segmented and traditional societies would be replaced by wealthier, more egalitarian, and participatory polities which would demand a suitably responsive political system. As Seymour Martin Lipset argued, democracy would be the outcome since it was the final 'mark of the efficiency of the total system'.[2] In contrast, leftist and socialist thinkers argued that it was only by breaking out of the stranglehold of the international capitalist system that a genuine and popular democratic system, providing the basic social and economic needs of all of society, could emerge. Without such a transformation, the masses of the Third World would be effectively controlled by small indigenous economically powerful élites, who were themselves subservient to the rich capitalist countries.

Despite the fervency with which the advocates of these opposing models supported their proposals, they rarely reflected the actual political evolution of countries in the developing world. The initial optimism of the modernization theorists of a fast 'take-off' to modernity was dampened by the failure of many countries in the late 1950s, such as the Congo or South Vietnam, to follow the prescribed path. As a result, a more cautious and conservative assessment emerged during the 1960s. Revisions were made to the theory which suggested that, unless political institutionalization developed in parallel with the socio-economic changes taking place, the more probable outcome would be authoritarian or totalitarian rule than democratic governance.[3] The underlying policy implication was that it might be necessary to defend pro-Western and capitalist-orientated authoritarian regimes to prevent the ascendance to power of anti-Western socialist or Marxist groups.

Subsequent Western support to 'national security' or 'bureaucratic authoritarian' regimes was quickly seized upon by leftist critics as the unmasking of the true intentions of Western promotion of capitalist development. The overthrow in 1973 of Salvador Allende's democratically elected government in Chile was seen as a paradigmatic example of Western support for authoritarian capitalism as against democratic socialism. For many élites in the Third World, the lesson learnt was the need for a more sustained attempt at radical reform, so as to disengage more effectively from the international capitalist system and thereby entrench genuine political and economic independence.

However, the expectation that an indigenous socialist-oriented form of economic and political development would lead to more responsive and participatory forms of government failed to materialize. Just as pro-Western capitalist countries tended to collapse into military dictatorships, the various leftist and socialist regimes generally degenerated into overbearing state bureaucracies which were mired in patrimonialism or attempts to assert totalitarian forms of social control. By the mid-1970s, the vast majority of developing countries, whether identified as capitalist or socialist, pro-Western or anti-Western, had some form of dictatorial rule, ranging from reasonably benign forms of authoritarian control to the most unspeakably brutal attempts to impose a totalitarian system.

Democracy in any recognizable form was present only in rare but honourable exceptions such as India, Botswana, or Costa Rica.

When even India's commitment to democracy came under threat by Indira Gandhi's imposition of martial rule in 1975, many analysts succumbed to a deep pessimism about the future prospects for democratization in the developing world. Not untypical was Daniel Moynihan's assessment that 'increasingly democracy is seen as an arrangement peculiar to a handful of North Atlantic countries'.[4] These gloomy prognoses were, however, to prove short-lived. Since the mid-1970s, there has been a remarkable trend towards increased democratization, a 'third democratic wave', following the two earlier waves of democratization after the First and Second World Wars.[5] In Latin America and sub-Saharan Africa in particular, but also to a more limited extent in East Asia and the Middle East, there have been a series of transitions from authoritarian to democratic rule through the holding of competitive elections. This process of democratization has been further consolidated by the collapse of the Soviet empire and the emergence of governments in Eastern Europe and the former Soviet Union formally committed to democratic values. The simultaneous discrediting of the socialist model of economic development, apparent even in countries formally committed to the tenets of Marxism-Leninism such as China and Vietnam, has further contributed to the recasting of the simple binary oppositions of the cold war period. The Manichaean struggle between socialism and capitalism, and their respective perceived linkages to democracy and authoritarianism, has been replaced by a more diffuse debate over the nature of capitalist development and its relationship to the social and political developments in different regions of the world.

The aim of this chapter is to contribute to this emerging debate by suggesting an analytical framework for assessing the implications of these recent developments for the political structures within developing countries. The first section will seek to isolate the most important structural and international factors which have contributed to the democratizing trend in the developing world. The second section will look beyond these general trends and assess the existing social, economic, and political conditions of most developing countries, focusing in particular on the continuing internal and external obstacles to democratization. The final section will attempt to draw from this analysis an overarching assessment of the direction of political change in the developing world and the most appropriate models or approaches for understanding the underlying dynamic of these changes.

II. THE THIRD DEMOCRATIC WAVE

The idea of a 'third democratic wave', like any single image of a complex set of developments, has its interpretive limitations, as the case studies presented in this volume clearly show. Yet, the metaphor does have value in describing the extent of the crisis of authoritarianism from the mid-1970s onwards. It highlights the extraordinary speed with which many authoritarian regimes were forced to accommodate demands for political pluralism, and the seeming domino effect of one country's democratic transition leading to a wider regional phenomenon, particularly in Latin America, Eastern Europe, and sub-Saharan Africa. During the 1970s and 1980s all the previously authoritarian regimes in Latin America and Eastern Europe succumbed to democratic elections; and all but a handful of Sub-Saharan countries had implemented political reforms which were intended to create more open political systems.

The process by which democratic reform appeared to gain a wave-like momentum can be seen most vividly in Western Africa in the late 1980s and early 1990s. The initiative of the Benin government in 1989 to hold a national conference to discuss political reform was swiftly replicated in practically every other francophone African country.[6] These conferences became a powerful catalyst for enforcing the rulers of the region to accept multi-party elections. Similarly in Latin America, the legitimacy of authoritarian rulers undoubtedly came under pressure when neighbouring countries were being forced to introduce liberalizing reforms as a result of popular protest. The demise of the Soviet empire, and its accompanying socialist ideology, also left the ruling élites of the newly independent countries without any apparent alternative to the introduction of a liberal democratic system.

However, the wave metaphor only captures some of the political dynamics in the developing world. For example, it ignores the fact that certain important regions cannot be said to have experienced a significant democratic transformation. In East Asia, the democratic reforms in South Korea and Taiwan have not been replicated in other countries of the region, most critically in China where the communist leadership remains deeply resistant to any form of political liberalization. In the Arab world, authoritarian and unresponsive systems of government are even more deeply entrenched and only a few countries, such as Jordan and Yemen, have experimented with any genuine political opening.

More substantively, the wave metaphor successfully isolates only the surface or secondary causes of the democratizing trend in developing countries. Authoritarian regimes were undoubtedly threatened by the example of neighbouring countries engaging in democratic reform. But it does not explain why these regimes were generally so weak and insecure in the first place. This requires an assessment of the deeper structural factors which had been instrumental in undermining the legitimacy of authoritarian governments. In particular, the economic crisis of the late 1970s and 1980s and the ending of the cold war, the two most visible developments of the period, must be weighed for their influence on the political changes in the developing world. The impact that these developments had on the relationship between the developed and developing world, between North and South, must also be assessed to gain a sense of the changing external international environment. In combination, these three factors provide significant additional insights into the principal underlying causes of the more hostile political environment facing most authoritarian regimes from the mid-1970s.

First, a major economic crisis afflicted most regions of the developing world from the late 1970s onwards, which was in stark contrast to the high growth rates of the 1950s and 1960s. As the industrialized world struggled with the consequences of the oil price rises of the 1970s, many developing countries became overwhelmed by mounting debts, poor growth rates, and increasing strains on resources. For Latin American and African countries in particular, the 1980s was a decade of economic stagnation and massive debt liabilities which resulted in zero or negative growth. The expense of maintaining swollen state bureaucracies, which had provided internal support and a source of legitimation for authoritarian dictatorships, became an increasingly unacceptable economic burden. The demands for cuts in the state sector became even more intense as the IMF and World Bank developed structural adjustment programmes, which ascribed the main causes of the economic crisis to the market imperfections sustained by excessive state intervention and the consequent inefficiencies in the allocation of resources.[7] Strict conditions were consequently imposed on recipient countries, including drastic cuts in the state budget, the adoption of strict monetary and fiscal policies, and the promotion of export-led growth.

However, the dynamic towards economic liberalization measures, with their associated reduction in state control, was not just due to the exertions of the Bretton Woods institutions. The empirical evidence of the economic success of many East Asian countries, which had limited the degree of state intervention in the economy, added to the political attraction of permitting a degree of economic pluralism.[8] On a more general systemic level, the globalization of the international economy, promoted by the Uruguay round of the GATT negotiations and the increasing mobility of capital, further undermined the viability of inward-oriented economic development. These cumulative pressures have meant that few developing countries now seek to resist the promotion of some degree of economic liberalization and the few exceptions, such as North Korea or Cuba, have only done so at the cost of increasing impoverishment.

Such radical changes to the economic structure of many developing countries have necessarily had significant political consequences. But they have not always led to a significant opening of the political system. China has continued to succeed in marrying radical economic liberalization measures with political repression. Even where increasing economic pluralism has led to greater political pluralism, it can be for very different reasons. For example, in Chile, South Korea, or Taiwan, the very success of the authoritarian regimes in implementing such reforms led to domestic pressure for political change. In other authoritarian countries, however, it has been the failures of past economic policies, combined with popular protest at the repressiveness and brutality of dictatorial rule, which has critically undermined the legitimacy of these regimes. But, with these qualifications in mind, it can still be said that the effect of economic liberalization, particularly in Latin America and sub-Saharan Africa, has been to open up a new political space, through which demands for political reform have been mobilized to the point where authoritarian leaders have been forced to respond.

The ending of the cold war provided a second major pressure on authoritarian regimes. Many years before the rise to power of Mikhail Gorbachev or the events of 1989, the structure of the cold war had been exerting less and less influence on the developing world. The power pretensions of both superpowers in the Third World had been radically undermined by the experience of Vietnam and Afghanistan. There also emerged a number of regional conflicts, such as the Iran–Iraq war, which were independent of the structure of a simple East–West confrontation. Although both superpowers suffered a loss of influence and prestige, it was the Soviet Union which suffered the most precipitous decline. In contrast to the period in the 1950s and 1960s when the Soviet developmental model seemed so attractive to many developing countries, the actual progress of those countries following the path of 'socialist orientation', such as Ethiopia, Angola, Mozambique, Vietnam, or Cuba, had considerably tarnished this model. By the early 1980s, even some Soviet analysts were questioning the validity of the non-capitalist path of development and recommended a decrease in Soviet foreign aid.[9] The growing evidence of the economic failures within the Soviet bloc itself further undermined the political attractiveness of imposing a command-administrative system allied to political repression. Indeed, by the time of *perestroika* and *glasnost*, the reality that the most salient feature of Marxist-Leninist regimes in the Third World was their commitment to terror and coercion could no longer be hidden under the veil of anti-imperialist revolutionary rhetoric.

The political environment, therefore, had already begun shifting before the late 1980s when the Soviet Union and the West began to cooperate in the Third World and to limit the economic, political, and military support to proxy dictatorial governments. The reduction in the level of superpower ideological confrontation merely intensified popular protest against the pretensions of many Third World dictators and their unfulfilled promises of a political nirvana in the future to justify repression and terror in the present. The fact that many of these leaders, rising to power after decolonization two or three decades earlier, had grown old, and in some cases senile, added to the momentum for change. The demise of the 'national security' justification for their authoritarian rule, with the associated superpower patronage which it provided, further contributed to the weakening of their power base. At the same time, the increasing demands by OECD countries for more responsive governments as a condition for the provision of aid added further pressures. Whilst earlier Western developmental institutions had often embraced authoritarian regimes as being better able to implement unpopular economic reform, the visible economic failure of many of the pro-capitalist authoritarian regimes in Latin America and the successful reforms initiated by incoming democratic governments weakened these anti-democratic assumptions.[10]

Such a shift in thinking in the OECD countries points to the third proposed systemic structural change influencing the political developments of the developing countries. This is the reduction in the degree of political tension between the developed and developing countries, at least in contrast to the intense confrontation of the North–South debate of the 1960s and 1970s. Clearly, such changes are intimately connected to the economic crisis and the decline of the cold war, but it is still a significant factor in its own right. In particular, it points to a dialectical process, where both sides have been more successful in finding mutually acceptable compromises to assuage their specific fears and concerns. This is not to suggest that the tensions have been eliminated, or that the earlier antagonisms might not re-emerge, but that a certain progress has been made in forging a less confrontational relationship.

The causes of this change cannot be seen as the result of some selfless moral international progress. For many developing countries, deference to the West has been imposed by the apparent absence of any other viable alternative, given the demise of socialism, the collapse of the Soviet Union, and the demands of economic liberalization. But there are also more positive factors which have been influential. The economic success of Taiwan, South Korea, Ghana, or Brazil has suggested that the international capitalist system might not be structured purely in order to impoverish the periphery and enrich the core. This has encouraged the view that joining the global economic system need not be a form of national suicide. Even India has succumbed to this logic and has relinquished its moralistic Nehruvian socialism and adopted a variety of economic liberalization measures. The consequence is that, in most developing countries, pursuit of material goods and the presence of an independent bourgeoisie is no longer seen as an imperialist threat to national independence.[11] Just as these earlier much reviled petty bourgeois figures have been resurrected, so the democratic ideal has enjoyed a similar revival. Ruling élites in developing countries have been less able to present all domestic civil and political protests as an externally fomented conspiracy.

For the developed industrialized countries, there can be seen an analogous process of pragmatic accommodation. In the 1970s, there was a widespread perception that the Third World represented a potentially serious threat to Western security and values. The OPEC oil price rises, and the effects of the 1973 Arab–Israeli war, were viewed as direct threats to both Western economic interests and its security interests in the Middle East. At the same time, the radicalization of the demands of the South for distributive justice, allied to the growing fear of the Soviet Union on the offensive in the Third World, undoubtedly unnerved the major industrialized powers. By the early 1990s, it was realized that such putative threats had been fairly easily contained and there was a far greater reassurance that the developing countries, barring the odd exception like Iraq, had broadly agreed to abide by the rules of international society. This, in turn, undermined the strategic arguments for sustaining authoritarian pro-Western regimes, which Jeanne Kirkpatrick memorably justified by saying that if 'they are sonabitches, they are our sonabitches'. At the beginning of the 1990s, it can plausibly be stated that the public Western commitment to the promotion of democracy was more closely correlated to actual practice than at any time since the Second World War.

Yet, these mutually reinforcing changes in the relationship should not hide the many sources of mutual distrust, which reflect a certain continuity with the earlier antagonisms of the 1970s. The demands of the IMF, World Bank, and the GATT negotiations are still viewed with deep resentment by most developing countries. The belief in the structural injustices of the international economic order have been far from lost. Analogously, the West's promotion of democratization, human rights, and environmental issues is rarely viewed as a dispassionate exercise of altruistic concern and rather more often as a form of neo-imperialist rhetoric, obscuring the real economic and developmental needs of the poverty-stricken South. From the other side of the dialectical relationship, the developed countries have not lost the fears of the non-Western world as a potential threat, as seen in the reaction to the rising power of Islamist movements and increased number of inter-ethnic and communal conflicts.[12] The early post-cold war optimism of an ineluctably pro-Western orientation of political change in the Third World has, as a consequence, been considerably qualified. Protectionist pressures in the mature industrialized countries have also led to a questioning of the social and political consequences of the enrichment of the non-Western regions of the world, most notably in East Asia.

These continuing tensions and conflicts highlight the need to adopt a certain caution in any analysis of the process of democratization. The end of the cold war has certainly transformed the international situation; and this section has argued that this new environment has so far been remarkably conducive to supporting the transition of many countries towards a more democratic system of government. But it has also been noted that this has been a far from a universal phenomenon, with some regions being more immune than others to the democratizing trends. There is no necessary reason why the future will remain as conducive to the further expansion or consolidation of political pluralism. The international political economy, which is so critical to the politics of the developing world, is evolving and changing so rapidly that it is almost impossible to predict its future demands.

In addition, it is vitally important to balance any account of the external international factors promoting or inhibiting democratization with an assessment of the internal structures and domestic challenges facing developing countries. Such an analysis usefully qualifies the nature of many of the democratic transitions in the 'third democratic wave' by bringing to light the internal difficulties and obstacles that need to be overcome before these fragile democracies can be consolidated. It also clarifies the advantages that authoritarianism appears to offer for many ruling élites. The next section, therefore, seeks to leaven the internationalist dough by highlighting some fundamental internal obstacles to democratization which confront many or most developing countries.

III. OBSTACLES TO DEMOCRATIZATION

There is a danger, which is present in much of the literature on democratization, of focusing on competitive elections, 'the competitive struggle for people's vote', as the primary unit of analysis.[13] Although elections are critical events in the democratizing process, too great an emphasis on them can obscure the social, political, and economic context within which any meaningful assessment of such political developments can be made. It can also divert attention from the continuing presence of a number of internal obstacles to the promotion or consolidation of greater political pluralism. This section will look at four of the most general and pervasive of these obstacles: (1) the problem that many of the states in the developing world are fundamentally weak and fragile; (2) that few developing countries possess strong civil societies; (3) that the process of modernization and economic liberalization threatens indigenous traditions and cultures of non-Western parts of the developing world; and (4) that the regional and international conditions only intermittently favour or protect the process of democratic consolidation.

1. The weakness of the state

The fragility of many states in the international system has become even more noticeable since the end of the cold war. Indeed, it is now clear that, despite its many inequities, the cold war sustained and supported a number of states which have now almost completely disintegrated. This not only includes the post-imperial fragmentation of the Soviet Union and Yugoslavia, where a number of ethnic, religious, and nationalist groups have been struggling over the carcass of the collapsed state. In Africa, countries like Somalia, Rwanda, Liberia, and Angola have essentially ceased to exist as sovereign entities. As such states fail to attract any popular allegiance, other forms of sub-state or supra-state identity have filled the ideological vacuum. Clan, tribe, ethnos, religion, and nation have all vied for the allegiance of communities and have asserted their pretensions through intolerance, violence, and conflict. The communal conflicts which now assail many parts of the developing world are the direct outcome of these struggles for identity and the attempts to secure a territorial basis for their consolidation.

Liberal political theory has been singularly unsuccessful in providing coherent explanations for the recurrence and virulence of these elemental struggles. The most common liberal reaction is a cosmopolitan disdain for the seeming return to a primitive tribalism. The sources of the liberal failure of imagination can best be seen in its proposed models of a social contract, such as those outlined by John Locke or John Rawls.[14] In these accounts, there is no hint of conflict as the pre-social nation decides through a process of consensus upon a liberal polity. Although this 'veil of ignorance' is a philosophical contrivance, it does reflect the way liberal thinking tends to overlook the highly coercive and conflictual process through most states have been formed. Only in very rare cases, such as in England, has the process been relatively conflict-free due to a variety of factors, not least the centuries rather than decades in which political liberalization and economic modernization took place. Most other states-in-formation have been far less fortunate and the emerging state has only gained its monopoly of the legitimate use of violence through coercing its peoples into a common culture and by forcefully subduing other claimants to power.

Most developing countries are themselves engaged in such a struggle, facing all the problems related to building strong centralized states. Many of them also have the additional problem of contending with unhelpful, artificial state borders. The most extreme examples can be found in sub-Saharan Africa, where the post-colonial borders rarely captured any pre-existing political entity but rather a multiplicity of segmented communities with their own distinctive identities. Most of the peoples of Africa still have no deep loyalty to their designated states, as is graphically illustrated by the many mass migrations which take place intermittently on the continent. As one commentator has suggested, in the *longue durée* Africa's most distinctive contribution has been the 'art of living in a reasonably peaceful way without the state'.[15] As a result, the supposedly sovereign state in Africa frequently designates nothing more than a lucrative source of revenues for competing élites representing one subgroup or another. In such circumstances, any attempt to introduce a democratic electoral process can be expected to result in a circulation or a perpetuation of ruling élites rather than a genuine transfer of popular power. Much of the recent democratization process in sub-Saharan Africa must, unfortunately, be seen in this light.

The problem of building strong states on divided, segmented societies is not, though, limited to Africa. The inter-ethnic conflicts in the former Yugoslavia and Soviet Union have shown that, even in Europe, the process of nation-building is far from complete. Underlying these tragedies is the fundamental problem that there are few models of multi-national and multi-ethnic democratic states which can easily be imitated. The Swiss and Belgian models have highly specific historical roots and the futility of transferring their political structures was cruelly exposed by the Vance-Owen plan for Bosnia-Herzegovina. The reality is that the examples of liberal multi-ethnic societies, of which India is the most notable example in the developing world, are more the exception than the rule. In most cases, the dynamic is towards making the people fit the state rather than the state the people and this necessarily entails varying degrees of compulsion or expulsion. A process of democratization can, unless very skilfully engineered, only contribute to the ensuing violence.

Even in states where a considerable degree of integration and centralization has taken place, past fears of a breakdown of social stability can act as a powerful deterrent against political liberalization. The Chinese communist leadership accrues considerable political capital by playing on the popular fears of a return to the warlordism and anarchy of the end of Manchu imperial rule. Similar justifications are used by other Asian leaders, who promote the Confucian tradition of political order and stability. In this Asian-Confucian context, Western promotion of democratization is often perceived as a neo-imperialist imposition which would undermine rather than strengthen society.[16]

Indeed, authoritarianism does have the political advantage of being preferable to anarchy or a complete breakdown of political order.[17] In many areas of the developing world, the perceived risks of political democracy descending into inter-communal conflict can provide a popular base for authoritarianism. In the post-Soviet Central Asian states, the effect of the Tajik civil war has been to undermine the attraction of a process of political liberalization.[18] Similarly, whether it is Deng Xiaoping or King Hussein, dictators can consolidate their legitimacy by intensifying the fear that 'après moi le déluge'. The associated argument that economic prosperity would be threatened by political liberalization provides additional support to the perpetuation of authoritarian rule.

There are, therefore, a number of reasons relating to the intrinsic weakness of states in most developing countries which limit the potential for democratic reforms. In certain instances, such reforms cannot be expected fundamentally to change the illiberal nature of society but will only perpetuate the exclusive possession of the state apparatus by small unrepresentative élites. In other instances, a process of political liberalization can be expected to harden rather than weaken existing social cleavages, whether based on ethnic, religious, or national grounds. In such cases, the perceived or actual weakness of the state will provide a strong legitimating justification for the continuation of dictatorial rule. In short, authoritarianism remains very much a live and viable option for many developing countries.

2. The weakness of civil society

A weak state necessarily implies a weak civil society; no vibrant civil society is possible without a state capable of safeguarding property rights and other civil and political liberties. But a strong state does not necessarily entail a strong civil society. Indeed, it is far more normal for states that have successfully accumulated power to their associated agencies to use those powers to subdue rather than empower their societies with genuine liberties.

Thus, the idea of civil society, which is at the centre of the democratic ideal, demands a remarkable degree of self-restraint on the part of the state. For a civil society to thrive, states must limit their recourse to force and establish an array of institutions which are committed to functional pragmatic compromise. The implications of this are far-reaching and profound. For example, it requires that politicians should not receive excessive rewards and should not be the preserve of any particular privileged groups; that the military or the police should strictly limit their duties to the defence of external and internal security without undermining economic and political freedoms; that those in charge of the economy should follow national objectives and not be tempted to emasculate the operation of the market or line their own or others' pockets. In terms of human history, such behaviour is highly abnormal for individuals who have gained access to the levers of state power.[19]

When even wealthy and consolidated liberal democracies find these conditions difficult to fulfil, it is hardly surprising that most developing countries lack strong civil societies. The position of the military in many developing countries highlights some of the dilemmas and problems. In much early developmental theory, the military was selected as an intrinsically modernizing force, given the relative openness of its ranks to the lower and middle classes and its frequent commitment to secular, modern values. In many parts of the world, as for example in Turkey, the military has played a generally positive role in guiding their societies through the process of nation-building and modernization. But, the ascendance of the military has normally been a double-edged sword; having tasted the rewards and privileges of power, they often show great reluctance to relinquish these to civilian control (and here Turkey is the exception). Even more dangerous has been the tendency of the military to consolidate their position by forming alliances with the landed aristocracy. This has been a regular political occurrence in Latin America, thereby undermining the political ascendancy of a commercial middle class, itself an essential structural precondition for political pluralism.[20] Much of the democratic struggle in Latin America has been, and continues to be, directed towards breaking the military-landowning stranglehold on civil society.

A similar set of problems is faced by developing countries in ensuring the equitable distribution of the economic resources accruing to the state. It is hardly a startling observation that the holders of political authority are frequently tempted to use such resources for a variety of regressive purposes; to enrich themselves or certain privileged groups; to oil the wheels of political patronage; or to undermine private property rights and contractual arrangements. How to create the conditions for containing corruption and for ensuring the most efficient and just allocation of state resources is one of the most difficult problems facing any state. In the context of a state without a strong civil society, initiating a process of democratization is not always the best solution, as has been demonstrated by the upsurge in criminality and mafia corruption in the states of the former Soviet Union. It is perhaps a sad truth that the direction of reform undertaken by China might ultimately be the more appropriate. If China continues to promote economic pluralism, together with the security of property rights and respect for contract, the transition towards a greater degree of political pluralism might, in the end, be less traumatic than has been the case in the former Soviet Union.

At a more fundamental level, these problems of consolidating a strong civil society mirror the obstacles to the promotion of a liberal democracy. In many developing countries, those committed to the promotion of civil society are the same small minority who are pressing for the institution of liberal democracy. But for the majority of the people in such societies, liberal democracy is in competition with, and frequently less attractive than, other more reassuring or populist ideologies. As one book on the Middle East has expressed it, the problem is how to promote democracy without there being democrats.[21] Certainly, the holding of competitive elections is an important stage in the democratic struggle but it only represents a beginning. Consolidation of a democratic culture requires the democratic process to be socially habituated, so that all groups accept the demands of political compromise and agree to a limited functional role for the state. As such, the struggle for civil society has still to be fiercely fought in most developing countries.

3. Preservation of tradition

It is not only developing countries which have been struggling with the dilemma of how to preserve traditional communal values in the face of the anonymous and socially dislocative forces of economic liberalization and globalization. In the mature Western democracies, a number of political philosophers and sociologists, who have been loosely grouped together under a 'communitarian' banner, have challenged the traditional liberal emphasis on individualism and its neutral stance towards the political goals of society.[22] They have argued that an individual's moral life cannot be abstracted from the common moral and political objectives of the community as a whole. Reflecting widespread concern at the increasingly atomistic and fractured condition of advanced liberal societies, they have recommended a return to a more holistic moral tradition which accords greater value to virtues over liberties and social obligations over individual rights. The political popularity of these views, even in such traditionally liberal countries as Britain and the United States, reflects a popular disenchantment at liberalism's seeming incapacity to safeguard social cohesion and defend such vital traditional institutions as the family.

If the mature industrialized countries are struggling with such questions, it is hardly surprising that the poorer developing countries face even greater challenges. The social costs of a rapid transition from a traditional to a modern industrializing society are far more damaging to existing social values and institutions than anything encountered in more mature industrial societies. The resulting sense of alienation and *anomie* breeds enormous social unrest and political instability. For non-Western societies, there is an additional problem that the cultural expression of the global economy and the international system appears to embody distinctively Western values, which can exacerbate the sense of alienation and mistrust. In particular, Asian and Islamic countries, which are inheritors of ancient civilizations as old or older than Western societies, are especially sensitive to any perceived imposition of alien values. The recent and still bitter memory of colonial rule in most of these countries further accentuates the desire to articulate a more authentic social and political model, which can be differentiated from the Western ideal of liberal democracy. During the cold war, socialism provided a potential alternative framework, offering a secular yet utopian ideology which could justify the sacrifices, social and political, needed to form a modern industrial society. The collapse of the Soviet Union considerably weakened the attraction of this model; but it has not ushered in the unchallenged ascendance of liberal thought. The success with which communist leaderships, particularly in Central and East Asia, have been transforming themselves into nationalists, whilst at the same time preserving many of the repressive communist structures, has revealed their political resilience and adaptability. A nationalist and capitalist form of Marxism-Leninism, as practised in China or Vietnam, is proving to be a formidable political hybrid. It reflects the legitimizing power of strong nationalist self-assertion as a means for consolidating the authoritarian rule of small unrepresentative groups. The highly illiberal Asian style of democracy, as advocated by President Lee Kwan Yew of Singapore, provides a similar ideological justification for such nationalist and cultural exceptionalism.

Nor has the demise of socialism stemmed the search for other potential universalist and internationalist forms of political legitimacy, even if it has shifted the focus. The rise of Islam as a political force in most Muslim countries is testament to the popular demand for an overarching moral framework for social and political activity, which Western-style democracy appears unable to provide. Islam's uniqueness is that, alone amongst the world religions, it has successfully resisted the process of secularization which has effectively marginalized other religions, and has remarketed its product for the needs of modernizing and industrializing Muslim societies. This success can, in part, be related to the egalitarian nature of its belief structure, which permits no exceptions, even for the political leadership, to the legal obligations as defined in the *shari'a* Islam's inclusiveness and the simplicity and coherence of its political ideology has a powerful mobilizing effect which few regimes in the Muslim world can afford to ignore. Unlike socialism, modern political Islam also has the distinct advantage that its fortunes are not tied to economic success or failure.[23]

It is a mistake, though, to treat the phenomenon of Islamic protest in an essentialist and undifferentiated manner.[24] The various Islamist movements in the Muslim world must be located in their specific socioeconomic and political context. Islamic protest is, in most cases, a genuine and legitimate reaction against repressive regimes, which have substantially forfeited any popular legitimacy. These groups often have a positive role in empowering civil society, through extending the welfare and social provisions which the states in the region have abjectly failed to provide. There is, therefore, no a priori justification for excluding Islamist groups from any prospective democratic process, since such incorporation would require them to assume political responsibility and learn the art of pragmatic political compromise. Advocates of this approach point to the success of Jordan's political experiment of including Islamist elements into a democratizing process, and contrast Jordan's example with the increasing descent into civil war in Algeria after the government's refusal to honour the Islamist electoral victory.[25]

However, such arguments have to be balanced by the reality that the central doctrines of political Islam rarely include an unqualified commitment to political pluralism. The implementation of *shari'a* law sets distinct limits to the permissable articulation of conflicts of interest. The possibility cannot be excluded that Islamist groups might not be converted to democratic norms merely by inclusion into the democratic process. Indeed, the long and bitter resistance fought by the Roman Catholic Church against the precepts of liberal political thought indicates the difficulty of reforming orthodox interpretations of divine law. With Islam gaining in strength and popularity, the temptation will remain for Islamist groups to seize power for the purposes of realizing the vision of a truly theocratic society.[26]

The rise of Islam, or as one commentator has called it 'la revanche de Dieu', is the most dramatic response to the desire for a more authentic political vision to counterbalance the corrosive effect of westernization and economic modernization.[27] But it is not an isolated phenomenon. For countries struggling on the tortuous and painful path towards prosperity, the articulation of a common moral endeavour based on the preservation of traditional culture and institutions has a powerful attraction. Liberal democracy, with its pragmatism and its functional instrumentality, lacks the moral force which many societies feel is necessary to legitimate the process of modernization. In many Asian societies, this has prompted a conflation of Confucianism and traditional authoritarianism to ensure social and political stability.[28] Other regions, such as Africa or Latin America, could find political solace by following a similar path, especially if the economic benefits of political liberalization fail to materialize.

In general, the struggle for democracy in most countries of the developing world has to contend with the attractions of a variety of populist, nationalist, or religious anti-democratic alternatives, which claim, however disingenuously, a greater traditional or cultural authenticity. Certainly, democratization is a process through which these other alternatives can be gradually de-ideologized and their ambitions constrained by the habituation to a political process of accommodation and toleration. Over time, it can also lead to the point where democracy is viewed as an indigenous tradition which is worth preserving. However, this is normally a long and difficult process, which is far from unilinear, with many prospective reverses and opportunities for backsliding.

4. Regional and international conditions

The relative historical contribution made by exogenous as against endogenous factors in the promotion of democracy is almost impossible to disentangle. What can be said without controversy is that many democratic transitions, which have subsequently led to the consolidation of a liberal society, were greatly influenced by external factors.[29] This is not just through the relatively consensual 'diffusion effect', where the example of democratization in one country spreads to other neighbouring countries. Historically, a more significant influence has been a coercive imposition of democratic governance, such as in Germany, Japan, and Italy after the Second World War, or in most post-colonial countries, such as India where the political system constructed by the withdrawing imperial power has unusually survived. The US invasion of Haiti in 1994 for the avowed purpose of restoring democracy indicated the continuing vitality of this model of quasi-imperialist external intervention for democratizing purposes.

The case of Haiti has been the exception in the post-cold war era. Coercive intervention has not generally been seen as an appropriate vehicle for promoting democracy.[30] Rather, hopes have rested on the expansion of democracy as a by-product of the increasing regional co-operation and integration evident in many areas of the world. The experience of the European Community, whose membership is limited to democracies, has acted as the most compelling paradigm of a regional body which has directly influenced the cause of democratic reform for countries on its periphery. The strict democratic conditions for entry into the EU, and the considerable economic benefits that membership provides, have been a catalyst leading to the transitions to democracy in Greece, Spain, and Portugal. Political developments in Turkey have also been affected by aspirations for potential membership of the Union. Democratic consolidation in Eastern and Central Europe can also be expected to be directly related to the expectation of eventual membership of the EC's single economic market.

However, in most other parts of the developing world the prospect of an institutionalized regional dynamic for democratization is considerably weaker. The exception might be Latin America, whose various regional bodies such as Organisation of American States (OAS), MERCOSUR, the Andean Pact, the Central American Common Market, and Caricom, provide in embryonic form potential EU-type bodies with commitments both to free trade and democracy.[31] NAFTA is also a potential forum contributing to democratization, though its acquiescence in President Salinas's gerrymandering of election results in 1988 revealed the limitations of NAFTA's commitment to political over economic liberalization. In other parts of the developing world, the prospects for regionalism acting as a democratic force have more tenuous foundations. In certain regions, the best that can be said is that the regional hegemon is formally committed to democracy and could become the catalyst for a regional democratizing process. The republic of South Africa and, more controversially, Russia could be such regional democratic hegemons. But, in regions where the political hegemon is deeply distrusted, such as Israel in the Middle East or India in South Asia, or firmly committed to authoritarianism as with China, regional organizations remain limited to economic rather than political issues and cannot be expected to contribute a decisive external influence towards democratization.

In reality, the majority of developing countries do not have a regional framework conducive to entrenching and consolidating democratic reforms. Partly in recognition of this, the OECD countries have sought to provide an additional impetus by incorporating common political conditionalities which have been linked to the dispensation of developmental aid.[32] These include attempts to coordinate standards over human rights, good governance, and demands for political participation, which have had some beneficial effects, particularly in encouraging multi-party elections in a number of African countries.

However, there are distinct limits to the application and universalizability of such common international standards on political practice. First, it is limited to those regions which are beneficiaries of such OECD aid. Countries enjoying private capital flows, such as in East Asia or Latin America, are relatively immune from such political conditions, leaving only the poorer countries being required to accommodate these demands. Second, even after the cold war, the developed world's interest in democratization is not an absolute concern; it can be overridden by other interests, such as a strategic concern for political stability or for supporting regimes committed to large-scale arms procurement. An example of this is in the Persian Gulf region where concern for the security of oil supplies, combined with the international embargo on Iraq and Iran, have led to *de facto* support for authoritarian and unrepresentative regimes in the Gulf Arab states. The argument, popular amongst disaffected developing countries, that the West imposes a democratic double standard cannot be easily evaded.

Finally, the inherent problems of creating a common set of democratic conditions reflecting the heterogeneous political realities in the developing world render a considerable subjectivity to the application of such conditions. The fact that the IMF and World Bank are precluded constitutionally from setting political conditions further complicates the issue. The preference for focusing on narrower and more quantifiable conditions, such as respect for human rights or demands for good governance, reflects an understandable pragmatic compromise. But it does mean that authoritarian regimes are not excluded from substantially fulfilling these less rigorous conditions.

IV. CONCLUSIONS

The starting-point of this chapter was the need to explain the sources and the significance of the large number of transitions to democracy, particularly in Latin America and sub-Saharan Africa, which have taken place since the mid-1970s, at a time when the prospects for such a development seemed so improbable. A number of factors were isolated of which the ending of the cold war was one significant element. However, as much if not greater weight was accorded to the changes in the international political economy, particularly in the context of the economic crises which confronted most of the developing world. The changing nature of the complex dialectical relationship between the developed and developing countries, creating a greater degree of trust and pragmatic accommodation than was present earlier, was also identified as a significant catalyst for political change. Thus, the ending of the cold war, however much it was an 'epochal event', was far from the sole or sufficient cause for this democratizing trend.

The degree of continuity over change was further emphasized by a closer analysis of the internal and structural constraints and obstacles with which most developing countries are forced to contend. The end of the cold war has only tangentially contributed to the resolution of the problem of the weakness of states in the developing world. Indeed, in some cases it has directly accentuated such problems, as the collapse of countries like Somalia or the former Yugoslavia have shown. Similarly, the institutions of civil society in developing countries, which generally remain weak and poorly grounded, have only been marginally strengthened, if at all, by the collapse of the bipolar system of superpower confrontation. The demise of socialism as an attractive and reproducible ideological model can be seen as undermining one important intellectual support for authoritarianism; but various forms of nationalist or cultural exceptionalism have taken up much of the slack and the drive to discover new all-encompassing illiberal ideological frameworks has far from disappeared. Finally, the hopes for new political structures supportive of democratic processes, based on greater regional integration and more consistent Western internationalist cooperation, have failed to materialize except in an incomplete and partial form.

These various qualifications indicate a more cautious and sceptical approach than that taken by many commentators in the immediate aftermath of the cold war, who presented a far rosier picture of the global prospects for liberal democracy. Francis Fukuyama's *The End of History and the Last Man* was respectively celebrated or denounced as the ideological icon of this neo-liberal optimism.[33] Although many of the subtleties of his argument have been lost in the subsequent debates, Fukuyama did suggest that the end of the cold war had finally lifted the last substantive obstacle to the ideological domination of capitalism and the inexorable expansion of democracy. In practical terms, it appeared as an elegant philosophical adjunct to the radical prescriptions of 'shock therapy', which sought to reduce the state to a nightwatchman role, providing the basic guarantee for law and order and the free and efficient operation of the market-place. The arguments presented in this chapter have sought to demonstrate the inappropriateness of this model of modernization and democratization and its limited applicability to most regions of the developing world.

However, the resurrection of more simplistic, unilinear models of modernization theory is not the only possible response to the ending of the cold war. There is another rich and historically well-grounded tradition of thought, which has remained relatively independent of the dualistic assumptions of the cold war. Ironically, the roots of this tradition lie with the great philosophers of the Scottish enlightenment who have been elevated as the ideological watchdogs of the neo-liberal orthodoxy.[34] Adam Smith and Adam Ferguson were, in reality, far from complacent about the 'invisible hand' of the market. They were greatly exercised by the potentially damaging consequences that the division of labour, free trade, and the market economy might have on the social and political framework of toleration and liberty. Most notably, Ferguson struggled with his fears that the social division between unarmed economic actors and a professional military might lead to a military dictatorship.[35] In this century, these concerns were readdressed by such thinkers as Karl Polanyi, Joseph Schumpeter, and Barrington Moore, all of whom noted the enormous social changes involved in the expansion of capitalism and the pressures that it places on democratic forms of political toleration and liberty.[36] Barrington Moore in his seminal work, *Social Origins of Dictatorship and Democracy*, provided a detailed historical and sociological account of the underlying structural factors which led to the emergence of a 'democratic version of capitalism' in England, France, and the United States; to a capitalist but reactionary form in Germany and Japan; and to communist regimes in Russia and China. Moore's analysis involved a dense historical understanding, allied with a complex evaluation of the contribution of the landed upper class and peasantry to the respective political institutions which emerged in the course of modernization. His work is a healthy antidote to the assumption that the progress of capitalism leads inevitably and inexorably to the consolidation of democracy.

The importance of this tradition of thought is that it does offer some basic insights which provide a fruitful analytical framework for thinking about the prospects and nature of political change in developing, modernizing countries. For a start, it militates against an over-optimistic assessment of the global prospects for democracy in the post-cold war era. In the larger historical perspective, there can be little justification for assuming that any single exogenous development, even as 'epochal' an event as the end of the cold war, can radically reorientate the political outcomes in the rest of the world towards a single evolutionary path. For countries engaged on the tortuous journey towards modern industrial societies, there will be a complex array of social, economic, and political challenges engendering a variety of political outcomes, depending on the domestic and international conditions and the strengths and weaknesses of the existing political leadership. Even if 'late' or 'late-late' developers can learn from the experience of those who now enjoy economic prosperity and political liberty, there is no simple emulative model available for economic growth or democratic consolidation.

Second, this tradition of thought points to a need to deconstruct the meaning of democracy and its exclusive identification with moral virtue.

Democracy, as suggested here, cannot be reduced simply to a procedural notion, such as the holding of competitive elections, however necessary such procedures are to the establishment and perpetuation of a democratic process. The substance of democracy involves a far more complex interaction between a strong state, capable of fulfilling its essential functions, and an independent society which can assert its civil and political liberties. In articulating these less quantifiable features of the democratic ideal, the notion of civil society has a valuable function. Particularly when looking at the developing world, it promotes a greater sensitivity to the essential nature of the different manifestations of political culture and social structures. It suggests, at the very least, the need for a taxonomy which differentiates between consolidated and transitional democracies; between genuine democratic transitions and essentially 'façade' democracies; and between authoritarian regimes which might have created the preconditions for political pluralism and those that have not. In addition, such an approach avoids the mistake of assuming that every democratic transition is a priori desirable; in certain instances, a process of democratization might unleash destructive forces, such as extreme ethnic or nationalist self-assertion, which had formerly been successfully constrained by authoritarian modes of governance.

Third, the advantage of this historical sociological tradition is that it offers a far more open-ended account of the nature of political change. If countries such as England, France, and Germany, which benefited from a common cultural legacy, had such diverse starting-points, differing trajectories, and final liberal end-points, the likelihood is that societies with radically different cultural, and social traditions, with very disparate historical experiences, should have similarly diverse paths towards modernity and the attainment of economic and political pluralism. This provides a welcome liberation from the constrictive dualism of the cold war ideological framework. Discussion of the nature and forms of capitalism has already benefited from this more open intellectual environment. Instead of a sterile debate between the benefits of capitalism against socialism, there is now a greater sensitivity to the various forms of capitalism and to the different ways in which states and markets can interact to increase productivity and efficiency. Analogously, there ought to be a similar approach for analysing the struggle towards political pluralism in different parts of the world and the ways in which social, cultural, and historical traditions condition the relations between individual states and their societies. Ultimately, it is only through such detailed and historically sensitive analyses that the political developments in any particular society or region can be adequately understood.

3

Developing States and the End of the Cold War

Liberalization, globalization, and their consequences

GAUTAM SEN

I. INTRODUCTION

The position of developing countries in the world political economy has experienced radical transformation since the mid-1980s. The transformation is both in measurable changes in their own objective circumstances as well as the wider context within which they operate.[1] There has also been a shift in the perceptions and attitudes of Third World élites and a loss of support from former third worldists in the West.[2] However, none of the economic transformations, to which this chapter primarily refers, can be adequately explained without taking into account the political and cultural aspects of global change in the aftermath of the Soviet collapse.

There are three interconnected historical events of dramatic significance that underlie change in the developing world or inform them in some way. The first is the collapse of communism, creating powerful new constraints as well as allowing fresh intellectual reappraisal of existing certainties. Its consequences are still reverberating intricately through parts of the developing world owing to the relatively sluggish transmission of ideas and information.

The second phenomenon, related to the first, but predating it as well as possessing a dynamic of its own, is the evident triumph of capitalism. The spread of market processes and privatization and attendant ideologies are of great importance because of the collapse of serious alternatives.[3]

The third dimension to this interpretation of the changes afoot is the emergence of the dialectical anti-thesis to the triumph of capitalism.[4] The defeat of the socialist challenge, at least for the foreseeable future, has not led to the disappearance of conflicts between social classes, regions, and countries. It has created new modes of disputation although their intellectual underpinnings are less coherent for the present.

The following section examines the political and economic conditions affecting developing countries. The two themes are the evolution of the international economy, especially since the 1970s, and the political impact of the ending of the cold war. The latter impinges on intellectual convictions and some established institutional practices. The subsequent section addresses the key issues of liberalization and globalization, which preceded the end of the cold war, but are now influenced by that climactic event. The differing impact of liberalization and globalization on developing countries and the significance of economic events of the 1980s are underlined. The next section identifies the deepening of liberalization and globalization as well as the phenomenon of regional integration and asymmetric competition between developed and developing countries. Aspects of the consequences of change within domestic society are also analysed briefly and the vulnerability of relatively weak societies to international economic forces is noted.

A more detailed discussion of two important expressions of liberalization and globalization follows. The importance of structural adjustment programmes for the advance of the new market forms and their associated ideology is investigated. The second event analysed is the GATT Uruguay round of trade negotiations, which is the basic institutional framework for liberalization and the future operation of the international economy. In each instance the political implications for developing countries are recorded.

The two final sections of the chapter evaluate the use of political power by developed countries to achieve economic ends. The role of diplomacy in altering market outcomes and the deployment of industrial policy to pursue competitive economic advantage are highlighted as particularly noteworthy. The discrepancy between the actual experience of successful developing economies and the recommendations of international agencies to other countries, purporting to be based on it, is then discussed. A final, concluding section assesses the possible future pattern of interaction between developed and developing countries. Although the latter description is now unambiguously imperfect, since socio-economic conditions in these countries have diverged substantially, it remains historically evocative and accurately underlines the relative asymmetry in power and influence in relation to developed countries that developing ones all share to some degree.

II. POLITICAL AND ECONOMIC CONTEXT
OF CHANGE

The historical context in which the above processes apply to different developing economies varies, although some broad economic and political issues of common relevance can be identified. Developing countries, with the notable exception of the Asian newly industrializing countries (NICs), have encountered recession (stagnation/low growth) in the world economy since the first oil crisis in 1973, which worsened during the 1980s. The economic slowdown undermined them in two interrelated ways: (1) the demand and prices of exports of a majority of countries were affected adversely; (2) it created a more hostile political reception in the advanced industrialized countries for the relatively successful exporters, for example, of Southeast and East Asia.

Two further problems created difficulties for developing countries. One was the need for much more sophisticated domestic financial management, because of the financial disarray which followed the end of Bretton Woods and the recycling of petrodollars and debt. The history of the debt crisis need not be recounted here, although the financial imbroglio continues for many developing countries and the source of indebtedness is more multilateral and bilateral intergovernmental than private. International banks involved, however, had ensured their own solvency by lowering debt equity ratios. By 1998 investors from developed countries found themselves, once again, facing major losses because of economic volatility and possible default by debtors in the developing world as financial crisis engulfed Asian economies. The other factor was the spectacular collapse of socialism as a competitor to capitalism, which can be regarded as virtually epochal. The origins of pro-market policies can be traced to the challenge of monetarist ideas and, at a more practical level, to the electoral victories of Thatcher and Reagan in the late 1970s and early 1980s, which some Third World élites subsequently sought to imitate. Economic transformation in the People's Republic of China (PRC) began just a year before the onset of these pro-market reforms in Britain, the US, and elsewhere in the world. But in conjunction with the Soviet collapse and the end of the cold war the spectacular march of capitalism in contemporary times has provided pro-market forces with unstoppable momentum.

The economic changes that are the principal focus of this paper coincided with major political changes in developing countries in the aftermath of the cold war. Specifically, the issues of political democracy in developing countries and of foreign policy options of major powers are both dependent on economic liberalization. As far as political democracy is concerned, the end of the cold war removed the rationale for Western support of authoritarian anti-communist regimes merely because they were allies against the Soviet Union and able to resist political forces perceived to be pro-Soviet. At the same time, similarly undemocratic regimes deprived of Soviet support found themselves vulnerable to challenge from domestic opposition groups that had hitherto been forcibly denied access to the political process. The only coinage of renegotiation between new political forces in such countries, in the absence of support for particular regimes from cold war protagonists, had to be pluralism. And pluralism implied democracy, which was the functional expression of its formal identity, even where it did not enjoy wholehearted domestic and foreign political support.

The relationship between liberalization and democratization was subtle and powerful where dirigiste formerly pro-Soviet regimes were concerned. In societies where state power and access to economic resources had been pre-empted by a particular group in society the advance of political plurality required, as its corollary, a reduction in state control over the economy. That by definition meant liberalization and market forces. By and large this phenomenon can be observed in much of pro-Soviet Africa as well as countries like Vietnam. The thinking of political movements like the ANC in South Africa and India's pro-Soviet political establishment has also altered in favour of market forms of economic activity, following the comprehensive chaos of socialist central economic planning.

The advance of political pluralism and democracy in pro-Western countries, where market economic processes were already prominent, did not imply a comparable economic transformation. Political pluralism in these countries in the aftermath of the end of the cold war was accompanied by an unexpected convergence of views between competing groups that eased political transition. On the one hand, the narrow political conception of markets by political and social élites, in terms of defending property rights against potential socialist threats, was complemented by a more dynamic view favouring competition and freer trade. On the other hand, the previously repressed political groups which pluralism and democracy now allowed to operate, ceased to espouse, like the ANC in South Africa, socialist collective ownership and direction of the economy as their main political agenda; the coincidence of liberalization and democratization eased the Latin American transition by creating a new consensus favourable to markets.[5]

The transformative political, economic, and intellectual impact of the cold war also reintroduced the issue of institutions and state capacity which had been overlaid by ongoing conflicts between North and South about outcomes and history. The preoccupation with economic injustices, both current and historical, had obscured the practical problems of effective management as an overriding factor in successful economic development—the real problem underlying the multiplicity of issues under negotiation and discussion between the North and the South. The end of the cold war finally dissipated the ideological glue that had distracted attention from the issue of economic and political management to the question of goals and the appropriate international economic environment for their achievement. But the sudden dissipation of cold war loyalties and accompanying intellectual fixations of the left and right suddenly exposed urgent problems of economic and political management. It might be argued, in fact, that completion of the Uruguay round, which had actually started in 1986, and the acceptance of many of its historically radical departures by the time of its conclusion in 1994 were influenced by the political earthquake of the Soviet collapse in the intervening period. The IMF and the World Bank had also discovered that programmes to dismantle pre-existing state economic involvement in the economy required a competent state, even a temporarily extended state organization.[6] The importance of such state capacity has been demonstrated by the economic successes of Asian NICs and the contestation of weak states as diverse as Bosnia-Herzegovina, Rwanda, and Uganda. The origins of coherent and purposive state and bureaucratic structures are apparently complex and their absence a serious barrier to economic development or even the mere survival of society.

One of the areas in which the weakness of post-colonial states has been evident, but never satisfactorily explained, is in their foreign policy conduct, an area of paramount importance to established societies. A study of regional integration efforts in West Africa, for example, demonstrates a remarkable lack of realism about constraints to cooperation between sovereign states. Much the same can be said of the attempts by post-colonial leaders as diverse as Nehru and Arafat to establish personal goodwill with foreign leaders in order to achieve their goals. A fundamental reason for this flawed method of pursuing policy goals is the embryonic stage of foreign policy institutions and consequent weak institutional memory in most post-colonial societies. The one area of colonial policy firmly located in the capital of the colonial power was its foreign policy. The foreign policy of a colonial possession was merely a factor in the wider foreign policy of the mother country. Thus once the colonial power departed, with independence, the newly independent country found itself making foreign policy in an institutional vacuum, sometimes filled by gifted amateurs, more often, by ideologues and adventurers. The consequences are there for all to see.

The end of the cold war requires a serious reappraisal of the formulation and implementation of foreign policy in post-colonial societies since familiar and therapeutic slogans cannot suffice, nor slavish adherence to the dictates of a relatively fixed and predictable world of bipolarity. The consequences of this rather sudden demise of certainty can be seen in the post-cold war confusion in societies as different as Saudi Arabia and India for whom the new world order offers no purchase for the posture of either ostriches, hiding inoffensively in the sand, or the assertion of ancient moral superiority.

III. LIBERALIZATION AND GLOBALIZATION

The two issues of particular interest to this volume, liberalization and globalization, are the specific factors which are considered to affect contemporary developing countries as a group as well as the formerly planned economies. In a sense globalization is the economic outcome of liberalization for which there are socio-economic and human consequences. It is appropriate to seek to offer a set of criteria by which these two phenomena may be detected.

Liberalization refers to measures extending and enhancing the operation of market forces. They include both microeconomic and macroeconomic aspects of the economy. The former includes the political and legislative measures enacted in a range of countries including post-Allende Chile, Thatcher's Britain, and Reaganite America to, for example, free labour markets and denationalize industry.[7] On the macroeconomic level the most significant retreat has been from the policy of demand management to reduce unemployment. The adoption of floating exchange rates and the abandonment of capital controls are also an aspect of macroeconomic liberalization.[8]

The dominant contemporary perception of liberalization is positive, particularly in the context of the dismal failures of various types of economic planning, both central planning and the dirigiste variety more common to developing countries. The argument is that economic mismanagement by politicians and the problems of rent seeking are chronic to major aspects of state involvement in the economy.[9] Thus it is predicted that the discipline of the market-place will result in fewer errors of judgement and those that occur will be on a reduced scale. Critics of marketization argue that the practical outcome of such liberalization policies is both a misrepresentation of the past (exaggeration of the failures of the state) and a vehicle for removing the few social measures which protect the weak from market failures and the exercise of political power.[10]

Globalization is counterposed to internationalization because it reflects the enhanced movement of goods and services across national borders and its organization on a transnational basis. Thus it refers to closer integration of the world economy as measured by trade/GNP ratios and international flows of foreign direct investment (fdi) and financial capital. But in contrast to national exports and imports of goods and services, the organization, flow and purview of fdi and global capital, undertaken by transnational corporations, assume a global market-place. It is also obvious that liberalization and globalization reinforce each other by combining pro-market policies that underpin the empirical reality of global economic integration. The historical sequence seems to be from separate national economies engaging in international economic relations to a global economic system in which the national economy, *mutatis mutandis*, is merely a piece of a global economic jigsaw puzzle, incomplete on its own.

The conventional view judges the process of globalization to allow, in the first place, the realization of static and dynamic efficiency gains through increased international specialization, in accordance with theories of international trade and foreign investment. Such a positive appraisal of the phenomenon also regards the increased flows of fdi and the mobility of financial capital as beneficial for both their owners and the locations which receive that investment. In popular imagination and scholarly perception this interdependence is binding the world in ways which are, finally, to be welcomed. By contrast, Immanuel Wallerstein, from a radical perspective views globalization as the highest point of global capitalism before the onset of its final historical phase. According to him and other world system theorists, following the end of further opportunities for spatial expansion the death throes of capitalism would be precipitated through a truly global class struggle.

But it is useful to pause to consider the historical dimensions of the apparent contagion of liberalization and globalization. On closer examination, it is clear that both of these facets were evident, to some degree, in a number of Asian countries, well in advance of the end of the cold war.[11] Another more geographically diverse group of countries exhibited the symptoms of both liberalization and globalization for a longer period. These countries include a number in Latin America and Africa (e.g. Malawi and Botswana). In any event, with the exception of the formerly centrally planned economies of Eastern Europe and the CIS, markets have coexisted with various types of state involvement in much of the developing world. The underlying economic catalysts of liberalization and its corollary, globalization, precede the subsequent causative political factor of the ending of the cold war as a matter of empirical fact.

While the end of communism is an important background variable, apparently vindicating and propelling market forces world-wide, more specific local factors and underlying changes in the international political economy are responsible for the advance of market reforms in the developing world.[12] In virtually all cases the immediate reason for the adoption of liberalization programmes has been a balance of payments crisis and a collapse of the exchange rate, usually accompanied by inflation and an unsustainable fiscal deficit. This situation is likely to have been preceded by stagnation or declining rates of growth, with all the social problems implied by high unemployment, especially with a rapidly growing workforce, common to much of the developing world. In a majority of cases the problems have been created by international indebtedness, intensified by it, or precipitated by it. Such a situation has led to structural adjustment programmes sponsored by international agencies and the pressure to liberalize as a condition for international assistance.[13]

The underlying changes in the international political economy exercise a more complex influence with general and specific implications for the individual developing country. There are three interdependent processes of change that can be identified. The first is the mobility of financial capital which has made it difficult for the state in both the developed and developing world (especially in the latter of course) to influence the terms on which it borrows.[14] The second is the apparent significance of fdi as a vehicle for exports and economic growth. The third is the dramatic perceptual impact of the phenomenon of high rates of growth in some parts of Asia on the hopes and anxieties of élites in the rest of the developing world.[15] In assessing the situation of developing countries it is possible to look at groups of geographical clusters which, with some exceptions, display common features.

By and large it is the decade of the 1980s which remains crucial as the period of change for developing countries. It ends of course with the collapse of communism, dating from 1989. But for many developing countries this was the decade of economic stagnation and the debt crisis, beginning with the Mexican default in 1982—the so-called 'lost decade'. During this period, as Jorge Heine discusses in his chapter, the Latin Americans as a group, and their most prominent members, Brazil, Argentina, and Mexico, suffered serious and historic reverses with zero or negative growth. Their poor economic performance is blamed on international indebtedness and inappropriate statist economic policies. Undoubtedly, this widely held view is partially tenable, but other factors like the world-wide economic slowdown and rising US interest rates during the early 1980s also had an important impact. What is much more significant, and here I take a somewhat less optimistic view than Jorge Heine, is the weak recovery in Mexico since the 1990s, despite the adoption of dramatic market-led policies, and the vulnerability of Latin American economies more generally to volatile international capital flows.[16]

Substantial reverses also occurred in much of sub-Saharan Africa. Their economic situation was worse in terms of debt/GDP and debt/service ratios. The combination of indebtedness and collapsing terms of trade and civil wars precipitated some of the worse conditions in post-war African history.[17] The Asians as a group defied the general economic situation and continue to advance. The uneven economic recovery of the major OECD countries during 1993, with the exception of the USA, but including Japan, has not undermined the buoyancy of the region. The non-inflationary economic recovery of the major OECD countries during 1994–5 and the widening of the opportunities for international trade with the successful conclusion of the Uruguay round of GATT suggested that the remarkable performance of the region would persist and improve. The dramatic turnaround of the Philippine economy, against expectations, indicates that remaining members of ASEAN may also join the virtuous circle of advancing countries. It also seems likely that Vietnam will continue to show improved economic performance and substantially enhanced international economic participation.[18] This is despite the major financial and economic crises that rocked Southeast and East Asia in 1997–8, the reasons for which will be discussed below.

IV. FUTURE EVOLUTION OF DEVELOPING COUNTRIES

The current situation in the late 1990s, against the backdrop of political change, new economic forces, and setbacks during the 1980s for quite a few, is establishing patterns likely to persist into the twenty-first century. These patterns display two prominent features: (1) liberalization, of course, and its consequence globalization; (2) the dramatic recovery of growth in some of the developing world (especially Brazil in Latin America and Ghana in Africa).

The process of liberalization and the resulting globalization needs to be viewed at the regional and domestic levels, in addition to the overarching systemic or international level. The international level is really a framework that constitutes the parameters for action for the individual actor or individual states acting in concert on a regional basis. As far as this systemic or international level is concerned, enhanced integration within the world economy introduces a new matrix within which decisions at the domestic and regional level become embedded. Thus monetary policy within each country of the European Union or MERCOSUR in Latin America is affected by regional concerns as well the relationship with the international currency, the dollar.

The way to look at the relationship between the systemic or international and the perspective of actors functioning at other levels is to conceive the latter either as price takers, the weak uninfluential states who are the small firms that take market prices as given, or the price makers, the large firms who can influence prices, the counterpart of the major powers in any given issue area. The relevant factors are size and per capita income as well as nationality, location, and alliances. Thus Kuwait is an unambiguous price taker on most non-oil issues compared to India, for example. The Netherlands, by comparison, can be regarded as an intermediate case, although it should be in a situation similar to that of Kuwait, except it has more space for manoeuvre because of nationality and geographical location.

Two groups of developing countries in Latin America and Asia are beginning to operate formally and informally at the regional level. Most impressive has been the debut and advance of MERCOSUR since 1991, encompassing Brazil, Argentina, Uruguay, and Paraguay (Chile and Bolivia have associate status), because they are important in size as markets and their potential is even greater. The gains of forming a common market with a common external tariff have been evident from the rapid growth of mutual trade despite adjustment costs and poor trade infrastructure. But the real motivation for the formation of MERCOSUR has been fear of other groupings like the European Community and NAFTA and the desire to improve bargaining capacity.

The disappointment of expectations from membership in a regional organization were evident in the marginalization of Latin America during the negotiations for the Uruguay round. The final stages of discussion on agriculture were, virtually exclusively, between the European Community and the US, and the Cairns group of developed and developing countries were excluded despite their significant interests in the issue of international trade in agricultural products. The Asia Pacific region, the subject of Chapter 6, is more complex because it needs to include the US and cannot really exist without it because of rivalries and mistrust among the Asians of the group. Despite the desire of Malaysia to form an exclusively Asian grouping, ongoing disputes between a number of Asian countries and the People's Republic of China and wartime memories of Japan make them insurmountably dependent on the US as a strategic counterweight.

The interlinkage between economic and other issue areas is not consistently direct although the diplomacy of war and oil, not unexpectedly, mingle more easily.[19] As a rule issues of security and diplomacy have a logic independent of the economic, except that the economic is a resource input. A price maker in the security area like the US is less constrained because none of the menu of actual operational choices are beyond its current budgetary and borrowing capacity. Developing countries, by contrast, have difficulty competing with developed countries because they have fewer resources in virtually every area. Argentina, for example, is unable to impose economic sanctions against the major powers that constrain its agricultural exports because of its modest international status and limited domestic market.

The dramatic economic collapse of 1997–8 in Asia, from the Republic of Korea to Indonesia, was a surprise that, in the light of pre-existing evidence, might have been anticipated. The collapse of the Mexican peso in 1994 and the widely recognized pitfalls of some types of international capital movements had already been causing concern. The IMF and Southeast Asian governments had been trying to identify appropriate policy responses to the particular dangers of rapid inflows and outflows of short-term capital. But a combination of complacency, stemming from overconfidence because of the record of economic success, and regulatory failures precipitated a serious economic setback. To give a sense of its extent, Indonesia's per capita income in March 1998 had declined to 1970 levels in dollar terms.

The regulatory failures in the region, owing to corrupt relationships between government and business, were an important reason for the downfall of these hitherto successful economies. However, they occurred in the context of economic conditions that were not wholly caused by policy failures. The problems of managing the exchange rate and the potential for catastrophe because of its inherent difficulties are not amenable to obvious solutions. The reform of political behaviour in these societies, as elsewhere in countries that suffer similar regulatory shortcomings, will have to be combined with the troublesome task of enumerating appropriate policy intervention to neutralize the potential dangers of exchange rate instability. The specific issue that exercises analysts is the relative merits of different exchange rate regimes and, given the experience of 1997–8 in Asia, the dangers of overvaluation within a relatively fixed exchange rate system. This is a major down side of financial globalization that impacts asymmetrically on developing countries at a stage of economic maturity that makes them attractive for speculative investment, but which remain vulnerable to sudden capital outflows.[20]

V. DOMESTIC POLITICS, LIBERALIZATION, AND GLOBALIZATION

It is difficult to generalize meaningfully about the impact of domestic circumstances of developing countries, as a group, on economic liberalization. The differences between regions (Uganda versus Singapore) and within regions (Haiti versus Argentina) are far too great. However, some issues do seem to recur. The first is the end of the ideological divide which, in previous decades, would have provoked more resistance to liberalization. It is of course true that some countries like Singapore and Hong Kong were already pro-market, but virtually all other countries, including other Asian NICs, have adopted a less statist stance, across the board, on economic policy. The common heritage of statist economic policy is being dissolved by the end of the cold war and the powerful surge of market forces world-wide. The underlying nationalist motivation for state control over major economic outcomes, despite differences in methods (export-led versus import substitution) has now given way to international economic openness and the conviction that it is unavoidable, despite some degree of anxiety over its appropriateness.

The second domestic aspect affected by the international is the social consequence of market forces. The growing interdependence of markets globally has undoubtedly resulted in a loss of state control over outcomes in virtually all countries and can be usefully encapsulated by the familiar concepts of 'sensitivity' and 'vulnerability'. Developing countries are 'vulnerable', across a majority of issue areas, because domestic policy responses do not deflect the impact of international change. Paradoxically, small countries, as price takers, are more likely to adjust successfully to international forces because they have to adapt constantly, since there is little room for them to attempt to aspire to price-maker resistance; the pace and cost of socio-economic adjustment also varies inversely with size. Of course, economic flexibility, signified by relative prosperity (e.g. the Asian NICs) is a positive factor. But the size of a country tends to be positively correlated with attempts to resist forces of change originating from abroad and frequently results in crisis and painful adjustments when they finally become irresistible.

A final comment about the relationship between the domestic, regional, and the international is that these are not linear ascending levels differentiated by relative size. Thus the domestic level is not a microcosm of the international or merely a smaller scale of economic activity. There are qualitative differences because competition at the domestic level is subject to democratic consent as well as political authority. International players like transnationals enjoy much greater freedom abroad and escape many constraints encountered by domestic players. The tensions between these two levels are the motive for regionalization. National political authorities, sanctioning both informal and formal regional identity, are attempting to reduce the power of international players by creating bigger spatial structures and enlarging their reach through regional arrangements. A major unintended outcome of regionalization is that, while it undoubtedly bolsters political authorities in the market-place, albeit by diluting sovereign autonomy in collective forums, it also instigates competition between regional organizations internationally and between states more generally. Hence, the proliferation of regional organizations among developing countries fearful of the EU and now NAFTA.

VI. STRUCTURAL ADJUSTMENT PROGRAMMES

In order to understand the impact of liberalization and globalization on the developing world two of its conduits provide an analytic focus—and the possibility of a critique of the new certainties. They are structural adjustment policies promoted by the IMF and the Uruguay round treaty.[21] Both are also connected to the three underlying long-run economic changes in the relationship between developing countries and world markets identified above (the mobility of financial capital, fdi, and the perceptions of élites in the developing world).

Structural adjustment programmes have been the response to economic crisis in developing countries. These programmes, under the auspices of the IMF and the World Bank, usually the former, provide financial assistance under certain conditions (so-called conditionality) with the purpose of restoring the financial viability and economic health of the economy.[22] Intervention in the running of the economy of developing countries by the IMF and the World Bank in return for financial assistance is significant because of its scale and the implications for traditional notions of national sovereignty. These programmes are the vehicle for promoting liberalization and markets in preference to state institutions and public ownership.

The intervention of international agencies can be criticized for tending to espouse the preferred solutions of the stronger party, the creditors, in negotiations with indebted countries. The former usually have the support of their own governments who have influence over international agencies. International institutions are thus especially concerned to ensure servicing of debt and repayment of capital rather than, first and foremost, restoring the economic health of the country concerned. The preoccupation with technical economic issues also underestimates the question of sovereign prerogatives and domestic political conflicts which are normal in any society. Structural adjustment programmes have been questioned because of their narrow orthodoxy and willingness to countenance harsh deflationary policies (and attendant social costs) to overcome inflation, and balance of payments and fiscal difficulties. The curtailment of social expenditure, privatization, and devaluation have been regarded by some observers as doctrinaire and failing to differentiate adequately between countries and circumstances. In recent years, the World Bank has shown some signs of flexibility and what Lance Taylor terms an 'intelligent conservatism', while the IMF seems to be more insular.[23] The disputes over prescription and the combination of policies appropriate to particular circumstances apparently harken back to a three-century-old disagreement between structuralism and monetarism.[24]

The political implication of structural adjustment programmes is therefore loss of economic sovereignty, formal niceties notwithstanding.[25] Of course there is a widespread conviction that such violations of sovereignty will lead to desirable outcomes. But such intervention is instituting profound changes to the relationship between developing countries and the world economy and international institutions. The programmes of liberalization imposed by structural adjustment result in globalization which, in turn, fundamentally alters the relationship between a given national economy and the international economy. The point is that such profoundly political outcomes are being driven by apparently innocuous technical decisions. To put it in comparative perspective, policies of comparable importance would require the assent of the Council of Ministers in the European Community. They could not be insisted upon by the European Commission without the prior assent of national assemblies, as in the case of the Single European Act or the Maastricht Treaty.

The nature of relations with the IMF are an index of the weakening resolve of developing countries as well as the retreat of statist models of economic development and management. The dependence of developing countries on the IMF and the World Bank, best exemplified by their role in the debt crisis, amounts to a greater erosion of national sovereignty than at any time since the end of anti-colonial struggles. The IMF both dictates and monitors the conduct of governments who take recourse to it. It acts as banker and legitimator for agreements negotiated between creditors and indebted countries. It not only negotiates on behalf of commercial banks but also acts as a surrogate for creditor governments when the debt is public, as in the case of most African countries. This is undoubtedly a political rather than a technical function although the IMF also offers modest credit facilities in the context of negotiations on behalf of creditor banks and countries.

A number of points need to be reiterated in order to underline the significance of the end of the cold war for the relationship between the major economic powers, represented by the IMF, and developing countries. The first is the absence of a Soviet presence to intervene in favour of developing countries politically and, on occasion, financially, as in the case of Cuba and Egypt. The second is the ideological change that has downgraded statist policies and eased the entry of market-led solutions via the IMF. Finally, even where such solutions are adopted with reluctance, the integration of world capital markets circumscribes room for manœuvre and makes necessary the official IMF seal of approval, its imprimatur, without which economic collapse is likely.

VII. THE URUGUAY ROUND AND LIBERALIZATION

Structural adjustment programmes affect specific countries, but the Uruguay round treaty of GATT, signed in 1994, is a turning-point for globalization because of its world-wide geographical reach. It is impossible to refuse to sign the treaty since that would imply being cut off from international trade because the MFN clause does not apply between non-signatories of the Uruguay round and countries which have withdrawn from earlier GATT treaties (e.g. Kennedy and Tokyo) superseded by the Uruguay round treaty. Thus a non-signatory would have to rely on the goodwill of countries with which it previously enjoyed most favoured nation relations under previous treaties once the latter signed the Uruguay round treaty and rescinded the earlier ones (at six months' notice).

Of particular relevance to the globalization of developing countries are the General Agreement on Trade in Services (GATS), trade-related investment measures (TRIMS), trade in intellectual property rights (TRIPS), and dispute settlement. The GATS hopes to prise open trade in services, including banking, insurance, consultancy, films, etc. and will eventually result in the dominance of a powerful group of global suppliers. They will originate in developed countries because the poorer countries do not enjoy the economies of scale or possess the know-how required to operate independently. TRIMS ease the operations of international oligopolies by instituting national treatment and curtailing domestic policy goals (e.g. ownership and local content requirements). TRIPS involve the monitoring and enforcement of the property rights of nationals, in practice of developed countries, in more comprehensive detail and for longer periods than has been the case historically. That will also result in a net transfer of resources to the developed world without increasing total world economic welfare.

The relatively weak provisions on dispute settlement are a contrast to the establishment of international obligations in the areas outlined above because they underline the failure to curb the unilateral conduct of the US and the European Union (EU). The predilection of the US and the EU to violate international trade obligations capriciously will continue because of the failure to subject anti-dumping codes and countervailing duties (CVDs) to effective international supervision.

The signing of the Uruguay round GATT accords is paralleled by moves toward regional economic integration, most notably in the case of NAFTA which includes Mexico and may embrace other economies of Latin America. Regional economic integration at a formal and informal level is also advancing more generally elsewhere in Latin America, Asia, and Africa. Their political implications are not entirely clear although they may improve the bargaining capacity of the developing countries concerned at international negotiations and perhaps promote a degree of political amity. What they undoubtedly achieve is the fulfilment of the classic Ricardian prediction of universal welfare gains because the markets involved in the process of economic integration are, with some exceptions, competitive rather than oligopolistic.[26]

VIII. POLITICS OF THE MARKET

The ability of international agencies and the US to compel developing countries to adopt particular policies has become pronounced in the aftermath of the victory of NATO in the cold war. Deprived of the counterbalancing presence of the Soviet Union many developing countries have been weakened politically, as the virtual collapse of Indian pretensions of economic independence demonstrates. It is true that the lack of a competing ideology has allowed more effective advocacy of market policies, but closer scrutiny of such policies reveals a more complicated story than the triumph of a particular model for the economy and society.

Despite the apparent advance of market ideologies, governments of developed countries continue to intervene politically in a mercantilist fashion to protect perceived interests. In the area of international trade the misuse of anti-dumping and CVDs is so blatant that leading advocates of freer international economic relations have been appalled. The US and the EU have successfully threatened exporters with anti-dumping actions (in particular) and CVD that defy logic and cannot be justified on economic grounds.[27] Thus a key component of the functioning of the international market is subject to the arbitrary political interference of the relevant authorities in Washington, DC, and Brussels. But the victims of these actions are primarily Asian countries. And because fdi flows are a defensive response by firms to protectionism, prompted by political actions of host governments rather than market imperatives, Asian fdi flows to the US and the EU have risen in response to the protectionist threat to Asian exports.

It is also noteworthy that US threats to subject countries like Brazil, Egypt, and India, as well as others, to the Super 301 and Special 301 provisions of the 1988 Omnibus Trade and Competitiveness Act were instrumental in ensuring their consent to various provisions of the Uruguay round treaty, particularly on the GATS and TRIPS. The persisting threat of Super 301 is a key element of US strategy in promoting the interests of US industry and US corporations, irrespective of the merits of such actions for the functioning of markets.[28]

Developed countries in Europe, the US, and Japan are also active in the area of technology policy to ensure competitive advantages in the twenty-first century. The public sponsorship of basic research, as well as collaboration between industry and basic science in the universities and government research laboratories, has intensified as a key aspect of contemporary rivalry between countries and nationally owned firms to gain and retain the upper hand in areas like new materials, biotechnology, etc.[29] The importance of government intervention in such areas in developed countries contrasts with their advocacy of a truncated state and market solutions for developing countries.

IX. ECONOMICS OF MARKET IDEOLOGY

Beyond the asymmetric outcomes of international trade negotiations between the developed and developing worlds, the advocacy of market solutions derives from the alleged experiences of the Asian tigers, a number of other high-growth Asian economies, and Chile. According to this view, these examples demonstrate unequivocally the merits of market forces and free trade as a vehicle for economic advancement and catch-up. It is perfectly true that economic growth in much of Asia, outside the South Asian subcontinent, has been nothing short of spectacular, led in the first instance by the Republic of Korea (ROK), Taiwan, Hong Kong, and Singapore. But it is now clear that the processes were complex and involved more than adoption of market mechanisms.

A number of scholars have now demonstrated that the involvement of the state in the economies of the Asian tigers, with the exception of Hong Kong, was decisive in allocating and pricing investment, controlling fdi as well as deploying protection against imports.[30] More recently, a major World Bank study has highlighted the significance of infrastructure provision, especially education, as an explanation for growth. Indeed, education has the highest coefficient for growth.[31] It is also important to recognize the unusual circumstances encountered by the ROK and Taiwan during the crucial period of the cold war in the 1950s and 1960s, enjoying US largesse and positive international economic conditions for growth. Other preconditions were also present in the form of a facilitating historically evolved social backdrop and land reform. The cases of Hong Kong and Singapore are impressive, but hold fewer lessons—as small islands located athwart major trading routes and lacking an agricultural hinterland—unless they are located appropriately in their original contexts of China and Malaysia, respectively.

The development experience of East and Southeast Asian countries and the recent progress of China does offer insights about the nature and causes of growth in the region. But the central problematic of rising productivity, as the source of sustained long-run growth, has been re-examined recently by Paul Krugman, Alwyn Young, and a number of other scholars.[32] They argue that in the newly industrialized countries of Asia, (*a*) total factor productivity growth has been negligible and (*b*) their high-growth performance is explained by increases in factor inputs and one-off improvements in educational standards. The conclusion is that these rates of economic growth cannot be sustained indefinitely and once these sources of expansion (savings, labour force expansion, and one-off educational factors) are exhausted, much more difficult achievements in the area of technology and innovation will be required. The inference is that the attempt to attain parity with the already developed countries is formidably difficult and even the tiger economies of Asia are unlikely to achieve it in the foreseeable future. Furthermore, contemporary technological and scientific changes make that even less likely.[33]

What is at issue is not so much the importance of markets, because their significance is generally acknowledged to have been underestimated, but the identity of the larger framework within which markets are situated.[34] The question of social and political stability, international conditions, and the existence of social and economic infrastructure loom large. Social and political stability can be undermined by insistence on some abstract welfare function for the economy. The distribution of political power and pre-existing historical pay-off structures may require apparently inefficient and unjust economic outcomes. The fact that many developing countries have poor government and incompetent economic mismanagement should not obscure the existence of unavoidable costs in preserving fragile socio-political structures. The failures of market coordination also remain an unresolved problem and a decision to annul state involvement is not the logical political inference to be drawn from bad government, even on grounds of economic effectiveness alone.[35]

Paradoxically, many developing countries are anxiously embracing the novel contemporary model of an unregulated market and its apparent virtues, and not merely at the behest of international agencies and the US. Three comments can be made with regard to this situation. First, the version developing countries would in fact prefer to adopt differs significantly from the model being imposed by international agencies and now also through the Uruguay round of GATT. For example, the urgent wooing of international investors by developing countries (for both fdi and equity investment) is a strategy of recent origin for some. They have reluctantly acceded to the particular framework adopted at the Uruguay round of GATT, which permits few national objectives to influence the operations of international oligopolies, for example, by ownership restrictions and local content rules. Secondly, they correctly perceive the futility of challenging the powerful agencies, oligopolies, and their governments who dominate the functioning of the international market-place. For example, the rapid growth of fdi in developing countries underlines the control of access to the principal markets of the world by international firms originating in the OECD.[36] The rapid growth of intra-firm trade (estimated at two-thirds of US imports of manufactures) makes it very difficult for newcomers to establish themselves as independent suppliers of key manufactures (with some exceptions) in the world market, except as affiliates of large corporations. In other words, the barriers to entry in many areas of economic activity are significant and protected by state policy in the OECD countries.

Thirdly, notwithstanding the validity of questioning the dirigiste economics that has been prominent for almost a generation in much of the developing world, the neophyte enthusiasm of Third World élites for markets is really enthusiasm for consumer goods, howsoever available. It is also an indication of the circumscribed intellectual autonomy of societies whose history is in such stark contrast to the five-century-long cultural, political, economic, and military triumph of Europe and societies of European origin.[37]

X. CONCLUSION

The end of socialism and the victory of capitalism also imply distinctive cultural and political representations of the conflicts of material and economic interest between countries. At one level, the profound weakening of universalist interpretive categories like class (in the social democratic sense) undermines the perception of vertical, transnational configurations of interest that such an analysis of conflicts insinuates. Thus, in the past, domestic protest in Third World settings usually left open the possibility of international alliances, mitigating the prospect of horizontal, national parameters of conflict and a totalizing polarization. Contemporary conflicts of economic interest are being depicted as more directly ethnic and/or religious in their connotations. They also display greater intensity and intractability.

Religious protest, in response to secular conflicts of interest, is now more widespread and not merely in the case of Islam. Economic distress often leads to the rise of religious movements rather than traditional class struggles of a socialist and internationalist character. For example, anti-imperialist protest during recent decades, in countries like Iran and Algeria as well as contemporary India and Pakistan, has taken a nationalist and religious form, with powerful elements of anti-foreign sentiment. Militant ethnic consciousness in the context of social and economic upheaval has also resulted very directly from the collapse of socialism in Eastern Europe and the CIS. The collapse of the former Yugoslav economy was a potent factor in the underlying discontent that led to its destruction. It is possible to predict that the Western response to this phenomenon will become more coercive than in the past.[38]

The public agenda of human rights and humanitarian intervention is regarded with cynicism by Western governments. The violators of human rights and the intended beneficiaries of international concern also regard the new agenda with understandable scepticism. The complicity of the UN Security Council in the genocide in Bosnia-Herzegovina has ended the polite fiction of substance in the human rights agenda. The interdependence between economic calculations and such political and human rights issues merely underlines the principles of Western statecraft and the primacy of the political. Economic interests prevail where no direct security and political questions impinge, as with the remarkable tolerance showed towards countries like China and Indonesia.[39] But when major security concerns exist, as with anxiety over potential Russo-German conflict through surrogates in former Yugoslavia, economic calculations are relegated and human rights concerns are vestigial. The state system and its relentless logic of real and imagined interests prevails without respite.[40]

The end of the cold war has intensified a notorious complicity between academic social science and the interests of the victorious powers. Discussions about democracy, human rights, and humanitarian intervention grimly dominate discussion of the principles and practice of Western foreign policy. Standard textbook theories of power politics and national interest are largely notable for their absence from reflections on policy and conduct. Thus commentary on the Gulf War portrays it as having been essentially about the rights of small nations and the determination of the Security Council to uphold them, rather than the more complex conflict that it was. The failure to consider what happens to an international system in which a single centre dominates security issues and exercises immense power in all other areas is a serious failing.

In the same vein, the economic choices being imposed on developing countries through international agencies prevail by default because statist policies of an earlier era failed. The intrinsic merits of these imposed choices are examined in abstraction, without sufficient attention to the practical politics of their actual operation. For example, the evidence that the IMF has primarily sought to ensure servicing of international loans by debtor countries, rather than seeking long-term economic change, is ignored. The success of the Uruguay round conceals the misuse of anti-dumping actions and countervailing duties which have now been officially legitimized by the new trade treaty. Nor is the most comprehensive and tightly formulated aspect of the Uruguay round, on trade-related intellectual property rights, recognized for the exercise in political muscle, rather than sound economic logic, which it is.

The fact that some parts of Asia advanced rapidly for three decades says little about the prospects for much of Africa, Latin America, or South Asia. The vulnerability of Latin America despite economic reform, achieved at high social cost, was dramatically highlighted by the collapse of the Mexican economy in December 1994 and the surrender of its oil revenues to the US government.[41] The future of the People's Republic of China is also uncertain as the spread of market forces from the coast to the interior signals the retreat of hitherto secure central political authority. The precise relationship between these two forces will then have to be renegotiated, the historical parallels for which are upheaval and discontinuity.

The idea that democracy will follow markets or that it will become the principal foreign policy goal of the US and Europe cannot be sustained on the basis of past evidence. The interdependence between democracy and capitalism is fortuitous and the dictates of foreign policy cannot endure electoral victories for Islamic groups like the FIS in Algeria or the kind of popular fervour induced in Jordan by King Hussain's reluctance to abandon the Iraqi regime during the Gulf War. On the basis of current evidence the only weak projection to be hazarded is that the coastal zones of countries and continents are likely to be precursors of economic change. In this regard, Taiwan, Singapore, and the west coast of India have something in common. On the face of it, major Latin American countries possess many of the conditions that can lead to economic growth within the appropriate policy framework, but social and political tensions remain unresolved in currently high-growth societies like Brazil. The inauguration of socio-political reform in South Africa has instituted the minimum first step towards economic growth in a large swathe of the African continent. But continued peace and the accumulation of social capital remain a prerequisite. In that context the prospects for economic growth in much of Africa remain uncertain.

In conclusion, it might be reiterated that the end of cold war politics and financial globalization are the two dominant factors influencing the contemporary international economy of the developing countries. The first circumscribes their room for diplomatic manœuvre and the second, as events in the latter half of the 1990s in Latin America and Asia show, highlights the temptations of international borrowing and its associated risks. It can be inferred that, for the present, the reaction of the US has to be weighed much more carefully by potential challengers to the status quo, in the absence of a serious alternative source of military and diplomatic support for dissent. The ability of global financial markets to cause the socio-economic counterpart of nuclear reactor meltdown is so significant that the choice it poses for affected states is the economic equivalent of military surrender.

4

Developing Countries and the Emerging World Order

Security and Institutions

AMITAV ACHARYA

I. INTRODUCTION

This chapter is a reflection on the relevance and role of the Third World in the emerging world order.[1] More specifically, it examines the extent to which the end of the cold war affects the insecurity and vulnerability of the Third World countries and the state of the North–South divide as it relates to the prospects for global cooperation and order-maintenance in the post-cold war era.

During the cold war, two fundamental and common factors shaped the Third World's predicament and role within the international system. The first relates to the relative abundance of violent conflicts within its boundaries. These conflicts (intra-state and inter-state) vastly outnumbered those occurring in the developed segments of the international system. One study by Evan Luard estimates that of the 127 'significant wars' occurring between 1945 and 1986, all but two took place in the Third World (Latin America, Africa, the Middle East, and Asia).[2] The Third World also accounted for the vast majority of the over 20 million war-related deaths during this period.[3] Thus, at a time when nuclear weapons had rendered war among the industrialized nations a highly unlikely prospect, the Third World came to be viewed by the First and the Second World as the principal source of insecurity, violence, and disorder within the established international system.

Apart from its security predicament, the Third World category during the cold war period was made distinctive by its political posture. This posture incorporated not only a quest for enhanced status, but also for economic justice in the face of a shared condition of acute poverty, underdevelopment, and dependence. While coping with insecurity within a rigidly bipolar structure, the Third World also worked, self-consciously and collectively, to alter its vastly inferior position *vis-à-vis* the developed countries of the North. Using Hedley Bull's expression, this process might be viewed as a 'revolt' against the North's (particularly the West's) superior economic and military power, intellectual and cultural authority, and its hold over the rules and institutions governing international society.[4] Despite its immense diversity, the Third World came to exhibit a remarkable unity of purpose in its struggle, as Bull put it, 'to destroy the old international order and establish a new one, to shake off the rules and institutions devised by the old established forces (in Sukarno's phrase) and create new rules and institutions that will express the aspirations of the new emerging forces'.[5]

To what extent will the combination of acute instability and self-conscious radicalism, which led the Third World to be labelled variously as an 'intruder' element within the established international system,[6] an 'international social protest movement',[7] and, somewhat pejoratively, as the source of a 'new international disorder',[8] survive the end of the cold war? What are the implications of the end of the cold war for Third World insecurity and the North–South conflict? Will a multipolar international system aggravate Third World instability? Will the end of the East–West rivalry also dampen the North–South conflict? Seeking answers to these questions is important not only for assessing the position and role of the Third World in the emerging world order, but also in evaluating whether the North's preferred reordering of international relations will succeed.

The discussion that follows is divided into three parts. The first looks at the question of whether the end of the cold war will increase or dampen instability and conflict in the Third World. This is followed by an assessment of emerging areas of North–South tension over world order issues, especially those which are associated with the North's ill-defined vision of a 'New World Order'. The third part will examine the changing role of Third World's platforms and institutions, both global and regional, in addressing the political, security, and economic concerns of the developing countries.

II. THIRD WORLD INSECURITY: A 'DECOMPRESSION' EFFECT?

As statistical evidence suggests, the cold war was hardly a period of stability in the Third World.[9] But some commentators have predicted that the post-cold war era might prove even more destabilizing for the Third World, with the emergence and/or re-emergence of conflicts that were 'overlaid' by superpower rivalry.[10] Thus, Jose Cintra argues that the cold war had suppressed 'many potential third-world conflicts', and while its end has led to superpower withdrawal from some regional conflicts, 'other conflicts will very probably arise from decompression and from a loosening of the controls and self-controls' exercised by the superpowers.[11] Robert Jervis believes that the cold war 'In the net . . . generally dampened conflict [in the Third World] and we can therefore expect more rather than less of it in future.'[12]

Several potential and actual implications of the end of the cold war justify such concerns. First, superpower retrenchment has led to a shift in the balance of power in many Third World regions, which in turn has created opportunities for locally dominant actors to step into the 'vacuum' with managerial ambitions that could fuel regional conflict.[13] Second, many Third World regimes (such as those in Cuba, El Salvador, Nicaragua, Cambodia, Somalia, Ethiopia, and North Korea), which had survived domestic challenges to their legitimacy with the help of superpower patronage, have now either collapsed or are faced with such a prospect.[14] In a related vein, the example set by the implosion of the former Soviet Union, itself linked to the end of the cold war, has fuelled demands for self-determination in Third World societies. Thus, the emergence of ethnic conflicts in the 'new' Third World, for example, the Balkans and Eastern Europe, which has been linked by some to the removal of superpower control, is also evident in parts of the 'old' Third World, particularly Africa. Fourth, the end of superpower protection creates pressures on their former clients to achieve greater military self-reliance. As one analyst puts it, the withdrawal of the superpowers from Third World regions 'entails merely that the Third World will do more of its own fighting'.[15] Such a trend is already evident in East Asia, where a competitive arms race appears to be in progress.

Finally, the end of the cold war also raises the prospects for greater inter-state conflict. While the vast majority of Third World conflicts in the cold war period were intra-state (anti-regime insurrections, civil wars, tribal conflicts, etc.),[16] some observers now foresee the prospects for a rise in inter-state territorial conflicts. Thus, Barry Buzan argues that 'If the territorial jigsaw can be extensively reshaped in the First and Second Worlds, it will become harder to resist the pressures to try to find more sensible and congenial territorial arrangements in the ex-Third World.'[17] Such a scenario applies particularly to Africa, whose established regional norms against violation of the post-colonial territorial status quo seem to be under considerable stress (especially with the separation of Eritrea from Ethiopia).[18] In Southeast Asia, the disputes over the Spratly and Paracel Islands in the South China Sea, as well as numerous other maritime boundary disputes, attest to the potential of territorial issues to threaten regional stability.

But concerns about greater incidence of instability in the post-cold war Third World could be overstated. To be sure, the vast majority of wars in the post-cold war era continue to be fought in the 'old' Third World. A recent survey by *The Economist* shows that twenty-eight out of thirty-two current wars—including, insurgency, civil strife, and inter-state wars—are taking place here.[19] The numbers would rise if, as some have suggested, one extends the Third World to include the Balkans and the former republics of the Soviet Union.[20] None the less, the consequences of the end of the cold war for Third World stability have not been entirely negative. Among other things, the political settlement of conflicts in Cambodia, Afghanistan, Southern Africa, and Central America was possible due to cooperation between the US and the Soviet Union/Russia. The end of the cold war has also contributed to the end of the apartheid regime in Southern Africa (which fuelled regional strife during the cold war) and the dramatic turnaround in the first half of the 1990s in the Arab–Israeli conflict. Moreover, the collapse of authoritarian regimes in the Third World has not always led to violence. In Latin America, the loss of Soviet support for leftist regimes and the end of American backing for right-wing authoritarian regimes have actually contributed to a largely peaceful process of democratization, as occurred arguably in Nicaragua and El Salvador.[21] Africa has seen several cases of peaceful transition to a multi-party system (in Benin, Burkina Faso, Congo, Côte d'Ivoire, Gabon, Mali, Tanzania, and Kenya).[22] In East Asia, the end of the cold war has reduced Western tolerance for authoritarianism, thereby encouraging local groups to demand greater political openness and leading to government violence in China in 1989, Thailand in 1992, and Indonesia in 1998. But in general, the new democracies of Asia, such as the Philippines, Taiwan, South Korea, and Thailand (after the 1992 bloodshed), have proved to be remarkably stable. (Cambodia, which was given a 'liberal-democratic' constitution by the UN-supervised elections, is an exception.)

The spread of democracy in the Third World might also eventually create better prospects for regional stability. Whether democracies tend not to fight with each other may be a debatable proposition in the West,[23] but in the Third World, there has always been a strong correlation between authoritarian rule and regional conflict, largely due to the tendency of internally insecure regimes to 'succumb to the temptation to consolidate their domestic position at the expense of their neighbours by cultivating external frictions or conflicts'.[24] Thus, by leading to the removal of the non-performing and repressive rulers and their replacement by regimes enjoying greater political legitimacy, the end of the cold war might create improved conditions for domestic political stability and regional security, although the transition to democracy could be destabilizing in the short term.

There are two other ways in which the end of the cold war improves the security outlook of the Third World. First, with the end of the US–Soviet rivalry, the North is becoming more selective in its engagement in the Third World. In a bipolar world, as Kenneth Waltz argued, 'with two powers capable of acting on a world scale, anything that happen[ed] anywhere [was] potentially of concern to both of them'.[25] With the collapse of the Soviet Union, the only power capable of global power projection, the US, is likely to limit its areas of engagement to a few areas such as the Middle East and East Asia and Central America.[26] While this means many Third World regions face the prospect of 'marginalization', where bloody conflicts might go unnoticed by the great powers and left to managerial action by local powers and regional security arrangements, it would also prevent the internationalization of local wars and localization of systemic tensions that was a marked feature of the cold war period. During the cold war, the maintenance of the stability of the central strategic balance rendered many Third World conflicts necessary, as the superpowers viewed these 'as a way of letting off steam which helps to cool the temperature around the core issues which are directly relevant and considered vital to the central balance and, therefore, to the international system'.[27] The end of superpower rivalry extricates the Third World from this unhappy predicament.

Secondly, with the end of the cold war, regional powers (including 'regional policemen' such as Iran under the Nixon Doctrine, or regional proxies for the Soviet Union such as Vietnam and Cuba) can no longer 'count on foreign patrons to support them reflexively, supply them with arms, or salvage for them an honourable peace'.[28] Without massive superpower backing, even the most powerful among Third World states may find it more difficult to sustain military adventures,[29] and may be deterred from seeking to fulfil their external ambitions through military means. The Iraqi experience during the Gulf War is illustrative of the predicament of regional powers deprived of an opportunity to exploit the superpower rivalry.[30]

Those who argue that the end of the cold war would be destabilizing for the Third World ignore the fact that the cold war itself was hardly a period of tranquility or order in the Third World, as evident from bloody and prolonged regional conflicts from Angola to Afghanistan. Moreover, many of the current or potential inter-state conflict situations, as in Southern Asia and the Korean peninsula, were conceived during the cold war and cannot be used as examples of post-cold war instability. While it is tempting to view the Iraqi invasion of Kuwait, thus far the major conflict of the post-cold war period, as an act of Iraqi opportunism in the face of declining superpower involvement in the region, the seeds of this conflict were planted during the cold war period, when Iraq received military hardware and economic support from Western nations even while its main arms supplier continued to be the Soviet Union.

It also needs to be emphasized that the end of bipolarity does not by itself alter the fundamental sources of Third World insecurity. As Halliday puts it, 'since the causes of third world upheaval [were] to a considerable extent independent of Soviet–US rivalry they will continue irrespective of relations between Washington and Moscow'.[31] The causes of Third World conflict, as highlighted by Ayoob, Buzan, Azar and Moon, and Sayigh,[32] continue to lie in weak state-society cohesion, problems of national integration, economic underdevelopment, and the lack of legitimacy of regimes. As in the past, these factors are likely to ensure that domestic conflicts along with their regional ramifications, rather than inter-state territorial conflicts, will remain the main sources of Third World instability in the post-cold war period.

Thus, in Africa many recent outbreaks of conflict have been linked to ethno-national cleavages within weak state structures as well as instability caused by a deepening economic crisis linked to structural adjustment policies imposed by international financial institutions. In Asia, a host of ethnic insurgencies and separatist movements, all dating back to the cold war period, remain the principal threat to stability. These include ethnic separatism in India (Assam, Kashmir, and the Punjab), Pakistan (demands for autonomy in the Sindh province), Sri Lanka (Tamil separatism), Indonesia (Aceh, East Timor, Irian Jaya), Myanmar (Karen and Shan guerrillas), and the Philippines (Muslim insurgency in Mindanao). In the economically more developed parts of the Third World, the primary security concerns of the ruling regimes have to do with what Chubin calls the 'stresses and strains of economic development, political integration, legitimation and institutionalization'.[33] In the Persian Gulf, rapid modernization has eroded the traditional legitimizing role of religion, tribe, and family, and contributed to the rise of fundamentalist challenges to regime survival. Similarly, in the affluent societies of East Asia, the emergence of a large middle-class population has contributed to demands for political openness and democratization. None of these problems can be realistically described as the result of a systemic shift from bipolarity to multipolarity.

To be sure, the end of the cold war does not have a single or uniform effect on Third World insecurity. In some parts of the Third World, such as in sub-Saharan Africa, the end of the cold war has been accompanied by greater domestic disorder, while in Southeast Asia it has seen increased domestic tranquillity and regional order (with the end of communist insurgencies and settlement of the Cambodia conflict). In the Middle East, the demise of superpower rivalry has enhanced prospects for greater inter-state cooperation, especially in the Arab–Israeli sector. In Africa, the end of the cold war has contributed to a sharp decline in arms imports, while in East Asia, it has created fears of a major arms race. Furthermore, the impact of the end of the cold war varies according to the type of conflict. Increased domestic strife in Africa contrasts sharply with the settlement of its long-standing regional conflicts (especially in Southern Africa), while in Southeast Asia the end of the cold war has led to greater internal stability while increasing inter-state tensions. Regional hegemonism is a distinct possibility in East Asia with China's massive economic growth and military build-up, but elsewhere, it is the regional powers, India, Vietnam, and Iraq included, which have felt the squeeze by being denied privileged access to arms and aid from their superpower patrons.

III. THE NORTH–SOUTH DIVIDE IN THE NEW WORLD ORDER

In the euphoria that accompanied the end of the East–West conflict, some Northern leaders (as well as the liberal perspective on international relations) were quick to raise hopes for a reduction of North–South tensions as well. As the former US President, George Bush, put it, the New World Order would be 'an historic period of cooperation . . . an era in which the nations of the world, East and West, North and South, can prosper and live in harmony'.[34] A more sober analysis, however, reveals that North–South divisions are not disappearing from the agenda of world politics. Specifically, one could point to four areas of North–South tension in the emerging world order.

The first relates to global environmental change. At first glance, this should be somewhat less political and ideological than other issues of contention in the North–South agenda. Environmental degradation affects the well-being of both the North and the South and can only be addressed through their mutual cooperation.[35] Yet, the global environment has become a focal point for a North–South policy divide in the post-cold war era. Marc Williams has identified four aspects of the South's position which forms the basis of this divide:[36] (1) that the industrialized countries bear the primary responsibility for the global environmental crisis; (2) that these countries should bear the major costs of environmental protection; (3) that the industrialized countries should ensure free transfer of technology to the South so that the latter can reduce its dependence on technologies damaging to the environment; and (4) that the industrialized countries should transfer additional resources to fund efforts by developing countries to ensure greater environmental protection.

The more extreme opinion within the developing world sees the North's interest in global environmental negotiations as a kind of 'eco-imperialism', motivated by a desire 'to protect its wasteful lifestyle by exporting the environmental burden to the South, and . . . to increase its political leverage by putting environmental conditionalities on the South'.[37] The North's expectation that the developing countries should adopt strict environmental standards is seen as self-serving and unfair. An editorial in the London *Times* described the Southern position in the following terms: 'The rich who consume four-fifths of the world's resources and account for most of its industrial emissions are asking the poor to invest in the conservation of natural resources, and to adopt more environmentally friendly policies than the rich world employed at comparable stages in its growth.'[38]

While critical of the North's push for global environmental protection, the South clearly recognizes the potential of the issue to extract concessions from the North and thus help its efforts at reforming the global economic order. As the North becomes increasingly concerned with the South's growing share of global greenhouse emissions and the increased outflow of Southern 'environmental refugees', the South senses a window of opportunity that the issue of environmental degradation can be used to press the North over a broad range of issues that have traditionally been of concern to the South, such as underdevelopment, technology transfers, and development assistance. As Malaysia's Prime Minister Mahathir Mohammed put it, 'Fear by the North of environmental degradation provides the South the leverage that did not exist before. It is justified for us to approach it this way.'[39]

A second issue of North–South conflict in the post-cold war era concerns the emerging frameworks for peace and security championed by the North. US President George Bush's vision of a new world order promised a return to multilateralism and the revival of the UN's collective security framework. But the first major test of this new world order, the US-led response to the Iraqi invasion of Kuwait, prompted widespread misgivings in the South. Although the UN resolutions against Iraq were supported by most Third World states, this was accompanied by considerable resentment of US domination of the UN decision-making process. US military actions against Iraq were seen as having exceeded the mandate of UN resolutions,[40] and US rhetoric about collective security was greeted with scepticism. Many in the South would perhaps agree with Zbigniew

Brzezinski's remark that 'once the symbolism of collective action was
stripped away . . . [the war against Iraq] was largely an American decision
and relied primarily on American military power'.[41] The Gulf War fed
Southern apprehension that in the 'unipolar moment', the US, along with
like-minded Western powers, would use the pretext of multilateralism to
pursue essentially unilateral objectives in post-cold war conflicts. Conflicts
in those areas deemed to be 'vitally' important to the Western powers will
be especially susceptible to Northern unilateralism.

From a Southern perspective, the ambiguities of the new world order
prevailing at the time of its birth (the Gulf War) have since been compounded by the North's championing of armed intervention in support of
humanitarian objectives. Ostensibly, the concept of 'humanitarian intervention'[42] calls for military action against regimes which are too weak to
provide for the well-being of their subjects (Somalia) or which are classic
predatory rulers that prey upon their own citizens (Iraq). But this has
caused genuine misgivings and apprehensions in the South. Scheffer captures some of these misgivings:

. . . there is a strong current of opinion among the nations of the developing world
and particularly China that upholds the principle of non-interference in the internal affairs of states as their only bulwark against the intrusive designs of the
West's 'New World Order'. These governments view humanitarian intervention
as a pretext for military intervention to achieve political or economic objectives.
Any effort to broaden the legitimacy of either nonforcible or forcible humanitarian intervention must therefore balance the political concerns of these governments with the humanitarian needs of their peoples.[43]

Mohammed Ayoob has offered a similar critique:

Recourse to humanitarian justifications for international intervention, as in the
case of the Kurds in Iraq following the Gulf War, would be greatly resented by
Third World states, above all because the logic of humanitarian intervention runs
directly counter to the imperatives of state-making . . . the primary political enterprise in which Third World countries are currently engaged. The dominant powers could persist in collective enforcement and international intervention
selectively, despite the opposition of the majority of Third World states (a majority of the membership of the international system). However, such actions, even
if ostensibly termed 'collective security', would lose much of their legitimacy and
could, in fact, seriously erode the idea of international society itself.[44]

Southern fears about a new and expanded framework of Western interventionism in the South are reinforced by the impact of the end of the cold
war in removing certain constraints on such intervention. Earlier, Hedley
Bull identified four major constraints on Western intervention in the Third
World during the later stages of the cold war period: (1) 'a remarkable

growth in Third World countries of the will and capacity to resist intervention'; (2) 'a weakening in the Western world of the will to intervene, by
comparison with earlier periods, or at least of the will to do so forcibly,
directly and openly'; (3) the growing Soviet capacity to project power,
which 'facilitated Third World resistance to Western intervention'; and (4)
'the emergence of a global equilibrium of power unfavourable to intervention', in the sense that 'there has emerged a balance among the interveners
which has worked to the advantage of the intervened against'.[45] Of these,
the collapse of the Soviet Union undermined the global 'power projection
balance' and deprived Third World states of a source of support against
Western intervention. Moreover, with the end of bipolarity, the Third
World states could no longer exploit great power rivalry to build immunity
from intervention. While the capacity of Third World countries to resist
military intervention has increased, so have the capabilities of the interveners to project power. In the 1980s, the projection forces of major
Western powers were substantially enhanced in response to growing
Soviet capabilities and to secure access to Middle Eastern oil. In the post-
cold war era, forces previously deployed in Europe are being earmarked
for Third World contingency missions.[46] At the same time, despite the
proliferation of indigenous defence industries in the Third World, the
North–South military technology balance remains overwhelmingly
favourable to the former. The advent of smart weapons makes it 'possible
for an intervening power to inflict severe damage on a developing nation
without its having to incur commensurate costs'.[47] The experience of the
US intervention in Iraq suggests that not even the most heavily armed
Third World power can offer effective resistance to the superior interventionist technology of Western powers.

A third area of North–South tension concerns the Northern approach
to arms control and non-proliferation. Some of the key regional powers of
the South, particularly India, object to the anti-proliferation measures
developed by the North, such as the Nuclear Non-Proliferation Treaty
(NPT) or the Missile Technology Control Regime (MTCR), which are
essentially supplier clubs that impose restrictions on export of military or
dual-use technology. Their misgivings, which were highlighted during the
process leading to the indefinite extension of the NPT in 1995 and which
are likely to persist despite the extension, focus on their selective application and discriminatory nature. As Chubin argues, in the case of nuclear
weapons, the North's anti-proliferation campaign 'frankly discriminates
between friendly and unfriendly states, focussing on signatories (and
potential cheats) like Iran but ignoring actual proliferators like Israel. It is
perforce more intelligible in the North than in the South'.[48] In a more
blunt tone, the Indian scholar K. Subrahmanyam charges that:

First, export controls are by definition discriminatory—they embody a fundamental double standard whereby nuclear weapons and missiles are deemed essential for the security of industrialised countries but dangerous in the hands of
developing nations . . . Above all export controls divide the world into North and
South, project a racist bias, and have proved to be inefficient instruments for pursuing global non-proliferation objectives.[49]

India's decision to carry out nuclear testing and declare itself a nuclear
weapons state in May 1998 needs to be seen in this context. Though partly
a product of domestic factors, especially an effort by the newly elected
Hindu nationalist government to shore up its popular support after failing to win an absolute majority in parliament, it also reflects New Delhi's
resentment of the existing non-proliferation regime, most recently
expressed in its refusal to sign the Comprehensive Test Ban Treaty in 1996.

Southern critics of the supply-side regimes also argue that the North's
aggressive campaign against the weapons of mass destruction is not
matched by a corresponding interest in restricting the flow of conventional
weapons to the South. On the contrary, the post-cold war era has seen
unprecedented competition among the major Northern manufacturers to
supply conventional arms to the more affluent segments of the South.
Despite their ostensible interest in restricting conventional arms transfers,
Northern governments (both Western and members of the former Soviet
bloc), as their Southern critics see it, have encouraged such transfers in a
desperate bid to save jobs at home.[50] To a significant extent, the current
military build-up in East Asia is driven by supplier competition in making
available large quantities of sophisticated arms at bargain basement
prices.[51]

A fourth area of North–South tension in the post-cold war era relates
to the West's advocacy of human rights and democracy as the basis for a
new global political order. The leaders of the West see the 'enlargement' of
democracy as a logical corollary to the successful 'containment' and
defeat of communism. The Western agenda on human rights is being promoted through a variety of means, including aid conditionality (linking
development assistance with human rights records of aid recipients), support for self-determination of persecuted minorities, and, as in the case of
Haiti, direct military intervention. All these instruments affect the political and economic interests of Third World states, many of which see these
as a threat to their sovereignty and economic well-being.[52]

Speaking at the 10th Non-Aligned Summit Conference in Jakarta in
1992, Egypt's foreign minister warned the West against 'interference in a
nation's internal affairs on the pretext of defending human rights'.[53]
Malaysian Prime Minister Mahathir Mohammed goes further; he sees the
West's human rights campaign as a device to perpetuate the condition of

dependency of the South. Citing the example of the former communist states of Eastern Europe, Mahathir contends that the campaign of human rights and democracy is a prescription for disruption and chaos in weaker countries, a campaign which makes the target ever more dependent on the donor nations of the West. Other critics of the South accuse the West of hypocrisy and selectivism in applying its human rights standards. The Foreign Minister of Singapore finds that 'Concern for human rights [in the West] has always been balanced against other national interests.'[54] To support this argument, Singapore's policy-makers contrast the US support for absolutist regimes in the oil-rich Arabian Peninsula with its response to the recent crisis in Algeria, in which Western governments acquiesced in the military *coup* that cancelled the electoral process after the first round had produced a strong Islamist victory.

The position of the South on the issue of human rights is marked by significant regional variations; the attitude of the Latin American nations contrasts sharply with those in East Asia, and even among the latter group differences exist between South Korea and Taiwan on the one hand and the ASEAN countries and China on the other. Moreover, the projection of a North–South divide on human rights is a state-centric understanding, as there is little disagreement between Northern and Southern non-governmental organizations over the issue of human rights. But there are a number of general areas in which the views of many Southern governments seem to converge. These include a belief that the issue of human rights must be related to the specific historical, political, and cultural circumstances of each nation. Governments in East Asia have added their voice to this 'cultural relativist' position by rejecting the individualist conception of human rights in the West, arguing instead for a 'communitarian' perspective that recognizes the priority of the 'society over the self'.[55] The developing countries in general have stressed that economic rights, especially the right to development, be given precedence over purely political ones in the global human rights agenda.

IV. INSECURITY, INEQUALITY, AND INSTITUTIONS

Any discussion of the South's role in the emerging world order must examine the role of institutions through which it could articulate its demands and mobilize its resources and response. During the cold war, the major Third World platform, the Non-Aligned Movement (NAM), spearheaded the South's conscious and collective challenge to the dominant international order. To this end, NAM pursued a broad agenda that included demands for a speedy completion of the decolonization process, superpower non-interference in the Third World, global disarmament, and strengthening of global and regional mechanisms for conflict-resolution.[56] NAM's record in realizing these objectives has attracted much criticism, but its achievements cannot be dismissed. Despite the diversity within its membership, NAM was able to provide a collective psychological framework for Third World states to strengthen their independence and to play an active role in international affairs.[57] Membership in NAM provided many Third World states with some room to manœuvre in their relationship with the superpowers and to resist pressures for alliances and alignment.[58] NAM led the global condemnation of apartheid and pursued the liberation of Rhodesia and Namibia with considerable energy and dedication. While NAM had no influence over the superpower arms control process, it did succeed in raising the level of ethical concern against the doctrine of nuclear deterrence. Through the UN disarmament conferences which it helped to initiate, NAM members highlighted the pernicious effects of the arms race and articulated the linkage between disarmament and development.

Yet, NAM's efforts to reshape the prevailing international order were seriously constrained. Permissiveness towards diversity within NAM with respect to external security guarantees—only states which were members of 'a multilateral military alliance concluded in the context of Great Power conflicts' were ineligible to join NAM; close bilateral relationships with superpowers were not an impediment—undermined the group's unity. It also made NAM susceptible to intra-mural tensions, as demonstrated over Cuba's unsuccessful efforts during the 1979 Havana summit to gain recognition for the Soviet Union as NAM's 'natural ally'. NAM's credibility suffered further from its poor record in international conflict-resolution. While focusing on the larger issues of global disarmament and superpower rivalry, it was unable to develop institutions and mechanisms for addressing local and regional conflicts such as those in the Gulf, Lebanon, Cambodia, Afghanistan, and Southern Africa. According to one observer,

During the last three decades, many non-aligned countries were involved in some kind of conflict, directly or indirectly, either with a fellow non-aligned country, or with great powers, or with some aligned countries. It is not difficult to comprehend the inability of NAM to prevent conflict within the group initially, and later, to resolve it quickly if the conflict had surfaced for one reason or the other.[59]

With the end of the cold war, NAM faced distinct risks of further marginalization in global peace and security affairs.[60] The collapse of the bipolar structure prompted inevitable questions regarding the movement's continued relevance. Despite a growing membership, the NAM's post-cold war direction remains unclear. Some members, such as India (perhaps reflecting its desire for a permanent seat in the UN Security Council), see the central role of NAM as being to push for democratization of the UN. Others, especially Malaysia, would like to use NAM to counter what they see as US propagation of a new world order. Indonesia, when chair of NAM, sought to shift the priorities of NAM from the political to the economic arena: 'We have to address the new concerns of the world—environment and development, human rights and democratisation, refugees and massive migration.'[61] Indonesia also led efforts to strike a moderate and pragmatic tone for NAM in global North–South negotiations.[62] In Jakarta's view, while the end of the cold war did not 'in any way diminish . . . the relevance and the validity of the basic principles and objectives of the Non-Aligned Movement', it 'like everybody else must adapt itself in a dynamic way . . . to the new political and economic realities in the world', realities which call for a posture of cooperation, rather than confrontation.[63] But Indonesia's efforts to revitalize NAM faltered as the Suharto government faced a series of economic and political crises at home, leading ultimately to its ousting in 1998.

Although NAM emerged primarily as a political institution, its agenda was broadened to the economic arena in the 1960s and 1970s. As Tim Shaw points out, while 'in its first decade it was a reaction to . . . international bipolarity; in its second decade, it has been a critical reaction to international inequality'.[64] The most important example of this was NAM's strong advocacy of the idea of a New International Economic Order, first voiced at the Fourth NAM summit in Algiers in 1973.[65] The concept of NIEO embraced a number of demands such as the creation of a new structure to regulate world trade in primary commodities, improved conditions for the transfer of Northern technology to the South, better market access for the export of Southern manufactured goods to the North, negotiating codes of conduct for multinational corporations, reform of the international monetary system to ensure greater flow of financial resources (both concessional and non-concessional), and the resolution of the debt problem and promotion of collective self-reliance through South–South cooperation in trade, finance, and infrastructure.[66] But the process of North–South negotiations aimed at the realization of these objectives has run its course without producing any significant breakthroughs for the South as a whole. The economic progress of the South has been disjointed. The list of achievements includes the ability of OPEC to raise the oil revenues of its members, the signing of the three Lomé conventions by sixty-four African, Caribbean, and Pacific states and the rise of the Newly Industrialized Countries of East Asia.[67] But the collective institutional framework of the South has not contributed to, or been strengthened by, these developments; instead, some of these regional successes have lessened the relevance and solidarity of the larger Third World platforms.

Among the major reasons for the failure of North–South negotiations[68] one must count the special hostility of conservative Western regimes (particularly Ronald Reagan and Margaret Thatcher) in the late cold war period. The Reagan administration viewed the North–South dialogue as an 'annoying distraction to the administration's goal of restoring American global influence'.[69] Under US leadership, Western governments downgraded the North–South dialogue by ignoring the South's established negotiating channels (such as the Group of 77) at the UN in favour of direct talks with Third World capitals. The handling of the debt crisis provided further evidence of this 'divide and rule' strategy pursued by the North, as the latter conducted debt-restructuring negotiations on a country-by-country basis by offering incentives to those who accepted bilateral deals.[70] Despite constant urging by Third World leaders for greater South–South cooperation on the debt crisis, the South was unable to develop institutional platforms to enter into collective negotiations with the North on the issue.

Overall, as the cold war drew to a close, Southern institutions seemed incapable of advancing their quest for economic justice for the world's poorer nations. The South's economic position has indeed worsened. The net flow of resources from the North to the South was reversed from a positive flow of US$43 billion to a negative flow of US$33 billion in 1988.[71] Moreover, the net value of development assistance from the North remained more or less stagnant during the 1980s. According to the then French President François Mitterand, the actual level of annual aid from the G7 countries was $130 billion short of the set target based on 0.7 per cent of their gross domestic product.[72] To compound matters, the end of the cold war presents new economic challenges for the South. The collapse of the Soviet bloc not only increases the pressure on the South to integrate more closely into the world capitalist order, but the South also faces the prospects of a redirection of Western aid and finance to Eastern Europe. (This fear might be overstated, however.)[73]

While NAM and issue-specific *ad hoc* coalitions in the South have found it possible to develop substantial unity on the issues of environment and development, this has not translated into concrete achievements in support of the South's demands. At the UN Conference on Environment and Development (UNCED) in Rio de Janeiro in 1992, the coalition of Third World states had to give up their demand for the North to double its aid to the poor countries by the year 2000.[74] While the North wants a Southern commitment to sustainable development, it is unwilling to make any specific pledge of financial aid beyond 'new and additional resources'. The cost of meeting the goals outlined in UNCED's 'Agenda 21' document is estimated at some $125 billion a year, far higher than the approximate US$55 billion the South was receiving in annual aid at that time.[75]

Will regional institutions fare better in addressing the security as well as economic and environmental concerns of the South in the post-cold war period? The Third World's interest in regionalism is not new. In the post Second World War period, several regional organizations emerged in the Third World with the objectives of pursuing conflict-resolution and economic integration.[76] But the promise of regionalism remained largely unfulfilled during the cold war. Superpowers were seen as ignoring, bypassing, and manipulating indigenous security arrangements in the Third World geared to pacific settlement of disputes, and encouraging balance-of-power arrangements that often aggravated ideological polarizations within Third World regions. As with security, during the cold war, the South's experiment with regional integration bore limited results. Although several such experiments were inspired by the success of the European Economic Community, regional economic integration in the Third World proved to be 'much more rudimentary than in Europe, more obscure in purpose and uncertain in content'.[77] Overall, regional integration in Africa and Latin America 'founder[ed] on the reefs of distrust, noncooperation and parochial nationalism'.[78]

In the post-cold war period, regional security frameworks have found a new appeal partly in response to the perceived limitations of the UN's peace and security role. Some Southern policy-makers see regional organizations as a way of ensuring the democratization and decentralization of the global peace and security framework. While the cold war was marked by a competition between global and regional security frameworks, the UN authorities now see regional action as a necessary means of relieving an overburdened UN. Moreover, the end of the cold war has lessened the polarizing impact of many 'successful' regional organizations in the cold war period, whose origins and role were closely linked to the ideological interests of the superpowers.[79]

As recent experience has shown, Third World regional arrangements could perform a range of peace and security functions. The role of ASEAN in the Cambodia conflict and the 'Contadora' and Esquipulus groups in the Central American conflict demonstrate that regional multilateral action can contribute to the management and resolution of local/regional conflicts.[80] In recent years, several other regional groups have developed mechanisms for a similar role, including the ECOWAS' creation of a standing committee for dispute-mediation in 1990 and the decision of the OAU summit in June 1993 to create a mechanism for

Amitav Acharya

preventing, managing, and resolving African conflicts.[81]Action by the Economic Community of West African States in deploying an 11,000-strong peacekeeping force in the Liberian civil war attests to the role of regional organizations in peacekeeping.[82] The OAS role in assisting the UN in investigating the human rights situation in Latin America suggests a potential for regional multilateral action in addressing internal conflicts (although the OAS could not pre-empt the US military intervention in Haiti). In Asia, ASEAN has assumed a significant role in regional security cooperation. The ASEAN Regional Forum seeks to develop confidence-building and transparency measures that would reduce the prospects for regional conflict and the threat of great power intervention.[83]

The effectiveness of Third World regional security arrangements is subject to distinct limitations. The first major conflict of the post-cold war period saw the virtual collapse of the Arab League and dealt a severe blow to the Gulf Cooperation Council (whose much-heralded collective security system failed to offer any resistance to the Iraqi invasion). In many of the Third World regional conflicts whose settlement was helped by US–Soviet/Russian cooperation (e.g. Afghanistan, Angola), the UN played a far more significant role than the relevent regional organization. Despite their apprehensions about external meddling, Third World regional groups have not been able to provide an indigenous regional mechanism to deal with humanitarian crises and thereby pre-empt external intervention. In Somalia, the UN Secretary-General sought to involve three regional groups—the OAU, the Arab League, and the Organization of Islamic Conference—but the latter two did nothing while regional action by the OAU 'proved largely irrelevant' in dealing with the humanitarian and political aspects of the crisis.[84]

In general, Third World regional organizations continue to lack the resources and organizational capacity to conduct major peace and security operations and are dependent on external support. Moreover, the role of a regionally dominant actor is problematic for regional peace and security operations. Some regionally dominant powers, such as India (in the case of SAARC) and China (in the case of the ARF), have been unsupportive of regional security arrangements for fear that multilateral norms might offset their relative power and influence over lesser regional actors. Others, such as Nigeria (in the case of the ECOWAS) and Saudi Arabia (in the case of the GCC), are seen by their lesser neighbours as using regional security arrangements as a tool to further their own strategic interests and ambitions. In both areas regionalism is subordinated to the interests of a dominant actor, and regional peace and security operations may not be perceived to be neutral or beneficial in a conflict situation. The problems encountered by the ECOWAS in the Liberian civil war are a case in point.

This operation has been been hampered not only by a scarcity of financial and organizational resources, but also by a perceived lack of neutrality on the part of Nigeria and resentment against its dominant role in the peace-keeping force on the part of other ECOWAS members.[85]

Finally, regional security arrangements in areas that are deemed to engage the 'vital interests' of the great powers have limited autonomy in managing local conflicts. In these areas, the dependence of local states on external security guarantees, hence frequent great power intervention in local conflicts, will continue to thwart prospects for regional solutions to regional problems.[86] In the Gulf, for example, Kuwaiti security agreements with the US came into conflict with regional security arrangements involving the GCC after the Iraqi defeat. Similarly, most developing nations of East Asia prefer bilateral arrangements with the US as a more realistic security option than indigenous multilateral approaches.

As in the field of security, Third World countries see regional cooperation as a necessary means for responding to pressures from a changing world economy.[87] During the cold war, the economic role of Southern regional organizations focused primarily on regional trade liberalization. Little attention was paid to addressing the wider range of economic and ecological security issues.[88] In recent years, regionalism in the South has been increasingly concerned with issues such as protectionism, low export commodity prices, essential raw material supply disruptions, and the debt burden. While regional cooperation is unlikely to resolve these problems, it might be useful in articulating areas of common interest and developing common negotiating positions.[89] In Asia, collective bargaining by ASEAN members with their Western 'dialogue partners' has already produced benefits such as better market access for their exports and the stabilization of the prices of their main primary commodity exports.

The 1990s are also witnessing a revival of Southern interest in regional trade liberalization. Recent examples include ASEAN's decision in 1992 to create a regional free trade area, the OAU's signing of an African Economic Community Treaty in 1991, and the emergence of two new trade groupings in South America (the MERCOSUR group including Argentina, Brazil, Paraguay, and Uruguay, created in 1991; the Group of Three including Mexico, Venezuela, and Colombia, established in 1994), and the Arab free trade zone launched in 1998.[90] The South's renewed interest in economic regionalism stemmed partly from doubts about the future of GATT (since dispelled) as well as fears about the emergence of protectionist regional trading blocs in Europe and North America. But old problems associated with regional integration in the South remain, especially the difficulty of ensuring an equitable distribution of benefits. The materialization of the proposed African Economic Community

Treaty has a thirty-four-year time frame, and the ASEAN framework is bogged down by inter-state suspicions over 'who gains most?' This problem also affects the 'market-driven' alternative to state-centric regional integration efforts, better known in East Asia as subregional economic zones or 'growth triangles'. In general, regional economic integration among developing countries will remain hostage to political and security concerns of the participating countries and their prior interest in fuller integration with the global economy through inter-regional trade and investment linkages.

The weaknesses of intra-South regional trade arrangements might be offset by the emergence of a North–South variety. The intended southward extension of NAFTA and Malaysia's proposal for an East Asian grouping under Japanese leadership are important developments in this regard. Such regional trading groups will expand market opportunities for the participating developing countries and alleviate their fear of protectionism in global markets. But they also pose a new set of dangers, such as the transfer of polluting industries to the developing countries and the dumping of unsafe and inferior Northern products in Southern markets. Buzan warns that the advent of regional trade blocs involving a North–South membership will increase the risk of 'exploitation of the periphery by the centre' unless there emerges a sense of genuine regionalism binding the hegemon and the less developed actors. [91] Moreover, such trade blocs will aggravate economic inequality within the South, since the opportunity to participate in such regional trading blocs is open only to those developing countries which have achieved relatively higher levels of economic success. While developing countries in Asia and Latin America can enjoy the benefits of closer integration with their developed neighbours, those excluded from such blocs (such as the African nations) will risk further marginalization in an increasingly regionalized global economy.[92]

V. CONCLUSION

Both realist and liberal theorists analysing post-cold war international relations appear to have come to the conclusion (albeit for different reasons) that the end of the cold war also means the end of the Third World.[93] This view rests largely on the increasing diversity and differentiation within Third World economies and on the obsolescence of its political and economic platforms. In particular, the adherents to this view point to the non-realization of the New International Economic Order and question the relevance of non-alignment within a non-bipolar international system structure. While realists point to the decline of the South's bargaining power (to compound its perpetual lack of structural power) as heralding the demise of Third Worldism, liberal theorists suggest a significant dampening of North–South polarization emerging from their growing economic interdependence[94] as well as the spread of democratic governance in the Third World. The latter perspective is buoyed up by the collapse of Marxism and the rise of the newly industrializing countries (both developments contributing to the further discrediting of the *dependency* school).

Yet, this chapter finds that the 'end of the Third World' may be somewhat simplistic and misleading. It is based on a narrow conception of the Third World's interests, position, and role within the international system. While it is easy to question the relevance of a Third World in the absence of the Second, several elements of the Third World's security predicament within, and political predisposition towards, the established international order have survived the end of the cold war and bipolarity.

In the post-cold war era, Southern instability has not disappeared, but rather has become more localized. Several parts of the Third World remain highly unstable despite the fact that the end of superpower rivalry has lessened the prospects for internationalization and escalation of its regional conflicts. (This does not mean the end of bipolarity is having a decompression effect; the fundamental sources of Third World instability remain independent of the structure of the international system.) The persistence of Southern regional instability contrasts with the situation involving the major Northern powers who, as some analysts see it, appear to be developing into a 'security community' with minimal prospects for the use of force in inter-state relations.[95]

The end of the Third World does not mean the disappearance of the North–South divide, it only means changes in the way in which the divide is being managed. As with insecurity within the South, the division between the North and the South survives the end of the cold war. North–South tensions encompass political, economic, ecological, and security issues, although the members of the South do not and cannot always agree on how best to address them. Greater economic differentiation within the South does not obscure the convergence of a critical interest among many developing countries in relation to a host of world order issues such as environmental degradation, disarmament, and intervention. Even a few of the NICs, considered by some to have graduated out of the Third World category, continue to harbour essentially 'Third Worldish' aspirations when it comes to the environment, human rights, and democracy.

To be sure, the post-cold war South faces simultaneous pressures for rebellion and adaptation within the established international system. The experience of the past decades has shown the futility of the South's confrontational approach *vis-à-vis* the North and induced a greater degree of pragmatism on its part in global negotiations. The major institutions of the Third World, their unity and credibility diminished, have accordingly adopted a more moderate attitude in pressing for the reform of the global economic and security order. But as the leading formal institutions like the NAM and the Group of 77 appear to be in a state of terminal decline, they are being replaced by more informal and *ad hoc* coalitions (as evident in the recent UN meetings on the environment and human rights) in articulating and advancing the South's interests in global North–South negotiations. Regional organizations can also play a useful role in accommodating the growing diversity of the South while projecting a basic and common outlook on political and distributive issues. But the absence of transregional effective institutions makes it difficult to speak of a Third World with a collective agenda to challenge the existing international system, an agenda that was a central element of the Third World's identity during the cold war period.

For these reasons, celebrating the end of the Third World on the part of the North seems highly premature. The North–South divide persists, even as Southern unity over these issues has collapsed. While the Third World (or South), never a cohesive or homogeneous political entity, has become even less so in the post-cold war era, many of the features of the international system which originally fuelled its political and economic demands and aspirations remain. Proclaiming an end to the Third World may seem a logical corollary to the West's 'victory' in the East–West conflict, but it obscures the persistence of the South's acute insecurity, vulnerability, and consequent sense of inequality in the emerging world order. These cannot simply be 'wished away' in any Northern construction of a new world order, since the Southern predicament of instability and inequality affects the economic and political well-being of the North itself, and since the major elements of the world order, including its ecological, human rights, and conflict-resolution aspects, cannot be realized without Southern participation and cooperation. For a genuine new world order to emerge, the concerns and aspirations of the South and its reservations about aspects of the Northern approach to order-maintenance must be recognized and addressed in the new agenda of global politics.

PART II

PART II

5

Latin America

Collective Responses to New Realities

JORGE HEINE

I. INTRODUCTION

The *anno mirabilis* of 1989, commonly used to mark the end of the cold war, was also a key turning-point in Latin America. With the fall of General Alfredo Stroessner in Paraguay in February, and the election of Patricio Aylwin as president of Chile in December—a scarce five weeks after the fall of the Berlin Wall—South America culminated its democratization process. The year was also the last of what the United Nations Commission for Latin America and the Caribbean (ECLAC) dubbed 'the lost decade', the one that started one weekend in August 1982 with the Mexican debt crisis and ended up engulfing much of the region in a vicious circle of debt and stagnation.[1]

One way to appreciate the magnitude of the changes Latin America has gone through since the end of the cold war is to look back to 1989 and consider how the situation in the region appeared at that time. Most observers would agree with the proposition that Latin America was then in dire straits. From 1980–1 to 1990–1, Latin America's GDP grew at annual average of only 1.3 per cent. With a population growth of 2.1 per cent a year, this resulted in a fall of per capita GDP of 9 per cent during the decade, with per capita consumption falling much the same. Not surprisingly, the number of people under the poverty line increased from 113 million in 1980 to 184 million in 1990.

The effects of the region's foreign debt have been analysed extensively and there is no need to recapitulate them here.[2] Latin America became the most heavily indebted region in the world in per capita terms. The adjustment programmes initiated to pay off that debt led the region to become a net capital exporter, remitting hundreds of billions of dollars abroad without making any appreciable dent in the total amount of extant debt.[3]

These adjustment programmes meant heavy sacrifices, not only for Latin American individuals, whose incomes fell drastically, but also of future growth, as investment rates were cut across the board to meet foreign obligations—often undertaken by the private sector, but quickly nationalized. Ironically, given the sort of ideology espoused by these regimes, those countries with large state-owned, natural resource industries (like Mexico, Chile, and Venezuela) had an easier time, for obvious reasons, in paying in orderly fashion these enormous debts, than those countries that did not (like Brazil and Argentina), where their leaky tax systems made it very difficult for the state to raise the necessary foreign exchange, leading to hyperinflation and serious fiscal management crises.

The rather bleak picture offered by Latin America in 1989–90 was, if anything, compounded by developments in Eastern and Central Europe. Precisely at the moment when the democratization process in Latin America was culminating and the possibility of starting to normalize the region's international economic relations loomed high, the 'Eastern European Communist threat', if there was ever such a thing, by disappearing became an even bigger threat to Latin America. By attracting huge amounts of capital, both from multilateral institutions, extant and especially created for that purpose, like the London-based European Bank of Reconstruction and Development, and from private investors, Eastern Europe became a powerful competitor to Latin America in the world's capital markets, and one with seemingly big advantages over the latter. Greater proximity to Northern markets, a better trained labour force, and a close cultural affinity to Western European mores were all seen as promising a huge influx of funds to the lands east of the Oder and the Danube, once again leaving Latin America stranded and marginalized.[4] In turn, the Single European Market, and Maastricht Treaty seemed to indicate that the protectionist tendencies manifested in Northern economies during the 1980s, which had made only more difficult Latin America's efforts to service its enormous, half-trillion dollar debt, would become even stronger, as Europe turned inward.

In short, the prospects for Latin America in 1989 were hardly encouraging—and in the minds of many commentators, frankly discouraging. Yet, nearly a decade later, it is difficult to escape the conclusion that Latin America is doing a lot better than expected, given the previous scenario.[5] The average annual growth rate of 3.3 per cent for the 1991–3 period rose to 5.3 per cent in 1994. As can be seen from Table 5.1, the tequila effect of the December 1994 Mexican peso crisis, though bringing down regional growth to an almost non-existent 0.3 per cent (largely caused by the Mexican and Argentinian downturns, of 6.6 and 4.6 per cent, respectively), was short-lived, with growth returning to a healthy 3.4 per cent in

TABLE 5.1. *Evolution of Latin American economies* (%)

	1990	1991	1992	1993	1994	1995	1996	Average annual accumulated growth	
								1981–90	1991–6
Growth of GDP	−0.3	3.4	2.7	3.8	5.3	0.3	3.4	1.1	3.1
Inflation	1,191.0	199.7	418.0	887.4	336.8	25.5	19.3		
Unemployment	5.8	5.8	6.3	6.3	6.4	7.3	7.7		

Note: The economies considered are: Argentina, Bolivia, Brazil, Chile, Colombia, Costa Rica, Dominican Republic, Ecuador, El Salvador, Guatamala, Haiti, Honduras, Mexico, Nicaragua, Panama, Paraguay, Peru, Uruguay and Venezuela. The figures for 1996 are preliminary estimates only.

Source: ECLAC, *Balance Preliminar de la Economía de América Latina y el Caribe* (Santiago: ECLAC, 1996).

1996. For a region traditionally riven by inflation, the steady decline of the latter, from 1191 per cent in 1990 to 19 per cent in 1996 has been especially gratifying, bringing a measure of price stability not seen in many decades.

Nor is this positive situation confined to the economic sphere. With the exception of Haiti and Suriname, very special cases for a variety of reasons, there has not been a successful military *coup d'état* in Latin America since 1982, when the one in El Salvador took place. To be sure, there have been a number of failed attempts—most notably in Venezuela, on several occasions—and Peru has been through some unorthodox constitutional situations. Needless to say, there is much that is fragile about the re-emerging democratic regimes; civilian control over the military is not yet fully reasserted; there are questions about the nature of constitutional liberalism;[6] legislatures need to become much more sophisticated in their processing of information and data to be able to play the role of countervailing power to the executive; corruption, rampant in some cases, may be undermining the democratic process; and judicial reform is an urgent task in the region. Still, the overall picture looks a lot better than most observers would have thought only a few years ago.

What are the reasons for this remarkable turnaround in Latin America's development? How has it become the fastest growing region in the world, after East Asia? What are the roots of its now rejuvenated democratic institutions? What sort of international role is it taking on now, after the end of the East–West conflict? Where does it place itself in the North–South cleavage that now remains as a key dividing line in post-cold war world politics?

The purpose of this chapter is to provide an answer to these and related questions by examining various aspects of the manner in which liberalization (i.e. economic reform), democratization and the new security challenges of the 1990s have been handled in the region, the impact they have had on Latin America's social and political structures, and the conditions they have created (or failed to create) to put the region on the road to self-sustaining economic development and political stability.

II. THE QUEST FOR ECONOMIC REFORM

Perhaps the most dramatic example of the limitations of democratization without economic reform was provided by Argentina's President Raúl Alfonsín, who, despite his accomplishments on the political front, had to leave office in 1989 several months in advance of the end of his constitutional term, to make room for his elected successor, President Carlos Menem, because of the rapidly deteriorating economic situation.

And the lesson has not been lost on most Latin American governments, which, by and large, have undertaken wide-ranging and extensive economic reform programmes. In fact, as Ben Ross Schneider has put it, 'In Latin America, the surprising record of the 1980s and early 1990s was one of radical economic reform with punishing social costs and without a wave of collapsing democracies.'[7] These economic reform programmes have been anchored in three key components: stabilization, liberalization, and privatization.

The scourge of inflation has, of course, been one of the main culprits behind the absence of an economic environment conducive to growth and development, and its ravaging effects made governments finally realize that drastic measures needed to be taken against it. Without macroeconomic equilibria, or so the reasoning went, not much could be done. That deficit spending and loose monetary policies were behind the region's high inflation rate—which averaged 67.5 per cent a year during the 1980–4 period, more than doubling to 164.6 per cent in 1985–9, only to reach 1191 per cent in 1990—had of course been known for a long time. Even so, decision-makers were simply not prepared to take the necessary measures to tighten the reins, as the political costs of so doing were often felt to outweigh the benefits of a lower inflation rate.

During the 1989–91 period, though, a number of factors converged to narrow significantly the range of policy options, and thus open the doors to the firm establishment of the so-called 'Washington consensus'.[8] The fall of the Berlin Wall and the subsequent dismemberment of the Soviet Union put paid to whatever hopes central planning and 'actually existing socialism' might have embodied for Latin America. The devastating effect this had on Cuba, whose exports dropped from US$9 billion to US$2 billion in a couple of years as COMECON came tumbling down, made it all too clear to Latin American countries that a different approach was needed to survive and prosper in the world of the 1990s.

On the other hand, the East Asian experience, in which countries like South Korea, Taiwan, and Singapore managed to grow at double-digit rates for long periods of time, seemed to validate the importance of high savings and investment rates, none of which are possible in an inflationary environment.

Drastic measures were needed and, in fact, were taken. As a result, the average fiscal deficit in the region fell from 4.25 per cent of GDP in 1988–9 to some 0.5 per cent of GDP in 1990–4.[9] Not surprisingly, inflation fell to 25.5 per cent in 1995 and 19.3 per cent in 1996, the lowest in a quarter of a century. Instead of trying to achieve multiple objectives, central banks focused on one: keeping inflation under control; and low inflation became the litmus test of a successful macroeconomic policy.[10]

Of course, however necessary, stabilization by itself is not enough to generate high growth. The opening of the economies to outside competition and their deregulation were also part of the new 'policy packages' being applied, and another prerequisite for the highly indebted Latin American countries to regain access to the international financial markets they had been excluded from after the debt crisis arose in 1982.[11]

Tariff-lowering and the removal of non-tariff barriers to trade, tax reform—with an emphasis on taxes on consumption like VAT as opposed to those that penalize savings and investment—and increased labour-market flexibility were among the key components of these liberalizing efforts designed to free economic agents from the shackles of decades of protectionism and over-regulation.

The third leg of these economic reform programmes was the privatization of state assets, in many cases important sources of the above-mentioned huge deficits in public spending. Though the picture of the privatization programme is necessarily a mixed one—it is not evident that the interest of the fiscus was maximized in the many often non-transparent transactions that have taken place over the past decade or so in the region—it has also turned out to be a key tool to attract foreign investment, from the region itself and from elsewhere.[12] And even Brazil, until now reluctant to privatize its enormous state assets, has put on sale its mining holding Compania do Vale de Rio Doce, arguably one of the 'jewels in the crown' of the Brazilian public sector, with an estimated value of US$10 billion, in one of the biggest privatization exercises ever undertaken.

Needless to say, these are all matters that pose complex challenges to policy-makers.[13] As the Mexican peso débâcle in December 1994 revealed, the massive inflow of foreign capital can be as much a threat to an economy's stability as its total absence, since its sudden withdrawal can launch the country into a crisis—and that can easily spill over into other countries, as shown by the 'tequila effect' in Argentina and elsewhere in the course of 1995.[14]

The timing, sequencing, and careful monitoring of these reforms is thus central for their success. Simply opening the capital account to the inflow and outflow of foreign exchange, without having undertaken the necessary reforms of the local financial institutions and their regulatory environment, can be a recipe for disaster—as shown by the Chilean banking crisis of 1982, which led to a 14 per cent drop in GDP.[15] Having learnt this painful lesson, and having been overwhelmed in the early 1990s by a huge inflow of short-term foreign capital which led to an appreciation of the Chilean peso and a dangerous overheating of the economy, Chile put in place checks and disincentives to short-term capital inflows, while facilitating long-term ones.[16]

That these reforms have a strong measure of staying power was shown by the aftermath of the Mexican crisis of the peso in December 1994. Although its effects on the Mexican economy were severe, this by no means led to a revival of protectionism or other policies of yesteryear, and in 1996 the country—and the region—rebounded.

Yet, the Achilles' heel of Latin America's economic reform programmes remains what we might call the social question.[17] Although renewed growth in a much more stable economic environment has meant a steady reduction in the number of people under the poverty line in countries like Bolivia, Colombia, Costa Rica, Panama, Peru, and Uruguay, in most cases this has only meant a return to the levels of income of the late 1970s which were severely cut in the 1980s; elsewhere, in countries like Brazil and Venezuela, not even that can be said.

The Chilean case is especially interesting because, although the number of people defined as poor has fallen from 39.4 per cent in 1987 to 24.1 per cent in 1994, it has become more and more difficult to cut into the core of 'hard poverty', and overall income distribution remains extremely unequal—despite an average annual growth of 6 per cent growth during the 1984–96 period, and 7 per cent during 1990–6.[18] The extreme inequality of Latin American societies—countries like Brazil have a Gini index of 0.59, among the highest in the world—remains one of its most distinctive features, and one unlikely to disappear simply as a result of economic growth, however high.

III. FROM TRANSITION TO DEMOCRATIC CONSOLIDATION?

As Gautam Sen argues in Chapter 3, the implementation of these economic reform policies requires a high degree of 'state capacity', leading to what has been termed the 'orthodox paradox'. In the words of Haggard and Kaufman, 'for governments to reduce their role in the economy and expand the play of market forces, the state itself must be strengthened'.[19] Moises Naim has illustrated well how some of the frustrations of the Venezuelan recent experience were precisely rooted in a weak and inefficient state, in need of modernization.[20]

In this context, perhaps the most remarkable feature of Latin America's political evolution in the post-cold war era has been the staying power of its democratic institutions.[21] With one or two exceptions, electoral democracy has become the norm throughout the region, in marked contrast to the situation prevailing in the late 1970s and early 1980s, when a vast majority of Latin Americans found themselves under military rulers. This remarkable change is even true for countries like Haiti, Nicaragua, and Paraguay, with little or no democratic history and democratic political culture to fall back on, but which have still managed to latch on firmly to the 'third wave' of democratization Samuel Huntington has referred to.[22] In cases where military rule was absent but democracy still limited, like in Mexico, there have also been significant advances. Today, the electoral authorities are independent from the blatant interference exercised in the past by the Minister of the Interior. The results of the July 1997 elections, when the PRI—the party that has long dominated Mexican politics—lost the majority in Congress and the mayorship in Mexico city, are evidence of these new trends.

None of this means that Latin American democracies are fully consolidated.[23] As Larry Diamond has argued recently, the political development challenges facing the region's democratic regimes are manifold: these relate to democratic deepening, institutionalization, and performance.[24] And although the military are not exercising political power in a direct fashion, they remain highly influential, often with 'reserved domains' of institutionality which limit the democratic space in the region's polities.[25]

The case of Peru in particular raises further questions, as the ambitions of President Fujimori to extend his mandate for yet another term pose serious doubts about the democratic nature of his rule. There are, in addition, factors outside the respective regimes which threaten the stability of the democratic processes. The emergent guerrilla movements in Mexico, and the assassination of Donaldo Colossio, have come as a surprise but also as a warning of how violent politics could turn. Violence has of course been a long-standing feature of the Colombian scene, where both guerrilla and drug-mafia organizations have become a major barrier to democratic developments.

The process of moving to eliminate these non-democratic bastions is a complex one, with political leaders having constantly to balance the need of moving forward and keeping the momentum of change with that of avoiding authoritarian regressions. For obvious reasons, this is an especially difficult balancing act in countries where the military regimes were particularly repressive, and the collective memory is still haunted by the suffering of the past.[26]

IV. THE DYNAMICS OF POLITICAL COOPERATION

One of the less appreciated aspects of Latin America's evolution over the past fifteen years is the degree to which the region's transition to democracy has given rise to extended political cooperation among Latin

American states. Breaking the pattern of mutual distrust and occasional conflict that has marked so much of the region's history, governments have started to work together on issues of common concern in an unprecedented fashion. Perhaps the most visible of these cooperation mechanisms have been the Summits of the Americas, of which the first took place in Miami in December 1994, and the second in Santiago, Chile, in March 1998, but there are many more expressions of the new vitality of Latin American collective diplomacy—one of the significant ways in which the region has responded to the post-cold war era.

What was perhaps the nadir of Latin American political fragmentation was reached in 1982, when the first Falklands/Malvinas War and then the erupting debt crisis were met by a divided and therefore ineffective response by the region's governments. Having repudiated previous regional integration efforts, 'the only common denominator of (those) military governments seemed to be brutal repression, the threat of war among neighbouring countries and their adherence to the national security doctrine sponsored by the United States'.[27] However, shortly thereafter, and as the Central American crisis moved into high gear, the emergence of the Contadora Group, formed by Colombia, Mexico, Panama, and Venezuela (and named after an island off Panama where the grouping's initial meeting took place), signalled a crucial turning-point in the region's collective response to the perverse, cold war-inspired conflicts in the Central American isthmus.

Originally formed to search for a peaceful solution to these conflicts— a quest in which the Contadora Group found itself at odds with a Reagan administration bent on imposing its own version of Pax Americana—it soon garnered additional support in South America. As can be seen in Table 5.2, the Contadora Support Group counted as its members countries as significant as Argentina and Brazil, as well as Peru and Uruguay, leading ultimately to the so-called Group of Eight. As time went by, however, the Central American predicament took second stage to the broader issue of ensuring the success of democratic transitions throughout the region. As these progressed, the Group of Eight expanded, giving way to the Rio Group.[28]

Quite apart from the nomenclature, an important qualitative change has taken place in the approach taken by these various groupings to the international agenda. Whereas as recently as 1989, the documents emanating from the G8 were in many ways prototypical of the 'cahier de doleances' school of diplomacy, i.e. the one specializing in conveying a long list of unmeetable demands to international public opinion, this has gradually changed to much more pragmatic and realistic concerns in specific issue areas—of which the agenda of the Iberoamerican Summit held

TABLE 5.2. *Latin America's evolving political cooperation*

	Mechanism	Members	Purpose
1983–1985	Contadora Group	Colombia, Mexico Panama, Venezuela	Peace in Central America
1985–1986	Contadora Support Group	Argentina, Brazil Peru, Uruguay	Peace in Central America
1986–1987	Group of Eight	All of the above	Support democratic transitions
1990–	Rio Group	All of the above, plus Bolivia, Chile, Ecuador, Paraguay, and the Central American and CARICOM states	Facilitate intra- and inter- regional dialogue on political and economic affairs
1991–	Iberoamerican Summits	All Spanish-speaking countries in the Americas, plus Brazil, Spain, Portugal	Political dialogue
1994–	American Summits	All countries in the Americas, minus Cuba	Political dialogue

Source: Jorge Heine.

in Santiago, Chile in November 1996, 'Towards an Efficient and Participatory Democracy', is in many ways emblematic.

As Latin American economies and policies gain strength and self-confidence, so does the participation of these states in world politics. And without the extensive political convergence and cooperation that has taken place since 1983, and which has gained momentum in the 1990s, the increased trend towards regional economic integration, a subject to which we now turn, would not have been possible.

V. GLOBALIZATION, REGIONALIZATION, AND REGIONAL COOPERATION

In this new environment, then, Latin America, far from being marginalized, as some observers thought in the early 1990s, has taken on the challenge of globalization and the related phenomena, regionalization and regionalism, with great verve.[29] I would argue that part of the reason the region has rebounded with such strength from the crisis of the 1980s is because it has adapted exceptionally well to the demands of a changing world economy.

Globalization and regionalization, of course, have a number of common elements, as in both investment flows play a key role and 'trade, which is often intraindustrial and intrafirm, is determined by the dynamic interdependence of decisions made by firms and markets'.[30] As Gautam Sen argues, it is the tension between the freedom of movement enjoyed by international players in the economy and those still constrained by national boundaries that lies at the root of regionalization. Globalization impels political authorities to liberalize their economies and open the doors to greater competition; at the same time, the creation of new regional structures allows them to reduce the power of these international players and have some say in the direction of trade and investment flows.

Regional integration schemes, of course, are not exactly new in Latin America. Inspired by the example of the European Community, the 1960s saw a proliferation of them—from the Latin American Free Trade Association (LAFTA), through the Andean Group, the Central American Common Market, and the Caribbean Community (CARICOM). Despite their promising beginnings—the Andean Group (originally named the Andean Pact), because of its daring commitment to set a limit on the profits to be made in the member countries by transnational corporations, was seen in the 1970s as an especially imaginative attempt to combat their power by creating a common front among a group of developing countries, thus avoiding the trap of competing among themselves in concessions to foreign firms—none of these agreements made much headway, with intraregional trade rarely reaching beyond 10 per cent of total trade.

In the 1990s, however, the emergence of what ECLAC has called 'open regionalism' in Latin America has given a new impetus to regional integration, a process that as recently as 1989 many believed to be a dead duck.[31] What we are witnessing is the rise of a complex set of intertwined bilateral and multilateral agreements that have considerably dynamized cross-border trade and investment. This has created a much more favourable situation, with countries showing a considerably greater willingness to open their economies.

This process has been fuelled by both intergovernmental agreements and market forces. On the one hand, 'the current trend toward the globalization of competition and the internationalization of production makes it imperative to open the economies to international trade and investment. [However], this does not exclude the possibility of a preferential, and therefore deeper, opening among those of the same region.'[32]

As Table 5.3 indicates, the new, open regionalism differs in important ways from the old, for want of a better term, 'closed' variety. To start with,

TABLE 5.3. *The old and the new regionalism in Latin America*

	Old Regionalism	New Regionalism
Economic development strategy	ISI	Export-led
Role of regional market	Buffer against foreign competition	'Trial run' for world market
Nature of integration	Shallow	Deep
Autonomy of economic policy	High	Low
Tariff liberalization	Positive lists of products included	Negative lists of products excluded
Implementation	Complex: item by item negotiation	Simple: straightforward deregulation

Source: Adapted by the author from various sources, including ECLAC, *Panorama de la Inserción Internacional de América Latina y el Caribe* (Santiago: ECLAC, LC/G.1941, 2 Dec. 1996).

of course, the notion that one could embark on ambitious regional integration plans while still sticking to import substitution industrialization (ISI) and 'desarrollo hacia adentro' (development from within) approaches to economic development cannot but strike one as wrongheaded; this was what in the end made it so difficult for LAFTA to succeed in the 1960s and 1970s. The highly gradualistic process of tariff liberalization, whereby lists of products to be included in the lowering of the often enormous tariffs were carefully negotiated on an item-by-item basis, led to a perverse dynamic: used to decades of protectionism, Latin American industrialists became adept at fighting tooth-and-nail against any dismantling of these protectionist walls, thus making progress toward freer trade in the region an exceedingly slow process. By proceeding thorough short negative lists of the relatively few products to be excluded, the new regionalism has turned the corner in this regard, allowing much swifter movement towards the opening of regional borders to trade and investment.[33] Partly as a result of this, intraregional trade increased from US$16.1 billion in 1990 to US$43 billion in 1995, with intraregional exports growing from 13 per cent of total exports to 19.5 per cent in the same period.

VI. THE CASE OF MERCOSUR

In February 1995, the common external tariff of the Andean Group (now renamed Andean Community) formed by Peru, Bolivia, Ecuador, Colombia and Venezuela came into effect with a maximum rate of 20 per cent and covering 95 per cent of all product items; the same happened a month earlier with the treaty of the Group of Three (formed by Mexico, Colombia, and Venezuela), committed to establishing a free trade zone by 2005, something already extant between Venezuela and Colombia. Many other bilateral free-trade agreements have been signed in the region over the past five years. Yet, with Bolivia having joined MERCOSUR as an associate member in December 1996, and Venezuela having expressed interest in doing the same, MERCOSUR, perhaps the most prominent example of the new regionalism, seems to be at the forefront of the integration process.

Founded in 1991 by Argentina, Brazil, Paraguay, and Uruguay, it is considered by many the single biggest success story in the history of Latin American regional integration, having contributed to increasing trade among its members from US$5.1 billion in 1991 to US$15 billion in 1995, an increase from 11 to 20 per cent of total trade.[34]

The history of Chile's on–off relationship with MERCOSUR is revealing of the new winds that are buffeting the Latin American economies. Though invited to join when the original MERCOSUR Treaty was signed in Asunción in March 1991, Chile backed off because it was not prepared to raise its own external tariff (then set at 15 per cent, later lowered to 11 per cent) to the higher levels set by the treaty. Yet, keen to leave an open door to Latin America's fastest growing economy, member countries included a tailor-made clause allowing Chile to join at a later date.[35]

Chile soon found out that, treaty or no treaty, its trade with MERCOSUR was growing in leaps and bounds—150 per cent from 1990 to 1995. Perhaps even more significant was its nature: 34 per cent of Chile's exports to these countries were industrial products, as opposed to only 12 per cent for total exports. In 1995, Chile's trade with MERCOSUR was a little less than a third of total intra-MERCOSUR trade of US$15 billion. In this context, to be left out of the subregional group's customs union instituted on 1 January 1995 would have meant paying increasingly higher duties, and thus being effectively shut out from some of Chile's fastest growing markets. Though offering a relatively small market (of only 14 million people with a per capita income of US$5100), Chile has provided MERCOSUR with much-needed access to the Pacific, as well as with a highly dynamic foreign trade—whereas MERCOSUR's population is 14.5

times that of Chile, its foreign trade is only 5.3 times as high—and an important source of capital (about which more below).

There is at least one school of thought, largely derived from neo-classical economics that condemns preferential trading agreements as conducive to trade distortions and a misallocation of resources.[36] Yet, as Uruguayan Foreign Minister Alvaro Ramos Trigo has pointed out, 'MERCOSUR is a clear example of a "natural" customs union based on geographical facts that clearly offset any trade diversion by actual trade creation.'[37] Moreover, as ECLAC has underscored, open regionalism in the developing world today has a strategic component. Given the difficulties Southern producers have in accessing Northern markets affected by low growth and high unemployment rates, the strengthening of regional markets in the southern hemisphere can play a vital role, allowing developing countries to adapt to the process of globalization without being excluded from it.

One of the reasons why MERCOSUR has done particularly well in this context is because it has reversed another legacy of the 1960s: that of the smaller and medium-sized economies being the keenest on regional integration, and the largest ones, like Brazil and Argentina, being much more inward-oriented and self-centred. By bringing together the two Latin American powerhouses—and the original impetus to MERCOSUR was really given in 1986 by Presidents José Sarney and Raúl Alfonsín in a bilateral cooperation programme aimed at expanding intra-industry flows—MERCOSUR has changed regional geopolitics and geoeconomics. With the two regional powers driving the process, progress is much more likely than with them standing on the sidelines. MERCOSUR has also shown that considerable differences in size (from Brazil's population of 154 million and Argentina's 34 million to Paraguay's 4.8 million and Uruguay's 3.1 million) and per capita income (almost as significant, from Argentina's US$8004 and Brazil's US$3465 to Uruguay's US$4511 and Paraguay's US$1400) need not stand in the way of regional integration.

MERCOSUR has several distinct features that may help explain its remarkable success. To start with, it is an intergovernmental, bare-bones organization with no aspirations of transforming itself into some sort of supranational body. Secondly, it is extremely flexible, allowing members to sign agreements with other parties, and being able admit not only full members, but also associate ones, as in the case of Chile and Bolivia. Thirdly, although it has a relatively broad mandate, it has targeted very specifically its objective of making the member countries' economies more competitive by increasing trade and investment flows, and it has succeeded in doing so to a remarkable degree.[38]

The down side of this new regionalism is its 'tremendously disordered and chaotic' character, as Carlos Mladinic, Chile's chief MERCOSUR negotiatior, has referred to it, because of the proliferation of regional, sub-regional, and bilateral agreements that have emerged in the last decade.[39] Yet, as long as each of them are seen as gradual steps toward global integration, and not as ends in themselves, this would not seem to be a problem.

VII. THE UPSURGE IN INTRAREGIONAL INVESTMENT

This rebound in the Latin American economies has also meant that the region has once again started to attract foreign direct investment (fdi). Thus, in 1991–3, Latin America was the destination of 31 per cent of all fdi directed to developing countries and some 10 per cent of all fdi world-wide, making for a total stock of US$186 billion in fdi in the region by 1994. Despite the Mexican crisis, fdi in the region actually increased, rising from US$20 billion in 1994 to US$27 billion in 1995.[40]

By far the most interesting phenomenon in this regard, though, is the emergence, for the first time in many decades, of strong currents of intraregional investment flows. The product of the growing internationalization of Latin American firms, they have become another important driving force behind the new regionalism. As has been established elsewhere, to keep its momentum, the process of regional integration cannot depend solely on trade flows, but must also trigger a dynamic in which the productive structures *in toto* adapt themselves to the opportunities offered by expanded markets.

Important magnets for cross-border investment have been privatizations, of which there has been a veritable flood since 1990, and the process has been given a considerable boost by the removal of almost all constraints on foreign investment and profit remittals. Public utilities have been a special target in that regard, and the pattern is for such flows to be especially strong among neighbouring countries: between Argentina and Brazil, Chile and Argentina, Mexico and Central America, and Venezuela and Colombia.

The country at the forefront of this process has probably been Chile. As Table 5.4 indicates, some US$12 billion in foreign investment abroad, largely in South America especially in Argentina—where over half of the electricity used in the province of Buenos Aires is now produced by Chilean-owned utilities—but also in Peru, Colombia, Brazil, Bolivia, and Mexico, have made Chilean companies leading players in the new intraregional investment game.

TABLE 5.4. *Chilean investment abroad,*
1990–1996

Country	Materialized Investment (US$)
Argentina	5,681.9
Peru	1,605.5
Colombia	944.8
Brazil	737.9
Mexico	478.8
Panama	387.5
Channel Islands Guernsey	298.1
Venezuela	286.3
Cayman Islands	241.4
Bolivia	235.0
Russian Federation	153.2
Others	1,134.5
TOTAL	12,184.9

Source: *El Mercurio* (11 Mar. 1997), B1, B5.

The irony, of course, is that Chilean business had for long been very sceptical of Latin American regional integration—the argument was often made that a fully open economy does not need it since it is 'integrated to the world'. It is now making the most of the natural advantages of geographical proximity and cultural affinity to bring to bear its accumulated experience in areas like electricity generation and distribution, financial services, and food retailing to the rest of South America. This is aided by Chile's high savings rate (28 per cent of GDP) and the relatively small size of its internal market, which forces it to look for additional outlets.

VIII. LATIN AMERICA AFTER THE COLD WAR

For students of Latin America, it often seems difficult to escape Lampedusa's well-known statement: 'the more things change, the more they stay the same'. Notwithstanding the cataclysmic changes we have witnessed in the international and political system in the course of the past decade, for those who waxed lyrical about the improved prospects for the region in mid-1994, three significant events in the last quarter of that year seemed not only an anachronistic throwback to earlier, less sanguine times, but also a confirmation that the region finds it impossible to break the 'boom-bust' cycle which has traditionally stood in the way of its road to self-sustaining development. The US occupation of Haiti in September, the Peru–Ecuador border conflict in November, and the débâcle of the Mexican peso in December, with their connotations of inter-American relations in the 1920s rather than in the 1990s, seemed to ratify for the region as a whole what has so often been said about Brazil: that it is the country of the future—and always will be.

Yet, from the vantage point of the mid-1990s, the ultimate denouement of those very same events provides elements for a rather different interpretation. Far from having been simply another invasion of yet another Caribbean country in defence of US corporate interests and those of its local allies—the comprador bourgeoisie—this US occupation of Haiti was designed to reinstate in power a left-wing, liberation-theology priest, Father Jean Bertrand Aristide, who had made much of his political career denouncing US imperialism. One immediate effect of it was the wholesale dismantling of the Haitian Armed Forces, for long the principal instrument of kleptocratic rule in the country of Henri Christophe and Toussaint L'Ouverture, and the laying of the foundations of what may still emerge as Haiti's first truly democratic government. The Peru–Ecuador border conflict, though it took longer to be brought under control than most observers expected, did not escalate into full-scale war, and ultimately proved to be a mere blip on the screen of the tremendous push for regional integration and cooperation that is taking place in Latin America. And the region's quick recovery from the 'tequila effect' by the second quarter of 1995, thus disproving any fears of it leading to another foreign creditworthiness crisis like the one generated by the self-same Mexico in August 1982, was the best demonstration of the region's newly found economic resilience and robustness—a far cry from the fragility and fickleness of earlier booms.

None of this is to say that Latin America has 'turned the corner', as it were, or that it is totally 'out of the wood' in terms of the many development challenges it faces and has to master. But it has been the central argument of this chapter that the region is better positioned to do so than it has been for a very long time and that this new situation is directly related to the considerable changes we have witnessed in the world political economy since the end of the cold war, and Latin America's creative response to them, one that in many ways has made the most of them. And in contrast to some of the other regions discussed in this volume, 'what makes the current reform process particularly attractive', in the words of Sebastian Edwards, 'is that it has taken place at a time when democratic rule has returned to virtually every country'.[41]

6

The Asia Pacific Region in the Post-Cold War Era

Economic Growth, Political Change, and Regional Order

AMITAV ACHARYA AND RICHARD STUBBS

I. INTRODUCTION

Any discussion of the Asia Pacific region in a book dealing with the place of the Third World in the post-cold war era must grapple with a difficult question: is 'Third World' an appropriate label for these states? Although economic and political conditions of the countries of this region vary widely, the region locates some of the most successful economies of the world. Their leaders and peoples no longer see themselves as part of the 'Third World'; indeed, even with the regional economic crisis that started in 1997, some have achieved levels of prosperity exceeding those of many of the traditional members of the 'First World'. Past outpourings of claims and generalizations about 'Asian values', 'the East Asian model of economic development', and 'Asian democracy' have not just been directed against the West; they have also been a strong indication of the confidence with which a sizeable number of Asian élites view their region as providing a model of successful economic and political development for the rest of the Third World to follow. Even with the economic crisis of 1997–8 which sapped some of the region's self-confidence, there is still a sense that the Asia Pacific has outperformed other parts of the Third World.

Yet, the category 'Third World' or 'South' is more than a matter of economic development alone. As the editors of this volume and the contributors to the thematic section remind us, being part of the Third World is also about having a shared security predicament, economic approach, and collective self-identification. This broader understanding of the notion complicates one's analysis of the position and role of the Asia Pacific region in the global economic and political order, since economic success has not necessarily delivered the region from traditional Southern insecurities (along with new ones), nor does it indicate a willingness to abandon entirely the confrontational posturing that had been a hallmark of the old 'South'. These contradictions are aggravated by the region's pursuit of a mode of capitalist development whose essential features differ markedly from capitalism in Europe or North America, and which, despite the economic crisis in some countries in the region, will not quickly be abandoned.

The main argument of this chapter is that the position and posture of the developing countries of the Asia Pacific region toward the emerging world order are marked by a great deal of complexity and ambivalence. This ambivalence or the state of apparent schizophrenia can be discerned from an analysis of some of the principal economic, security, and political developments in the region in recent years, especially in the wake of changes brought about by the end of the cold war. The following sections provide a closer analysis of these developments in four key areas: economic regionalization, problems of security and stability, human rights and democratic governance, and regional institution-building.

II. ECONOMIC PREDICAMENT

The spectacular economic success story of the Asia Pacific region, which until the crisis of 1997–8 had lifted many regional countries out of poverty levels characteristic of the Third World, is well-documented. A brief overview here will therefore suffice. The developing countries of the Asia Pacific region include many of the world's best performing economies. The share of the Asia Pacific region of the world economic output was 26 per cent in 1993, compared to 4 per cent for all of Asia in 1960. The four newly industrializing countries (NICs) of South Korea, Taiwan, Hong Kong, and Singapore averaged growth of 8.3 per cent during the 1980s.[1] The average annual GDP growth rates for the 1965–80 and 1980–88 period were 9.6 and 9.9 per cent for South Korea, 9.7 and 6.8 per cent for Taiwan, 8.6 and 7.3 per cent for Hong Kong, 10.1 and 5.7 per cent for Singapore, 7.2 and 6.0 per cent for Thailand, 8.0 and 5.1 per cent for Indonesia, 7.3 and 4.6 per cent for Malaysia, and 5.9 and 0.1 per cent for the Philippines. Percentage growth rates for the 1988–91 period were 7.4 for South Korea, 5.7 for Taiwan, 2.7 for Hong Kong, 7.9 for Singapore, 9.8 for Thailand, 6.7 for Indonesia, 9.0 for Malaysia, and 3.8 for the Philippines.[2] During the early 1990s, the four NICs have averaged a growth rate of over 5 per cent, while the countries of Southeast Asia have managed average annual growth rates of 7 per cent.

While rapid economic growth sets the region apart from other parts of the global capitalist economy, equally important are the distinctive features of capitalist development and the process of economic integration evident in the region. The development experience of the Asia Pacific region has attracted much attention, leading to considerable theorizing about indigenous 'East Asian models' of industrialization.[3] These models challenge the validity of classical theories of development derived from Western Europe, home of the Industrial Revolution, which was once regarded as a 'universal' model for latecomers to emulate. They reject neo-classical assumptions about the invisible hand of the market-place, which had underplayed the role of the government while stressing the role of 'vigorous, competitive and entrepreneurial private business'.[4] Moreover, the fact that rapid economic growth and industrialization occurred in countries highly dependent on the core industrial powers also raised serious questions about the validity of the dependency theory which held that the world capitalist system had locked the Third World into perpetual underdevelopment. More recently, theorizing about the development experience of Asia Pacific countries has taken stock of cultural variables. As Chan and Clark point out, the 'East Asian miracle' has two features that were disregarded by the Modernization and Marxist schools: 'The first was the role of a strong developmentalist state, and the second was the impact of indigenous culture.'[5]

While some analysts remain sceptical of the existence of an 'East Asian model' of growth,[6] there is little dispute that the developing countries of the Asia Pacific are increasingly woven into an economic region by the southward movement of Japanese capital. During the 1988–93 period, Japanese fdi in the Association of Southeast Asia Nations (ASEAN) totalled over US$22 billion.[7] The end of the cold war has served to accentuate the regionalization process further. Between 1990 and 1993, Japan's direct investment in five main ASEAN economies amounted to US$15 billion, compared to US$10 billion by the US.[8] The integration of Northeast and Southeast Asian economies in the area of industrial production, the role of overseas Chinese production networks, and the emergence of transboundary 'growth triangles' has created a regional economy which has furthered the collective identity of the developing countries of the Asia Pacific region within the global economy.

The breakdown of the cold war structure that ordered international relations for so long has prompted a greater degree of fragmentation and regionalization in international affairs. In the Asia Pacific region this has accelerated trends in the regional economy that were already becoming apparent by the mid-1980s. The economic dynamism of the region and the challenge this represented to the American economy were noticeable well before the end of the cold war. However, the collapse of the Soviet Union has meant that there is now no overriding political reason for the US to continue to tolerate what is considered in Washington to be the unfair economic competition from Asia's rapidly expanding economic powers. Japan, of course, has been a target of US attempts to restructure its economy for over a decade. But in recent years China, once thought of as a necessary ally against the Soviets, and even the members of ASEAN, important to the US in the Vietnam War and the later fighting in Cambodia, have also come under increasing scrutiny as free-riders in the US-led open international trading regime.

There is an irony in this turn of events because the cold war and the containment policy followed by the United States were key factors in the economic rise of Japan and the NICs (South Korea, Taiwan, Hong Kong, and Singapore) and near-NICs (Malaysia and Thailand) of Asia. The flow of American dollars into the region, prompted initially by the Korean War but extended because of the continuation of the cold war, resuscitated a region that had been devastated by the Second World War and its aftermath. American aid to the front-line states in the battle against Asian communism—Japan, South Korea, Taiwan, and Thailand—allowed for the importation of industrial machinery and raw materials as well as the development of their economic and social infrastructures. Inflated commodity prices as a result of fears of a communist takeover of the region generated by the Korean War, and later the general regional prosperity created by US spending on the Vietnam War, also bolstered the economies of Singapore, Malaysia, and Hong Kong. Moreover, mobilizing resources and allocating US aid to build a defence against the communist threat helped to expand the powers and capabilities of the governments of the region. Strong authoritarian states, then, became a characteristic of the region and their intervention to facilitate the expansion of particular industrial sectors of their economies was a significant factor in the rapid economic growth they enjoyed.

Hence, the end of the cold war has highlighted the fact that the United States is now at odds with the very countries whose remarkable economic rise it sponsored. It must face the fact that a very distinct form of capitalism appears to be emerging in the Asia Pacific region. While it has its roots in American Fordism, it is very different from the form of capitalism entrenched in the North America Free Trade Agreement (NAFTA). In Asia there is clearly a major role for a facilitative state that is prepared to help national industries gain a competitive advantage. The Japanese have also adapted American industrial practices to their own needs. As a result, and in sharp contrast to American multinationals, Japanese firms empha-size, among other factors, a willingness to engage in joint ventures, the formation of subcontracting networks or complexes of production, flexi-bility so as to adapt quickly to rapidly changing market demands, and innovation in production processes.

Most importantly this form of capitalism has spread throughout the region. This is in part because the developing countries of the Asia Pacific region have chosen to adopt the Japanese model of development as opposed to the American model. For example, the Malaysian government explicitly followed a 'Look East' policy in the hope of emulating Japan's economic success. And in part this Asian form of capitalism has been dif-fused throughout the region as Japanese firms have been forced to relocate manufacturing production in lower cost countries such as Thailand, Malaysia, Indonesia, and China. Indeed, it has been American attempts to create 'a more level playing field' by driving up the price of the yen that has given the most recent boost to the economy of the Asia Pacific region. The Plaza Accord of September 1985 and the doubling of the value of the yen in the following three years produced a great wave of Japanese foreign direct investment throughout East and Southeast Asia. Initially, Japanese companies looked to South Korea and Taiwan, but then, as the South Korean and Taiwanese currencies also began to appreciate, a significant number of Japanese companies turned to the ASEAN region and to China. During the first half of the 1990s Washington continued to keep up the pressure on the yen in an attempt to reduce the Japanese trade surplus with the United States. As a result Japanese investment in the ASEAN economies reached a record $5 billion in 1994.[9]

The economic battle between Japan and the US has produced a number of crucial consequences for the rest of the Asia Pacific region. The fact that Japanese firms have been seeking out low-cost production platforms in China and Southeast Asia forces their competitors in the NICs to do the same. Hence, in 1994 Taiwanese businesses constituted the largest group of foreign investors in Malaysia, businesses in Hong Kong were the largest investors in China and Indonesia, and Singaporeans were the largest group to invest in Vietnam.[10] Moreover, in 1993 both the ASEAN states as a group and China exported more to the NICs than to the United States or Japan.[11] The resulting rapid integration of the Asia Pacific economy has been reinforced by the development of production networks and com-plexes which often include both Japanese and family-run overseas Chinese companies and which cut across state boundaries.

There is no doubt that the economic crisis of 1997–8 created an oppor-tunity for the US, through such institutions as the IMF, to impose neo-liberal economic practices on countries such as South Korea, Thailand,

and Indonesia. However, it is by no means certain that the distinctive Asian way of doing business will be radically altered. The cultural underpinnings of Asian business practices cannot be easily or quickly transformed.

III. THE INSECURITY DILEMMA

During the cold war, the security problems facing the developing countries of the Asia Pacific region closely paralleled those found elsewhere in the Third World. For these countries, the threat from within was considered to be more serious than the threat from without. In Southeast Asia, most of the newly independent states were confronted with the twin problems of ethnic separatism and communist insurgency. In many cases, these internal threats invited and were aggravated by superpower intervention, producing two of the biggest cold war flashpoints in Korea and Vietnam.

In the post-cold war era, some of the internal sources of instability in the developing states of the Asia Pacific region have lessened. This includes, most notably, the total collapse of communist insurgencies in Southeast Asia. Rapid economic growth has reduced the prospects for domestic challenges to regime legitimacy. At the same time, there has been a shift in the traditional inward-looking view of security in the region. Now, external threats to national security are receiving more attention, with a corresponding shift in their security posture from counter-insurgency to conventional warfare.[12]

Among the principal external sources of threat perceived by Asia Pacific countries is the region's shifting balance of power. The US Secretary of Defense under the Bush administration, Dick Cheney, spoke in 1990 of the danger that the withdrawal of the US forward deployed forces from the Asia Pacific region would upset the regional balance of power, leading to 'a vacuum' which 'almost surely would [lead to] a series of destabilizing regional arms races, an increase in regional tension and possibly conflict'.[13] Southeast Asia's leaders have expressed concerns that the end of the cold war order could be followed by strategic competition among a host of powers, including China, Japan, the US, and India,[14] leading to a highly unstable regional balance. It is being seen throughout the Asia Pacific region as a potential catalyst of new forms of regional conflict, including conflicts previously suppressed by superpower rivalry. Early in the post-cold war period, the Director of the US Defense Intelligence Agency warned of the emergence of 'regional flashpoints' in the Middle East, East Asia, and South Asia, because the end of bipolarity 'has removed the tampering mechanism that often kept these situations under control'.[15] In a similar vein, Singapore's Lee Kuan Yew has warned that the end of the cold war and the consequent reduction in the US military presence in Asia may lead to a situation in which 'all the latent conflicts in the region will surface'.[16]

Potential inter-state conflicts in the Asia Pacific region can be categorized in terms of their intensity and escalation potential (see Table 6.1). At the upper end of the spectrum are high-intensity conflicts with significant escalation potential, such as a possible war in the Korean peninsula or confrontation between China and other claimants to the Spratly Islands in the South China Sea. The two conflicts are not strictly comparable, however. The Korean peninsula problem is a legacy of the cold war which has been aggravated by North Korea's nuclear ambitions. It is partly driven by the North Korean regime's shaky domestic position. In contrast, the Spratly Islands dispute is primarily over territorial jurisdiction, compounded by competition for resources and strategic access. It is a prime example of the rising importance of territorial disputes in the post-cold war Asia Pacific. As a former armed forces commander of the Philippines, General Lisandro Abadia, predicted, 'the future area of conflict [in the Asia Pacific region] may shift towards the maritime area, specifically the territorial dispute of the South China Sea'.[17]

TABLE 6.1. *Potential inter-state conflicts in Asia Pacific region*

High-intensity/worst-case
Korean Peninsula (North Korea, South Korea, the United States)
Taiwan Straits (China, Taiwan)

Medium-intensity
The Spratly and Paracel Islands (China, Taiwan, Vietnam, the Philippines, Malaysia, Brunei)

Low-intensity (select)
The Northern Territories Dispute (Japan, Russia)
Takeshima-Tokdo Dispute (Korea, Japan)
Senkaku Islands (China, Japan)
Sipadan and Ligitan Islands (Malaysia, Indonesia)
Pedra Branca Island (Singapore, Malaysia)
Sabah Dispute (Malaysia, Thailand)
Limbang territory (Malaysia, Brunei)
Gulf of Thailand (Vietnam, Cambodia, Thailand, Malaysia)

Source: Amitav Acharya, 'Preventive Diplomacy: Concept, Theory, and Strategy', paper prepared for the International Conference on Preventive Diplomacy for Peace and Security in the Western Pacific Jointly Sponsored by the 21st Century Foundation and the Pacific Forum CSIS, 29–31 Aug., 1996, Taipei, Taiwan.

At the other end of the regional conflict spectrum are low-intensity conflicts over contested maritime borders and economic zones. Examples of such conflicts in Northeast Asia include the unresolved Northern Territories question between Japan and Russia and China's dispute with Japan over the Senkaku (Diaoyu) islands in the East China Sea. In general, however, these have yet to become a military issue comparable to regional tensions over the Spratlys.

Despite the seemingly greater concern with external threats, issues of domestic security and stability continue to preoccupy the developing countries of the Asia Pacific region. Issues of state-building and regime legitimacy remain important, in some cases aggravated by the end of the cold war. In East Asia during the post Second World War period, regimes which sought legitimacy through rapid economic growth and prosperity also stressed the need for political stability and continuity (as well as quality, although in this respect, the performance was uneven) of leadership over political participation in the Western model of liberal democracy. But sustaining these 'soft authoritarian political structures' on the basis of economic performance alone is no longer an easy task. While economic performance has in the past enhanced the legitimacy of authoritarian regimes in the short term, it may also contribute to what might be called the 'performance paradox' in which greater prosperity has worked against authoritarian rule by fuelling the political aspirations of an expanded middle-class population, by energizing the civil society, and by creating divisions within the ruling élite. While the claim that capitalist economic development promotes transitions from authoritarian rule is a major, if highly contested, element of the liberal ('new world order') thinking, there is little doubt that, throughout East Asia, rapid economic growth emerged as a possible catalyst of political change. Moreover, the crisis of 1997–8 also acted as a force for change, as the inability of a number of governments to deal with it clearly called into question their capacity to guarantee prosperity and thus undermined their legitimacy.

In addition, it has to be noted that the legitimacy of the region's regimes has rested on the fact that they have provided security in the face of both internal and external communist threats. Being on the front line in the cold war has meant that the populations under siege have been generally willing to cede considerable authority to those in power. And success in fending off the threat from Asian communism has certainly bolstered the claims to political authority made by governments in the region. However, the cold war, despite still being a factor in the stand-off on the Korean Peninsula, is essentially over. As a result, these traditional forms of threat to the state cannot now be used as a means of mobilizing people and resources, and justifying the actions of states. Together with the recent crisis in the regional economy this turn of events would suggest that the legitimacy of the region's governments will be called into question and space may be made for more democratic institutions.

To be sure, the legitimacy of the region's governments may be more robust than is generally recognized. The past economic success of the region's economies is being credited to the 'soft authoritarian' or, as Scalapino calls it, the 'authoritarian-pluralist'[18] state and there will be a reluctance, especially if the economic crisis is quickly overcome, to alter the political structure that has generated such a high level of prosperity. In particular the policy networks that link governments and the business community are likely to continue to buttress the political authority of the current regimes. Nor should the habit of acquiescence, built up over a period of time, be underestimated. On top of this most governments in the region have proven themselves to be flexible in dealing with threats to their political authority. For example, the legitimating geopolitical threats associated with the cold war have been replaced by geoeconomic threats associated with survival in an increasingly competitive global economy.

None the less, the powerful forces of rapid economic growth and upheavals which drive social changes in the Asia Pacific region are also challenging the equally powerful forces of entrenched political structures which claim to have been responsible for past and current successes. Under these circumstances the possibility of some form of democratization in parts of the region does exist. While élite consensus is reasonably firm in places like Singapore and Malaysia, cracks are appearing in places like Taiwan, Thailand, and, as became especially evident in May 1998, Indonesia. However, nowhere is radical change likely and if there is to be greater democratization it will be a distinctly Asian form of democracy which will continue to have a significant amount of authoritarianism mixed in with it. All of which adds to the sense of uncertainty that has been engendered by the ending of the cold war and its impact on the region.

A key issue here is whether transitions to more democratic rule will promote or threaten the region's stability. This question has important ramifications for the region's economic future, given the widely held view among the region's policy-makers that continued economic growth can only be achieved in a climate of political stability and regional order. Violent conflict resulting from leadership transitions and demands for greater political openness in authoritarian polities is not without precedent in the region. The Tiananmen Massacre (1989) in China, the 'People's Power Revolution' in the Philippines (1986), and the Bloody May episode in Thailand (1992), attest to this possibility. The downfall of the Suharto regime in Indonesia in May 1998 continued this trend. It should be noted that, as the case of Iran after the Shah shows, upheavals associated with leadership succession are not just a domestic problem, they could also have implications for the wider region if the regime which comes into power seeks to legitimize itself by creating frictions with its neighbours. While violent demands for political change may seem unlikely in countries in which rapid economic growth has benefited large sections of the society, order may be seriously threatened in the event of a major economic downturn. This is a possibility that no Asia Pacific nation can afford to overlook. Moreover, the global democratic revolution that accompanied the end of the cold war, and policies of the Western powers seeking to promote democracy, have given encouragement to pro-democracy groups in the region, including segments of the civil society pressing for greater respect for human rights. Thus, the question of domestic political openness and change has become an area of contention in the foreign policy and national security agenda of Asia Pacific countries.

IV. HUMAN RIGHTS, DEMOCRACY, AND THE NORTH–SOUTH DIVIDE IN THE ASIA PACIFIC CONTEXT

Perhaps nowhere is the tendency of the developing countries of the Asia Pacific region to identify with the Southern position more apparent than with respect to human rights and democratic governance.[19] Governments of Singapore, Indonesia, and Malaysia have been strong in their criticism of Western conceptions of human rights and democratic governance and have instead championed 'Asian values' as the basis for regional political order. Under Prime Minister Mahathir Mohammed, Malaysia has been particularly active in championing Third World causes. Mahathir has emerged as a leading critic of the West on issues of environment, human rights, democracy, and collective security.

The West tells us that democratic freedom and human rights are fundamental for the achievement of economic and social development. We in ASEAN never disputed that democracy for the people and opportunity for the individual to develop his or her own greatest potentials are indeed important principles. We disagree, however, that political systems qualify as democratic only when they measure up to certain particular yardsticks. Similarly, the norms and precepts for the observance of human rights vary from society to society and from one period to another within the same society. Nobody can claim to have the monopoly of wisdom to determine what is right and proper for all countries and peoples. It would be condescending, to say the least, and suspect for the West to preach human rights to us in the East.[20]

Speaking at the Vienna UN World Conference on Human Rights, Indonesian foreign minister Ali Alatas argued that Indonesia and the developing world have to maintain a balance between an 'individualistic approach' to human rights and interests of the society as a whole. 'Without such a balance, the rights of the community as a whole can be denied, which can lead to instability and even anarchy.'[21] The developmentalist argument on human rights, a common aspect of Third World platforms, has also found a particularly powerful echo among governments in Southeast Asia. At the Vienna World Conference on Human Rights, Malaysia called for a universal conception of human rights to go beyond political rights, and establish 'particularly its linkage with development'.[22] The argument is that, unless they fulfil the basic economic needs of their societies, developing countries cannot ensure the necessary conditions under which to uphold the political rights of citizens. 'Only those who have forgotten the pangs of hunger will think of consoling the hungry by telling them that they should be free before they can eat . . . economic growth is the necessary foundation of any system that claims to advance human dignity and order and stability are essential for development.'[23]

Mahathir has gone further in arguing that the human rights campaign of the West is an instrument of dependency. Citing the example of the former communist states of Eastern Europe, Mahathir contends that the campaign of human rights and democracy is a prescription for disruption and chaos in weaker countries, a campaign which makes the target ever more dependent on the donor nations of the West. In a similar vein, he sees Western attempts to link economic relations with human rights as a new set of 'conditionalities and protectionism by other means', aimed at undermining the economic prosperity and well-being of the East Asian region.[24]

Many Southeast Asian governments consider the rising prominence of human rights in recent years as a direct result of the end of the cold war. The anti-communist thrust of Western policy, which tolerated blatant human rights abuses by pro-Western Asian governments in the past, is no more. Instead, promotion of human rights constitute the core element of the 'new world order'. In responding to the human rights campaign of the West, Southeast Asian leaders often accuse the West of double standards. Foreign Minister Wong Kan Seng of Singapore argues that 'Concern for human rights [in the West] has always been balanced against other national interests.'[25] Attesting to 'hypocrisy' in the West's application of its human rights standards, Kishore Mahbubani, a senior Singaporean Foreign Ministry official contends:

. . .while human rights campaigns are often portrayed as an absolute moral good to be implemented without qualification, in practice Western governments are prudent and selective. For example, given their powerful vested interest in secure and stable oil supplies from Saudi Arabia, Western governments have not tried to export their standards of human rights or democracy to that country, for they know that any alternative to the stable rule of the Saudi government would very likely be bad for the West.[26]

Asia Pacific governments have viewed the enforcement of human rights standards by the West as not only selective, but also intensely political. Thus Ali Alatas wondered whether there are any 'disguised political purposes' behind the West's human rights campaign, designed to 'serve as a pretext to wage a political campaign against another country'.[27] Furthermore, this campaign is reflective of the power disparities in the international system. As the Malaysian Foreign Minister Ahmed Badawi put it: 'Attempts to impose the standard of one side on the other . . . tread upon the sovereignty of nations.'[28] Indonesia also sounded a warning as chair of the Non-Aligned Movement, arguing that 'In a world where domination of the strong over the weak and interference between states are still a painful reality, no country or group of countries should arrogate unto itself the role of judge, jury and executioner over other countries on this critical and sensitive issue.'[29] The rebellious posture toward Western-dominated international institutions extends to non-governmental organizations in the region. In Malaysia, for example, the US handling of the Gulf War came in for strong criticism from groups such as Aliran, which attacked what it saw as a new era of American unilateralism masked by the slogan of the new world order.

V. INSTITUTION-BUILDING

During the cold war, many Southeast Asian countries followed the path of other developing countries by joining Third World political and economic platforms such as the Non-Aligned Movement and the Group of 77. Moreover, the emergence of regionalism in Southeast Asia was strongly imbued with a quest for regional autonomy and collective self-reliance that would shield them from the danger of superpower rivalry. One of the founders of ASEAN articulated this perspective in the following terms:

Southeast Asia is one region in which the presence and interests of most major powers converge, politically as well as physically. The frequency and intensity of policy interactions among them, as well as their dominant influence on the countries in the region, cannot but have a direct bearing on political realities. In the face of this, the smaller nations of the region have no hope of ever making any impact on this pattern of dominant influence of the big powers, unless they act collectively and until they develop the capacity to forge among themselves an area of internal cohesion, stability and common purpose. Thus regional cooperation within ASEAN also came to represent the conscious effort by its member countries to try to re-assert their position and contribute their own concepts and goals within the on-going process of stabilization of a new power equilibrium in the region.[30]

The end of the cold war has been acompanied by changes in the regional countries' commitment to regional autonomy. For example, ASEAN's traditional policy of seeking the neutralization of Southeast Asia through the establishment of a Zone of Peace, Freedom, and Neutrality (ZOPFAN) has now given way to a more inclusive approach toward the role of outside powers in regional security.[31] Yet governments in Southeast Asia have continued to support Third World political and economic platforms. Indonesia's chairmanship of the Non-Aligned Movement in 1991 attested to the value it continues to attach to an institution now widely believed to be obsolete. Similarly, the Malaysian Prime Minister continued to defend the relevance of the NAM. In his view, although the world was no longer divided into two major blocs, the word 'non-aligned' remained relevant because of the dominance of the US. 'We are still non-aligned because that one bloc may jointly apply pressure on us. Thus, we still need to protect ourselves.'[32]

With the weakening of the Third World's global platforms such as the NAM and G77, regional institutions are seen by some Third World analysts as the best avenue for mobilizing Southern resources for a more equitable world order. In the Asia Pacific, while regional institution-building in both the economic and security arenas has brought together the developed Western states with the developing countries, signs of North–South polarization within these groupings remain unmistakable.

The Asia Pacific Economic Cooperation (APEC) forum, which was established at a ministerial meeting in Canberra in November 1989, and which includes as member economies the ASEAN states at that time— Brunei, Indonesia, Malaysia, the Philippines, Singapore, and Thailand— as well as Australia, Canada, Chile, China, Hong Kong, Japan, Mexico, New Zealand, Papua New Guinea, South Korea, Taiwan, and the United States, has been the only formal region-wide multilateral organization to emerge dealing with economic issues. While in some respects it has moved member economies fairly quickly down the road to greater interaction and limited institutionalization it has yet to make a significant impact on the way in which regional economic conflicts are resolved.

In good part this is because of divisions along North–South lines which have undermined the prospects for a clear consensus on the way forward for APEC. The governments of the US, Australia, and Canada, for example, tend to see APEC as a chance to tie as many regional economies as possible into an open, market-led, regional arrangement that would undercut any trend towards protectionism in the global economy and demonstrate the benefits of economic liberalization. In contrast to this approach to APEC's development is an influential view in Japan that sees APEC as a Pacific version of the Organization for Economic Cooperation and Development. According to this view APEC would hold discussions and policy dialogues, attempt to develop a common understanding on measures to strengthen regional cooperation, and help with policy-making at the regional and national levels.[33] Then there is the sceptical view of Malaysia's Prime Minister, Dr Mahathir, who is concerned that ASEAN might be swamped as an organization and that APEC might be used by the US to push its views on such issues as environmental and labour standards, and human rights. In addition to differences over goals there are also differences over process. The US, Australia, and Canada appear to be arguing for immediate and decisive action while many of the Asia Pacific governments are arguing for measured progress based on lengthy discussions and consensus.

Perhaps the most important limitation for APEC is that the membership has no sense of a shared history, culture, or set of political institutions. There is no common identity or sense of community which might unite APEC and allow for the development of a shared vision of APEC's future. In this respect Dr Mahathir's proposal for an East Asian Economic Caucus (EAEC) which would bring together the ASEAN states, along with China, Hong Kong, Japan, South Korea, and Taiwan, is more likely to emerge as an important forum for regional integration, if only because they do share aspects of recent history, similar political values, and a common approach to ordering their economies. The EAEC has been incorporated into APEC as a caucus of the larger grouping. But its future and the possibility that it will compete with APEC has to be considered. As Higgott and Stubbs point out,

. . . there are elements of North–South politics involved in support for EAEC as a potential counterweight to US hegemony. Mahathir was instrumental in establishing the group of fifteen developing countries which first met in Kuala Lumpur in 1989 to promote South–South economic ties. Moreover, Mahathir has been seen as a leader in defending the South's and indeed Asia's, interests on issues such as the environment and human rights . . . He has consistently railed against American hegemony and what he sees as attempts by the North to 'subject us to imperial pressures' . . . Mahathir's interest in developing the EAEC is, therefore, consistent with his concern not to have the United States dictate economic policy in the region. This clearly has some attractions for a number of regional governments.[34]

As with APEC, there are some important North–South divisions within the ARF. Formed in July 1994 with eighteen founding members, including the seven ASEAN states, the US, Australia, Canada, China, the European Union, Japan, Laos, New Guinea, New Zealand, Papua, South Korea, and Russia, the ARF is a somewhat unique regional security institution. As a grouping with a strong Northern representation, its formation and agenda-setting has been controlled by a coalition of developing states. Alarmed by what they see as attempts by the US and Australia to wrest control over APEC, ASEAN wants to retain its 'driver's seat' in the ARF.[35] Within the ARF, there remain important differences between its Western and Asian members. Canada and Australia want quick progress by the ARF in developing concrete measures of security cooperation. The ASEAN states have adopted a much more gradual, informal, and cautious approach to institution-building and explictly rejected the need to emulate Western models of security cooperation, particularly the Organization for Security and Cooperation in Europe.[36] Furthermore, the ASEAN states and China are also of the view that the ARF should not develop into a forum for promoting human rights and democracy because this will lead to the interference of Western powers in their internal affairs. These differences have raised some doubts as to how soon the ARF will be able to provide practical solutions to regional security problems.

VI. CONCLUSION

The foregoing analysis of economic, security, and political trends in the Asia Pacific region has important implications for developing countries in general and especially for the sense of identity of those countries which have thought of themselves as members of the Third World. The Asia Pacific region locates some of the most successful economies in the developing world, ones whose leaders no longer see themselves as being part of the 'Third World'. Instead, they claim to provide a 'model' for the rest of the developing world as the latter searches for ways to overcome the predicament of underdevelopment, dependence, and insecurity. Yet, although some of the region's countries have industrialized economies which are more akin to the developed world, their lack of political development and their military vulnerablilty mean that they still have as much in common with most Third World states as they do with the developed world of industrialized liberal democracies. Furthermore, as the economic integration of the Asia Pacific region, fostered in good part by Japan, gathers momentum, the resulting North–South links may weaken the sense of common cause that countries of the region have traditionally had with other Third World countries.[37]

Overall, there is an increasing ambivalence within some countries of the Asia Pacific region about their identity as members of the Third World. While their economic development suggests that they have moved closer to the developed world, their avowed distrust of aspects of Western liberal democracy, their limited ability to defend themselves, and their continuing institutional links with other Third World countries through such organizations as the G77, the South Commission, and the Non-Aligned Movement mean that the idea of the 'Third World' still has some resonance within the region. The term remains an important factor in the region's collective identity, and a determinant of the effectiveness of regional multilateral institutions and its relationship with the outside world.

7

Africa After the Cold War

Frozen Out or Frozen in Time?

KEITH SOMERVILLE

The end of the cold war is the 'wind from the East that is shaking the coconut trees'. (President Omar Bongo of Gabon, April 1990)

The end of the cold war and the success of US and international diplomacy over the politics of superpower confrontation has paved the way for 'democracy and political reconciliation in this vast region . . . [African dictators] have lost their freedom of manoeuvre'. (Chester Crocker, former Assistant Secretary of State for African Affairs under President Reagan, *High Noon in Southern Africa: Making Peace in a Rough Neighbourhood*, New York: W. W. Norton, 1992)

These are just two of the many statements of apprehension or hope from African and world statesmen on the effects of the cold war on Africa's domestic, regional, and international politics. Whether they feared, as Bongo appeared to, or hoped, as did Crocker, that the end of the cold war would by its very nature lead to a rapid political metamorphosis in Africa, some African political leaders and most Western politicians concerned with Africa believed that as a result of the fall of the Berlin Wall and the rapid dismantling of the communist states of Eastern Europe in 1989 and 1990, obstacles to democratic reform, national and regional reconciliation, and continental peace had been removed.

These expectations were heightened by the progress towards the independence of Namibia, the hopes for realistic peace talks between the warring parties in Angola, the release of Nelson Mandela and the unbanning of the ANC in South Africa, and an upsurge in demands for greater democracy and popular participation across Africa. Politicians and commentators talked of a New Wind of Change in Africa, though not all of us saw this as bringing with it unmitigated benefits.[1] The optimists, including Chester Crocker and Baroness Chalker, believed that the end of superpower confrontation and intervention in regional disputes, the removal of Soviet support for socialist-oriented governments, the declining need of

Western governments to support dictators such as Mobutu Sese Seko of Zaire and Hastings Kamuzu Banda of Malawi purely because they were anti-communist, and the demise of the socialist model of political and economic development would enable Africa to move towards Western-style democratic systems of government and solve the national and regional conflicts which had been a fact of life in Africa since independence.

The pessimists—some commentators and former politicians,[2] who feared that the mere removal of one set of problems would not be a panacea for all of Africa's ills, and some African presidents who for reasons of their own political fortunes believed and sought to make sure that the changing international political environment did not mean automatic changes in the African political environment—did not see things in such a rosy light. They believed that, despite the high profile periodically accorded to African conflicts (Angola, the Horn of Africa, and South Africa) in the arena of superpower confrontation, US–Soviet competition and rivalry had never had more than a superficial effect on Africa and that the departure of the superpowers from the African scene would not have a decisive effect on the pact or nature of the continent's political development.

Both the optimists and the pessimists were wrong in their ways, but many of them had reached very quick conclusions in the immediate wake of the events of 1989 and 1990 in both Europe and Africa. Now, with the luxury of nearly a decade of hindsight and observation, more measured conclusions can be reached about the effects of the end of the cold war on Africa and of the responses of African states and political leaders.

In taking advantage of hindsight it is necessary to take into account a number of seemingly contradictory sets of influences exerted by the changing global balance of power. As Roland Dannreuther pointed out earlier in this volume, the ending of the cold war contributed to a general global impetus towards consolidating democratic political structures and encouraged among Western policy-makers the view that democracy represents the major objective of contemporary political development; but he also highlights the reality that the end of the cold war 'has not magically dissolved the many structural obstacles' in the way of greater democracy. A related point is that the retention of those structural obstacles, combined with the stripping away of the structural restraints imposed by the bipolar global system created by superpower competition, have released forces or uncovered power struggles or undemocratic forces that the cold war held in check. This duality of effect works not only on the prospects for democracy, however one chooses to define it, but also on security in the developing world, as Amitav Acharya has identified in this chapter. It should not be taken as a foregone conclusion that the ending of one form of global conflict would automatically dampen conflict in the developing world. The changes in the international environment also have the potential for increasing or unleashing conflict where it has been lessened or overlaid by the effects of US–Soviet competition.

What also has to be borne in mind in considering the effects within Africa of the end of the cold war is that there is a two-stage process at work. The end of the cold war removed what Acharya has called a 'structural element in the international framework facing the developing countries', that is, the global competition between the superpowers and the consequent search for allies/proxies in the developing world, but the end of competition meant a decisive change in Western policy towards developing countries, particularly the poorest of the poor in Africa: they could no longer expect to be able to use their strategic position, mineral resources, or political support in regional conflicts as bargaining chips with the superpowers.

Against the background of these structural changes I will examine the effects of the end of the cold war on three specific areas which profoundly effect Africa's current political, economic and social development: (1) the international environment within which African states operate; (2) the effects of structural change in this environment on the evolution of African political systems; and (3) the consequences of the changes for continental and regional security and the prevention or solution of regional conflicts.

I. THE INTERNATIONAL ENVIRONMENT

Political and security issues

Africa has never been at the top table when it comes to decision-making in world affairs. For the first sixty years of this century, Africa's decisions were made for it by its colonial masters—even the two independent states of Ethiopia and Liberia were subject to the tutelage of the great powers. At independence, African states were bequeathed economies dependent on the export of agricultural produce, unprocessed minerals, and other primary commodities to Western Europe and North America, political systems drawn up in London, Paris, or Brussels, and borders which generally bore little or no relation to historical, cultural, or ethnic entities which had existed before colonization.

Not surprisingly, Africa struggled to cope with independence and was accorded a peripheral status in international institutions. African states became members of the United Nations and sought to use the organization as a forum for advancing the cause of continental decolonization, opposition to white minority governments, protesting at interference in the internal affairs of African states, and seeking a more just world economic system. But the fiery rhetoric of African politicians at the UN could achieve little, as little in fact as the annual bouts of rhetoric at the club of African autocrats, the Organization of African Unity. UN member states from Africa could sound off in the General Assembly or from their two seats on the Security Council, but they could not force the UN to act, dominated as it was by the five permanent members of the Security Council and limited in its freedom of action by the need to get agreement between the United States and the Soviet Union (and later China) on Security Council resolutions that would be mandatory and involve either the imposition of sanctions or the taking of action.

The only source of influence for Africa within the UN was in terms of the relative value of its General Assembly and Security Council votes. These could be used as levers to gain concessions, aid, or other benefits from either the Soviet Union or the United States—and both superpowers certainly took very seriously the business of accumulating votes and of monitoring which states voted which way and over which issues. After China's emergence from the throes of the cultural revolution it provided a third source of aid, political and military support which could be bargained for by African states and movements.

But from the very start of the post-independence era, African states experienced persistent problems in finding a coherent continental strategy in dealings with major international actors. One of the driving forces behind the formation of the Organization of African Unity had been the Ghanaian president, Kwame Nkrumah, the most vocal proponent of pan-Africanism as a means of unifying Africa politically. His pan-African vision was not just of concerted African action to achieve common goals, but of eventual federation of all African states. Nkrumah and his supporters saw this as a long-term goal and the OAU as the first step towards it. But this path was too radical for many leaders—notably Emperor Haile Selassie of Ethiopia, President Houphouet-Boigny of Côte d'Ivoire, and President Banda of Malawi. If they saw the OAU as having a major role to play (and Banda certainly doubted this), it was as a continental forum for discussion of common political, social, and economic problems and as a means of aggregating African energies to increase the diplomatic influence of African states. They did not see the OAU as a step on the road towards political integration or the gradual withering away of borders. They argued bitterly with the radicals such as Nkrumah, Modibo Keita of Mali, and Ahmed Sekou Toure of Guinea. The differences undercut the ability of the OAU to act as an international voice for Africa and enabled external powers to use the obvious cleavages to their own advantage.

Pan-Africanism never really got off the ground as a blueprint for Africa's interactions with the international community or a guide to future cooperation, let alone integration, in Africa. The OAU and African heads of state would periodically pay lip-service to the concept of pan-Africanism in their resolutions or in the formation of bodies such as the Pan-African Freedom Movement for Central and Southern Africa (PAFMECSA), established to channel African moral, diplomatic, and, on a limited basis, material support to the liberation movements of central and southern Africa; but pan-Africanism was just the rhetoric not the motivation of state policy. Continental bodies like PAFMECSA were short-lived, but their work and the broad concept of pan-Africanism lived on in the Liberation Committee of the OAU. This sought to advance the cause of liberation, notably in southern Africa, by attempting to channel foreign economic aid and military assistance to the liberation movements and by seeking to persuade the movements themselves to cooperate.

Attempts were made under the auspices of the Liberation Committee to bring the rival nationalist movements ZAPU (Zimbabwe African People's Union) and ZANU (Zimbabwe African National Union) together in Zimbabwe and to mediate, during the war against the Portuguese, between the competing Angolan movements. But the Liberation Committee and the OAU were only ever the sum of their parts, they never developed sufficient autonomy or established policy on the solution of disputes to act independently.

The Liberation Committee and, on a wider scale, the OAU were unable to overcome the differences within the organization in order to follow a consistent and united policy and were as a result unable to make serious progress in mediating between rival liberation movements. When the Angolan civil war started in 1975, Zaire committed troops in support of one faction, Zambia supported another, and Congo a third. This made OAU mediation impossible—whatever was achieved under OAU auspices was immediately destroyed by the actions of individual states. The OAU was consistent in its attempts to prevent inter- or intra-state conflict and to instil a sense of continental unity. This was only successful when the issues involved were such that there were not serious divisions within the OAU itself, such as opposition to apartheid, support for decolonization, and pressure on the international community to assist in both of those campaigns (though even in those cases, Malawi did not follow OAU policy, cooperating openly with the Portuguese in Mozambique, the Smith government in Rhodesia, and being the only African state to open formal diplomatic relations with the white government in South Africa).

Even when it came to the attempts of the OAU and the Liberation Committee to assist in liberation struggles, they were able to play a limited role in material terms. The majority of liberation movements organized their own bilateral relations with external sources of support and finance and OAU supplied only a fraction of their aid. OAU attempts, for example, to get the Soviet Union to assist Robert Mugabe's ZANU movement in the closing stages of the war in Zimbabwe failed totally because of the existing relationship between Moscow and Joshua Nkomo's ZAPU. The OAU also established a Mediation and Conciliation Committee to attempt to resolve disputes between or within member states. But, as will be seen later in this chapter, the mediation committee's work was hampered by regional and political rivalries, by a lack of funds, and poor organization of peacekeeping operations.

Africa had even less power to influence external institutions such as the International Monetary Fund and the World Bank than it did to forge a common policy on regional conflicts. African states could be members and have a vote, but their economic weakness and dependence on Western aid and investment and the dominance of the United States and Western Europe (and latterly Japan) meant that in practice that African states were subject to the decisions of these bodies and not party to the making of the decisions. The whole structural adjustment system, the economic (and in the 1990s political) conditions attached to institutional aid, and the lack of effective consultation with African states made Africa vulnerable in both practice and perception to the actions of institutions which were theoretically international and independent of the superpowers but which were in effect dominated by the developed industrial nations. The Economic Commission for Africa was set up under the UN and in cooperation with the OAU, but it has never functioned as anything more than a think-tank and a weak pressure group. It has not succeeded in coordinating African economic policies, trade policies, or Africa's attempts to bargain with international institutions or major trading partners.

The only leverage African states were able to exert to prise aid and other forms of support from the industrialized nations and the socialist countries involved manœuvring between the superpowers and China. The global nature of superpower competition meant that states could enhance their diplomatic, military, and economic positions by becoming allies (temporary or permanent) of the powers competing for influence in Africa.

In the wake of independence—but with Portugal clinging on to its colonial possessions (Angola, Cape Verde, Guinea-Bissau, and Mozambique), with Rhodesia, South Africa, and Namibia under white colonial rule, and with border or ethnic disputes outstanding in the Horn of Africa, Sudan and, Chad—African states and movements needed political and military support from outside the continent to achieve their aims, and states also sought to maximize their access to investment and economic assistance. To further their political causes and to garner financial aid, states and movements played the superpower game—though in turn their conflicts and development objectives became subject to attempted manipulation by the powers from which they sought help.

If one examines the major areas of conflict or foreign intervention in the first three decades of independence, it is possible to trace the origins of foreign involvement to the need of the African participants in those conflicts for assistance, be it training and weapons for their armed forces, diplomatic support, financial aid, or even military personnel to enable them to achieve their aims. The massive Soviet presence in Somalia in the 1970s resulted from the search by the post-independence government in that country in the 1960s for sources of weapons and military expertise to help it build a modern army and air force capable of territorial defence and of enabling the government to pursue its aim of regaining areas of Ethiopia, Djibouti, and Kenya which Somali nationalists claimed were rightfully part of Somalia.

The same process could be seen at work in Ethiopia, Sudan, Angola, Mozambique, and Zaire. Regimes or movements sought foreign aid to entrench their power, to fight colonial or minority rule, or to fight off domestic opponents. There is no case of the Soviet Union, Cuba, China, or the United States intervening unilaterally. France, when it overthrew the self-styled Emperor Bokassa of the Central African Republic (CAR) on 20 September 1979, did take the initiative to rid itself of an increasingly embarrassing ally, but only with connivance of military and political leaders in the CAR and after gaining a position of influence in the country with the help of the government and the military. France was allowed to station over 1,000 troops in CAR under a defence agreement with Bokassa and French personnel had assisted Bokassa (along with commando units from Zaire) in suppressing anti-Bokassa riots in Bangui in January 1979.[3]

Those states which did intervene forcefully and uninvited in the affairs of African states were in every case other states on the continent—be it Libya in the case of Chad or South Africa in Angola, Mozambique, and Lesotho. Even in those cases the intervening power had already been involved in the conflict in support of or at the request of factions within the countries; though in the case of Mozambique, the rebel Renamo movement was created from a variety of dissidents by the Rhodesian intelligence service and then built into a rebel army by South Africa. The interventions by Libya and South Africa pushed the targets of their intervention into escalating foreign involvement in the conflicts.

The prevalence of foreign intervention in African conflicts and the periodic bouts of open superpower competition in Africa were indicative not only of the interest of foreign powers in intervening in Africa to pursue their own global or regional policies, but particularly of the weakness of African state systems, the potential for domestic and regional conflict built into the political map of Africa by the colonial powers and by the dominance of what could be called 'the winner takes all' approach to political activity in Africa. These factors, characteristic of African political development during the cold war, were the dominant ones in shaping the political systems, regional relations, and Africa's place in world affairs between independence and the end of the cold war.

The disappearance of superpower conflict and competition in Africa and the advent of Western policies based not on containment of the Soviet Union but on the promotion of 'good governance', the dismantling of state-centred economic development, and greater respect for human rights, all engendered expectations among the leaders of democratic movements in Africa and the West that political cultures developed during a century of colonization and three decades of independence could be changed almost overnight. As President Bongo's comments at the start of this chapter make clear, even strongly pro-capitalist autocrats believed that the events in Eastern Europe would have a profound effect on Africa.

And it was undeniably the case that the popular demonstrations and uprisings in Eastern Europe, the fall of Soviet-backed governments, came just as the supporters of greater democracy in Africa were making their voices heard. As people were gathering in the squares of Leipzig, Prague, Sofia, and Bucharest to call for an end to one-party rule, the crowds were also gathering in Cotonou, Abidjan, Lusaka, and Dar es Salaam. But it would be wrong to posit direct causal relationship. Although the Zimbabwean Foreign Minister had obvious political interests in denying in March 1991 that the events in Eastern Europe would give birth to similar events in Africa, he had a point in saying that political systems in Africa had not been modelled on those in Eastern Europe and that the political dynamics in Africa and Eastern Europe were very different. He stressed that the decision of President Gorbachev to allow Eastern Europe greater political freedom and his reversal of the Brezhnev Doctrine, which had led to Soviet intervention in Czechoslovakia in 1968, had been crucial in enabling popular protests to succeed in bringing down governments.[4] There was no dominant continental power in Africa which kept governments in power, it was the military of each African state which had the ability to protect or destroy indigenous African governments; though one could add that African governments had utilized foreign support, even foreign troops, to enhance their power to destroy military or political opponents.

France has military forces stationed in at least six of its former colonies, has military cooperation agreements with eighteen African states, and has intervened militarily in Africa on at least twenty occasions since 1960. But its operations were not usually linked with cold war-related objectives. France was concerned with maintaining its allies in power, extending French political influence (particularly by superseding Belgium as the main European political, military, and economic partner in Zaire, Rwanda, and Burundi) and projecting itself as a global rather than just a European power. This role has been maintained in the post-cold war period with French troops being deployed, not always to good effect, at times of crisis in Djibouti, Rwanda, and, most recently, the Central African Republic. France's ability and willingness to intervene has remained unaffected by the end of the cold war and the disappearance of superpower competition from the African equation. Despite planned changes in France's military structures (notably the phasing out of conscription), the country will retain the capacity and clearly still has a great propensity to intervene in the affairs of former colonies or in those states with which it has defence agreements. It is arguable that willingness to intervene will have been reduced by the failure of the French to maintain Mobutu in power in Zaire (now Democratic Congo).

The forms of intervention which have disappeared or are in the process of disappearing since the end of the cold war are Soviet military support for pro-Marxist African regimes, the Cuban military presence in Angola, and unquestioning US and Western support for strongly anti-communist and pro-Western governments and leaders. In general terms, as Barry Buzan has identified

the effect of the end of the Cold war is generally less dramatic in the Third World than in Europe, but the principle is the same: a much weakened superpower presence leaves more room for local security dynamics to take their own shape, and to operate more on the basis of local resources and local issues . . . In some areas the superpower withdrawal seems to have facilitated reconciliation and moves towards the establishment of security regimes. In others it seems to have unleashed higher levels of conflict and rivalry . . . In Africa . . . the immediate military effect of the ending of the cold war is fairly small, and the longer-term effect is unclear . . . Security problems are more domestic than inter-state, and spillovers from domestic conflicts are more significant than international wars.[5]

The realization that in the post-cold war world regional or purely internal conflicts in Africa remain largely unaffected by the decline in superpower conflict and the increasing demands being made upon the United Nations to deal with conflicts across the globe have combined to give rise to calls for regional organizations (in Africa's case the OAU, ECOWAS, and the

Southern African Development Community) to play a greater conflict prevention, resolution and peacekeeping role.

Former UN Secretary-General, Bhoutros Bhoutros Ghali, called on regional organizations and groups of states to play an ever greater role in maintaining security in their areas and promoting development and inter-state cooperation. While still US Ambassador to the UN, the current US Secretary of State Madeleine Albright called on the OAU and regional organizations in Africa to play a greater role in security and political affairs and to take on responsibility for providing the military personnel for peacekeeping and humanitarian operations in Africa to reduce the load on the underfunded and inadequately staffed UN peacekeeping structures. But Africa is lagging far behind in regional organization. The OAU is now into its fourth decade but it lacks political credibility, the framework for efficient and effective military cooperation, and any viable economic role.

In the first six years of the 1990s, the OAU and groups of member states issued a series of well-meaning but empty declarations on the development of a conflict-resolution and peacekeeping role. This of course has been tried in the past and proved a failure, but the new impetus given by the decline of the superpowers and the encouragement (one could almost say the threat) of complete international withdrawal from African diplomatic and security affairs implied by the Albright position has led the leaders of African states to try again. Fresh enthusiasm has been provided by new heads of state voted in place of the long-standing autocrats. South Africa's transition to non-racial democracy has also provided a gleam of hope that a regional power is emerging which could have the diplomatic clout backed by military power to drive forward a regional security initiative. To this end, OAU summits and meetings of interested nations in Cairo, Kampala, and Yaounde between 1993 and 1996 have discussed the way forward and failed to come up with viable answers. The OAU proved powerless to stop or even lessen the extent of the Rwandan genocide and has proved equally impotent in the continuing Hutu-Tutsi conflict in Burundi. ECOWAS failed initially in Liberia and it is not clear that the peace will last there. The warring sides in Angola have not proved susceptible to the diplomatic overtures of southern African states and the grudging progress in the peace process owed little to African regional organizations. There is no sign that the OAU or its subgroups have the capability to develop anything other than a diplomatic good offices service, particularly as most of the conflicts in Africa are intra- rather than inter-state, even though peacekeeping exercises have been held in Africa involving forces from African states.

Economic weakness and peripheralization

Another major change in the international environment since the end of the cold war, and one that is continuing to have major consequences for Africa's perceived international weakness, is the growing stress in international relations on economic conflict and the regionalization of economic and political power. This globalization of economic issues has served to institutionalize still further a hierarchy that places Africa at the bottom of the heap economically and therefore in terms of political and diplomatic influence.

Africa's lack of effective continental or regional organizations and its economic backwardness are increasing its peripheralization now that it has lost its ability to trade on its value as an asset or an arena in superpower competition. The world is increasingly dominated economically (and to a lesser extent politically) by North America (United States, Canada, and Mexico, who have come together in NAFTA); Japan, ASEAN, and the Pacific Rim; and Western Europe (grouped around the European Union). They may not all be formalized as regional organizations or have overt political roles, but 'they are set apart from other regions because they have the ability to project themselves outwards [and] . . . the economic might of the three regions already gives them great leverage in some spheres of international activity, and they have the potential to play a wider role'.[6]

States falling outside these core regions are increasingly peripheral but seek to increase their international potential by seeking admission to the core groups or association with them—notably the bids by Scandinavian and Eastern/Central European states for membership of the EU, growing Latin American overtures to NAFTA, and the closer economic links being developed by Asian states with the Pacific Rim powers. Africa has no such opportunity of association, let alone membership of the core regional groupings, and its own regional organizations (the OAU, ECOWAS, and the SADC) have yet to develop the economic, let alone political, cooperation common to the other groups. The only manner in which Africa currently projects itself outwards is as a recipient of aid, as the sick man of the international community in need of rapid humanitarian intervention and as an undemocratic and conflictual region which lags far behind in terms of security, stability, and fulfilment of basic human needs and freedoms.

The end of superpower competition, as Acharya notes, has removed just one structural element of Africa's international environment. It has not significantly changed the economic environment in which Africa has to operate (except to remove a failed model of economic development and a relatively minor source of economic aid) and has not directly affected the basic political, economic or social forces at work in Africa. For Africa, the end of the cold war has brought no peace dividend. The post-cold war world is a less hospitable place for Africa than the cold war world, for now Africa has no clear international role and no influence. It is more likely to be seen as a pariah or a pauper than as a junior partner or even a pawn in world politics.

Porous politically and in security terms, Africa has been even more susceptible to the economic power of the outside world. It is no exaggeration to say that many of the major decisions about the management of African economies are taken not in Nairobi, Lagos, Abidjan, or Kinshasa but in Washington, Paris, London, and, increasingly, Tokyo. Whether it is World Bank and IMF policies and initiatives or the investment decisions of major multinational corporations, they can have a decisive impact on the health and direction of African economies but it is beyond the power of most African states to influence them. The technological revolution in communications, financial movements, and control of commodity markets has led to a breaking down of national barriers across the globe. Strong, economically organized, and politically unified states are well adapted to coping with such changes, economically weak, technologically deficient, and politically unstable states are not. Africa is further disadvantaged in the global market-place by every advance in the reach of the Internet and the scope of electronic commerce.

Africa's global economic weakness is of course compounded by the consistent failure of African governments (with honourable exceptions such as Botswana) to establish a reputation for probity, transparency, and good governance. The failure of the 1990s wave of democratization truly to change the course of African political development has not only meant that the majority of Africans are still ruled arbitrarily in most states, but also that there has not been the hoped-for accountability around management of the economies. The new rulers of the 1990s (Soglo, Chiluba, Muluzi, etc.) all inherited the government structures, well-entrenched networks of nepotism and corruption, unfair terms of trade, and huge debt burdens of their predecessors. Some of these factors were and still are beyond their powers of influence, others—the lack of government control and accountability and the fight against corruption—are within their competence but have not been tackled. So Africa, whether under old or new leaders, retains the international image of an economic pariah, a sinkhole for aid, and a basket case of bribery and bad debts.

II. AFRICAN POLITICAL EVOLUTION SINCE
THE COLD WAR

In one period of eighteen months between the beginning of 1990 and mid-1992 eleven African heads of state fell from power, four of them voted out of office in newly established pluralist elections (in Benin, Cape Verde, São Tomé, and Zambia). In Côte d'Ivoire, the doyen of African autocrats, Felix Houphouet-Boigny, had bowed to domestic and French pressure, established a multiparty political system, and been forced to run against a vociferously critical opponent in a truly competitive presidential election. Along the West African coast in Nigeria, a military-led return to civilian politics was grinding slowly towards local and then national elections. Across the breadth of Africa, in Tanzania, the ruling Chama Chap Mapinduzi (CCM) had conceded that one-party rule was not working and that a gradual move towards the legalization of other parties was inevitable. The founder of the Tanzanian one-party experiment, Julius Nyerere, who had stepped down voluntarily as president in 1985 and retired totally from active politics in 1990, came out in 1991 and admitted that single-party rule was stifling participation, and leading to political and economic stagnation and to corruption and ineffective government.

These developments had at a stroke changed the whole direction of political evolution in Africa. The direction of that evolution had, since independence, been away from a plurality of parties and towards single-party (often single-leader) rule or government by unelected and dictatorial military regimes. In the closing two years of the 1980s and the opening years of the 1990s, the drift towards increasing autocracy was halted abruptly. In 1988 and 1989, there were serious riots by students and civil servants in Benin, student protests in Côte d'Ivoire, demonstrations by disgruntled miners and trade unionists in Zambia's Copperbelt, signs of growing popular discontent in Mali and Niger, and increasingly outspoken criticism of authoritarian rule in Kenya, Tanzania, Rwanda, Zaire, Madagascar, and Ghana.

The speed of the changes and the timing—as the barriers were coming down in Eastern Europe—convinced many analysts that this was a new beginning, some called it a Second Independence, and that the total demise of authoritarian politics was on the way.[7] They were bolstered in their opinion by the referendum in Ghana on 28 April 1992, which endorsed the calls for a return to multiparty politics; by Congo's adoption of a multiparty system; and by the development in a range of West and Central African countries (including Mali, Niger, and Zaire) of the

National Conference as a means of negotiating their way towards participatory politics.

The big question being asked was what had caused this massive political upheaval. Was it the result of the end of the cold war and the destruction of one-party regimes in Eastern Europe, was it the fruit of Western policy changes which emphasized the pursuit of democracy and accountability in Africa rather than regime stability, or was it simply the inevitable outcome of the disintegration of unpopular and weak governments? The most popular answer was that the influence of the cold war had been paramount as it had deprived African regimes of the authoritarian, statist model provided by the pre-Gorbachev Soviet Union and by the socialist states of Eastern Europe. Furthermore, Marxist-oriented states (such as Angola, Benin, Congo, Ethiopia, and Mozambique) had lost the military, political, and economic support of their socialist patrons. Finally, the end of superpower confrontation had enabled Western governments to review their support for authoritarian regimes whose sole appeal to the West was that they were anti-communist and so constituted bulwarks against Soviet influence.

The problem with emphasizing the cold war factor was that the pressures for change had in many cases predated the uprisings in Eastern Europe and, that in the case of Angola Soviet military aid had increased dramatically in 1989 and 1990 just at the time that diplomatically Gorbachev was stressing peaceful solutions to regional conflicts. Nor had the end of superpower conflict led to declining French military, political, or economic involvement in Africa nor, despite protestations that Paris supported the restoration of democratic politics in Africa, any withdrawal of French support for its traditional allies. Yet francophone Africa was leading the way in the move away from military or single-party rule.

Instead of there being one basic cause, the nature and erratic course of political evolution in Africa in the 1990s (despite the hopes generated by the early successes for multiparty movements) suggested a number of influences which varied in their efficacy and consequences in different regions. Carol Lancaster has identified a number of factors,[8] which are elaborated on here.

1. 'The most important is the failure of African governments to fulfil their end of an implicit social pact with their people: African autocrats promised economic progress in exchange for restrictions on the political rights of their citizens . . . it was evident that economic progress in much of Africa had stalled or had been replaced by economic decline.' Africans had been told by their leaders that democracy was a luxury the continent couldn't afford; —it became clear that they could not afford dictatorship or authoritarian rule either. Falling living standards had sparked off

student demonstrations in Côte d'Ivoire, protests and rioting by civil servants and teachers in Benin, and unrest in Zambia's Copperbelt.

2. Economic reforms necessitated by economic decline or imposed by the World Bank, IMF, or donor nations had led to a decline in the power of the state and required greater diffusion of power, initially economic power, to private individuals. In Tanzania, for example, the break up of parastatals, the growth of privatization, and the need to encourage private initiative in the economic sector deprived the state of some of its hold over the business sector and urban élite and gave urban groups the economic power base to mount a political challenge to the government.

3. The democratic reforms and uprisings in Eastern Europe and the Soviet Union, 'widely reported even in the restricted African media, had a visible impact on the African political élite, as well as amongst the general population'. Although not limited to Marxist-oriented regimes, the demise of communism in the USSR and Eastern Europe could not but shake what remaining faith Marxist leaders in Africa had in the applicability of Marxist formulas to African political and economic development.

4. 'Perhaps the most important factor stimulating demands for political reform in African countries was the "diffusion effect" of reforms in other African countries. This is nowhere more evident than in francophone Africa . . .'—though proponents of multipartyism in Tanzania and defenders of the plural system in Zimbabwe have stressed the impact on their thinking of the re-emergence of multiparty politics in Zambia in December 1991.[9] Later, when the demands for reform pushed the intransigent President Banda into holding a referendum on the political system in Malawi in 1993, it was clear that the example of neighbouring Zambia and the willingness of the newly elected government in Zambia to assist Malawian political movements in their campaign for change had been crucial in the pace of developments. The opening up of South Africa's political system, the release of Nelson Mandela, and the unbanning of the ANC, SACP, and PAC also had a profound influence elsewhere in Africa.

5. The growth in the number of educated but unemployed urban dwellers throughout Africa, particularly among the young, created an articulate but alienated pool of potential supporters of reform. As Lancaster points out, in Zimbabwe only 10 per cent of those graduating from school or university each year find jobs. This is a common problem across Africa, even in relatively prosperous and open societies such as Botswana. I would add that in addition to the problem unemployment and poor living standards, the youth of Africa are more aware of Western freedoms, lifestyles, and wealth than their forefathers and are less prepared to listen to the hollow promises and justifications of a failed generation of political leaders. Prior to his electoral defeat, President Kaunda of

Zambia told me in March 1991 that: 'I realised that out of our population of nearly 8m, about 7m had not known the struggle for independence, the reasons why we opted for one party . . .When I told my National Council that we needed change, I was thinking of these 7m young Zambians who want something new.'[10]

6. 'Finally, the role of foreign governments and international institutions must be considered in the political changes taking place in Africa. Although it is incorrect to attribute these changes to the manipulations of external actors, those external forces have often played roles supportive of change.' And such support has included freezing aid to countries like Kenya and Malawi pending progress towards political freedom and respect for basic human rights. Such policies were hardly evident before the end of superpower competition, but since 1990 have been a very prominent part of Western political and economic policy in Africa.

A combination of these factors has been at work in Africa since the early 1990s and the exact mix has differed from country to country. But what is clear is that the impetus for political change came from within Africa, most frequently arising out of widespread popular anger over declining living standards and growing government repression, mismanagement, and corruption. The manifestations of this anger led either to government concessions or attempts at suppression. The successes of the uprisings in Eastern Europe then provided examples of what could be achieved through sustained and courageous protest, as well as a warning to authoritarian governments that they were vulnerable. This dual effect was evident in Tanzania, where multiparty supporters told me that their resolve had been bolstered by events in Eastern Europe and government ministers said that they had been shaken by the fall of their former allies in Europe, notably the ousting and execution of President Ceauşescu of Romania, which took place during a visit by a high-ranking Tanzanian government delegation. It has to be said, though, that in one area at least, the Horn of Africa, the withdrawal of the Soviet Union and the collapse of the Soviet model very rapidly pulled the rug from under the feet of a pro-Soviet government. Haile Menistu Mariam's wannabe Marxist regime in Ethiopia was militarily dependent on Soviet aid not just in the fight to keep hold of the northern territory of Eritrea but to hold on to power, too. Years of repression, economic mismanagement, and unresourced and misjudged socialist agricultural experiments had engendered such intense opposition that a plethora of armed opposition groups had come into being. They ranged from radically Marxist but ethnically based movements such as the Tigre People's Liberation Front (TPLF, led by the current Ethiopian president, Meles Senawi) to the Ethiopian People's Revolutionary Party (EPRP, based more on political opposition to

Mengistu than ethnic or regional factors) and the purely ethnic Oromo Liberation Front. Fighting a variety of fronts on a number of fronts, the regime was dependent on massive and regular supplies of Soviet arms and military advisers, economic assistance, and political support. When these were withdrawn, Mengistu was rapidly defeated, militarily and politically.

Western pressure also played its role in effecting change following the end of the cold war. As with the effects of the changes in Eastern Europe, the application by Western governments and donor agencies of pressure through conditionality and the withholding of economic assistance did not in itself generate demands for political reform. Western pressure encouraged those campaigning for change and, at times, put limits on the repressive responses of authoritarian governments. The change in the balance of power internationally meant that Africa was no longer a weight to be put on one side of the scales. Western policies shifted from supporting anti-Soviet or pro-capitalist allies to pressing for democratic reform and greater accountability.

In the cases of Kenya and Malawi, the cutting of Western aid did put pressure on Presidents Moi and Banda to adopt a more conciliatory approach, though it did not lead to any change of heart by those leaders. They instituted constitutional changes that allowed the formation of opposition parties but fought to maintain their own unchallenged power. Although the actual conduct of the Kenyan elections was viewed as free and fair by foreign observers, the preparations for the elections and the registration of candidates had been far from fair and it was clear that the government had used every instrument at its disposal to harass opposition parties, enabling Moi to emerge the victor. Although he now has to contend with opposition MPs in parliament, he has been able to use his presidential powers and the coercive machinery of the one-party era to ensure that multiparty politics have not meant a strong and functioning opposition that is able to act as a check on the untrammelled power of the KANU government. Yet, because Moi met Western conditions regarding the freedom to organize opposition parties and because he held elections, economic relations have been restored. In 1997, Moi repeated his policy of holding multiparty elections but using state power to hamstring the opposition.

In Malawi, Banda tried to follow a similar course, but a better organized opposition campaign and a greater level of popular disenchantment with thirty years of Banda's rule meant that he fell from power and a more participatory political system has emerged, though the new government of President Bakili Muluzi has had no greater success than its predecessor or its neighbours in dealing with its basic debt and trade problems. Malawi had one major advantage over Kenya, and that was that although the country had three distinct regions with three parties each with strong support within one particular region, there was no distinctly ethnic or regional edge to the campaigning. In Kenya, the Kikuyu had been politically dominant under Moi's predecessor Jomo Kenyatta, with the Luo (who supported the veteran politician Oginga Odinga) as the second most powerful group. Moi was from a smaller ethnic group, the Kelenjin, and was able to forge an alliance of non-Kikuyu, non-Luo groups (particularly those from the Rift Valley who were ethnically linked to the Kalenjin and from among the Masai) and to play on fears of renewed Kikuyu dominance. This ethnically based approach led to bloody communal violence in the Rift Valley, which has continued since the elections and threatens to create permanent tensions and blood feuds.

The Kenyan example of the utilization of ethnic or regional differences by politicians to serve narrow political interests has been repeated elsewhere in Africa in the last five years. The most appalling example and the one which has done the most to destroy the illusion that Africa as a whole was moving towards a more peaceful and harmonious political future has been Rwanda. This tragic state is the clearest example of how the basic political divisions within African states have been totally unaffected by the intervention of the superpowers in Africa and by the end of the cold war.

Even before its independence in 1962, Rwanda's Hutu and Tutsi were at war with each other. Their conflict was chiefly a product of the distortion by colonial rule of the political, social, and economic hierarchy which had previously existed in the region which now constitutes Rwanda and Burundi. The Tutsi monarchy had ruled the region through control of cattle, land, and military power, with the Hutu playing a subordinate role. The Germans and then the Belgians ruled through the Tutsi monarchy, which in turn used the colonial repression of anti-colonial revolts to increase its power. It was only as the era of decolonization began, after the Second World War, that the Belgians began to dilute Tutsi power just as Hutu nationalists began to press for independence and an end to Tutsi privilege. Hostility between these movements and the Tutsi hierarchy led to widespread violence in 1959. In 1961, the Belgians cooperated with the Hutu élite to destroy the Mwami's power and to replace Tutsi chiefs with Hutus. Nationwide violence ensued in which at least 10,000 Tutsi were killed and 130,000 fled into exile in neighbouring countries (Uganda, Tanzania, Burundi, and Zaire). Independence came in July 1962 with a Hutu élite in power and the Tutsis subjugated.[11]

The independence period saw the election of a solely Hutu government and the start of a guerrilla war by Tutsi insurgents. A Hutu backlash followed, with tens of thousands of Tutsis killed or driven into exile. Splits also developed between southern and northern Hutu communities in

Rwanda. When Tutsi-Hutu violence in neighbouring Burundi in 1972–3 prompted communal violence in Rwanda, the army stepped in to over-throw the government and place the northern Hutu Javenal Habyarimana (the army chief of staff) in power. His authoritarian military government restored order and maintained tight political and security control for the next seventeen years. Tutsis, with the exception of a few token appointees, were excluded from positions of political and economic power.

The latest bout of genocidal violence emerged from the political devel-opments in Rwanda and neighbouring Uganda at the end of the 1980s and the beginning of the 1990s. Uganda was host to tens of thousands of (chiefly Tutsi) Rwandan refugees. Many of them joined Yoweri Museveni's National Resistance Army, which overthrew President Milton Obote and the short-lived military government which succeeded him. Rwandans rose to senior positions in the army and subsequently in Museveni's govern-ment, though they did not give up the hope of returning to Rwanda. Many belonged to a Tutsi-led movement, the Rwandan Patriotic Front (RPF). By 1990 RPF leaders were intent on launching an invasion of Rwanda.

The RPF's plans coincided with growing pressure from the Hutu élite in Rwanda for political reform. Encouraged by events elsewhere in Africa, aware of the growth of the RPF among the exile community, and deter-mined to spread the benefits of political and economic power beyond the small élite grouped around Habyarimana, Hutu political groups suc-ceeded in getting the president to change the constitution, allowing for the formation of opposition parties and competitive elections. This process was getting under way when the RPF invaded northern Rwanda in September 1990. Most Hutus, even those opposed to the president, saw the RPF as a Tutsi movement. The civil war which ensued both galvanized Hutu militants and hurried the process of political reform, as Habyarimana sought both domestic and international support to with-stand the RPF offensive.[12]

The moves towards multiparty politics—hardly taken with the greatest enthusiasm or with a belief in the necessity of more democratic struc-tures—muddied the Rwandan political waters by injecting aspects of Hutu factionalism and party-political competition into what could have been seen simplistically as a Tutsi versus Hutu conflict with minor splits among the Hutu. But the situation also goaded extreme Hutu supremacists into action. The latter group had support within the military, police, civil ser-vice, and the ruling MRND party led by Habyarimana. When peace talks started between the government and the RPF, the militants made little secret of the fact that they had no intention of allowing Habyarimana to come to an agreement with the RPF which would bring Tutsis, moderate Hutus, or the RPF into a power-sharing government. They tried to block

progress at the peace talks hosted by Tanzania in Arusha and were vehemently opposed when Habyarimana finally agreed to sign the Arusha
accord of August 1993, which provided for a ceasefire, a token RPF military presence in Kigali, and the formation of a power-sharing government
to prepare for democratic elections. Habyarimana was unhappy with the
agreement, but he could see no option as the Rwandan army had been
unable to defeat the RPF.

Habyarimana's own wariness, plus the opposition of the militant Hutus
(who formed the Coalition for the Defence of the Republic, CDR),
delayed the implementation of Arusha and he came under pressure from
Tanzania and other regional states to make more progress. It was when he
and the president of Burundi were returning from Tanzania, following
Habyarimana's agreement to speed things up, that his plane was shot
down and both leaders were killed. Although responsibility for the killing
has not been established, it is believed that Hutu extremists in the army or
even the presidential guard were responsible. His death gave them a pretext for destroying the accord and launching an all-out war against the
RPF, Tutsis, and moderate Hutus. The path of the RPF-led government
since 1994 has been far from smooth, despite having a major role in assisting Laurent Kabila to overthrow Mobutu in a civil war in Zaire which
grew directly out of the overflow from the Rwanda conflict. International
efforts to halt the conflict in Zaire failed because of clear splits between
Washington and Paris over policy and a general unwillingness of the international community to commit troops or resources.

The lesson of Rwanda is not that ethnic conflict is the principal obstacle to peace and democracy in Africa but that political forces desperate to
retain power or deny a share of power to others will utilize every means
possible to achieve their aims. Ethnic tensions exist—they are a fact of life
in colonially created states—but do not automatically lead to political let
alone violent conflict. Tanzania has a mass of differing ethnic and linguistic groups but has not suffered from ethnic conflict or violence, even when
hundreds of thousands of Hutu and Tutsi refugees fled there from
Burundi and Rwanda in the 1960s and 1970s.

If the tragedy of Rwanda indicates one outcome of insincere or incompetent attempts at political reform, countries such as Kenya, Côte
d'Ivoire, and Zambia indicate that the existence of a multiplicity of parties
and the holding of elections does not in itself indicate real progress
towards democracy. The former two states are still ruled by the parties
which held power under the single-party systems. Although during the
elections they had to compete for power, they did so using the full state
machinery, including the media and the security forces, to support the
party campaigns, to deny media coverage to the opposition, and to place

every conceivable obstacle in the way of their opponents' campaigns. Since the elections, they have largely acted as though they were still running a one-party system. And even in Zambia, where Frederick Chiluba's Movement for Multiparty Democracy (MMD) defeated Kaunda and his UNIP party in a free election, the new constitution and a freely elected parliament and government have hardly led to a more tolerant political system. The opposition parties have accused the government of harassment, a brief state of emergency was imposed, and the government has been seen as corrupt and authoritarian. In 1997 and 1998, Chiluba's government detained opposition leaders and put Kaunda under house arrest after a failed farcical *coup* attempt by junior army officers.

But the main disappointment for those who looked to multiparty politics as the panacea for Africa's ills or as at least the starting-point on the road to political and economic recovery has been that elections or a multiplicity of parties do not in themselves ensure democracy (a point made in Roland Dannreuther's chapter) and certainly do not ensure economic rehabilitation. For democracy to develop, a culture of political tolerance, a free press, independent national institutions (the judiciary, the legal profession, churches, trades unions, etc.), a politically neutral civil service, and armed forces loyal to the constitution and the government and institutions, but not loyal to a party or particular leaders, are all required. With the exception of Botswana, Senegal, and arguably Zimbabwe and South Africa, the states in Africa which have moved towards more democratic systems have lacked these vital ingredients. Furthermore, political activity throughout Africa has remained predominantly urban-based, rendering the majority of the population which lives in the rural areas politically peripheral. These problems were inherited from colonialism, which inhibited rather than encouraged the development of independent institutions, and have been made worse by decades of authoritarian rule.[13]

If the basic elements of what could be called 'civil society' are lacking and will continue to inhibit the development of democracy and its likely lifespan in African states, just as important is economic rehabilitation and improved welfare provisions and living standards. African governments have not delivered the promised benefits of independence in the economic sphere and continue to mismanage their economies and resources. This failure to deliver was a major factor in generating impetus for political change. But is there any reason to believe that freely elected governments will have more success and be able to achieve rates of economic growth and improvements in living standards that will provide the basis for political stability?

Economic decline and the failure of political reform

Since its seminal report in 1989, *Sub-Saharan Africa: From Crisis to Sustainable Growth*, the World Bank has argued that 'political legitimacy and consensus are a precondition for sustainable development . . . underlying the litany of Africa's problems is a crisis of governance'.[14] A similar view was adopted by the IMF and by Western donor nations, notably Britain and the United States, plus the European Union in its role as an institutional donor. African proponents of greater democracy were equivocal in their view of Western intervention in the internal affairs of African states, but they, too, viewed accountability as necessary for an end to corruption and incompetence in the management of African economies or took the view that there was a clear correlation between the lack of democracy and deterioration of African economies.[15]

Those who campaigned for change in the early 1990s certainly believed that if economies were no longer treated as the personal fiefdoms of presidents or as the treasuries of ruling parties then reconstruction and reform would be easier to achieve.[16] Olusegun Obasanjo, the former Nigerian head of state, while not directly calling for Western economic sanctions against dictatorial governments, certainly held the view that Western economic pressure could assist pro-democracy movements and, in the longer term, that this would lead to more balanced and competent economic management.

But in the wake of the restoration of multiparty rule across Africa, there has been little evidence that the hopes of the democracy activists and the beliefs of the World Bank have been converted into reality in the short term. President Chiluba's government in Zambia experienced forty industrial strikes in the first six months of rule, indicating that trade unions and workers were no more prepared to accept austerity policies from an elected government than they had been to accept them under a single-party system. This was one of the factors that pushed Chiluba into a more autocratic style of rule. He used a state of emergency to keep the lid on opposition outside his own party and became increasingly unaccountable within the MMD, leading to several damaging resignations from the government and defections from his party. Now more than five years after his overwhelming election victory, Zambia's economy is in as much of a mess as it ever was under Kaunda, and Chiluba has lost much of his democratic credibility at home and abroad. His attempts to privatize the loss-making copper mines have not borne fruit and his management of the economy has failed to convince the population that he will deliver better living standards in the future.

It is harsh to judge the economic performance of the new governments after relatively short periods in office. What must also be taken into account is the catastrophic economic inheritance they received from their predecessors. An analysis of the indebtedness of African states at the end of 1993 indicated that twenty states had debts in excess of their total GNP (these included Côte d'Ivoire, the darling of Western governments and bankers for its free-enterprise economic policies and adherence to World Bank and IMP-approved policies). A further twenty have debts equal to between 50 and 100 per cent of GNP. The most indebted nations include the more prosperous economies (to which lenders are keen to advance loans) and the poorest countries which are totally unable to survive without incurring massive debts.[17] The level of indebtedness imposes a heavy debt-service burden on the annual budgets, depriving countries of development capital and leading to austerity programmes which end up reducing economic growth (at a time when most African countries have population growth rates exceeding their GNP growth and a steadily rising rate of youth unemployment).

While Western governments have supported democratic change in Africa by putting political as well as economic conditions on aid, they have done nothing to assist newly elected governments by writing off debts or improving the terms of trade which continue to punish African economies. In this there has also been a definite post-cold war effect: aid has flowed to former communist countries and their debts have been reduced massively to assist their transitions to democracy. Poland had 50 per cent of its total debt written off by the West, 'in contrast to its unwillingness to do anything comparable for Africa'.[18] Furthermore, Africa's peripheral status has put it in an ever more precarious position regarding future disbursements of aid and, especially, when it comes to the possibility of attracting much-needed private investment. Even South Africa has had a disappointing response to its attempts to attract foreign investment.

Far from benefiting from political reform or from Western-inspired structural adjustment programmes, African states have experienced steady decline. UN figures show that Africa's share of global GNP fell from 1.9 per cent in 1960 to 1.2 per cent in 1989, with its share of global trade down from 3.8 to 1.0 per cent. Foreign investments fell by over 38 per cent in the same period. The consequences of economic as well as political peripheralization are that even if democratically elected governments set out with good intentions to reform economic management, divest the state of the economic burdens of loss-making parastatals, and liberalize trade and financial systems, the domestic environment within which they have to operate is one which is inimical to economic progress. Africa remains and will continue to remain for the foreseeable future in debt, lacking in foreign investment, and of little economic consequence to the rest of the world. Africa has no voice in the decision-making of the major international financial institutions and was powerless in the long-running GATT negotiations under the Uruquay round. Its export base remains dependent on agricultural produce or unprocessed/semi-processed minerals. Despite years of structural adjustment there has been little economic diversification.

There is no real hope for African governments of being more able than their predecessors to meet the economic needs of their populations. They may become more efficient and accountable but that will do nothing to lift the overall debt burden. In addition, harsh austerity programmes, rigorous IMF-inspired structural adjustment programmes, and unpopular but necessary policies will be harder for accountable governments to impose than their authoritarian predecessors. Under a participatory system with regular elections, governments have to meet popular demands and needs or face electoral defeat. Africa's economic weakness and its poor chances of recovery in the short, medium, or long term will continue to act as a destabilizing influence politically and inhibit the prospects of a democratic culture developing. The failure to deliver economically will create the conditions for industrial, social, and political unrest and be a breeding ground for military intervention (as we have seen recently in Gambia) or a return to authoritarianism as is happening in Zambia. The hoped-for development of participatory politics and transparent economic management has not developed from the democracy movements. Many incumbent presidents remain impregnable and unaccountable, while newly elected leaders have been swamped by economic crises or have adopted tried-and-tested methods of authoritarian rule. There is no certainty that democracy as understood in Western Europe and North America will be at the end of the political road along which many African states are struggling. Some countries may be able to stay on the road and make gradual progress towards a more durable and stable democratic form of government, with continued help from donors and international institutions, 'but it is hard to avoid the conclusion that many other African states, in the absence of constant munificent benefactors (and when the global fervour with 'democracy' possibly goes out of vogue?) will be seen as a bad bet and let loose to drift their own way, backsliding into political strife, social chaos, single-party and military rule'.[19]

III. SECURITY AND CONFLICT

One of the great hopes which arose during the period of *glasnost* and superpower cooperation, and which was then magnified at the end of the cold war, was the expectation that the end of Soviet–US confrontation would lead to a more secure world and to the resolution of regional conflicts. Chester Crocker firmly believed that conflicts in Africa, notably the civil war in Angola, would have their best chance of solution once the superpowers ended their involvement as sponsors of arms suppliers to those engaged in these conflicts and replaced it with joint initiatives to find peaceful solutions—stating in his account of diplomacy in southern Africa that it was only with the end of superpower confrontation and the withdrawal of the Cubans that 'Angolans could now begin to shape their own destiny after centuries of foreign domination, living with foreign legacies and foreign conflicts'.[20]

The view that the end of superpower confrontation would lead to a new and more secure era for Africa was also held by some commentators in the region. The South African analyst Simon Baynham has argued that there were a number of factors involved in the signing of the December 1988 New York Peace Accords on Angola and Namibia and later the Angolan peace agreement, but 'the first and most critical of these was the growing convergence of interests between Washington and Moscow during the Gorbachev era of new thinking'.[21] There was a feeling, too, among African diplomats and politicians that they were emerging from 'an era in which Africa saw herself dragged into the divisive and destructive politics of the cold war between contending ideologies'.[22] Those were the words of the OAU's special representative in South Africa, Joseph Legwaila, in assessing influences in Africa's security agenda.

But I would argue against the view that 'the divisive and destructive politics of the cold war' had been dragged into many of Africa's most intractable conflicts and areas of national, regional, or ethnic tension. If you examine the major armed conflicts in Africa during the first three decades of the independence period, they all sprang from indigenous causes rather than being generated by superpower or other external involvement.[23] Furthermore, as MacFarlane and Dannreuther have argued earlier in this volume, the cold war may in some instances have enhanced stability or overlaid deeper indigenous conflicts and thus given the impression that the withdrawal of the superpower factor would radically reduce the potential for conflict, when in fact the end of the structural divide in global politics actually served to unleash or reveal deep-seated tensions within or (and this is not generally the case in Africa) between nations.

Chester Crocker, cited above on the effects of the foreign withdrawal on the ability of Angolans to shape their own destiny, was particularly concerned, as US Assistant Secretary of State for African Affairs, with Angola and Southern Africa. The civil war in Angola and the regional conflict in southern Africa had a level of superpower involvement that exceeded anything else seen on the continent (with the possible exception of the Horn of Africa between 1976 and 1978). But the regional and national conflicts did not have their origins in superpower conflict, were not shaped decisively by that conflict, and their post-cold war evolution has indicated the predominance of national and regional factors when it comes to security and political developments. I will use the examples of Angola and southern Africa as a whole to expound the view that the end of the cold war and superpower intervention have had remarkably little effect on security and that in the future regional initiatives or *ad hoc* bilateral/multilateral initiatives will be more important for the region than international ones, though an international commitment to support regional security programmes or structures will assist in providing the foundations for a more peaceful and stable region.

The Angolan conflict became a major international crisis in 1975/6 when Zairean, South African, and Cuban military intervention and US/Soviet sponsorship of rival movements internationalized what had been a national liberation war in which the liberation movements were as keen to fight each other as they were to fight the Portuguese. Zaire supported the northern Angolan, Bakongo-based FNLA movement led by Holden Roberto—which also received South African assistance, US funding and military equipment, and Chinese weapons and military advisers. The Luanda-based, multi-ethnic (though chiefly Mbundu) MPLA was backed by the Soviet Union (which supplied arms and financial aid), Cuba (which supplied troops), East Germany, Bulgaria, and Yugoslavia (which supplied smaller quantities of arms plus military and intelligence training). UNITA, led by the flamboyant Jonas Savimbi, was based on the Ovimbundu people of central and southern Angola and received Chinese and South African support, including the commitment of South African ground forces, and was loosely allied with the FNLA against the MPLA.

The rivalry between the movements derived from their different regional and ethnic power bases, their divergent political and religious cultures, and their varying experiences of Portuguese colonialism.[24] The civil war which followed the demise of Portuguese colonial rule followed inevitably from the hostility of the movements. The scale and longevity of the war was a result of regional and extra-African forces providing the military and financial backing for the combatants, but they would have fought each other regardless of the availability of huge quantities of arms. The conclusion of the December 1988 peace accord was a result of the political and military stalemate resulting from the siege of Cuito Cuanavale and from the South African realization that it was losing military dominance in southern Angola. US–Soviet *rapprochement* and co-operation over Angola and Namibia assisted a process of disengagement and negotiation but did not give rise to the basic conditions which led the South Africans and Angolans to opt for a political solution. And no amount of superpower pressure or bribery convinced the MPLA and UNITA of the need for real reconciliation or political accommodation. It took two and a half years of continued war in southern Angola for the MPLA and UNITA to realize that they had reached military stalemate. Even then, the US/Soviet/Portuguese brokered talks failed, ultimately, to achieve a lasting and stable peace deal. There is little common ground between the MPLA and UNITA and so the war resumed when UNITA could not accept electoral defeat and when the MPLA used the outbreak of fighting as a pretext to attempt to destroy the UNITA leadership in Luanda. Despite the November 1994 ceasefire, Angola remains the most serious threat to security in southern Africa and the strongest example of the failure of the new world order to provide the basis for regional security. By March 1998, the peace process had still not been completed, not all UNITA forces had been demobilized, and there still remained the possibility of the resumption of conflict.

Insecurity in Africa was not a product of superpower conflict, rather it was the case that insecurity and conflict in Africa opened the door for superpower involvement. In the post-cold war order, the disappearance of superpower conflict, the potential military, political, and economic dominance of the United States, and the new interventionist role of the United Nations, have had remarkably little effect on Africa's basic security dilemma. On the contrary, one could argue that in some ways the post-cold war environment has helped to expose the already fragile legitimacy of many African states. Across the continent the challenges from below have become increasingly acute. As Barry Buzan correctly argues, 'many of the region's states are weak and internally unstable. Security problems are more domestic than inter-state, and spillovers from domestic conflicts are more significant than international wars'.[25] Even in southern Africa, where the democratization process in South Africa, the independence of Namibia, the withdrawal of foreign forces (apart from mercenaries) from Angola, and the Mozambican peace process have all improved the regional security outlook, the improvements have been a result more of regional and national factors rather than the overall international environment, though the end of the cold war did remove one layer of conflict and simplified conflicts such as those in Angola and Mozambique by removing the ideological and geopolitical factors from the equation. One other positive effect of the end of the cold war for southern Africa was the way that the momentous global changes and the effective demise of communism assisted in the process of changing white South African attitudes and helping them adapt to regional and national changes.

Africa in the 1990s is peripheral to international security and cannot expect its problems to be of vital or lasting concern outside the continent. The soundbite politics of contemporary North America brought about the US intervention in Somalia (albeit under the auspices of a UN humanitarian mission). The scenes of human misery nightly on US TV screens, combined with George Bush's desire to be seen to be contributing to world peace as he was preparing to leave office, led to an over-rapid and ill-planned intervention which went far beyond the UN mandate of facilitating aid deliveries and became a peacemaking operation and a war against one faction in Mogadishu. There was no clear political objective and no cooperation with Somali factions, political leaders, or traditional centres of authority. The operation brought in aid but failed to achieve lasting security, political stability, or reconciliation.[26] The US forces withdrew in some disarray and factional conflict continues, though now no longer in the glare of international media attention—which, in African terms, has shifted briefly to Rwanda. And in neither Somalia nor Rwanda was there the possibility, as arguably there is in West Africa (see below) and southern Africa, for a regionally powerful or influential state to play a leading or even a supporting role to back up UN and US efforts. In the past, Kenya has been seen as a possible focus for regional political or security cooperation in East Africa and the Horn. However, Somali–Kenyan tensions over Somali claims to parts of northern Kenya inhabited by Somali speakers, a persistent problem of Somali banditry in Kenya, and the West's disenchantment with Kenya over the Moi government's's resistance to viable political reform, all counted Kenya out in this case and there seems no prospect of regional cooperation guided or powered by one particular regional hegemon or influential state.

There is no prospect of the UN or international community becoming seriously involved in reconciliation attempts in Africa, other than to provide inadequate forces with weak mandates to supervise the disengagement of combatants, observe ceasefires and disarmament programmes, or establish temporary safe havens of dubious humanitarian or political value. In Rwanda, the UN security/political role has been ineffective and was brought into disrepute by UN backing for French unilateral action to support its old Hutu allies. The latest Angolan peace deal, signed on 20 November 1994, led to the deployment of over 7,000 UN military personnel. But the UN force was poorly funded and had insufficient logistical support. It has helped keep the warring sides apart but cannot lessen the basic hostility between the combatants in Angola. By 1998, it had been scaled down further in size and funding, despite the failure to implement fully the peace process.

Workable, adequately funded, and uniformly directed security institutions for Africa still seem a distant prospect, as do institutions to integrate or at least aggregate African economic and trade policies. The nature of the continent's conflicts, the weakness of the state structures and the basic lack of viability of many of the existing states suggest continuing insecurity, political instability, and economic peripheralization even beyond the low status currently suffered by Africa. Only a radical change of direction by African political leaders, a major rethinking of the whole state system and political culture, sympathetic help from the international community, and the development of effective regional and continental organizations can do what over thirty years of independence, experiments with multiparty, one-party and military rule have failed to achieve. There is no question that the emphasis in African security and political developments will remain on the state, despite the lack of serious inter-state conflict and the prevalence of intra-state conflict. But the major impetus towards establishing greater security and towards conflict prevention and resolution is likely to come about on a regional basis.

So far, the history of regional peacekeeping in Africa is far from encouraging. Although the OAU has been active in trying to resolve conflicts between and within member states, it has not had a good record of success. Numerous attempts at mediation between the Sudanese government and successive southern-based rebel movements have failed to end the war or move towards any lasting political solution there. In West Africa, Nigeria's competition for power and influence with France and the leading francophone African states has undercut the ability of the regional organization ECOWAS (the Economic Community of West African States) to operate as a united body in seeking to end conflicts. This first occurred in Chad in the late 1970s and early 1980s, when Nigeria's suspicion of French policy prevented the forging of a common West African position on the war there. Instead, Nigeria's dithering left the field open for France and Libya to intervene in Chad to pursue their own interests. Nigeria, as the most politically, economically, and militarily powerful state in the region would have been conveniently placed to have led a regional conflict-resolution attempt. But its narrower suspicions of France, Côte d'Ivoire, and Senegal prevented wider interests from being considered.

Similar political and regional factors have undercut the active role played by ECOWAS in Liberia. From the start of the conflict, Côte d'Ivoire and Burkina Faso were divided from the rest of ECOWAS members over Liberia. Those two states supported the rebellion by Charles Taylor against President Doe and since the latter's overthrow and subsequent death have continued to back Taylor in the face of the ECOWAS intervention. Nigeria's long-standing suspicion of French and

francophone influence exacerbated the splits within the ECOWAS operation and led to accusations within West Africa, and particularly among
Liberia's warring factions, that the regional organization's military forces
were nothing more than a Nigerian attempt to impose its will on Liberia.
That operation continues but has proved to be as politically fragmented
and as controversial as previous African peacekeeping attempts. The
ECOWAS problems suggest that, at least in West Africa, there is not a
sufficiently strong or widely accepted regional power or hegemon which
can take the leading role in regional organizations. The split between
anglophone and francophone countries and Nigeria's own domestic political instability suggest that regionalism is not going to be a convincing or
lasting solution to regional conflicts in that part of Africa.

In Central and East Africa, the situation is not so obviously polarized
but again there is not a powerful regional hegemon which could take on
the role of peacemaker or at least be the driving force behind regionally-
based attempts to develop structures or institutions for conflict-
resolution, peacekeeping, and security. Zaire (Democratic Republic of
Congo) is the most powerful state in Central Africa and it has strong
influence over events in neighbouring Rwanda and Burundi. But like
Nigeria, its own domestic instability, even under the new regime of
Laurent Kabila, inhibits its ability to play a constructive role. Mobutu,
despite his cooperation with French intervention, had little ultimate influence over events in Rwanda in 1994, despite the presence of French and
some Belgian troops under UN auspices. This operation actually demonstrated the drawbacks of Zaire's role and its international affiliations. The
French intervention rapidly became seen as an attempt to prop up the
brutal and discredited Hutu militias and remnants of the Bahyarimana
government and Zaire was seen by many international observers and
African states as backing what was effectively a unilateral intervention by
France rather than a credible international attempt to alleviate suffering
and limit the violence in Rwanda. Mobutu's cooperation with the French
there did not elicit sufficient support to maintain him in power. As in West
Africa, the Central African region is afflicted by splits between pro-French
states and those suspicious of France. Uganda, whose government is close
to the new Tutsi leadership in Rwanda, opposed the French intervention
and was part of the anti-Mobutu coalition which helped Kabila's forces to
overthrow him. French influence in Central Africa plummeted with
Mobutu's fall and led to the ascendancy of a Uganda/Rwanda/Kabila
group seen as being close to the USA and anglophone states in Africa,
including South Africa. As noted above, although much of the heat has
gone from the regional conflict in the Horn of Africa following the end
of superpower involvement, there is no credible regional grouping or

dominant power that could assist in finding security and political solutions in Somalia, between Somalia and those of its neighbours with Somali-speaking populations, and encouraging regional security cooperation.

The only region where there is a credible move towards a regional approach to security is southern Africa. Several years have gone by since the election of the power-sharing government in South Africa, yet the prospects of a South African-led regional security framework are looking reasonably good. Even before the elections of April 1994, when De Klerk was still President, South Africa cooperated closely with Botswana and Zimbabwe (at the request of the strongly anti-apartheid Robert Mugabe of Zimbabwe) to work on a multilateral basis to end the army mutiny in Lesotho in January 1994 and to establish peace. Later in the year, the three states worked in harmony to reverse a constitutional *coup* by King Letsie which overthrew the elected government and threatened further violent conflict. Using a combination of combined political influence, the threat of economic sanctions by the states of the Southern African Development Community (of which Lesotho, South Africa, Botswana, and Zimbabwe are all members), and even the implicit threat of military action led by South Africa, worked to end the crisis, see the restoration of the elected government, and set the precedent for further regional intervention to assist Lesotho in resolving its political problems.

This assistance went on as South Africa was trying to establish its own political *modus operandi* following the elections and against the background of a growing debate within South and southern Africa over the possibilities of regional security cooperation under SADC auspices. Many South African analysts, such as the influential Jakkie Cilliers of the Institute for Defence Policy in Johannesburg,[27] urged a cautious functional approach to security and other spheres of cooperation. But the debate itself, combined with the success in Lesotho and the wave of optimism following Mandela's inauguration, led to a growing interest regionally in establishing something other than *ad hoc* operations to avert or resolve crises. Some have argued for moving rapidly towards the formation of an all-encompassing set of regional institutions which would not only lead to security coordination but to joint approaches to economic, environmental, migration and other issues. Such an institutional framework would, Ohlson and Steadman argue, 'address regional interaction in a multidimensional way, including politics, economics and military security. It would also have to consider the linkages between subnational, national and regional levels'.[28] The slow transitional process for South Africa's armed forces has led to a reassessment of the pace of regional security cooperation, but *ad hoc* cooperation worked in Lesotho and long-term planning continues.

Such an approach is undoubtedly what is needed in the long term, with issues of subnational conflict, economic viability, national stability, and regional cooperation all being addressed within the same framework. The South African writer Laurie Nathan has identified the range of non-military factors which threaten peace and security in southern Africa, including 'underdevelopment and poverty; fragile democracies and authoritarian rule, internal political and ethnic conflicts; AIDS and other diseases; environmental degradation; and large numbers of refugees and displaced people'.[29] And the ANC, to whom Nathan submitted his ideas, have in their foreign policy discussion documents stressed the need for South Africa to work with SADC, of which it became a member in August 1993, and on a wider basis with the Preferential Trade Area for Eastern, Central and Southern Africa, to 'craft an appropriate institutional basis for the promotion of mutually beneficial cooperation and integration' to include regional security and human rights institutions.[30]

Most regional states agree with South Africa on the need for a framework for cooperation and policy coordination. The Secretary-General of SADC, Kaire Mbuende, told the author in London in October 1994 that the organization was moving ahead with plans to increase coordination in the area of security (giving this wide parameters to include issues of cross-border crime, the illegal arms trade, illegal migration, and environmental threats) and he said that the framework would be established to go beyond the sort of *ad hoc* multilateral conflict-resolution measures seen in the case of Lesotho. This became more concrete in mid-November 1994 when SADC agreed to set up a SADC Rapid Deployment Force. However, this would not be a standing force and, as President Ketumile Masire of Botswana told the BBC World Service on 27 November, there is currently no funding for a permanent force or command structure.

The drawbacks to the plans for institutional frameworks are that funding is non-existent. South Africa is for the foreseeable future going to be consumed with its own domestic reconciliation and reconstruction programmes and there is no precedent in Africa for successful integration of policies across such a wide range of issues and of sustained political cooperation between states. But southern Africa does have significant advantages over the rest of Africa. Despite the setbacks of the Angola accord of 1991, the region's states have shown a sustained willingness to attempt negotiations and conflict-resolution, even at the height of the cold war and the regional conflicts between white-ruled South Africa and its neighbours. There were attempts at regional *détente* and reconciliation in 1974, led by President Kaunda and Prime Minister Vorster of South Africa. The Frontline States and future SADC members were involved in the international negotiations which led to Zimbabwe's independence in 1980 and states as diverse as Angola, Mozambique, and Botswana negotiated military disengagement or non-aggression pacts in 1984 (although South Africa did not stick to its side of the agreements). Namibia's independence involved regional negotiations once a military settlement was reached in 1988 and in 1992 South Africa, Botswana, and Zimbabwe worked closely together to combat a particularly severe drought. South Africa, Botswana, Lesotho, Namibia, and Swaziland also have the experience of working together, not always amicably, within the Southern African Customs Union.

This suggests better prospects for institution-building in southern Africa than in the rest of the continent. However, there will be problems of military cooperation given the different sizes, levels of training and discipline, and political roles of the regions' armed forces. For this reason, I would err on the cautious side of the debate and agree with Jakkie Cilliers that

ambitions should be limited to realistic and feasible sequential steps. The early implementation of continental schemes, such as the institution of an African peace-keeping force under the auspices of the Organization of African Unity (OAU), is unmanageably ambitious . . . Africans need to adopt a cautious approach, not only towards what is possible and what is not, but also in building from national institutions upwards and not from regional institutions downwards.[31]

In continental terms, the prospects for multilateral attempts to cope with the political, economic, and security problems of Africa in the post-cold war world are patchy. In southern Africa, the desire for cooperation is evident and the regionally dominant power, South Africa, is prepared to play a major role in the process of institution-building and functional coordination of policies. South Africa is concerned that it should not get too involved in regional events to deal with its own massive nation-building tasks, but as Ohlson and Steadman argue, 'the notion that South Africa—the region's giant—will be too inwardly focused to take the lead in creating an equitable regional mistakenly assumes that such a task would impede the resolution of its domestic crisis. In fact, a growing, developing Southern Africa can help meet the needs of South Africa's people'.[32] Self-interest as much as regional altruism can be the basis for progress. But elsewhere in Africa the prospects are not good. Despite the existence of Nigeria as a potential regional giant, West Africa has failed to overcome the hurdle of political rivalries within ECOWAS and Nigeria would not be accepted by francophone states as a first among equals within regional institutions. In East Africa, the Horn, and Central Africa, prospects are even worse, with few institutional frameworks for cooperation and weak states operating without sufficient common ground for coordination with neighbouring states.

In the long term, a successful transition in South Africa and the development of SADC institutions could both provide a model for other regional groupings to follow and the nucleus of a wider African security and cooperation framework. In 1957, Karl Deutsch analysed the role played by the United States in helping to forge the Atlantic alliance within NATO structures. South Africa could play the role of benign giant within Africa, but Africa currently lacks the level of economic development, the history of working democratic institutions, and the social cohesion of Europe after the Second World War. The slow rate of economic growth and the cautious foreign policy approach in South Africa could also inhibit the country's ability to provide a role model and a dynamo for reform and growth.

In the wake of the cold war, Africa remains politically unstable, lacking a democratic culture, lacking the institutions of civil society that can help entrench greater democracy and accountability, and beset by military conflict and basic human insecurity (in terms of threats to life, health, civil and political rights, and economic well-being). In a few states, more democratic governments have been installed and there is some hope that they will prove more durable and accountable than their predecessors, but overall the 'winner-takes-all' mentality rules. The continent is peripheral to world security and to the world economic system and is viewed as a basket case deserving sympathy and periodic humanitarian aid but no more.[33]

While there have been some advances in terms of security since the end of the cold war, some as a result of the structural changes in the international environment and some as consequences of regionally driven factors, the replacement of bipolarity with an unstable mixture of unipolarity and multipolarity have not had the universal effect of dampening conflict. Structural change has had a dual effect on security—helping the resolution of those conflicts where superpower rivalry had exacerbated or generated divisions but revealing or releasing conflictual forces which had been overlaid or suppressed by superpower competition. And as Roland Dannreuther contends, although there have been dynamic forces working on behalf of democracy globally, the disappearance of cold war conflict has not dissolved the obstacles to democracy. In Africa, ethnic, regional, political, religious, and economic obstacles still exist and have remained largely unaffected by the changes in the international environment. The major positive change for Africa has been the withdrawal of foreign intervention (the ubiquitous and tenacious French excluded) from most African state, inter-state, or regional conflicts.

On Africa's prospects for the millennium, five concluding points might be made:

1. The basic desire for more equitable, accountable, and participatory political and economic systems remains intact. The impetus for democratic change in 1989–90 came from within Africa itself. That impetus has not been lost entirely, though it has slowed down and has suffered setbacks. The continent is still undergoing a generational change and as the old, authoritarian rulers and their supporters simply die or become physically incapable of rule, the new generation of leaders may prove more amenable to change (though the examples of military *coups* in Sierra Leone, Gambia, Niger, and the setbacks for democracy in Nigeria in recent years show this could be an illusory hope).

2. South Africa has emerged from its bloody and conflictual transition period with a popularly elected, power-sharing government which has the potential to oversee a successful metamorphosis from racial hegemony to multiracial democracy. If the system works and elements of power-sharing can persist, along with devolution of political and economic power to the provinces, then an African country will have provided a model for its neighbours to follow. Power-sharing and real devolution of power could prove to be the answers to regional and ethnic conflicts which have plagued Africa. But they need to be seen to succeed in one country if others are to adopt them.

3. There is a growing desire in southern Africa to see the Southern African Development Community, now including South Africa, develop not only economic cooperation but also security coordination. There is no immediate prospect of a NATO equivalent in the region or of the establishment of permanent multilateral peacekeeping forces. But South Africa, Botswana, and Zimbabwe have been working closely to bring about military security and political reconciliation in Lesotho, hand in hand with the competing factions there. They have not sought to impose themselves militarily or to dictate to Lesotho, rather they have used political persuasion (backed by the threat of economic sanctions) to try to restore constitutional rule in Lesotho and to use that as the basis for finding a political solution. What is likely to result is a cautious and incremental approach to regional security, encompassing issues such as border security, drug smuggling, protection of maritime resources, and controlling human migration across borders, as well as the more obvious military threats to security.[34]

4. Successes on a regional basis could help in converting the OAU from a meeting place for autocrats and military leaders into an increasingly effective continental forum bolstered by functioning regional organizations whose activities range across economic, security, and humanitarian issues. The short-term prospects for this are not good, but this should not stop us from investing hope in the longer term.

5. The major negative factor for Africa is the continuing economic peripheralization. Economic globalization harms rather than helps Africa. As Claude Ake emphasizes: 'What is globalised is not Yoruba but English . . . not Senegalese technology but Japanese and German . . . Globalisation is the hierarchisation of the world—economically, politically and culturally—and the crystallising of a domination.'[35] Africa is dominated by world economic forces and is at the same time pushed further into the periphery.

8

South Asia After the Cold War

Adjusting to New Realities

P. R. KUMARASWAMY

Unlike some of the other regions described in this volume, the cold war was not a prime cause of prevailing political tension and insecurity in South Asia.[1] The continuation and intensification of various ethnic, sectarian, religious, and linguistic conflicts and tensions rooted in colonialism also indicate the inadequate policies and practices of the newly independent states. Without creating any ideological division in South Asia the cold war accentuated the situation and—often against their will—the countries of the region were drawn into the great power rivalry. The close ties that region sought to develop with the rival blocs of the East–West divide affected the security as well as political and economic policies of this impoverished region. In some ways this external linkage facilitated the prolongation of some of the critical regional tensions and disputes.

The end of the cold war opened a new era in South Asian politics and has exposed the region to an unpredictable and unstable future. Like much of the rest of the world, the countries of the region were poorly prepared for the transformation of Europe and needed considerable time to recognize and adjust themselves to new realities. The disintegration of the Soviet Union eliminated some of the immediate threats that had faced South Asia in preceding years but simultaneously rekindled other contentious issues. The new inclination of the United States and Russia to adopt a common posture towards certain fundamental security issues and the emergence of the US as dominant global power had a profound impact upon the policies and options of South Asian leaders. The impact of these changes was more acute in India and Pakistan, the principal protagonists of South Asia, and less acute elsewhere.

The author is grateful to the Leonard Davis Institute of the Hebrew University for its support in the preparation of this chapter.

Though the region was not actively involved in cold war power politics, India and Pakistan had developed special relationships with Moscow and Washington respectively. These relationships, dating back to mid-1950, extended to a wide range of political, military, and economic assistance and support. Strong external linkages enabled the two rivals to address and mitigate larger security concerns. In the process they developed a dependent relationship with their respective patrons.[2] This precarious situation was further exacerbated by the decision of both countries to abandon their nuclear threshold status and conduct a series of nuclear tests in May 1998.

For India as well as Pakistan this prolonged dependency proved to be the major security and foreign policy challenge of the post-cold war era, and demonstrates how major systemic change interacted centrally with regional developments.[3] In aspiring to retain their erstwhile strategic relationship, these two countries looked for new leverage that would still make them attractive assets for the great powers. At the same time they were coerced into diversifying their search for economic, political, and military partners, where hitherto one had sufficed. In this process sacrosanct foreign policy postures and mantras were made redundant and countries of South Asia had to look for new issues and platforms from which to reach out to the world. The end of the cold war significantly challenged the relevance and influence of once-important Third World bodies such as the Non-Aligned Movement (NAM). As a result, the countries involved are either knocking at the doors of existing multilateral forums or searching for new bodies.

Yet while the parameters of the local security environment have changed, to a large extent politics of the region remain dominated by the conflicting relationship between India and Pakistan.[4] And their interactions, differences, disputes, and conflicts continue to have significant bearing upon South Asian security and stability.

A second systemic challenge with major regional implications has been the pressures of economic liberalization and globalization. Regionalism has been a major outcome of these pressures. Indeed the fall of Eastern Europe corresponded with a new South Asian approach towards regional cooperation. Issues of economic cooperation have, for a number of countries, displaced hitherto popular foreign policy postures. Economic liberalization is now seen as an important, if not essential, tool in regional development and progress and as a vehicle for interaction at the global level. Even though countries like Sri Lanka had already taken this path in the late 1970s, the post-cold war period saw further significant moves in this direction. After protracted negotiations and delays the countries of the region agreed to forge an economic bloc, SAPTA (South Asian

Preferential Trading Arrangement), that is committed to accelerating economic integration and bringing down trade barriers.

A third challenge can be identified at the domestic level. The end of the cold war saw South Asia enter a period of serious domestic turmoil and transformation. With the exception of Bhutan all countries are gradually moving towards democracy, and far-reaching political changes are being brought about by ballots rather than bullets. With all their imperfections and inadequacies, elections have become part of the emerging political culture in South Asia and legitimacy and accountability are tested and validated at polls. This process of democratization has been partly undermined by the escalation of existing conflicts or the emergence of political tensions within various countries, which in turn have contributed to a state of uncertainty. At times communal hostilities, ethnic conflicts, linguistic discord, and other sectarian differences challenge the social fabric and political governance. The destruction of the disputed mosque in Ayodhya by extremists of the majority Hindu community was a milestone in post-independence India and posed a severe challenge to its commitment to secularism. Most of these substate-level developments are largely independent of the emerging new world order, and yet they seriously affect the ability of these countries to appreciate and understand the nature of the post-cold war world and readjust their policies accordingly. Inconclusive and disputed popular verdicts have contributed to political instability in a number of South Asia countries. When governments are struggling for survival, politicians have less time for foreign policy and are even less inclined to adopt a long-term view.

As suggested above, a significant part of these changes and resulting new orientations were made necessary and facilitated by the end of ideological conflict in Europe. The task of this paper is to unpack further these different levels of change and determine how, and to what extent, the end of the cold war has been a long-term determinant in defining the region's foreign and domestic policies.

I. THE SECURITY DIMENSION

The principal regional protagonists adopted a diametrically opposite view of the cold war and its relevance to South Asia. The nationalist leadership in India viewed insulation of the region from the negative consequences of the cold war as a prerequisite for post-colonial nation-building and was determined not to become a 'plaything of others'.[5] Sensitive towards hard-earned independence and sovereignty, Jawaharlal Nehru, the architect of India's foreign policy, was determined to keep aloof from the great power rivalry and pursue a non-aligned foreign policy. For Pakistan, the situation was different. In creating a 'homeland' for Indian Muslims, the partition of the subcontinent had created peculiar security dilemmas and economic hardships for Pakistan. India's acceptance of partition was coupled with its rejection of the 'two-nation theory'[6] and for long there were fears in Pakistan over India's acceptance of the partition. Furthermore, New Delhi's opposition to extra-regional involvement in South Asia as well as in the Indian Ocean sounded in Islamabad like explicit signals for post-partition Indian hegemony. So India opted for a non-aligned foreign policy based on Afro-Asian solidarity and sought a political relationship with the outside world including Moscow, while Pakistan preferred the strategic path and emerged as a partner in anti-communist military alliances established by Washington such as CENTO (Central Treaty Organization, erstwhile Baghdad Pact) and SEATO (Southeast Asian Treaty Organization).[7] Similar security considerations eventually compelled India to sign a peace and friendship treaty with Moscow in 1971. Though less than a military alliance, it was primarily aimed at counteracting emerging security cooperation between China and Pakistan, two states with whom India has serious border disputes and had fought in the past. In short, both countries exploited the cold war tension between the two superpowers to achieve their own ends—usually in opposite directions.[8]

Furthermore since partition there have been serious differences and apprehensions over India's role and position in South Asia. Even without a big-brotherly attitude or ambitions of domination, India's regional importance is enhanced by various historical, geographic, economic and demographic considerations. Committed to supporting anti-imperialist and anti-colonial struggles, Indian leaders were unwilling to abdicate what they considered a legitimate leadership status for India. New Delhi's support for Afro-Asian solidarity and the Non-Aligned Movement and the recent campaigns for permanent membership of the United Nations Security Council were part of this search. Following the decisive military victory over Pakistan in 1971 most countries of the world have recognized India as a major regional power. This view is not shared by others in South Asia, especially by Pakistan. In its view, there is no place for 'India's dominance in South Asia', especially when New Delhi was considered as the principal source of threat.[9] On occasions the foreign policies of countries such as Bangladesh, Nepal, and Sri Lanka were significantly influenced by their apprehensions over Indian designs and hegemony. Against this background the fall of Eastern Europe and collapse of the Soviet Union had a profound impact upon the South Asian security environment in four distinct areas: Soviet withdrawal from Afghanistan; the demise of external patrons; the growing American concerns over non-proliferation in South Asia, and the ethno-national conflict. In some ways all these issues have influenced the foreign policy of the region.

The Afghanistan crisis

The announcement by Mikhail Gorbachev of the start of withdrawal of Soviet troops from Afghanistan by May 1988 was the development that marked the end of the cold war in South Asia.[10] Directly or indirectly this development affected the security considerations of India as well as Pakistan. Ever since the December 1979 invasion, the presence of Soviet troops in Afghanistan had severely undermined the regional balance and eliminated Afghanistan as the traditional buffer between Russia and the subcontinent. This uncoordinated Soviet action proved to be an embarrassment for India. It was not willing to endorse a great-power invasion of a fellow member of the NAM. At the same time, growing military cooperation with Moscow, as well as renewed American interests in anti-communist alliances, inhibited New Delhi from joining the Western chorus against Moscow. Its opposition to 'all foreign interference' in Afghanistan was insufficient and paved the way for serious doubts about India's commitment to a non-aligned foreign policy. For its part Pakistan found itself encircled by two unfriendly partners, namely India and the Soviet Union. If geographical proximity traditionally inhibited India from assuming an anti-Soviet posture, the same consideration made Pakistan wary of Moscow's intentions. The invasion led to fears of the further dismemberment of Pakistan and the influx of Afghan refugees, which at one point passed the three million mark, posed serious security and social problems and undermined the Pakistani economy.

Yet the Afghan crisis was not without its positive attributes. It enabled General Mohammad Zia ul Haq to legitimize and consolidate his position.[11] The legal execution of former Prime Minister Zulfikar Ali Bhutto did not enhance Zia's position and Moscow provided an escape route. The crisis in Afghanistan was preceded by the Islamic revolution in Iran that eroded vital American interests in the Middle East. Zia thus saw the Soviet invasion as an important opportunity to promote Pakistan, and by extension himself, as a dependable Western ally against communism and offered a whole range of political and military support for the anti-Soviet coalition. At the political level Pakistan launched an aggressive campaign in the Organization of Islamic Conference (OIC) and fostered an Arab and Islamic consensus against Moscow. By providing training facilities to Afghan mujahidee ('holy warriors') and shelter to fleeing refugees he earned Western admiration and support. The election of a Republican president obsessed with 'evil empire' obliterated any American concerns about Zia's legitimacy or restoration of democracy. In short, while Indian Prime Minister Indira Gandhi was reluctant to take a stand against the Soviet Union, General Zia proved to be a dependable ally and a front-line state in President Ronald Reagan's crusade against communism.

Furthermore, by successfully exploiting the Afghan crisis, General Zia succeeded in diluting Washington's concerns over and commitments to non-proliferation. Apprehensions over Soviet designs in the Persian Gulf compelled Washington to reorient its strategic policy. Many legislative measures initiated by the Jimmy Carter administration were either put on hold or overruled by Ronald Reagan and George Bush.[12] In return for its critical support Pakistan was rewarded with US$3.2 billion in economic and military assistance from Washington and another $1.1 billion worth of advanced weapons paid for by the Saudis.[13] These measures sent different signals to New Delhi. Though most of this military assistance was provided to Pakistan in the context of Afghanistan, the growing strategic relationship between Washington and Islamabad threatened India's security interests and led inevitably to a South Asian arms race in the 1980s.

On the whole, the eventual Soviet withdrawal from Afghanistan in February 1989 was a political as well as diplomatic victory for Pakistan's steadfastness. The Soviet withdrawal signalled the end of bloc politics and lessening of tensions between Moscow and two of Pakistan's key allies, China and the US. Above all, for Pakistan, the disintegration of the Soviet Union meant the removal of Moscow as the principal patron of its rival, India. However, despite Moscow's ignominious pullout, the Afghan problem still haunts Pakistan. The Geneva agreement that was to enable a post-Soviet political order in Kabul was doomed from the beginning and nearly a decade later the country is still tormented by internal strife and political instability. The battle lines are far from clear and fluctuate regularly. The social cost for Pakistan of this lingering crisis is severe and the easy availability of sophisticated weapons has significantly contributed to the intensification of sectarian violence in various parts of the country. Moreover the 'Afghan crisis' is often blamed for rampant drug abuse among the younger population.[14] Even after the Russian departure, Pakistan is yet to be liberated from the Afghan entanglement.

Demise of external patrons

Since Nikita Khrushchev's historic visit in 1955, Moscow has been an important player in India's foreign and defence policies. The disintegration of the Soviet Union came as a serious blow to the Indian defence establishment. The problem for India had three dimensions. Beginning

with the MiG deal in 1962, vast amounts of India's defence needs including sophisticated weapons and systems were met from Moscow.[15] By the
end of 1980s 60–70 per cent of total military supplies came from this
source and this dependency was acutely felt in the air force; for instance,
Soviet inventories account for thirty-two of the forty-one combat
squadrons. Second, largely to consolidate the political relationship,
Moscow supplied the most advanced weapons in its inventories without
undue political restrictions and enabled India to counter Pakistan's US-
supplied inventories.[16] Third, these sophisticated weapons were supplied
with a host of financial incentives such as 'friendly prices', credit arrangements with low interest rates, repayments in Indian currencies, or barter
trade. Moreover, unlike Western suppliers, the Soviets were willing to supply technology and grant production licences to India.[17] Its ability to
maintain defence expenditure at around 3 per cent of the GNP and pursue military modernization without unduly straining its scarce financial
resources should be attributed to its dependence on Moscow.[18] On various
occasions India sought to escape from this dependency and to diversify its
military needs by looking for alternate suppliers. Beginning with the
Jaguar deal approved by the Janata government in late 1978 New Delhi
signed major deals with the West. This approach induced the Soviets to
offer more advanced systems and the Western option turned into a means
of leverage *vis-à-vis* Moscow. Diversification remained elusive as financial
difficulties and technological hardships prevented India from actively pursuing indigenous defence production.[19]

   The fall of Eastern Europe suddenly brought home the negative side of
the special relationship and the military establishment woke up to its worst
nightmares. The situation was worse than that which confronted Israel following the French embargo shortly after the June war of 1967. In certain
key areas such as land-based air defence systems and tracked armoured
vehicles Indian dependency was total. Availability and guaranteed supply
of spare parts and maintenance facilities became the primary concerns
facing the defence establishment.[20] Any outbreak of hostility with
Pakistan or China then would have severely exposed India's military vul-
nerabilities. If shortage of spare parts was immediately felt, there were
fears over the long-term dislocation of supplies, especially when these
inventories were produced by a wide network of factories scattered across
the former Soviet Union. Rapid *de facto* devaluation of Russian currency
exposed India to the negative implications of rupee-rouble trade. At the
end of December 1989 Indian debts to the former Soviet Union stood at
9.9 billion roubles or Rs.196 billion and arms imports constituted the bulk
of this amount. According to one estimate when the Russian currency was
trading at 309 roubles to a dollar, the dollar value of Indian debts plum-

metted from 'US$13.4 billion to US$34 million'.[21] However, Russian refusal
to re-evaluate the exchange rate with market values and their insistence on
hard-currency payments for military transactions intensified the pressures.
By threatening to auction the debts Moscow in March 1993 successfully
secured a debt-repayment agreement based on an artificial and highly exag-
gerated exchange rate.[22] There were indications that the finance ministry was
exploring the possibility of settling this debt early by hard-currency repayment.[23] It is in this context that one should examine India's growing military
contacts with Israel[24] and economic relations with Southeast Asia. Initial
hopes of India coping with the loss of a traditional patron by evolving a new
strategic relationship with Washington[25] proved to be illusive and premature. Moreover, strong-arm tactics and pressure from Washington compelled
Moscow to modify its earlier commitments in India.[26]

Pakistan's fortunes were less fluctuating. Soviet withdrawal diluted its
position as a front-line state and compelled Islamabad to seek alternative
leverage on Washington. This led to two distinct phases which approximately coincided with the Republican and Democratic administrations in
the White House. Pakistan's ability to secure tacit American acquiescence
if not indifference towards its nuclear posture came under stress. After the
US Congress passed the Pressler amendment in July 1985, both Reagan
and Bush continued military aid to Pakistan by formally certifying that
Islamabad did not possess a nuclear device. This presidential waiver that
ran counter to American intelligence assessments was facilitated by
Pakistan's geo-strategic role and cooperation in the Afghan crisis. The
administration argued that 'constructive dialogue' was a more effective
means of pursuing the non-proliferation objective. However, the end of
the cold war and the weakening of Pakistan's importance led to a reappraisal of this approach. At the time of the Kuwait crisis, President Bush
refused to guarantee Pakistan's non-nuclear status and thus brought the
country under the Pressler amendment, suspending military aid. This was
a belated American acknowledgement of nuclear Pakistan. Around the
same time the State Department also accused Pakistan of supporting various anti-Indian terrorist groups. In January 1993, as Bill Clinton assumed
office, Pakistan earned the dubious distinction of being placed on the
watch list of suspected state-sponsors of terrorism. It was on the verge of
being classed together with countries such as Iran and Libya.

Indian hopes of total American abandonment of Pakistan were quickly
dashed as both countries began to develop a new formula of friendship,
and the inauguration of Bill Clinton accelerated this process.[27] Unlike the
Afghan crisis there was no definite development that modified the
American posture but the return of Benazir Bhutto as Prime Minister of
Pakistan in August 1993 greatly facilitated this process. Committed to the

policy of 'dual containment' of Iran and Iraq originally articulated by Martin Indyk, former US ambassador to Israel, the administration took a different view of Pakistan's utility. Under a woman premier, Pakistan was seen and projected as a progressive and modern Islamic state committed to democracy and hence an important ally in the Middle East and Central Asia.[28] Even Bhutto's electoral defeat in March 1997 did not significantly diminish the administration's assessment of Pakistan. Furthermore it was perceived as a key player in the American objective of securing and establishing a regional arms control mechanism in South Asia and frustrating India's strategic aspirations. Reversing the earlier posture, the administration established strong cooperation with Islamabad in its fight against terrorism. For its part Pakistan arrested and deported key suspects wanted for various terrorist activities in the US and has enhanced cooperation with the American drug enforcement agencies.[29]

However, the most significant progress in US–Pakistan relations emerged in the nuclear arena. Soon after assuming office, the Clinton administration sought to repeal the country-specific Pressler amendment and to supply twenty-eight F-16s (fighter aircraft) for which Pakistan had already paid or to return the money. After prolonged lobbying in August 1995 the US adopted an amendment introduced by Republican Senator Hank Brown that partially lifted the Pressler amendment sanctions imposed five years earlier. The administration felt that the supply of $370 million worth of arms was essential both to retain American influence over Pakistan and to maintain the regional security balance in South Asia. This move was projected as a compromise between delivering all the equipment that had been paid for by Pakistan and not supplying any weapons. The former would undermine American non-proliferation objectives and the latter would alienate Islamabad. This was a personal victory for Prime Minister Bhutto that underscored her country's importance in the post-cold war environment. Even though the impact of the Brown amendment upon Pakistan's military appears moderate, the move succeeded in damaging America's relations with India. Various analysts and media pundits castigated Washington for its insensitivity. Informed observers in New Delhi moreover seriously refute the financial implications of the Brown amendment and according to one Indian analyst:

Taking into account the current published prices for weapons systems, as well as the cost of support package consisting of spares and components accompanying them (which are all too often disregarded in calculations of price), the total value of arms package to Pakistan is estimated at over $1 billion. In addition, the US House-Senate Conference also recommended the sale of American surveillance equipment, radar, and radar warning receivers to Pakistan, for border security.[30]

Likewise, the administration's position that this was a 'one-time exception' had few takers in New Delhi. Prime Minister Narasimha Rao expressed his apprehensions that the move could trigger the first post-cold war arms race in the region.

Non-proliferation

The diminished power of its rival and newly earned sole global power status enabled Washington to redefine its strategic objectives and to adopt an activist and interventionist posture *vis-à-vis* non-proliferation. Without Moscow's countervailing influence non-proliferation became a primary foreign policy objective. Since global disarmament ran counter to its vital national interests, the US sought to promote various regional non-proliferation measures that would contain and remove potential threats to itself and its regional allies. South Asia emerged as a primary target and President Clinton was unambiguous: 'we will encourage India and Pakistan to proceed with multilateral discussions of non-proliferation and security issues, with the *goal of capping and eventually rolling back their nuclear and missile capabilities*'.[31] In recent years various officials and political leaders have viewed India's strategic programmes and ambitions as a long-term threat to the US. This approach also reflects the conventional Western tendency to view India's security concerns and military build-up through a narrow Indo-Pakistan lens that conveniently excludes or belittles the Chinese dimension.[32]

This ambitious non-proliferation agenda has been manifested in American policy towards issues such as missile programmes in South Asia, extension of the Nuclear Non-Proliferation Treaty (NPT), and the conclusion of Comprehensive Test Ban Treaty (CTBT). On all these issues the positions of India and Pakistan are far from similar. One opted for a regional approach and strengthened its ties with Washington and the other preferred a global framework and weakened its position. The American approach on all these regional issues enjoys the understanding and support of Pakistan. Above all it had repeatedly endorsed the idea that any regional approach to non-proliferation in South Asia should be conditional upon India's acceptance of similar American demands. Though merely a tactical move, this approach proved to be an effective public relations exercise *vis-à-vis* India. Conversely, Indian positions on these issues are at odds with Washington. The principal American non-proliferation concern revolves around India's endeavours to develop the intermediate-range ballistic missile (IRBM) Agni (fire) and tactical battle field support missile Prithvi (earth).[33] Right from the inauguration of the Clinton administration Washington repeatedly expressed its concerns at

India's indigenous efforts in this direction. By a host of political and economic pressures the administration appears to have slowed down the development phase of Agni and the deployment phase of Prithvi. This is in contrast to American indifference towards suspected Pakistan import of Prithvi-like missiles from China, or the test firing of a 1500 km-range Ghauri surface-to-surface missile in April 1998.[34]

India found itself at odds with the American endeavour to secure an indefinite and unconditional extension of the Nuclear Non-Proliferation Treaty (NPT). From its inception the non-proliferation regime was unacceptable to India. While the US saw it as an arms control mechanism the latter took a more idealistic approach and demanded total disarmament. Though it never campaigned against the treaty, New Delhi considered NPT an instrument that legitimized nuclear weapons and restricted its possession to the five permanent members of the Security Council. The US–Soviet rivalry during the cold war temporarily insulated India from undue pressures over its non-proliferation posture. When the treaty came up for extension in 1995, the situation was different. Rejecting various more adventurous suggestions, Indian Prime Minister Rao adopted a rational response that involved an understanding with Washington without compromising its traditional position.[35] Though domestically unpopular, this approach provided a temporary respite for India.

Both India and the US were at loggerheads over the comprehensive test ban. From the early 1950s New Delhi consistently championed the proposal for a comprehensive and non-discriminatory test ban. All the major powers were indifferent towards such 'utopian ideals' and conducted nuclear tests to improvise and modernize their arsenals. Technological advances and the lessening of international tensions enabled the US to re-examine its traditional position and to conclude a comprehensive test ban. At the same time India moved in the opposite direction and began to examine the wisdom of its conventional stand. It views the treaty as a means of foreclosing its nuclear option in an area still threatened by nuclear weapons. Its decision to link CTBT to a time-bound global nuclear disarmament was unanimously rejected by all the five nuclear weapon powers, who instead decided to make New Delhi's acceptance a precondition for the coming into force of CTBT.[36] Overruling India's objections to such a blatantly coercive and unprecedented move, on 24 September 1996 the CTBT was opened for signature.

Having refused to endorse the CTBT, India conducted five nuclear tests, which it said included a themonuclear device and sub-kiloton devices, on 11 and 13 May 1998. These tests revealed its suspected nuclear capabilities and the technological progress it had achieved since 1974. Although the preparations had been under way for some time, successive Indian governments had avoided crossing the threshold until the electoral victory of the BJP. Because of the past policy of nuclear ambiguity and the refusal to renounce the nuclear option, most of the domestic criticism (including from the various communist parties) was directed not at the tests but rather at their timing. Internationally, the Indian tests were perceived primarily as a populist measure aimed at consolidating a fragile coalition. On the other side, faced with mounting domestic pressures, Pakistani Prime Minister Nawaz Sharif's political survival depended on giving 'a strong rebuttal' to the Indian tests. Pakistan accordingly conducted six nuclear tests towards the end of May, confirming the nuclearization of South Asia. Its decision reflected the view that the response of the international community to the Indian tests, especially the US sanctions, was minimal and inadequate. Ironically, the Indian nuclear tests provided an opportunity for both India and the US to reach an understandig over the CTBT.[37] None the less, by underscoring the limitations of the international non-proliferation regime, a development viewed with interest by other nuclear threshold or aspirant states in the Middle East and East Asia, the Pakistani striving for 'parity' with India and Indian concern with the growing strategic capabilities of China have only added to the uncertainties of the post-cold war world.

Internal threats and violence

These post-cold war developments have their origins outside the region and smaller countries of South Asia largely remained immune to such debates on non-proliferation and external security linkages. On the contrary the security of these countries has largely been threatened from within and even the two big powers are not immune to domestic violence based on ethnicity or religious differences. Among the handful of sectarian and communal conflicts in South Asia, the Punjab and Kashmir problems are directly related to regional security. From the early 1980s troubles over Sikh separatism in Punjab dominated the Indian political scene and took thousands of innocent lives on both sides of the communal divide. The intensity and extent of violence raised genuine doubts about the nature and durability of the Indian state and its ability to function as a home for different ethnic, religious, linguistic, and social populations. The dismantling of the Soviet Union with its multi-ethnic and multinational population raised apprehensions over India's future. The resolution of the Punjab problem was a major achievement of P. V. Narasimha Rao.[38] The death and disappearance of key protagonists from the political scene, unrestricted military action, intensified political moves, and accelerated economic growth led to a new phase. Though a boycott of leading Sikh parties contributed to the dismal popular participation in the 1992 assembly election, the restoration of a popular government in Punjab after many years of direct rule from New Delhi facilitated rapid economic growth and return to normalcy.

The situation in Kashmir is different and has emerged as the most serious and contentious issue that could spill over into a fully blown Indo-Pakistan conflict. The dispute over the political status of Kashmir dates back to partition days when both countries considered the Himalayan province as an integral part of their territory.[39] The issue is not yet another border dispute but has become ideological. Neither the passage of time nor the bilateral Simla agreement of 1972 led to any fruitful results. The protracted conflict has been both the cause and symptom of the prevailing relations between the two countries. The political leaderships in both countries have adopted an uncompromising position towards Kashmir and they are as far apart as they were in 1947.[40] Their mutual opposition to an independent Kashmir appears to be the only common ground between the two countries. During the cold war years support given by their patrons enabled both parties to maintain the status quo. The current phase of hostilities coincided with the end of the cold war and the Soviet withdrawal from Afghanistan. From the summer of 1989 Kashmir became the venue for a protracted low-intensity conflict between India and Pakistan. New Delhi was determined to use all its military might to prevent a cession of Kashmir from India, while Pakistan provided military and training facilities to those fighting against India.[41] Suggestions of greater autonomy for Kashmir within the Indian union are vehemently opposed by various separatist groups in Kashmir as well as by Pakistan, as both are unanimous in demanding a plebiscite to determine the future of Kashmir. Along with the rest of India, Lok Sabha (the lower house of the Indian parliament) elections were held in Kashmir in May 1996. Though popular participation was meagre, the move initiated a political process and was followed by assembly elections a few months later. Fighting on a platform to secure greater autonomy for the state, in October the National Conference led by former Chief Minister Farooq Abdullah was voted to power. Restoration of a popular government after a gap of seven years significantly diminished the threats of militancy. The importance of National Conference support for a United Front as well as BJP governments at the centre has brought about greater political understanding between the state and the rest of India.

Foreign policy

Closely related to the new security environment is the changing South Asian perception about the content and direction of foreign policy. Earlier rhetoric gave way to economic realism and key regional players are increasingly looking for new friends and political blocs. Prime Minister Rao's decision to establish full diplomatic relations with the Jewish state was the most visible manifestation of new openness in Indian foreign policy. Even though it had granted formal recognition in September 1950, a number of national and regional developments inhibited India from proceeding with normalization. Shortly after taking office in 1984, Rajiv Gandhi tried to improve the situation and initiated certain key steps in this direction but the task of completing this process fell to Rao.[42] Though not all were happy with the move, the decision did not affect India's ties with the Arab and Islamic countries. Rao's preference for a foreign policy based on economic cooperation and political realism enabled him to enhance India's relations with a number of countries in the Middle East and elsewhere. In a significant move in April 1995 India opened a non-official commercial office in Taipei and entrusted the mission to a retired career diplomat. Though this move was primarily aimed at promoting economic and commercial relations, it is difficult to ignore the political implications.[43]

There are indications that Pakistan is actively considering moving closer towards the Jewish State and the Israeli media often discuss increased contacts between the two countries. Nepal, which has maintained relations with Israel for a long time, appears to be promoting Israel–Pakistan relations.[44] Sri Lanka on the other hand has travelled in the opposite direction. In the 1980s when Israel was still facing international condemnation and isolation, Colombo took an unprecedented step and sought Israeli military assistance in waging its ethnic conflict with the Tamil minority and even allowed an Israeli 'interest section' under the American umbrella. Even though this involvement did not alter the outcome of the ethnic conflict, Sri Lanka received vital military supplies, training, and advice from Israel.[45] India was not happy with this development and the Indo-Sri Lankan accord of July 1987 called for an end to Israeli involvement. The government eventually succumbed to domestic pressures, especially from Muslim circles, and in April 1990 President Ranasinghe Premadasa, known for his populist foreign policy, terminated relations with Israel.[46] This move proved to be untimely. Just over a year later a host of major powers including India were re-evaluating their Middle East policy and began establishing normal relations. Sri Lanka had looked to Israel when not many were willing and able to involve themselves in its ethnic conflict, and its sudden decision to cut off such crucial assistance was not looked on kindly in Israel. Even though subsequent Sri Lankan efforts to normalize relations were not reciprocated, both are maintaining regular contacts through third countries and even renewed arms trade.[47]

Iran is another country that attracts considerable attention in South Asia. Under Prime Minister Rao, Iran occupied an important position in India's Middle East policy.[48] Economic considerations aside, New Delhi sought to influence and mellow Tehran's positions on crucial issues such as Kashmir. Even though some observers have questioned Iran's *locus standi* on Kashmir, aware of its importance in the Islamic world, Rao was keen to wean Tehran away from Pakistan and paid a highly successful state visit to Iran in 1993. This was reciprocated by President Ali Akbar Hashemi Rafsanjani's visit to India in 1995.[49] On a couple of occasions Tehran prevailed upon Pakistan to desist from raising the Kashmir issue in international forums. During Rafsanjani's visit both countries signed a host of agreements, some involving third parties, to promote trade cooperation between India, Iran, and Central Asia.

Pakistan on the contrary is adopting a delicate policy towards Iran. The expansion of the Economic Co-operation Organization (ECO) in February 1992 provided a framework for Pakistan's endeavours in Central Asia.[50] Traditional ties, geographic proximity, and the Islamic orientation of its foreign policy potentially make Iran an important friend and ally. In the post-cold war period American leniency towards Islamabad, especially on issues such as non-proliferation, has been explained by Pakistan being a 'modern' Islamic state fighting against Islamic fundamentalism. Given the American preoccupation with Iran, Pakistan's dilemmas are considerable. Politically it needs Iranian support to consolidate its credentials as an important player in the Islamic world and to promote its new-found economic relations with Central Asia. But security considerations, especially *vis-à-vis* India, compel Pakistan to remain dependent upon Washington. In short, Pakistan seeks to project its Islamic identity towards Tehran while emphasizing modernity in dealing with the West.

At another level, the Non-Aligned Movement, still the largest forum of developing countries, appears to have lost its importance for the region. The organization is yet to identify against whom it is non-aligned. The disappearance of East–West confrontation has not led to North–South cooperation. On the contrary, various technological and economic barriers are being raised to inhibit, if not prevent, the development of the South.[51] An unwieldy, unmanageable, politically heterogeneous, and consensus-bound NAM does not appear to be a realistic forum for collective bargaining with the North. Traditional perceptions of its utility however are difficult to change and hence the South Asian leaders, like their counter-parts in other parts of the world, are officially committed to a non-aligned foreign policy. Other traditional forums are also actively used to promote respective national interests and positions. Multilateral forums, such as provided by NAM and Commonwealth summits have been transformed into venues for Indo-Pakistan rivalry. [52] With the Kashmir dispute occu-pying a prominent position in its foreign policy, the OIC continues to be an important forum for Pakistan. The organization's inability to influence and significantly modify Indian positions towards the problem has not diminished its utility in embarrassing India.

At the same time, compelled by political needs, these countries are searching for new political allies. They have realized the importance of smaller and more coherent multilateral forums to promote economic as well as political cooperation. In a significant development in June 1990 India along with fourteen other countries formed a forum called G15[53] to promote North–South and South–South dialogue and cooperation. Though small and cohesive, it is yet to emerge as a major player in the South. The former Regional Co-operation and Development grouping (RCD) was revitalized and relaunched as the Economic Co-operation Organization (ECO). Geographic proximity and Islamic identity would enable this group, consisting of Iran, Pakistan, Turkey, and the newly independent countries of Central Asia, to promote economic cooperation. While visiting India in November 1993, South African Foreign Minister Pik Botha called for a forum of Indian Ocean countries. This received a further impetus when President Nelson Mandela endorsed the idea during his state visit to India in January 1995. In March seven countries of the region met in Port Louis, Mauritius, for an intergovernmental meeting to launch the Indian Ocean Rim Initiative. Efforts by Australia to place secu-rity high on the agenda have been thwarted by others. After months of deliberations a fourteen-member Indian Ocean Rim Association for Regional Cooperation (IOR-ARC) was launched in March 1997. In its infant stage, it is primarily concerned with promoting economic coopera-tion among member states.[54]

Simultaneously however, India, Pakistan, and Sri Lanka are actively campaigning for membership in the Association of South East Asian Nations (ASEAN). After decades of neglect, indifference, and occasional disdain and disregard, New Delhi had woken up to the importance of Southeast Asia. Without undue publicity under Rao, the region, especially ASEAN has emerged as a dominant factor in Indian foreign policy.[55] At the fourth ASEAN summit in 1992 India was recognized as a 'sectoral dia-logue partner', a status that enabled it to participate in areas such as trade and investment, joint ventures, science and technology cooperation, tourism, and human resource development. It took Rao numerous visits to the region, personal meetings with various leaders, and increased economic interaction to upgrade this relationship. Singapore has emerged as the focus of Indian endeavours and a strong supporter. In December 1995 India was admitted as a full dialogue partner of ASEAN and the following May New Delhi was admitted into the ASEAN Regional Forum (ARF), a body that deals with security issues. This move is interpreted in New Delhi as a step towards India's entry into the Asia Pacific Economic Co-operation forum (APEC). Conscious of the advantages, Pakistan has used its Islamic identity to influence countries such as Indonesia, Malaysia, and Brunei. While Pakistan was granted dialogue partner status together with India, economic considerations and fears over ASEAN meetings degenerating into a political forum for South Asian rivalry appear to have prevented the organization from upgrading that status.[56] For its part, since May 1981 Sri Lanka has been unsuccessfully seeking ASEAN membership and in January 1996 became the first South Asian country to apply for APEC membership. Economic incentives, the pro-Western orientation of previous United National Party (UNP) governments, and frustrations over lack of progress on South Asian regional cooperation appear to have strongly influenced Colombo's interests in Southeast Asia.[57]

II. DEMOCRATIZATION IN SOUTH ASIA

The end of the cold war and the emerging new international order initiated and accelerated certain political changes in Eastern Europe, Latin America, and Africa, and to a lesser extent in the Middle East. Democracy became an acceptable norm in certain dictatorial states. These developments facilitated far-reaching internal changes in South Asia and to a certain extent accelerated the process of democratization. One of the most striking features of the post-cold war era is the slow and gradual consolidation of democracy in South Asia. Since 1988 South Asia has witnessed as many as twenty-six new governments and, for a change, all of them came to power through democratic process.[58] Unlike other domestic developments, this process is significantly influenced by the rapid political changes in Eastern Europe. Occasional internal strife and civil war situations did not inhibit India and Sri Lanka from pursuing democratic governance after independence. Other countries are less fortunate and for long democracy remained more of a utopian ideal and experiment than a reality. Popular rebellion against dictatorial regimes in Eastern Europe inspired similar movements in Nepal, Bangladesh, and to some extent Pakistan. Leaders gave in to public pressures and relinquished their autocratic and dictatorial rule in favour of popular government. In December 1990 General H. M. Ershad, who had ruled Bangladesh since March 1982, was forced out of office, paving the way for fresh elections under a neutral care-taker government headed by Chief Justice of Supreme Court Shahabuddin Ahmed.[59] The Nepalese monarch opted for a less painful course. Developments in Eastern Europe and support by key Indian political fig-ures intensified the pro-democracy struggle in the Himalayan kingdom. This took a dramatic turn in January 1990 when it transformed into a mass movement and began to threaten not only the thirty-year-long party-less system but also the survival of the monarchy. On 8 April the Palace gave in and announced the end of the party-less system, lifting the ban on political parties. Under a new constitution proclaimed on 9 November 1990, Nepal was transformed into a constitutional monarchy.[60]

The situation was somewhat different in Pakistan, where democracy was nothing more than an experiment. Except for brief intervals, military or non-democratic rule was the norm. In successfully pursuing this non-democratic governance, Islamabad enjoyed the tacit support and approval of Washington. At times the military has forged a better relationship with the US than the civilian politicians, and under the military dictatorship of General Ayub Khan (1958–68) and General Zia (1977–88) the relation-ship became stronger. A major aid recipient during the cold war years, Pakistan's military rulers could have not survived without a clear political understanding with Washington.[61] This relationship resembled Washing-ton's close ties with similar dictatorial regimes elsewhere. Notwithstanding public commitments to promoting democracy, different US administra-tions found 'friendly' dictators useful for promoting larger political goals. Internal repression and lack of legitimacy were subservient to geopolitical realities and the containment of communism was more important than democratization. By successfully exploiting the Soviet invasion of Afghanistan, General Zia not only promoted the image of Pakistan as a strategic ally of the US but also consolidated his personal stronghold over the country. He soon became as important as Ferdinand Marcos of the Philippines or the erstwhile Shah of Iran and even managed to execute the only popular leader since Mohammed Ali Jinnah without any American reprisals.

Two crucial developments threatened Zia's position. From her return to Pakistan in April 1986, Benazir Bhutto had emerged as the focus of anti-Zia agitation and a natural leader of the Movement for Restoration of Democracy (MRD). Faced with frequent agitation and protest, Zia reluc-tantly announced that elections to the National Assembly and the provin-cial assemblies would be held, but on a non-party basis, in November 1988. Meanwhile, Soviet withdrawal from Afghanistan further undermined his position. Under the four-power Geneva agreement signed in April 1988, the Soviet Union agreed to complete the pullout by the following February. General Zia thus ceased to be an important ally for the US and could be dispensed with like other Third World dictators. Under these changed circumstances on 18 August 1988, General Zia, a host of senior military officials, and the US ambassador in Islamabad were killed in a mysterious air crash. This incident could hardly have come at a more appropriate time. Zia's continued presence during and after the November election could have led to a serious internal crisis reminiscent of those of the Philippines and Romania. Without much difficulty the US was able to discard its prolonged association with dictatorship and endorse and support the re-emergence of democracy in Pakistan. In September, the judiciary which had hitherto been subservient to military rule began to assert its independence, ruling that all political parties were eligible to contest the November elections.[62] Following the elections on 16 November 1988 Ms Bhutto became the first democratically elected woman Prime Minister of an Islamic country. Though three subsequent governments have since been dismissed under controversial circumstances, the process has not lost its momentum.

Transparency of the electoral process is another sign of consolidation of democracy. Supervision of elections under a neutral caretaker government has also contributed to the democratization of Bangladesh. A non-party government headed by Chief Justice Shahabuddin conducted a free and fair election in February 1991 that saw Begum Khaleda Zia of the Bangladesh National Party (BNP) coming to power. Begum Zia's rejection of such an election contributed to prolonged political unrest during 1994–6 and the opposition boycott of general elections in early 1996. The political stalemate was defused when the new BNP-dominated parliament amended the constitution and paved the way for a neutral caretaker government to supervise parliamentary elections. In April retired Chief Justice Habibur Rahman was sworn in as head of the interim government to supervise fresh elections. This was a clear victory for the opposition, and a coalition government headed by Sheikh Hasina Wajed of the Awami League assumed office. A number of opposition politicians are looking for the same system in Pakistan where a supervisory role has been played by the army. However, demands for a neutral caretaker government frequently aired by opposition parties in India remain unfulfilled, despite election promises, although the presence of a constitutionally guaranteed Chief Election Commission does mitigate the situation. Since T. N. Seshan was appointed to this post in December 1990, the Election Commission ceased to be yet another official body in India. The Indian media and various political parties were highly critical of his personal style and autocratic behaviour. Yet Seshan conducted free, fair, and transparent elections, vigorously enforced laws concerning electoral financing, and enhanced the status and position of the Election Commission.[63]

The judicial system has also shown signs of maturity and has actively intervened in crucial national debates. Besides passing judgements on political decisions, the courts are asserting their role as legal custodian and defender of the constitution. In the case of India, they have transformed themselves as the last avenue for a disillusioned public to rein in corrupt and autocratic politicians and bureaucrats. Most of the ongoing criminal proceedings against a host of leading Indian politicians are largely due to active judicial intervention. In some countries the courts have passed landmark judgements over the constitutional validity of the powers of the executive. The democratization process enabled the judiciary in Pakistan to break out of its traditional servility to the executive. Asserting its independence on 26 May 1993 it ruled that the dismissal of Nawaz Sharif's government and dissolution of parliament by President Ghulam Ishaq Khan was unconstitutional and ordered the restoration of parliament. Though the Sharif government did not last long and Pakistan went to the polls in October, the ruling was an important step in ensuring the supremacy of the judiciary in safeguarding constitutional norms in Pakistan. In Bangladesh, the judiciary has emerged as the only body that enjoys the trust and confidence of the public. The two free and fair elections that took place in 1991 and 1996 were both conducted by caretaker governments headed by incumbent or retired judges.

A development with far-reaching consequences took place in Nepal. In June 1995 the opposition-led Nepalese Congress tabled a no-confidence motion against Prime Minister Man Mohan Adhikari. In an unprecedented move 103 of 205 Congress members signed a petition to the king demanding the formation of a new government. Rather than face impending defeat, Adhikari advised the king to dissolve parliament and order fresh elections. The king could have rejected this recommendation and explored the constitutional possibilities of forming another government. However, overruling the advice of the communist prime minister would have raised serious doubts about the king's commitment to democracy and could even have precipitated domestic unrest and anti-monarchical sentiments. So acting on this advice the king dissolved parliament and ordered fresh elections. The judiciary, however, intervened and rescued the transition to democracy. In a landmark judgement the Nepalese Supreme Court overruled King Birendra's decision and reinstated the parliament. On 28 August 1995 an eleven-member special bench of the high court declared that the recommendations of the prime minister were unconstitutional.[64] Even though in the past the king had accepted the recommendations of the

Prime Minister and dissolved parliament, the situation in June 1995 was different. Under the court ruling, the king reinstated the parliament and on 12 September a four-member cabinet headed by Sher Bahadur Deuba assumed office.

The fragility of democracy in South Asia is both an indication and outcome of military intervention and, except for India, armed forces occupy a prominent role in South Asian politics. Even in Sri Lanka the prolongation of the ethnic crisis has significantly enhanced the role of the army, especially in influencing government policy concerning Tamil separatism. The situation is acute in Pakistan. Perennial political instability enhanced the role of the military and it quickly emerged as the key player. Even the restoration of democracy in the late 1980s has not diminished its role as the final arbitrator. The military still has a large say in critical domestic and foreign policy issues. The dismissal of the Benazir government in 1990 and the downfall of the Nawaz Sharif government three years later primarily reflected the army's lack of confidence in the politicians. Furthermore, under a controversial amendment introduced by General Zia, the president was given *inter alia* the powers to appoint the chairman of the joint chiefs of staff and three armed forces chiefs. Under a democratic arrangement this unique privilege fuels and exacerbates tension between the President and Prime Minister. Both Ms Bhutto and Sharif sought to annul this contentious eighth amendment and restore control of the military to the cabinet headed by the Prime Minister. Their attempt only led to a confrontation with President Ghulam Ishaq Khan (1988–93) and Farooq Ahmed Leghani (1993–8) which partly contributed to their downfall. Likewise, the army's reluctance to endorse the imposition of martial law appear to have contributed to the eventual downfall of General Ershad.[65] In the Maldives, though Maumoon Abdul Gayoom had successively won four presidential elections since 1978, political stability of this tiny country was frequently threatened by the possibility of a military *coup*. Events took a different turn in November 1988 when a Maldivian businessman hired mercenary Tamil militants to overthrow Gayoom.[66]

Internal violence

The democratization process does not imply that South Asia has remained peaceful. Indeed, there is a strong argument that democratizing states, as opposed to stable democracies, are particularly violence prone.[67] Since early 1980s internal ethnic violence has intensified and at times has erupted into civil wars. South Asia is a cosmopolitan basket of different ethnic, cultural, religious, and social groups. The end of colonialism and emergence of new states and the process of modernization have accentuated internal contradictions. Greater social mobility, increased educational opportunities, and rapid urbanization enabled hitherto deprived segments of the population to demand a greater share of economic and political power. Geography plays a crucial role when such demands take on ethnic or religious overtones. When legitimate demands of certain sections of society are met with prolonged indifference and are treated as 'law and order' problems, the seeds are sown for protracted violence. If this sense of political neglect and alienation secures external understanding, sympathy, and support, conditions are ripe for turmoil. The intensification and prolongation of such conflicts often leads to a separatist path whereby a particular ethnic or religious community seeks to secede and form an independent national identity. One can find these traits in a number of ongoing communal conflicts in South Asia, and of course outside the region as well—the Kurdish question in the Middle East providing one obvious example.

While some older problems have died down, new ones are cropping up in different parts of the region. Though the prolonged Sri Lankan civil war draws widespread attention and interest, others cannot afford to be complacent. What began as a demand for greater protection and autonomy for the Tamil minority was soon transformed into an ethnic conflict between minority Tamils and majority Sinhalese. In a significant departure from past policy on 3 August 1995 President Chandrika Kumaratunga came out with a 'devolution package' that offered far-reaching and unprecedented concessions to the Sri Lankan Tamil population. It recognized Sri Lanka as a multi-religious, multi-lingual, and multi-cultural 'union of regions' where all communities should be given 'space to express their distinct identity'.[68] Internal opposition compelled Kumaratunga to significantly dilute the proposal and any political settlement remains as remote as it was in the early 1980s.

Continued sectarian violence in Karachi has undermined Pakistan's political cohesion, economic stability, and international confidence. The idea of *mohajirs*, 'refugees', in a state conceived as 'homeland' for Muslims of the subcontinent is an anachronism. Conflict over mohajirs, post-partition migrants from India settled in Sindh, simmered from the beginning of the independence period and took a violent turn in the mid-1980s.[69] Since its formation in March 1984 by the maverick Altaf Hussain, Mohajirs Quami Movement (National Front of Refugees, MQM) has been a dominant factor in Karachi, where they account for two-thirds of its twelve million population. It subsequently took part in the election and formation of provincial as well as national governments. However, although the MQM joined hands with Ms Bhutto in the 1988 elections, the alliance was short-lived and the MQM crossed over to the opposition.

Yet in June 1992 prolonged violence compelled Prime Minister Sharif to send the army to Karachi, a move which only alienated the mohajirs further. Following the inglorious army pullout in November 1994, Ms Bhutto reluctantly initiated a political dialogue with the MQM, a body she despised as a terrorist organization. These talks legitimized MQM and enhanced Altaf Hussain's position but do not seem to be leading towards an amicable settlement. Sectarian violence is not confined to mohajirs alone. Since the early 1990s the Shia–Sunni sectarian divide has often turned into violence and led to a series of attacks on mosques worshipped by rival supporters. The failures of political leaders and the flow and easy availability of arms during the Afghan crisis are blamed for the prolongation of the sectarian violence in Karachi and other parts of Pakistan.

At times ethnic crisis has an explicit foreign element. The questions of Sri Lankan refugees in India, Pakistani refugees in Bangladesh, Bangladeshi refugees in India, or Bhutanese refugees in Nepal, are indications of political tensions between various segments of these populations. Unprotected and easily accessible borders enable a large influx of foreigners into India. The presence of a large number of illegal Bangladeshi nationals often contributes to social and political tensions in north-eastern states in India.[70] The presence of hundreds of illegal Bangladeshi nationals in Pakistan is attributed to domestic economic hardships. Afraid of its population being outnumbered by foreigners, Nepal is keen to monitor the flow of Indian nationals into the kingdom. It seeks tight border controls to prevent the flow of criminal elements into Nepal. At the same time Kathmandu adopts a different attitude concerning the presence of people of Nepalese origin in Bhutan. The exodus of around 100,000 Bhutanese refugees into Nepal in recent years underscores the demographic nightmare of small states.[71] The presence of Sri Lankan Tamil refugees in the southern state of Tamil Nadu inevitably leads to increased Indian involvement in that ethnic conflict.[72] In the early 1990s the prevailing violence in Kashmir led to an exodus to New Delhi and other parts of northern India.

South Asia is not immune to the growing religious revivalism that is sweeping a large number of countries in the world. The most visible manifestation of this trend has been the worsening of Hindu–Muslim relations in India. The emergence of Bharatiya Janata Party (BJP) as a major force in the Indian political arena and its emphasis on *Hindutva* (Hindu-ness) posed a serious challenge to traditional Indian understanding of and commitment to secularism.[73] Though it had accepted partition, the Congress party rejected the two-nation theory, and the rise of BJP undermined this basic premiss. For a party that was decimated in the 1984 Lok Sabha elections, the rise of the BJP was extraordinary. Its electoral success in a series of national and state assembly elections implies that this growth is not an aberration but an emerging realignment.[74] The growth of BJP also coincided with the increased tension between Hindus and Muslims. Partition did not solve the problems of the Muslims of the subcontinent and since the 1970s areas with significant Muslim populations have been the scene of communal riots. Perceived Congress appeasement of fundamentalist demands on issues such as payment of alimony to divorced Muslim women and the controversial ban of Salman Rushdie's *Satanic Verses* has intensified the tension.[75] Inter-communal relations reached their nadir in December 1992 when the historic mosque at Ayodhya was destroyed by Hindu extremists.[76] This was followed by a series of communal riots in various parts of the country leading to huge loss of human life and property. The failure of the central government to foresee such an eventuality and its inability or unwillingness to take preventive measures before the destruction of the mosque was colossal. The success of the BJP in the 1998 parliamentary polls and the election of Atal Bihari Vajpayee as prime minister in March 1998 thus marks a new era in Indian politics. Its willingness to dilute or sidestep controversial and contentious issues enabled the BJP to forge a fragile coalition with a number of smaller regional parties. The ability of the party to provide a stable government, however, depends upon its willingness to adhere to national consensus and to be accommodative towards the Muslim minorities.

III. ECONOMIC LIBERALIZATION AND REGIONAL COOPERATION

Cooperation between former enemies and rivals has been one of the positive outcomes of the collapse of the East–West divide. Political and security differences have given way to economic cooperation and integration. Market and economic reforms coincided with political reforms and in varying degrees the countries of former Eastern Europe have discarded the command economy of the Soviet model and are moving towards integration into the global economy. As Gautum Sen has noted, one finds similar trends in South Asia, and the inauguration of SAARC (South Asian Association for Regional Co-operation) in December 1985 in Dacca was a major step towards regional agreement and cooperation. A number of regional factors, however, make the process slow and minimal. It would be unrealistic to think otherwise. Constituting one-fifth of global population, South Asia is one of the poorest regions of the world and accounts for only 1.3 per cent of world GDP and 3.4 per cent of global trade. This trend is likely to continue for some considerable time. It is neither an attractive

market nor a vibrant economy. Political leaders of South Asia have to confront prevailing poverty, population explosion, growing unemployment,
social inequalities, lack of basic amenities, and poor infrastructure. While
the economies of Pakistan and Sri Lanka are significant, Bangladesh,
Bhutan, Nepal, and the Maldives fall in the category of Least Developed
Countries and are extremely dependent upon external aid and assistance.
India, which accounts for 73 per cent of collective South Asian GDP, is
not an important player in international trade.[77] The projection of India
as an important player in the emerging new markets is a recent phenomenon and a result of the economic reforms and liberalization process
authored and introduced by Narasimha Rao and his technocrat-turned-
Finance Minister Manmohan Singh. It would take considerable determination and effort for India to realize fully its potential and aspirations for
a major economic power. Furthermore, India's exports to SAARC
account for only 0.03 per cent of its total exports and just 1 per cent of its
total imports.[78] Where inter-regional trade is so limited—and this picture
is reflected elsewhere in this volume—the prospects for economic integration and cooperation are poor. Except for the smaller countries, all major
powers have been hostile towards SAARC. India has traditionally viewed
the grouping as an attempt by small countries to form a common platform
against itself while Pakistan regarded it as an acceptance of Indian domination in South Asia. For Sri Lanka, SAARC is merely a consolation prize
for its inability to join the more attractive ASEAN.

At the political level, prolonged hostilities and unfriendly relations
between the two principal players have proved to be the most important
impediment to regional cooperation in South Asia. Indo-Pakistan rivalry
remains as intense as the Congress–Muslim League animosity and competition during the pre-partition years. The passage of time has not modified the
situation: as one veteran Pakistani diplomat suggested, the present state of
affairs may continue 'for another two generations'.[79] Indo-Pakistan rivalry
over issues like Kashmir have soured many meetings of multilateral and
international organizations such as the Commonwealth and the Non-
Aligned Movement. Partly to avoid similar experiences, ASEAN, as noted,
has been somewhat reluctant to upgrade Pakistan as a full dialogue partner
or to invite it to join the ARF. India's exclusion from the Organization of
Islamic Conference endows Pakistan with yet another forum in which to
build support against India. Interestingly, recent multilateral forums, such as
G15 and the Indian Ocean Initiative where New Delhi plays an important
role, have conspicuously excluded Pakistan. As a result Indo-Pakistan
rivalry has severely undermined any efforts at regional cooperation. This
political rivalry often spills over into economic interaction. Bilateral trade
between the two is extremely restricted and limited to a select number of

items. Unilateral Indian moves to bestow Most Favoured Nation status upon Pakistan have not led to any reciprocal gesture. For its part Islamabad feels that economic ties with India are unacceptable to its people while the core issue, namely the Kashmir dispute, remains unresolved. The inordinate delay in the formulation of an economic framework for SAARC and enforcement of Southern Asian Preferential Trading Arrangement (SAPTA) was largely due to the Indo-Pakistan rivalry.

Fear of Indian hegemony remains a major obstacle to regional co-operation.[80] While many regions or regional groupings contain actual or potential hegemons South Asia is perhaps unique in its domination by a single power.[81] While it is difficult to ignore this basic reality, countries of the region differ widely over India's legitimate role and influence. At one time or another, India has had serious political differences and economic disputes with all the other countries of the region and even its legitimate security concerns are seen as harbouring hegemonic pretensions. Its traditional ties with Nepal did not inhibit escalating tension and economic boycott towards the end of Rajiv Gandhi's tenure.[82] Its vital role in the formation of Bangladesh did not prevent recurrence of anti-Indian sentiments in Dacca. Its vehement opposition to the creation of a separate Tamil state in Sri Lanka and its willingness to suffer military casualties in trying to disarm Tamil militants did not endear India to Colombo. Fierce attacks against India and its policies by rival parties reach their crescendo during election campaigns and often the extent of animosity towards India becomes the barometer of nationalism.

At times fear and apprehension over India's ambitions drive these countries to look to China as a possible ally and partner. Pakistan is not the only country that exploits the Sino-Indian conflict and perceives the former as an ally in countering India. Beijing is a major arms supplier to Bangladesh and the Nepalese decision to secure arms from its northern neighbour significantly contributed to its tensions with New Delhi. Landlocked Nepal's dependence upon India for access to ports and sea routes inflames the situation further. There were apprehensions that these countries would use SAARC to air their bilateral differences with, and possibly isolate, India. Cancellation of the 1990 SAARC summit scheduled to be held in Colombo and postponement of the 1992 summit in Dacca were attributed to political differences between the hosts and India.[83] Coupled with Indo-Pakistan rivalry, apprehensions over Indian hegemony lead to another vital doubt: how can economic cooperation be developed in the absence of political understanding?[84] Under Indian pressure contentious bilateral issues were excluded from the SAARC charter. In recent years countries such as Bangladesh, Maldives, Nepal, and Pakistan have been asserting that real progress is not possible when serious disputes are unresolved. It is no coincidence that the bilateral disputes of these countries involve India and hence the latter is extremely reluctant to amend the charter.

The end of the cold war approximately coincided with the arrival of Narasimha Rao as India's prime minister. Coming amid serious of political uncertainties, social tensions and above all the brutal assassination of Congress President Rajiv Gandhi, he provided a much-needed healing touch. Inheriting the habit of previous Congress Prime Ministers such as Nehru and Mrs Gandhi, he was actively involved in foreign policy and consciously tried to mend fences with his smaller neighbours. The early 1980s had witnessed a gradual deterioration of relations between India and countries such as Bangladesh, Nepal, and Sri Lanka. An insensitive approach towards these countries generated genuine concerns of Indian hegemony. While Pakistan continued to dominate the headlines, Rao sought to rectify past misunderstandings and adopted a more generous approach towards other countries. Resolution of the vexed Tin Bigha corridor issue with Bangladesh, voluntary repatriation of Sri Lankan Tamil refugees, an agreement to develop the Mahakali river with Nepal, and the opening of border trade with Myanmar are significant moves in this direction. Besides increasing economic aid and assistance, Rao, unlike his predecessors, was willing to accord importance to smaller countries both within South Asia and outside.[85] Moreover, active Indian involvement in the regional economy seems vital for smaller powers and even a major economy like Sri Lanka is keen to attract foreign capital involvement from India. In short, despite anxieties about political hegemony, Indian involvement appears essential to the economic progress of South Asia.

SAARC took a concrete step in April 1993 when the Dacca Summit saw the signing of SAPTA, which came into effect in December 1995. Under SAPTA member countries identify items and commodities to be awarded import tariff concessions. Though these concessions are not uniform, three major economies, namely India, Pakistan, and Sri Lanka, agreed to provide special and more favourable treatment to the other four.[86] For its part Nepal introduced a unilateral across-the-board 10 per cent tariff concession on all products imported from member states. Even before SAPTA came into force, Indian leaders were hopeful that by 2000 SAPTA would be transformed into South Asian Free Trade Area (SAFTA). Such a move, it is argued, would enable unrestricted movement of goods and services among member states. Interestingly, Indian trade with Nepal and Bhutan is now totally free of tariffs.[87]

Any significant improvement in economic cooperation among South Asian states, however, will depend on the success of the ongoing economic reforms and liberalization being undertaken by various countries. In 1977

Sri Lanka became the first South Asian country to introduce substantial economic reforms. The newly elected pro-Western President J. R. Jayawardane was well suited to a market-oriented economy. Irrespective of their positions in the past, once voted to power every political party in South Asia has followed this path. Attracting foreign investment has become a constant foreign policy theme. The most significant economic reforms in South Asia were preceded by an acute foreign exchange crisis that faced the newly installed Indian government headed by Rao. While both Mrs Gandhi and her son Rajiv pursued economic reforms, the situation was different in June 1991: India was on the verge of becoming a defaulter. With precarious foreign reserves and possible loss of international confidence, Rao opted for economic liberalization. This involved devaluation of Indian currency, deregulation, dismantling of the notorious licence-*raj*, decentralization, and privatization of state industries.[88]

Notwithstanding criticism and shortcomings, economic performance was not insignificant. Growth rose to 5.3 per cent in 1994–5 as against less than 1 per cent in 1991–2; in March 1995 foreign exchange reserves reached $20 billion, and after the introduction of reforms exports went up by over 50 per cent. In spite of the political differences over issues such as non-proliferation, Indo-US economic cooperation has improved significantly. Rao hosted visits by a series of American officials and business leaders during his tenure. The reform process did not please all sections of society and it became an important factor that worked against the Congress party in various national and provincial elections after June 1992.[89] However, every Indian state, including communist-ruled West Bengal, is committed to economic reforms. The differences lie more in the nuances than in substance. The United Front government—a coalition of fourteen parties that came to power after the inconclusive May 1996 Lok Sabha elections—was committed to an investment-friendly economic policy. Likewise, the BJP-led government which came to power in March 1998, though vocal on *Swadeshi* (self-reliance) vowed to continue the economic reforms. While the need for liberalization has been reasonably settled, the direction and speed of reforms are problematic. The process is greatly influenced by the ability of these reforms to bring benefits to the economically and socially underprivileged sections of society. It seems reasonable to argue that the process is likely to be slow and laborious.

IV. CONCLUSIONS

As a region swamped with a huge population, high levels of human misery, and socio-economic underdevelopment, South Asia is not an important player in the international arena. Except for the Afghan crisis and frequent doses of internal violence it rarely draws outside attention. Even half a century after decolonization, the international influence of the region that accounts for over one-fifth of humanity remains marginal. The ability of this region to transform its position will largely depend upon the success of ongoing economic reforms currently being undertaken by various countries of South Asia. Political freedom in itself does not imply freedom from hunger, illiteracy, underdevelopment, and backwardness. The absence of economic development and power is bound to lead to the erosion of political independence of South Asia. For a long time the West was generally indifferent towards issues such as democracy, human rights, or child labour. These were made subservient to the larger political agenda of fighting the 'evil empire'. This preoccupation fell with the Berlin Wall, and the countries of South Asia are realizing that these issues are no longer dormant in the post-cold war world. Important as they are, it would be impossible and even irresponsible to ignore the political motives behind such Western demands. Though economic liberalization is essential and overdue, the success of the process will depend on South Asian, especially Indian, ability to define priorities. Basic necessities such as drinking water, education, and health facilities must take precedence over fast-food chains or designer clothes.

Democratization has been the most significant political manifestation of post-cold war South Asia. Since 1988 the region has witnessed as many as twenty-six governments elected by popular mandate. The legitimacy and accountability of the leaders are tested and validated at elections. This process is not without its share of drawbacks. Political instability and uncertainty have become a chronic disease in the region. Without charismatic leaders, popular verdicts are contested and government formation becomes a Herculean task bringing together strange bedfellows. Forced to depend upon unwieldy coalitions, many leaders find it extremely difficult to complete their full term in office. Day-to-day government survival thus takes precedence over long-term national planning. Furthermore, this process of democratization does not imply that the region is free from violence. Every major player in the region is suffering from internal violence born out of ethnic, religious, or linguistic divisions.

It is perhaps in the security arena that one witnesses the maximum impact of the end of the cold war. The post-war ideological division of Europe had little relevance for South Asia and yet it was unable to escape from the consequences of cold war politics. Rivalry between India and Pakistan brought the region closer to rival blocs. Gradually key players of the region became identified with and dependent upon the superpowers for political support, military needs, and security guarantees. For their part, driven by strategic considerations, the superpowers overlooked the internal contradictions between their political orientation and the prevailing situation in South Asia. If Moscow tolerated India's non-authoritarian political order, Washington felt more comfortable with military rulers in Pakistan. On contentious issues such as Kashmir and non-proliferation their support for their respective regional allies prevented them from seeking a negotiated settlement. Soviet withdrawal from Afghanistan significantly diminished Pakistan's role as a front-line state for Washington. There was even a fear that Pakistan would lose its erstwhile patron to its arch-rival India. The inauguration of a Clinton administration obsessed with Iran, and the re-election of Ms Bhutto, significantly changed the situation. Pakistan is perceived and projected as a modern and democratic Islamic state and a possible model for the Islamic countries of Middle East and Central Asia. Furthermore, pressures on Pakistan's nuclear programmes are gradually being replaced by American determination to establish a regional arms control arrangement in South Asia.

The end of the cold war and loss of the Soviet Union are even more acutely felt in New Delhi. Prolonged dependence upon Moscow exposed Indian vulnerability to sudden dislocation and uncertainty over the guaranteed flow of spare parts and maintenance facilities. When Russia refused to adjust the value of its currency to market conditions, the rupee-rouble trade proved to be a long-term liability. Changes in the international environment enabled Moscow to re-examine its former refusal to supply arms and technology to China. The loss of the Soviet veto exposed Indian vulnerability to Western pressures over Kashmir. However, initial hopes of forging a strategic partnership with the US proved to be unrealistic. Nearly a decade after the disintegration of the Soviet Union India is yet to redefine its position *vis-à-vis* the post-cold war world. Compelled by issues such as military supplies, it is still hopeful of rejuvenating its relationship with Moscow, while the ongoing economic reforms drive it closer to the West. Moreover, the disintegration of the Soviet Union clearly underscored the futility of building military might upon a weak economic foundation. Therefore, India's aspirations to be a major player in the international arena, with or without a seat in the Security Council, depend entirely upon its ability and willingness to discard the Soviet model of military power and strive for economic power. Unlike Germany or Japan, however, it will have to pursue this path without any protective security umbrella from Washington. Ironically, its striving for great power status by undermining the international non-proliferation regime that had failed to address its security concerns has come in an era when the centrality of nuclear weaponry is itself in question.

9

Globalization Manqué

Regional Fragmentation and Authoritarian-Liberalism in the Middle East

YEZID SAYIGH

The Middle East offers a particularly good case-study which not only brings out the practical consequences of the end of the cold war for one region of the developing world, but also raises questions about the validity of its continued definition as a region. It also reveals effectively the methodological complexity of distinguishing between the manifestations of change on the one hand and its causality on the other, in its national, regional, and international settings.[1] A related, but distinct problem is that of 'ascribing structural significance to what may be conjunctural and temporary changes, dramatic though some of them may have been'. These issues are brought out with special immediacy in the case of the striving by the Middle East state to reassert its domestic power in one externally related context—that of internationalization and liberalization—while resisting the more fundamental challenges of changing ideational values and identities in another—that of globalization.

There can be little doubt that the end of the cold war has had a dramatic impact on the Middle East. This is manifest at the strategic level, as the Gulf War and partial resolution of the Arab–Israeli conflict underline the degree to which patterns of inter-state conflict and diplomacy have been affected. The question that arises, however, is whether or not the states of the Middle East will come, any more than previously, to seek stability and prosperity by institutionalizing their regional order and promoting common norms and rules. In the second place, the end of the cold war has had a far-reaching impact on national economies and domestic politics, although it is in this regard that change is the most difficult to assess and the relationship between systemic and local processes the most subtle. Yet the apparent discrepancy between widespread expectations of political change in the Middle East in 1989–90 (at the time of the East European revolution) and subsequent reality is deceptive, since it obscures the depth of the structural crisis facing states in the region. This crisis, which is often discussed in terms of the impact of globalization on local political, economic, social, and cultural institutions, may yet necessitate fundamental changes in those institutions and in all cases is likely to cause deep social *anomie* and political instability.

The purpose of this chapter is to outline the main strategic, economic, and political changes in the Middle East, and to account for the linkages between them. It argues, first, that a combination of external and internal factors has reinforced the fragmentation of the Middle East state system and further undermined prospects for regional cooperation or integration in the security, economic, and political spheres. The chapter then examines the record of economic liberalization, before analysing the process of political liberalization. In both cases the focus is on the state, since that is the level at which management of the domestic and external environments is conducted, criticism of the conventional focus in academic literature on the Third World state notwithstanding.[2] This allows consideration in the conclusion of the extent to which changes in the region can be directly attributed to the end of the cold war, and of the assumptions about the relationship between the international system and its regional and national units, particularly with regard to the impact of globalization on the nation-state and domestic structures of political power.

I. REGIONAL SECURITY AND THE LIMITS TO COOPERATION

The most immediate, and dramatic, effects of the end of the cold war for the Middle East came at the strategic level. Nowhere was this brought home with greater force than in the Gulf, where the Iraqi invasion of Kuwait in August 1990 not only led to massive military intervention by an unprecedented US-led international coalition, but also set the stage for the successful relaunch of the Arab–Israeli peace process. The legitimation of a permanent American military presence in the region and parallel assertion of US political and economic influence, the relegation of Soviet (and then Russian) interests to subordinate status, the deep divisions among the Arab states, and the initiation of formal diplomatic and commercial ties between a growing number of them and Israel reflected the sea-change in the strategic landscape.

More to the point, sweeping strategic changes have altered fundamentally the context within which the Middle East state system has operated since 1945. The implications for regional cooperation and integration are

especially pertinent in a purportive new world order characterized at the
security level by growing access to destabilizing military technologies and
enhanced ability to project power, at the economic level by intensifying
competition (including the formation of regional trading blocs) and interdependence, and at the political level by increasing recourse to ethnicity,
nationalism, and religion for mobilizing purposes as the social crisis
acquires cultural expression. Elsewhere, one response has been to upgrade
regionalism—witness the launch of the EU, MERCOSUR, and NAFTA
or the revival of ECOWAS and even the OAU—but Middle East governments remained unable in the 1990s either to adapt existing multilateral
institutions at the regional and subregional levels, or to devise new ones
better able to meet common challenges and seize opportunities. This was
due largely to the impact of three factors: the special role of the US, particularly in relation to security issues; economic trends; and the conflicting
foreign policy agendas of individual states. (Domestic constraints will be
touched on later.)

The United States: Restrained hegemon

Speaking towards the end of February 1990, only months before launching the invasion of Kuwait, Iraqi president Saddam Hussein warned that
the erosion of the USSR 'as the key champion of the Arabs in the context
of the Arab-Zionist conflict and globally' left the US as 'the country that
exerts the greatest influence on the region, on the Gulf and its oil' and
allowed it to 'consolidate its superiority as an unrivalled superpower'. His
conclusion was that the US would penetrate the Arab world further and
commit 'follies against the interests and national security of the Arabs',
unless they utilized their various assets to defy it. Sweeping global change
posed a challenge, but equally it offered the Arab states an opportunity to
unite their forces and strengthen solidarity between them.[3]

In the event, the Gulf crisis divided Arab ranks deeply, perhaps irrevo-
cably, and confirmed the hegemonic position of the US regionally.
However, although seeking since then both to retain the strategic advantage and maintain regional stability, the general effect of US policy has
been to impede movement towards the institutionalization of regional
security and cooperation. This is neither to overlook the obstacles presented by local actors, nor to attribute deliberate obstructionism to successive US administrations, but rather to emphasize the degree to which
the most important external power has none the less reinforced the impediments to regional organization since the end of the cold war. It has contributed to this outcome in part by adopting axis-building and bilateral
alliances as the basis for regional security maintenance, and in part by

discouraging the formation of broadly based multilateral institutions that might place allies at a relative disadvantage and grant actual or potential rivals significant strategic and commercial gains.

Axis-building and bilateral alliances were not typical of US policy initially. Speaking in September 1990, for example, the then Secretary of State James Baker preferred creating 'a regional security structure that is able to contain the aggressive tendencies of a leader like [Saddam Hussein]'.[4] He later endorsed the agreement reached in Damascus in March 1991 by the eight Arab member states of the anti-Iraq coalition to form the nucleus of a wider Arab security framework, while Assistant Secretary of State John Kelly confirmed the US position as 'encouraging close defence cooperation among the states of the region'.[5] The Bush administration's striving for regional consensus was also evident in its determination to involve all but the most hostile regional parties in the multilateral working groups that were set up in parallel to the bilateral Arab–Israeli peace talks.[6] However, the preference for consensus-building did not survive the transition to Clinton. In part this revealed growing awareness that, even as 'the dominant power in the region', the US has 'reduced military and economic means to influence events'.[7] It is also partly a reflection of the influence, at times described as a stranglehold, of the pro-Israel lobby within the administration.[8] At a minimum, resource constraints have made it less feasible for the US to promote actively the institutionalization of regional security and cooperation in the Middle East. US policy equally reflects decreasing interest in the region, given the decline in its strategic importance following the end of the cold war and its relatively limited attractiveness as a target for overseas investment. Curiously, this extends to the flow of oil and global energy security, towards which the US has shown a distinct lethargy despite according it a high priority among what remain of its key policy objectives in the Middle East.[9]

Also encouraging the trend towards axis-building is the absence of a serious challenge from other global powers. Ironically, the realization that too much causal importance was attributed to Soviet policy in the region during the cold war has weakened any residual incentive for the US to invest material resources and political credit in enhancing or establishing Middle Eastern organizations to promote collective security and cooperation.[10] Indeed, it suggests that there is a minimal political cost attached to axis-building, since friendly local actors can be tied into bilateral alliances while hostile actors lack a strategic alternative in the absence of geopolitical competition from the USSR (or any other global power) and can therefore be safely excluded. The trend towards placing relations with a few key allies (especially Israel) above others was reinforced by a Republican-dominated Congress determined to cut foreign assistance substantially and generally hostile to the commitment of US resources globally.

There have been further consequences of the declared elevation under the Clinton administration of US–Israeli ties, described routinely since 1966 as a 'special relationship', above those with any other state in the Middle East.[11] One was to allow Israel to escape pressure to accede to the nuclear Non-Proliferation Treaty when it was indefinitely extended in 1995, despite the damage to US–Egyptian relations and the resultant suspension of the multilateral working group on arms control and regional security. Another was the emergence in 1996 of an axis comprising Israel and Turkey (and tacitly Jordan), with the implicit objective of isolating Syria and weakening its position in the peace talks with Israel.[12] The focus on bilateral peace treaties and associated military provisions between Israel and each of its Arab neighbours has left the Jewish state in control of security management in its immediate region, and undermined its incentive to concede this role to a multilateral framework. For the Arab states, conversely, the costs of pursuing a course antithetical to US interests have become prohibitive, resulting in at least tacit acquiescence with US policy on most issues.[13]

US policy has accordingly had adverse effects, both direct and indirect, for regional organization in the Middle East. An obvious example is the designation as 'pariah' or 'rogue' several Arab states—Libya, Iraq, and Sudan—and Iran. The leading US role at various times since 1990 in initiating and maintaining United Nations sanctions against the first three underlined the ineffectiveness of the League of Arab States (LAS), to which they belong, and similarly brought into question the standing of the Arab Maghreb Union (AMU), to which Libya also belongs. In addition, the US policy of 'dual containment' against Iraq and Iran, announced in May 1993, impeded any inclination among the southern Gulf states to set up a regional forum for dialogue with their ostracized northern neighbours.[14] This confirms the move away from the stance taken by Baker during the Gulf War, that 'no regional state should be excluded from these [security] arrangements. Post-war Iraq could have an important [role] to play. And so could Iran as a major power in the Gulf.'[15] The Bush administration failed to pursue this approach, but its successor subsequently sought with even greater vigour 'to keep Iran artificially separate from the Gulf states'.[16]

Relations with the member states of the Gulf Cooperation Council (GCC)—comprising the six 'petro-monarchies' of the southern Gulf—offer another instance of the adverse, if unintentional, impact of US policy on regional organization in the Middle East. Starting in September 1991 the US, followed by Britain and France, concluded a series of bilateral defence, basing, and arms acquisition agreements with individual GCC member states. Assured of active intervention when needed, the GCC attached less significance not only to regional security arrangements with other Arab states, but also to collective defence among its own members.[17] Massive arms contracts have long acted as an 'insurance premium' by recycling petrodollars and supporting Western defence industry jobs—Saudi Arabia, Kuwait, and the United Arab Emirates alone accounted for orders worth US$44.2 billion in 1990–4.[18] Admittedly, the ineffectiveness of the GCC as a security alliance is largely due to the structural weaknesses—military and demographic—of its member states, and to their perception that the best guarantors of their security remain the US and its Western allies. This is graphically reflected in the continuing inability of GCC member-states to coordinate military policy (including arms acquisitions and compatibility) and in their repeated refusal, even in the wake of the Gulf War, to consider, let alone implement, an Omani proposal for a 100,000-strong deterrence force under unified command. Yet the US arguably reinforced the tendency among them to seek bilateral, rather than collective security arrangements, in part through its effort to capitalize on its role during the Gulf crisis to secure multiple military and commercial contracts and deny the lucrative Gulf market to its main Western competitors.

Economic and political competition with Western allies was also a factor in the negative attitude of both the Bush and the Clinton administrations towards proposals, endorsed in the early 1990s by some European governments, for the replication of the Helsinki process and the construction of a Conference on Security and Cooperation in the Mediterranean and the Middle East (CSCM).[19] For the same reason the US consistently opposed the institutionalization of the multilateral working groups formed as part of the Arab–Israeli peace process (although their format closely resembles the Helsinki-type 'baskets'), and insisted on limiting the role of the European Union (EU) and United Nations.[20] The EU appeared to gain a significant advantage by assuming responsibility for the multilateral working group on economic development, but the US made little effort to pursue the establishment of a proposed regional bank for economic cooperation and development. Instead it encouraged the Middle East/North Africa Summit—a loosely structured convention of government and private sector representatives that has met annually since 1994—prompting the EU to launch a parallel Euro-Mediterranean dialogue and to devote ECU4.7 billion of grant assistance and a similar amount of loans from the European Investment Bank in 1996–9 to the establishment of a 'Euro-Mediterranean Economic Area'.[21]

Despite commercial competition, the US has not faced a serious political challenge from the EU, which until the late 1990s effectively foreswore an independent Middle East policy.[22] The same is largely true of Russia, which, despite adopting a more activist Middle East policy after 1993, generally sought to avoid alienating the US and to benefit economically from the region.[23] The successor states of the former Soviet Union and Eastern Europe were generally more interested in deepening ties with Israel as a means of access to US and West European markets and to Western Jewish and US investment, than in promoting regional organization in the Middle East.[24] Alternatively, Russia has focused on its 'near-abroad', competing with the US particularly in the Caucasus and Central Asia, which was set to emerge in the early twenty-first century as a major energy-producing region and potential rival to the Middle East in strategic importance. Yet in seeking contradictory political and commercial goals, US policy has led to increased economic penetration of the region by other global powers. A case in point is the presidential ban in 1995 on all trade and investment in Iran, which abandoned that market to European competitors.[25] Russia and China, neither a real challenger to the US, were also ready to risk its displeasure in order to sell weapons and nuclear technology to Iran, partly so as to secure gas and oil supplies, and by 1998 were diverging openly (along with France) from US policy towards Iraq.[26] Indeed, the growth of commercial, rather than political, competition reflects increased economic pressures since the end of the cold war and shapes the attitude of Middle East governments towards regionalism.

Economic internationalization, regional fragmentation

Four external factors account for the increased economic pressure on Middle East states since the end of the cold war, and affect moves towards regional organization. One is the sharp decline in the strategic 'rent' they can obtain from advanced industrialized countries, affecting not only the supply of free or cheap arms, but also the extension of budgetary assistance and interest-free or 'soft' economic development loans. To make things worse, second, the successor states of the Soviet Union and Eastern Europe have turned from suppliers of assistance into competitors for foreign direct investment and aid from OECD countries. Third is the double negative impact of the launch of the EU: on the one hand the European economies of the Mediterranean littoral have become more oriented to the north than the south since 1992, while on the other the structure of trade agreements has treated Middle East partners individually but the Europeans as a bloc, strengthening the bargaining position of the latter group and enabling them to maximize their commercial advantage.[27] The fourth factor is the impact of depressed oil prices, which, although not directly attributable to the end of the cold war and indeed predating it, has become more marked since the massive expenditure of the Gulf War.

These factors might have been expected to prompt Middle East states to pursue regionalism more actively. The breakthroughs in the Arab–Israeli peace process, moreover, raised the possibility of building on the peace dividend and extending such arrangements beyond the Arab states to include Israel. Additionally, the fact that the US, while of the greatest military and strategic significance to most states in the region, is of less economic and commercial importance than Europe, suggests that it does not offer a long-term alternative to a regional approach.[28] Elsewhere, the economic consequences of the end of the cold war and the challenges of global economic competition and interdependence have led to the formation of new regional trade blocs or renewed interest in existing treaties and agencies. Indeed, the Arab states formally launched a free trade area on 1 January 1998, raising hopes in some quarters that the Arab Common Market established in 1964 might be revived. Yet the trend towards regionalism in the Middle East appears weak, and at times to move in the opposite direction. External factors have tended instead to accentuate structural biases in national economies, further impeding any inclination seriously to promote or institutionalize regional cooperation, let alone integration.

If anything, it can be argued that external developments have underscored the virtual absence of a regional economy, even in relation to the twenty-one members of the League of Arab States. It is striking that for this group, which has one of the highest ratios of imports and exports to GDP in the world, intra-Arab trade as a whole has remained stubbornly below 10 per cent of total external trade. Only for the smaller Arab economies has regional trade been significant, but this is true neither for the larger non-oil economies (such as Egypt or Morocco) nor for the oil-exporting ones. Furthermore, the greater part by far of all Arab (and non-Arab Middle Eastern, for that matter) external trade is with OECD countries, a pattern mirrored in the concentration of technological, military, and strategic ties. Oil wealth, which briefly gave rise to what might loosely be called an Arab 'oil economy', ultimately integrated national economies even more tightly into the global economy, rather than a putative regional one, by fuelling external debt, consumerism, and industrial and technological dependency.[29] The decline of oil revenues since 1982 has severely reduced the once-extensive cross-border flows of labour and capital within the region; in any case, even at their peak in the 1970s, the often personal manner in which official transfers were made, monetary controls, and the weakness of capital markets in the region did little to encourage the development of regional financial institutions and networks.

The incompatibility of economic (and political) systems has acted as an additional impediment to regional cooperation and integration, as have the generally poor state of intra-regional infrastructure and a combination of tariff barriers, remaining financial controls, and overlap rather than complementarity in agricultural and industrial output. Overlap has moreover been an obstacle rather than a cause for healthy competition, because it is between state-subsidized and tariff-protected sectors. Economic and financial liberalization measures, including the lifting of foreign exchange restrictions and currency inconvertibility, may encourage the return of flight capital and eventually improve the prospects for regional integration. However, the relative tardiness of integration with global financial markets—compared to other developing regions—means that many local economies remain unable sufficiently to utilize trade as a channel for the mobilization of investable resources.[30] Besides, some national governments remain fearful that integration will simply skew the distribution of costs and benefits further and exacerbate the skills and brain drain, since development and investment capital (as well as labour) move naturally towards more developed areas and better infrastructure. Governments also lack the political will generally to risk job losses.[31] Yet the real obstacle to integration lies in their perception that the procedural and operational requirements of regional political and economic institutions threaten their national sovereignty.[32]

Major differences in resources (such as oil), product diversification, per capita income, and state capacity have moreover led to significant subregional variations and weakened self-identification with a wider collectivity. This is evident among the Gulf petro-monarchies, yet while organizations such as the GCC have achieved modest cooperation in some areas, there has been little integration at the subregional level.[33] This is also true of the AMU, formed in February 1989, which has been hamstrung by the conflict between the national political agendas and economic systems of its members, resulting in resistance to free movement, monetary unification, and implementation of the agreed objectives of establishing free-trade zones, a common market, and joint economic projects. As a result of such disincentives and the disparate opportunities for investment, government-backed assistance agencies based in the Gulf, such as the Kuwait Fund for Development and the Islamic Development Bank, have increasingly targeted their concessional lending towards non-Arab developing economies, including Turkey and the Central Asian republics.[34] Similarly, the apparently healthy degree of diversification in the Middle East economy as a whole (in terms of production, export markets, and import sources) is belied by wide disparities in product diversification and trade openness at the level of individual economies, reflected, for example, in the concentration of EU trade relations with the Gulf and Maghreb (and with Israel and Turkey) and their decline with other Arab states.[35]

What emerges clearly is that Middle East states have responded, individually and separately, to the challenges of the post-cold war era and globalization with *sauve qui peut* strategies. Arguably this is not new, but it has become more salient as changes in the external economic environment—such as the loss of preferential access to certain markets—have brought long-standing structural defects in national economies increasingly to the fore.[36] In this context some medium non-oil Arab economies have discovered that the end of the cold war and developments in the global economy have not left them cornered, contrary to expectation, and they have therefore been able to avoid radical shifts in their foreign policies and regional relations. A good example is Syria, which has managed the crisis by combining controlled commercial liberalization at home and modest oil revenues, on the one hand, with the revival of economic and trade relations with Russia and East Europe and the expansion of ties with China and North Korea, on the other.[37] Jordan, conversely, has sought relief through the bilateral economic agreement signed with Israel in 1994 and modest debt write-offs and rescheduling by the US and Europe. The smaller economies may still be keenest to integrate—because the limited size of their domestic markets restricts import substitution and requires active export links to achieve economy of scale—but as the Syrian and Jordanian examples show, the availability of external palliatives has further inhibited moves towards regionalism.

The unwillingness of some capital-scarce economies in the region to commit themselves to an institutionalized framework for regional exchanges reveals a relative gains syndrome: they are reluctant to enter into multilateral arrangements because they expect the greater rewards to accrue to other member states.[38] For others, the priority in the post-cold war era is to minimize losses, rather than maximize gains.[39] The most graphic reflection of this trend was the unification of the two Yemens in 1990, as the northern government contemplated the failure of the Arab Cooperation Council (ACC), which it had helped found a year earlier, and its southern counterpart faced the bleak economic and strategic outlook resulting from the cessation of Soviet aid.[40] The combination of political rifts and economic retrenchment in the oil-rich economies has severely circumscribed the rent factor in inter-Arab relations, moreover, as highlighted by the evident lack of interest among the GCC petro-monarchies in activating the 'six-plus-two' alliance announced with Egypt and Syria in March 1991 or in channelling substantial aid towards either state. The decline of rent also explains the disappointment, for example, of

Jordanian and Yemeni hopes that membership in a regional body such as the ACC would ensure continued budgetary assistance.[41] In such a situation capital-scarce economies, in particular, have arguably become even less likely to replace traditional trading partners or seek major new sources of investment and assistance outside the OECD countries. This, coupled with the perception of US economic primacy and domination in international financial institutions, also explains Arab willingness to accept the unstructured 'talking shop' offered by the US-sponsored MENA annual summit, rather than emulate the European experience in regional institution-building.

The preceding comments apply mainly to the Arab states, but are supported by the counter-examples of Israel, Turkey, and Iran. Israel reaped substantial economic dividends in the wake of signing peace accords with the Palestine Liberation Organization and Jordan in 1993–4. The lifting of the secondary and tertiary commercial boycott by most Arab states proved the least significant reward, in fact, compared to a 21 per cent increase in trade with East Asia in the first year and the prospect of a long-delayed association agreement being ratified by the EU.[42] As foreign minister and then as prime minister, Shimon Peres may have envisaged a Middle East zone of 'cooperation and prosperity', and Israeli businessmen and economists may have hoped to wed Israeli technology to Arab capital and labour, but the reality is that Israel has no vital need for regional economic cooperation and integration, let alone a shared institutional framework with its neighbours.[43] Turkey, though experiencing far less of a boom than Israel in the early 1990s and faced with capital constraints and the severe social and material costs of structural adjustment and Kurdish insurrection, similarly remained more interested in deepening ties with the EU than with the Middle East to its south. Indeed, it also appeared more interested in the Central Asian republics and in drawing them into the Economic Cooperation Organization (ECO) formed with Iran and Pakistan to replace the moribund Regional Cooperation Development (RCD, established in 1964).[44] Much the same is true of Iran, which has reoriented a major portion of its external trade and economic relations towards Russia and also sought a role in Central Asia through bilateral agreements, the ECO, and Caspian Sea grouping, in response to US exclusionism and Arab ostracism in the Gulf.[45]

The foreign policy agenda: Reluctant regional partners

As the latter examples suggest, political disputes continue to bedevil relations between Middle East states. Much as in the case of economic pressures, the political factors that might have prompted Middle East states to pursue more effective regional cooperation and integration amidst the dramatic changes in the strategic environment have instead only reinforced their divergence. The first of these factors is the change in the notional boundaries of the Middle East, drawing the former Soviet republics of Central Asia into the politics of its northern tier and restructuring in particular the regional alignments of the three key non-Arab states, Iran, Turkey, and Israel. A particular reflection of this shift is the debate about the identity of the desired regional order: should it be Arab, Middle Eastern, or Mediterranean? By posing challenges, second, these factors highlight the often divergent foreign policy agendas of the Arab states and their inability to develop common responses or truly effective regional organizations. Lastly, Arab attitudes additionally reveal the continuing impact of the policies of the main global powers towards the region.

In the first instance, Central Asia and the Caucasus have been the main focus of shifts in the regional policies of Turkey and Iran since the end of the cold war. The dissolution of the USSR provoked immediate competition between the two countries for strategic and commercial advantage. In the Turkish case the eastward turn was partly a response to reduced prospects in the post-cold war era of joining the EU, due to demographic, cultural, and economic impediments.[46] Caution subsequently replaced early, fanciful notions of regional influence based on Turkic ethnic solidarity, and Turkey remains primarily westward-looking.[47] Its trade with the Middle East has declined (while that with the OECD has grown), and relations with its southern neighbours have focused mainly on security issues. Water-sharing, Kurdish rebellion, and oil bring it into constant interaction with Syria and Iraq, but this is usually a source of tension, and the only southward relationship that was institutionalized to any degree after the end of the cold war was the emerging military axis with Israel. Growing Iranian interest in the former Soviet republics, conversely, was the result of a foreign policy shift from the 'neither East, nor West' tenet of the Islamic revolution to a 'both North and South' orientation.[48] Iranian fear of Soviet military presence on the northern border was replaced with a dual policy of political and economic engagement in the less-developed Central Asia and Caucasus and closer ties with industrialized Russia. Yet this only underlines the irony that Iranian foreign policy is now based to a significant degree on a cold war tactic: using Russia to balance and neutralize US and other Western pressure.[49]

Unlike Turkey and Iran, the principal arena for Israeli regional politics has remained the Middle East as conventionally defined, especially the Eastern Mediterranean. The end of the cold war and the outcome of the Gulf conflict fundamentally undermined the utility of war as an instrument of policy in the hands of its Arab rivals, while the relaunch of the peace process opened previously unthinkable prospects for Israeli membership in formal regional associations along with Arab states.[50] Yet this outlook was impeded by the Israeli preference, especially under the right-wing nationalist government of Benjamin Netanyahu that came to power in May 1996, for power politics and axis-building, reflected among other things in military cooperation agreements with Turkey and the putative, if troubled, alliance with Jordan under the joint US umbrella. In this sense Israel proved to have, much like Turkey, little real interest in regional institution-building. The main determinant of its foreign policy—again much as in the case of Turkey and, in a contrary manner, Iran—remains the state of relations with the US, around which it patterns its regional ties.

However, the ambivalence of non-Arab neighbours should not obscure the reluctance or at times contradictory role of the Arab states, which have longer collective experience of Middle East multilateral institutions and arguably exert the determining influence in moves towards regional cooperation and integration. A fundamental obstacle remains their unwillingness to compromise on national sovereignty in any way; indeed, most governments are unwilling to cede to regional organizations the kind of powers they refuse to allow domestic institutions.[51] A particularly telling example of this is the lack of any formal mechanisms for dispute-arbitration or conflict-resolution within the framework of the League of Arab States. The outcome was most graphically displayed during the Gulf crisis; the League proved similarly unable to respond when asked by the UN to play a role in Somalia in 1992, nor did it mediate effectively in the Yemeni civil war of 1994. Nor was it able to play an effective role in resolving the disputes that left three of its members—Iraq, Libya, and Sudan—under international sanctions. Certainly little effort has been made by the Arab states to restructure their collective international relations, 'by developing new institutions, norms, and rules'.[52] Thus nothing came of the charter for cooperation and security proposed by the League in March 1995, which called for a court of justice to resolve inter-Arab disputes, a peacekeeping force, and a parliamentary body.[53] Further indications of the low standing of the League are the failure of some member states to pay budget dues, and repeated consideration since 1990 of its formal dissolution. In this context the LAS decision in June 1997 to soften the blockade against Libya, and the decision by most members to boycott the US-sponsored MENA summit in November and to oppose US-led punitive action against Iraq during the weapons inspections crisis of early 1998, point not to collective policy-making but rather to a collection of individual responses to domestic pressures and a low-key return to balancing politics.

Arab subregional groupings have not, however, offered a viable alternative to the LAS. This is partly because they have been established in response to existing or developing dangers—political, military, or economic—with the primary aim of enhancing the security of domestic regimes, rather than to promote the declared objectives of mutual co-operation for development.[54] The divergent foreign policy agendas of individual member states, which have in turn been influenced by the policies of the global powers, may equally have been at fault. Even the most successful subregional grouping, the GCC, was unable to build on the common vulnerability of its member states after the Gulf War to co-ordinate foreign policy towards Iraq and Iran, let alone promote collective security. The compatibility of their political systems has ensured neither internal cohesion nor the formulation of a common foreign and defence policy; at times only the preponderance of Saudi Arabia has contained the damaging effects of relatively minor territorial disputes between neighbours such as Qatar and Bahrain. Distrust of other Arab states and the evident superiority of Western strategic, logistic, and military support moreover explain the stillbirth of another subregional grouping, the Damascus Declaration or 'six-plus-two' alliance formed in March 1991 by the GCC and Gulf War partners Egypt and Syria.

Much the same can be said of the AMU, which was motivated primarily by the common sense of economic vulnerability among the Maghrebi states (and secondarily by a wish to contain Libya). Yet it, too, has foundered on the incompatibility of the economic and political systems of its member states, and on their equal unwillingness to compromise on national sovereignty and security.[55] Conversely, the lack of shared threat perceptions or sufficient reciprocal benefits helps explain the failure of the short-lived ACC (1989–90), a curious combination of geographically and politically disparate states. Thus Egypt, which resented Iraqi primacy in the subregional grouping, sought instead to confirm the League of Arab States as the vehicle for asserting its own regional stature.[56] Similarly, fear of Israeli economic and strategic domination explains Egyptian (and other Arab) opposition to inclusion of the Jewish state in Arab multilateral institutions despite the progress of the peace process (a position shared, for reasons more to do with Islamic legitimacy, by Saudi Arabia).[57] It is in this context, too, that the dispute over Israeli non-accession to the NPT and support for the Palestinian Authority have been used as means to reassert Egypt's regional leadership and to compensate for the erosion of its strategic importance following the end of the cold war, its inability to promote itself as a guardian of Gulf security, and the loss of its role as a key broker in the Arab–Israeli peace process.[58] Yet dependence on US annual aid and goodwill in international financial institutions has demonstrably limited Egyptian ability to incur the costs of the sort of foreign policy initiatives required to assert regional leadership.

The preceding survey confirms that any assumption that the end of the cold war would necessarily lead to regionalist initiatives in the Middle East is questionable and lacks empirical evidence. The passing of bipolarity and relaxation of systemic constraints at the international level have if anything enabled regional actors to realign more freely, and permitted strains within existing structures to come to the fore. Multilateral institutions in the region were not strong at any time during the cold war; the subsequent transition in the international system, coupled with growing economic challenges, has led to increased fluidity in regional alignments. The fact that the more pressing threats are increasingly diffuse in nature—emanating from global processes and societal *anomies*, and often taking cultural expression—makes the deterrent alliances of the past less relevant. This is even more the case where the US and other global powers maintain a ceiling on inter-state conflict, effectively suspending the unifying effect that external threats exerted previously. Ironically, it follows that the regional relations of most Middle East states remain largely subordinate to, although not derivative from, their ties to the global powers. However, the conclusion that systemic factors are more determining than regional or domestic ones must be suspended until the implications of economic and political liberalization in the Middle East states have been assessed.

II. ECONOMIC LIBERALIZATION

Significant as the strategic repercussions of the end of the cold war have been for the Middle East, the most pervasive consequence has arguably been to propel virtually all states in the region into varying degrees of economic liberalization. A substantial number had in fact already initiated reforms considerably before the fall of the Berlin Wall, not least in response to the decline in oil-based wealth or transfers, but the passing of superpower rivalry imparted new energy to the process, breaking the resistance of some governments to serious reform and offering others the opportunity to implement structural adjustment programmes with less risk of political instability. The conclusion of the Uruguay round of GATT and establishment of the World Trade Organization (WTO) moreover highlighted the continuing structural distortions of trade in many Middle East countries, despite its status as one of the world's most globalized regions in conventional terms of 'trade openness'. In this environment even oil-rich Arab states have been compelled to adopt austerity measures and greater budgetary discipline, whether due to the financial burden of the Gulf War (GCC member states) or to international sanctions (Iraq and Libya). The crucial point for all in the region is that the restructuring of national economies poses a direct challenge to the function and nature of the state, at a time when the meaning of sovereignty is already under question as a result of globalization.

Crisis of capital

The economic impact of the end of the cold war has been most acute for those Middle East states that were heavily dependent on 'strategic rent'. However, most economies in the region suffer from intensifying competition for external capital flows (whether in the form of aid or investment) from emerging markets in other regions. Indeed, a particular irony is that the successor republics of the former Soviet Union and the countries of East Europe have not only ceased to be sources of economic assistance and credit, but have become direct competitors for official and commercial transfers from OECD countries. The latter group have moreover reduced foreign aid, placing Middle East recipients in direct competition with each other. This has necessitated a shift from accommodational or international strategies—in which local societies and economies were spared the full burden of social, foreign, and defence policies—to a restructural one—in which substantial changes must be made to economic policy and to social alliances in order to increase domestic resource extraction.[59] Yet liberalization has revealed basic weaknesses in many national economies, and has moreover been slowed in some countries by opposition from societal coalitions, which confront the alliances that have similarly emerged between domestic and external business interests. The outcome of such contests has varied, but in all cases the state has shown a striking ability to adapt and modify its economic role. Indeed, the experience of liberalization to date suggests that many Middle East governments still see it primarily as a means of crisis management and avoiding financial collapse.

The nature and scale of the challenge facing Middle East economies are evident in the problem of assuring capital flows. The region received very high flows in 1970–90, with the net inflow averaging 16 per cent of Gross National Product (GNP) for the Arab countries of the Eastern Mediterranean, for example.[60] Indeed, for several economies this was a more important source of foreign exchange than exports of goods and services. However, these flows were accompanied by equally high levels of debt and capital flight, reaching 80 per cent and 120 per cent of regional GNP respectively by 1991. By way of comparison, in Latin America the same ratios were only one-half and one-third these levels.[61] Furthermore, most Middle East debt is bilateral, and so Brady-style multilateral initiatives offer little relief, and the trend is to seek debt write-offs instead. Economic liberalization poses an added pressure, since it strikes at the ability of Middle East states to control prices and to tax external trade, upon which many are dependent for revenue. Political disputes between states in the region and declining oil wealth have meanwhile led to a sharp drop in intra-regional flows—in the form of remittances from expatriate labour and official budgetary assistance—which previously provided an important means of relieving balance of payments deficits.

Economic growth has been difficult in these circumstances, especially for countries with serious debt overhang and resultant high service obligations, such as Syria and Jordan. The decline of official transfers (whether from within the region or from global powers) has greatly increased the importance of foreign direct investment (fdi) and domestic savings abroad. However, the average annual flow of private fdi flows to the Middle East actually dropped from 2.3 per cent of world totals for 1984–9 to a mere 1.5 per cent in 1990–5, with only $3.2 billion entering the region out of $315 billion world-wide in 1995.[62] As significant is the fact that the Middle East performed poorly even in comparison to the rest of the developing world, attracting only $2.7 billion, or 3.2 per cent, of the $84 billion in private investment flows to the latter group in 1994.[63] This modest performance is hardly surprising given the reluctance of flight capital—estimated variously at between $350 billion and $800 billion, at least half of which emanates from GCC states—to return to the region. Furthermore, such capital as has returned has generally been directed into speculative activities offering quick profit, such as purchasing real estate or financing luxury imports, rather than invested in productive enterprises.[64] This has been due in part to the slow pace and modest scale of privatization, with the region accounting, for example, for only 3 per cent of the $130 billion raised from sell-offs in infrastructure in the developing countries in 1988–95. The pace of privatization in some Middle East countries picked up in the mid-1990s, but World Bank data still showed the combined value of actual sales in infrastructure since 1984, coupled with those officially in the pipeline as of 1997, at under $9 billion, compared with a world total of $649 billion.[65]

The low levels of investment in productive sectors and of returns on privatization are partly a reflection of the shallowness of capital markets in much of the region. Of the non-oil economies in the Middle East only Israel and, albeit to a considerably lesser degree, Turkey have been able to raise much capital locally. Another indication of this problem is the modest capitalization of stock exchanges and financial markets, several of which were opened or relaunched in the early 1990s.[66] The weakness of private capital, the result of decades of massive state intervention in the economy, has led paradoxically to two unwanted consequences in the context of liberalization. One is the concentration of privatized stock in the hands of a few, large capitalists, resulting in oligarchy. An acute, if extreme, example of this is the experience of the sweeping Iraqi privatization programme of 1988–90, which 'simply meant the transfer of public monopolies to private monopolies'.[67] The second consequence is to increase foreign ownership of privatized stock, provoking a nationalist backlash in Turkey and Egypt, among others. Sensitive to the charge that they are selling their countries to foreign capital, some governments have set limits on foreign ownership, although this has provoked criticism from international financial institutions and creditors and resulted in undercapitalization of privatized stock. The fact that many existing private companies are family-owned further complicates the raising of capital in the context of Middle East financial systems, in which stockmarkets and competitive credit facilities and interest rates are not yet the norm.[68]

Private sector: Entrepreneur or parasite?

The question of capital reveals additional obstacles to liberalization in the Middle East, relating to the economic position and operation of the private sector. One obstacle is its focus on commerce and construction, even in the Gulf, where private capital is readily available. This is because risk is seen as lowest and return as highest in such activities, in contrast to productive enterprises and infrastructure.[69] The pattern is partly due to a heritage of nationalization of industry and banking and state appropriation of surplus wealth from agriculture. As the case of the Gulf petro-monarchies shows, however, it is equally due to the parasitic relationship between the private and public sectors, as the former benefits from the latter's ability to award contracts and maintain protectionist tariffs. Indeed, the private sector, long battered into political submission and dependent on the state for market creation and access, has not sought privatization across the board, preferring instead to maintain its privileged, if restricted position.[70] For their part governments in non-oil economies have found it politically and financially rewarding (at least initially) to allow controlled liberalization of commerce, since increased imports bring rises in customs revenue. Indeed, the Egyptian model of *infitah istihlaki* (an 'open door' policy on the import of consumer goods), rather than *infitah intaji* (liberalization of production), was typical of much of the region until the late 1980s.[71]

The symbiosis between the principal private-sector capitalists and the state has moreover tended to confine smaller investors to non-productive ventures. This is obvious, for example, in the case of returnee labour, which has generally tended not to invest remittances earned abroad in small-scale businesses, but rather to retire or to invest in property and live off rent.[72] Elsewhere, continued state domination of the economy has resulted in the rise of unregulated labour, illicit commerce by petty traders and *trabendistas* exploiting regional variations in subsidies, and the growth of alternative economic networks and extensive parallel economies.[73] North Africa offers several examples, as do wartorn countries such as Iraq since the Gulf War, and the Syrian-Lebanese nexus. When it has been invested in the formal economy, entrepreneurial capital has generally found more profit in services and tourism than in manufacturing and large-scale commercial agriculture.[74] The result is something of a double-bind: the state initially crowds out entrepreneurs, yet when economic controls are relaxed a major problem undermining effective liberalization is the difficulty of reinvigorating the entrepreneurial class.[75] At the end of the day, entrepreneurs remained deterred by the extent to which the state still governs the economy. The issue is not simply one of the rule of law, security against confiscation, or fear of excessive interest and currency conversion rates, important as they are.[76] Rather, it is one of the continuing power of the state to determine transaction costs in the economic sphere, whether by regulating activity, formulating policy, or negotiating with external (and domestic) actors.

Social coalitions and economic policy

By the same token, the nature of state-society relations exerts considerable influence on the scope, scale, and pace of economic reforms. In Syria, state managers and the military have managed to preserve their position in relation to a growing private sector by forming a coalition at one and the same time with labour and the 'state-bred new capitalists'—large-scale industrialists intimately tied to the regime and rich agriculturalists who benefited from the limited liberalization of the 1980s.[77] Although some sons of senior officials support liberalization in order to expand their own business activities, there remains a broad consensus that the public sector should at most be reformed, not abolished, and that incrementally, lest rushing into a market economy trigger Soviet-style economic collapse.[78] In Iraq, conversely, the greater autocratic power of the regime—resulting from its reliance on oil for revenue rather than socially productive labour, and reflected in a weak labour movement—made it easier to privatize major state enterprises in 1988–90, with close relatives and favoured clients again the main beneficiaries.[79] The case of Algeria reveals both outcomes: the concentration of political power in the triangle of army, government party (the FLN), and bureaucracy allowed it first to oppose serious reforms successfully until 1988, and then to implement sweeping liberalization and privatization despite entrenched clientilism within and civil war without.[80]

External factors play an important part in the strength of social coalitions. In Syria, the state-led coalition has been able to preserve its dominance over the private sector thanks to its continued ability to direct investment from the Gulf and the capital flows resulting from oil sales or transit fees into public-sector enterprises, and to revive or develop economic ties with the former Soviet bloc, China, and North Korea.[81] Israel offers two additional examples. On the one hand, the end of the cold war greatly increased pressure on the government to liberalize the economy, since it could not afford to provide housing, job creation, and other physical and social infrastructure for the massive influx of Jewish immigrants from the USSR that started in 1990.[82] On the other hand, continued military and economic grants and housing loans guarantees from the US have enabled the Netanyahu government, which came to power in May 1996 partly on the strength of its espousal of neo-liberal economics, to postpone major cuts in social spending for the duration of its term. Turkey similarly shows how the combination of societal pressures and favourable external circumstances—in this case its new importance as a regional actor in the wake of the Gulf War—has prompted a succession of populist governments to slow down stabilization measures since 1991.[83] However, Egypt offers the clearest example of the domestic-external linkage, as the local agents of foreign companies and import agents, who dominate the *infitah* bourgeoisie, are the strongest advocates of economic reforms.[84] The pattern moreover extends into the state sector, not least among the military: in several countries they control substantial unseen funds, and have switched their original social alliance from the lower middle class to the private sector and developed their own links to international business.[85]

As the above examples suggest, continued access to external flows of capital contributes to the resistance of Middle East governments to deeper economic liberalization. High levels of debt acount for this, despite declining strategic rent, low levels of fdi, and sharply reduced intra-regional official transfers. Debt write-offs and other forms of Western aid—motivated, for example, by the wish to assist friendly governments threatened by Islamist opponents, or to reward them for supporting Arab–Israeli peace or the blockade against Iraq—have encouraged a form of 'aid addiction', even when donors expect privatization in return.[86] Major consequences are the attempt to retain social spending and consumer subsidies, avoid cutbacks in public sector employment or ownership, and maintain protection of local private sectors, even as regional and international economic pressures make it necessary to impose austerity measures, increase direct taxation, and incur new debt.[87] This applies equally to the oil-rich economies, whose governments have generally been unwilling to use their wealth to cushion the effects of stablization measures, let alone privatization. Only belatedly have some petro-monarchies initiated stabilization measures—under the combined pressure of declining oil revenues and Gulf War expenditure—and even then with obvious reluctance and as minimally as possible. Needless to say, there has been little change in the appropriation of oil revenues, with 18–29 per cent of the totals in all GCC member-states (except Oman) failing to appear in state budgets and presumed to be diverted partly into defence and partly into private accounts of ruling family members.[88]

Numerous governments in the Middle East have been able to point to the threat of food riots in order to resist reforms, much to the anger of Western donors, who contrast their attitude with the eagerness of their counterparts in Eastern Europe to liberalize.[89] When pressed, however, they have proved ready to divest themselves of those state-owned enterprises (SOEs) that provide basic consumer goods, freeing themselves of direct responsibility for inflation, shortages, and black markets in goods, currencies, and services, and shifting the political onus of social discontent to the private sector.[90] It is in this sense that the experience of Eastern Europe has been relevant, by impressing Middle East state managers with the lack of labour resistance to reform.[91] Indeed, the public in the Middle East has also shown itself willing at times to accept economically painful liberalization measures, even while opposing their social costs. A case in point is Iranian president Hashemi Rafsanjani's proposal in the early 1990s to raise taxes, rationalize interest rates, cut subsidies, standardize exchange rates, liberalize trade, and link wages to productivity.[92] Highly unpopular as his 'perestroika' was, the electorate voted none the less for the most like-minded candidate, Muhammad Khatami, to replace him when his term ran out in May 1997. Generally, implicit or explicit social coalitions may form in order to limit the extent and impact of economic reform, but these may also fragment when crisis makes such reform inevitable, as each member adopts a *sauve qui peut* strategy in the hope that others will bear the burden of social costs.[93]

Balance sheet

In many Middle East countries the result of stabilization and structural adjustment programmes has been drops in price inflation and budget deficits and parallel rises in growth rates and hard-currency reserves, but only at the cost of sharp drops in real wages and per capita income and equally steep rises in unemployment (often affecting female and expatriate labour most severely) and corruption. The paradox is that welfare policies are not always at fault, but rather policy decisions by political leaders and inefficiency in SOEs. Yet the readiness of Middle East governments, under pressure, to cut social expenditure has not been matched in relation to privatization of economic assets. Divestiture has increased noticeably since 1990, especially in favour of Build-Own-Operate-Transfer joint ventures with foreign capital, but the general trend is to shift from SOEs to parastatal companies, in which the state retains ownership but delegates management.[94] Sell-offs have often been of hotels rather than industry, although the state is involved even then through the role of public-sector banks.[95] More typical is the approach of Libya, which abolished the state monopoly on import and export in 1988, but avoided real privatization and retained control of distribution.[96]

Furthermore, the willingness and ability of Middle East governments to embark on serious economic reform is mostly tied to external circumstances that affect capital inflows. Egypt is a good example: after a previous agreement with the IMF in 1987 had stalled, liberalization only picked up pace when Egyptian debts worth up to one-half the total of $50 billion were written off by GCC and Western governments in 1990–4, slashing the service obligation and making sustained growth possible. The Egyptian government moreover achieved this by implementing a structural adjustment programme far more gradual than the IMF wished, and without devaluing its currency. Yet Egypt still faced major problems, not least the need to create 50 per cent more jobs by 2025 (or more, if female participation in the workforce rises), a predicament shared by other countries in the region.[97]

The response to the challenges and opportunities presented by external factors varies across the region. Liberalization has prompted private-sector interest in developing regional ties, although it tends equally to deepen globalization, rather than regionalization, of national economies, since the overriding tendency is to deal with established sources of capital, technology, and manufactured goods in the OECD countries.[98] Indeed, any 'horizontal' spread of economic activity (such as investment) in the region tends to operate 'vertically', that is, by way of Western financial centres and joint ventures with Western firms. Concurrently, parasitical domestic sectors that continue to benefit from state protection oppose regional integration precisely because it would require more extensive economic liberalization and so threaten their privileged position in ways that globalization has not.

The lack of committed 'change teams' indicates that for many Middle East governments the purpose of liberalization remains limited to crisis

management and avoiding financial collapse. The task is especially daunt-
ing for countries (such as Egypt, Algeria, and Morocco) that most acutely
face the three core challenges of providing growing populations with jobs,
food, and money.[99] (The case of Saudi Arabia, where rapid population
growth and declining oil revenue brought per capita income from about
$19,000 in 1980 to $6,900 in 1996 and may have pushed unemployment up
to 20 per cent, shows that even the oil-rich economies are no longer
immune to the same problems.)[100] In these and other non-oil exporting
middle-income countries in the Middle East (such as Syria, Jordan, and
Tunisia), the effect of decades of under-investment in the traditional agricultural sector, massive rural-urban migration, and high levels of illiteracy—in the latter case inhibiting the growth of the middle class, often
regarded as a motor of economic liberalization—also means that despite
high levels both of human capital and of unemployment, the Middle East
is still not competitive when compared to Eastern Europe or Southeast
Asia.

What emerges from this survey, finally, is that whereas Middle East
economies have become increasingly internationalized (in terms of cross-
border exchanges) and liberalized (in terms of open-border relations),
most are far from being truly globalized (in terms of the supraterritoriality
of communications, business and other organization, trade, finance, ecol-
ogy, and consciousness).[101] Evidently not all face the same critical combination of challenges and handicaps, but the crux of the matter lies in the
striving of state actors for a new understanding that cedes significant freedom of economic activity in certain areas to domestic and external actors,
yet leaves key economic levers, as well as political power, in its own hands.
Its immediate dilemma is how to accommodate international economic
expectations without upsetting local political arrangements, and, indeed,
without entirely ending its protection of the domestic private sector. The
response may be to seek an extended lease of life by changing patterns of
allocation rather than ownership, while farming out the costs of maintaining clients and ensuring social stability.[102] The purpose remains the
same as it was during the cold war: regime survival. Yet the attempt to
maintain the state's economic role while increasing that of the private sector is leading to bifurcation in economic policies, which may produce
intra-regime conflict as new vested interests and social coalitions emerge
and realign.[103] The question is how long the state can have it both ways,
'conserving its power and autonomy while selectively unloading economic
decision-making onto a protected marketplace'?[104] The answer lies in the
political domain, since structural adjustment alters the use, production,
and distribution of resources and so profoundly affects relations between
people.[105]

III. POLITICAL LIBERALIZATION

The fall of the Berlin Wall in December 1989 and the rapid demise of one communist regime after another in Eastern Europe sent shock waves through much of the Middle East. The contrast was strongest in authoritarian, single-party states such as Syria, where the unseating of Romania's Nicolae Ceauşescu had particular resonance, but the expectation that long-overdue democratization was imminent was widespread in the region. Yet Middle East states have generally proved more resilient than initially expected, and pressures to achieve political change, whether from internal or external sources, have been qualified and contingent. That most governments have none the less embarked on varying degrees and forms of political liberalization is not the direct result, therefore, of the end of the cold war or of the example of Eastern Europe, although these major events necessitated a political response (as well as increasing the economic pressures). Rather, it reflects the understanding by incumbents that the state cannot safely curtail the economic patronage it provides without finding new ways to maintain the social contract: that is, the political relationship between state and citizens. The alternative, and there are Middle East examples of this, is an increase in coercion, repression, and illiberalism.

In pursuing the aim of regime survival, Middle East governments have demonstrated three propositions. First, although democracy may arguably be necessary to achieve genuine economic and social development, experience in the region lends weight to the argument that democracy and free-market reforms do not necessarily reinforce each other, and indeed may be mutually detrimental. Second, whether for this reason or in the interest of maintaining existing political systems and structures of power, incumbents have almost invariably implemented political liberalization that falls significantly short of democratization. The third proposition is that the central purpose of political liberalization, as with its economic counterpart, is crisis management in the face of a variety of internal and external pressures, most of which predated the end of the cold war but have intensified since then. In response, the general trend has been towards a fusion of moderated political authoritarianism with varying degrees of economic liberalism. What have determined the outcome in each case are the nature of existing state-society relations and the continued availability to the state of non-socially extracted economic resources.

Contending with Islam

The preceding explains the varying answers offered by different Middle
East countries to two questions: what makes political liberalization problematic, and what allows the state to 'win'? In the first instance, governments intent on economic liberalization are concerned to deny its victims
the opportunity to mobilize. After all, although in the short term political
liberalization may help attract a dwindling amount of foreign aid, in the
long term investors seek low wages.[106] Having embarked on limited political liberalization, governments are moreover anxious to prevent alternative forces, most commonly Islamists, from filling the resultant 'political
space', especially among the social strata most directly affected by economic reform. In certain cases political liberalization can lead to mobilization along communal lines—ethnic, confessional, or regional—and so
to the generation of centrifugal forces that threaten the structure of the
state, especially if its power derives from rent and if there is overly rapid
deregulation of the economy. In the second instance, the outcome of the
contest over the nature and extent of political reform depends heavily on
the attitude of social forces which have been deeply affected, and at times
even formed, by decades of state-led development, and on the degree to
which reform leads to a separation of political power and economic ownership. This explains in particular why the middle class—marginalized
politically and coopted economically by the state—has generally not
played its presumed role in democratization. It also explains the prominence of Islam as a political force throughout the Middle East, especially
as a mobilizing agent among the social strata that have been most affected
by the onset of economic crisis and reform.

Contrary to perceptions common in the West, Islam is neither inherently antithetical to democracy nor monolithic.[107] There is little that is
inevitable or preordained in its political role, which in fact varies widely
across the Middle East and is contingent in each country on the history of
state-society relations and on the nature and source of state power. Indeed,
Islam provides the formal ideology of several states in the region, yet each
has adopted fundamentally diverging modes of political participation,
economic management, and social control. This is not to deny certain sim-
ilarities, but these relate predominantly to shared cultural values and
social norms. The resort to Islam as a tool of opposition to domestic,
regional, or global order is in reality the cultural expression of widespread
social crisis or *anomie*, a response to the massive impact of demographic
changes, universal education, global economic competition, and the revolution in information technology in the past five decades and to the challenge they pose to patriarchal systems.[108] To the degree that Islam is a

political response to secularization—above all the emergence of the interventionist, territorially bound national state—then this is largely because the latter process has meant the exclusion of 'traditional' social forces or interest groups that have tried to hold the state accountable and opposed its use of populism to maintain a political system characterized by the lack of genuine representation.[109]

Consequently, political Islam has had a major influence on the pace and extent of liberalization in the Middle East. As Islamist private voluntary organizations have emerged to offer services once provided by the state, the latter has on occasion offered greater political space to its citizens in order to involve them in the ratification of economic reforms.[110] The problem for governments in such a situation is that Islamist movements have proved adept at filling such space, benefiting from the low levels of political institutionalization caused by restrictions on party politics and from government repression of labour and trade unions (intended to stifle organized resistance to reforms).[111] Political Islam has also been the unintended beneficiary of the cultivation by the state of the territorial ethos and downgrading of pan-Arabism, since this has undermined the state's ideological legitimation and placed the onus for economic failure squarely on its shoulders.[112] Economic reforms have deepened this crisis, since they signal the end of an era in which governments equated development with nationalism and attempted to monopolize both, in order to deflect attention from domestic problems and blame economic problems on exogenous forces.[113] The outcome has been the newfound assertiveness of Islamist groups in Tunisia in the 1970s and 1980s, substantial parliamentary gains in Jordan since 1989, growing Islamist insurgency in Egypt in the 1990s, and the stunning electoral success of the Front Islamique de Salvation and other groups in Algeria in 1988–92 and stubbornness of their subsequent challenge to the military regime.

As these examples suggest, Middle East governments have responded to the Islamist challenge in a variety of ways. Most common has been to distinguish moderates and radicals, in the hope of co-opting the former and thus enabling stringent security measures to be applied to the latter. This was most effective in Morocco, Jordan, Yemen, and, arguably, Sudan, but in Algeria the army's decision to rob the Islamists of their electoral victory in 1992 plunged the country into civil war. Ironically it was in Turkey, with its strong secular tradition, that an Islamist government finally reached power through the ballot box in 1996, although there too the army subsequently engineered the downfall and dissolution of the governing Islamic Welfare Party (Refah). The key difference was that Turkey had experienced democratic, multi-party politics since 1983, in which the government was able to muster public support for reforms, whereas the breakdown in Algeria was more clearly a legacy of the one-party system and rentier politics. In Egypt, conversely, the government replaced two decades of top-led liberalization intended to gain allies among the beneficiaries of *infitah* with a policy of political closure as it deepened economic reforms in the 1990s, excluding the influential Muslim Brotherhood Society from national politics and taking control of the professional syndicates in which it had a strong following.[114] The problem still facing governments in the region, however, is that economic liberalization has sharply widened the income gap in their societies, providing a perpetual source of radicalism expressed through religious, ethnic, or other forms of communal politics.

The role of political Islam also underlines the ambivalent position of secular forces, especially on the left, and the middle class more generally in relation both to the state and to political liberalization. The fact that political Islam appeals strongly to the deprived prompts the middle class to support the status quo, while the desire of leftists and secular nationalists to defend secularism drives them into the arms of the government and debilitates them as advocates of the victims of economic reform.[115] Yet the role of the middle class as a force for democratization has been undermined in additional ways. Indeed, what is seen as the exceptional resistance of the Middle East to political liberalization, human rights, and democracy can be ascribed to the fact that a large proportion of the middle class (including the intelligentsia) is employed by the state or directly dependent on its monopolies.[116] In contrast to the developed, liberal democracies, where there is often a net transfer of resources from the middle class to the state, the situation is reversed in the rentier economies of the region.[117] An independent bourgeoisie is on the rise in some countries such as Egypt, and with it pressures for a reformed legal-constitutional framework, but the more common picture is of a class first stunted in growth by colonial powers and then overwhelmed by the overdeveloped state inherited from the colonial era.[118] Even in the affluent member states of the GCC, oil-based rent has marginalized the role of the once influential merchant class.[119] The further implication, as the creeping deliberalization of Egyptian politics in the 1990s shows, is that the erosion of liberties is not only a result of the state's contest with Islamist opposition, but is moreover a corollary of financial crisis and the economic reforms initiated to overcome it.[120]

Liberalization versus democratization

The example of the middle class lends weight to the wider conclusion, that ruling élites and coalitions of state managers and large private sector capitalists have a stake in opposing democratization so long as the institutions of rule and the mechanisms through which domestic surplus is appropriated are not separated.[121] Yet the need to reduce the welfare state's social burden and raise capital has compelled Middle East governments to liberalize politically in other ways, in an attempt to relegitimate their rule. The challenge has been to do so without seriously increasing the risk of political instability. In Syria, for example, the regime has conducted political 'decompression', using economic liberalization to broaden its political base without democratization. This approach, applied in varying degrees in other countries of the region, has seen censorship relaxed, arbitrary action by the security services curtailed, public criticism of civilian ministries tolerated, the role of the ruling party reduced, professional syndicates revived, and political exiles (including Islamists) permitted to return home.[122] Elsewhere there have been clearer moves towards 'pacted democracy': the added freedom to form political parties and to compete in general elections to parliaments that are allowed to do somewhat more than rubber-stamp government directives. Examples are Jordan, Yemen, Kuwait, Lebanon, Tunisia, and Morocco, although in each case there is either a formal charter or an informal understanding that ensures the continued role of the military (or outside hegemon, as for Syria in Lebanon) and autonomy of the ruling élite or family.[123] The exact path taken depends on the availability of material resources to the state, the willingness of opposition groups to accept its terms and limitations, and the failure of its attempts at repression, especially at a time when it needs both to attract flight or entrepreneurial capital and to secure societal acceptance of painful economic reforms.

What the evidence suggests is that Middle East governments have continued to employ strategies of repression or, more often, revision, but not of fundamental political reform. They have succeeded in most cases, an obvious exception being Algeria, where failure to reach a pact triggered the army's intervention. Yet although incumbents remain firmly in control of economic and political levers, decades of state-led development policies have promoted the emergence of social forces with diversified economic resources and potential political autonomy. Economic and administrative reforms have allowed these forces to broaden formerly circumscribed bases of civil society, affecting not only private voluntary organizations but also formerly docile bodies such as state-controlled trade and labour unions.[124] However, the revival of civil society does not necessarily presage democratization (although it is an important precursor and constituent of democracy), and is not without critical problems. There remains a non-nurturing environment—in terms of the independence of the judiciary or security of property rights, for example—but paradoxically civil society cannot survive without the legal and institutional continuity provided by the state, which is a crucial prerequisite for democracy.[125] This is demonstrated clearly in countries where there is an extensive parallel economy, and the state is unable to regulate and tax: democracy is an inadequate mechanism when social and political actors do not converge in a single 'national economy'.[126] The same circumstances, moreover, impede the emergence of a genuinely shared or consensual political culture, which is necessary both for economic and administrative regeneration and for social stability in a rapidly changing world.[127]

In any case, political liberalization is concurrently affected by the impact of globalization on national economies and social forces. As the example of Morocco shows, greater reliance on international capital for local development can actually increase the allocative power of the state and lead to 'recentralization' of political power, as lower-level brokers lose control over resources or are supplanted by alternative channels for capital flows.[128] Similarly in Egypt, the commercialization of the traditional agricultural sector and cessation of USAID loans has weakened the patronage of rural notables and prompted the Ministry of Interior to replace elected village mayors with its own appointees.[129] Recentralization has arguably allowed ruling élites to renew the neo-patrimonial basis of their power, thus restraining centrifugal communal forces that might question the geographical boundaries and legal justification of the state.[130] It has also allowed élites and key 'brokers' to benefit from the globalization of their economies and capture the new domestic links to international capital, in the process reconstituting their patronage networks and adapting the manifestation and exercise of their power.[131]

Two additional factors assist recentralization. Not least is the fact that democratization is not on the agenda of the US or major international financial institutions, which are more concerned with governance (that is, good public administration and managerial skills).[132] These global actors moreover tend to overlook authoritarianism in the often-intertwined causes of combating political Islam and of overcoming domestic resistance to economic liberalization. As a result, secondly, the domestic and expatriate entrepreneurs who might be the potential engines of civil society are equally likely to fuse with the political élite in a property-owning class and collude in the construction of authoritarian liberalism.[133] Through most of the Middle East, the presumed impact of democracy as a global political value has in fact largely been contained by such mechanisms as periodic elections to assemblies with severely constrained powers or appointment to consultative councils with none; ironically, the new freedom in a few countries to form political parties has not compensated for the loss of protection previously offered to lower income groups by corporatism in the welfare state.

In conclusion, what emerges from a survey of the Middle East is that rentier states will not democratize, although financial pressures may compel them to embark on limited political liberalization. This reflects the realization by some ruling élites after the cold war that steps were needed both to ease the economic crisis and to lessen political malaise: liberalization has remained a tactic to relieve pressure rather than a goal, and has not been allowed to threaten the established order.[134] The main exceptions are industrializing economies such as Israel and, to a lesser degree, Turkey. Egypt, Morocco, and, especially, Tunisia are potential candidates due to the relative importance of their manufacturing sectors and rising bourgeoisie and to the incipient globalization of their economies, but they are impeded by the bifurcation of economic policy, renewal of patronage networks, and disengagement of substantial societal forces into parallel economies. In these and other countries political liberalization may at most produce polyarchy or 'low-intensity' democracy, and reform is likely to be put on hold if political instability causes investors to flee and external aid is resumed.[135] For all, the problem lies in the time-lag between incurring social costs and receiving tangible returns on reform: economic exigency requires rapid change, but because it is more difficult to improve living standards (the concern of the masses) than to implement political liberalization (the concern of élites) the latter tends to be limited and gradual.[136] In this context, democratization is increasingly likely to come (if at all) by way of social upheaval and conflict, and to build initially on 'bread riots' of the sort that brought down the Sudanese regime in 1985, forced the (short-lived) opening up of the Algerian political system in 1988, and prompted the invigoration of parliament in Jordan in 1989; or else they might occur in the wake of major external crisis, such as momentarily threatened the Iraqi regime and assured the restoration of the Kuwaiti parliament in 1991.[137]

IV. CONCLUSIONS

Examination of the Middle East since the end of the cold war sheds light on three inter-related dynamics that are fundamental to the debate about the nature of the international system and the relationship between its different components and levels.

The first of these dynamics is that the conjunction of various trends at the national (domestic), regional, and international levels poses a challenge to the basic unit of system, the state. Most significantly, economic reform alters the function, and potentially the nature, of the state at a time when changes in global trade, finance, communications, and information technology are already eroding conventional notions of borders and sovereignty. Democratization is inherently destabilizing in such a context and may trigger the disintegration of the state, in societies in which primordial solidarity ties (such as sect, clan, region, or ethnic group) remain an effective means to mobilize or acquire resources and contend for political power.[138] The state is the source of patronage and is the prize for social contenders, for whom control over power rather than production remains the key asset.[139] Social cleavages are hardly new, but the point is that they gain new roles in the context of structural realignments in the domestic and international economies. This is true of much of the Middle East, yet the region also offers concrete evidence that the state has proved adept at retaining means of leverage and control and at reclaiming its central role. It has been helped in part by the continuing emphasis of the international system on Westphalian notions of statehood and sovereignty, but equally by the fact that the reforms demanded by the new economic orthodoxy require a capable and even strong state—in political as well as managerial terms. Only such a state can be an effective guarantor of a free-market economy, civil society, and, ultimately, democracy.

As the challenge to the state shows, the relationship between political and economic power remains at issue, and the contest between social actors to impose the superiority of one form over the other is reflected in a variety of institutional arrangements at the domestic and international levels.[140] The outcome will be determined not by the combination of economic and political liberalization, but by the manner of their interaction.[141] The critical dynamic is the way that social forces, both within and without the state, gain new roles and sources of wealth and form coalitions in the context of economic reform. The resulting changes in the social base of the regime and realignments in domestic politics are further influenced by the opportunity provided by globalization to form additional coalitions with external forces and interests. None the less, Middle East states have demonstrated their ability to recentralize even in such circumstances, reasserting themselves at the interface between globalizing forces and domestic actors. Indeed, authoritarian regimes in the region have proved better able to ensure their survival than their Eastern European counterparts precisely because 'a mixed economy can more readily generate class and primordial support than a totalitarian one'.[142] Despite economic hardship and social crisis, therefore, Middle East states have for the most part moved from the historic phase of state formation to a transitional one of reform and consolidation characterized by a new fusion of economic liberalism and political authoritarianism.

The preceding points to the importance of the second dynamic, the relationship between external and internal factors in shaping the challenges and opportunities that confront the state—especially in developing countries—and the strategies it adopts in response. This raises in particular the question of regionalism, since it should be at this level that states can do most to shape their external environment. Previous patterns of balancing and bandwagoning politics have become less pronounced since the end of the cold war, but Middle East states have not sought to promote regional order by institutionalizing cooperation (especially in security) or integration (especially in trade and infrastructure, if not in national economies generally), preferring instead, whenever possible, to replicate past attempts to obtain capital through accommodational and international strategies (rather than restructural ones). They have remained unwilling to relinquish aspects of sovereignty, accept relative gains disparities with their neighbours and partners, or cease protection for privileged economic sectors (including the private), through which they might maximize the potential rewards of region-wide economic liberalization and minimize its social costs in the medium and long term. Instead they have preferred defensive, nationally focused strategies that seek to minimize short-term economic costs and maximize the concentration of political power—not entirely an unreasonable calculation given the strikingly low level of regionalization of most of their economies.

Regional alignments in the Middle East remain largely derivative of the international relations of individual states, for which the overall trend remains to be integrated, separately and to unequal degrees, into the wider international system, and more specifically with principal linkages to the OECD economies. Integration proceeds at different rates and through different mechanisms, since the states of the region have evolved along distinct, at times dissimilar, historical, social, and institutional paths. There is some scope for more effective subregional groupings—since countries within the same geographic area may share institutional characteristics 'linked to underlying historical, socio-cultural, and politico-ideological factors'—but these are impeded by the fact that their member states are firmly set on established trajectories that tend to integrate them ever more deeply into the international system.[143] An additional impediment is the varying impact of the nuanced partnerships and competitive associations between the external powers involved in the Middle East. On the one hand, the preponderance of US strategic, military, and political influence inhibits inter-state war and lessens the incentive for regional cooperation in the security sphere. On the other hand, local states are less likely to seek regional integration or construct viable intergovernmental institutions over the medium to long term so long as the multipolarity of global competition for commercial advantage offers more immediate economic and political opportunities. Indeed, it is questionable whether the Middle East can be usefully conceived of as a single state system any longer, not least, ironically, because the very balancing politics that helped give it shape during the cold war have now lost much of their strategic impact.

The third dynamic, finally, relates to the vexing question of causality between different levels of analysis. To what extent, and by what analytical means, can developments in the Middle East since 1989–90 be attributed specifically to the end of the cold war? And does this indicate international 'system'-dominance, or does the operation of relatively autonomous processes at the national and regional levels throughout the cold war and since demonstrate 'agent'- or 'subsystem'-dominance? The experience of the Middle East, catchily described as 'the most penetrated international relations sub-system in today's world', suggests that even there the abstract contraposition between system and agent or subsystem domination is unsound.[144] The system may have provided the context and contributed to local processes, but the outcome in each case has resulted from the interaction and convergence of trends at the national and international levels. There has been more than a simple correlation, therefore, but the case of the Middle East supports the argument that causation is not only multi-layered and multi-faceted, but also more protracted and interactive a process than conventional frameworks of analysis suggest; causality lies in the inter-linkages rather than the parts.[145]

It is in this context that the impact and meaning of globalization can be seen. The Middle East has proved resistant to globalization, perhaps exceptionally so, but this is due not to innate cultural characteristics, but rather to the ability of incumbents to adapt to externally linked changes and utilize them in order to renegotiate and reconstruct political power internally. It is perhaps a fitting irony that the retreat of economic nationalism has not deprived ruling élites of the basis of their political power, even as they have overseen ever closer integration into the global economy. Potentially, the processes of globalization may erode the power of these élites while empowering other social forces, but Middle East experience suggests that the latter are just as likely to forge alliances with the former and so reinvigorate the state, albeit increasingly in an intermediary role between local and international actors. Whether this is done in the name of furthering modernity, secularism, and the liberal order, or of protecting indigenous systems of political governance and traditional social values and cultural norms (with all terms in heavy inverted commas) reflects the 'transference of political costs as mediated through states' between the international and domestic spheres, but cannot obscure the continuing integration of national economies into the global one.[146] If, in closing, the end of the cold war has contributed in any way to this process in the Middle East, then that is primarily by propelling the state and key domestic actors more quickly towards a new fusion of political authoritarianism and economic liberalism. It is this fusion that lends credence to the fears of pessimistic observers that globalization, while ushering in historic transformations in the nature and form of economic activity, will challenge citizenship and democracy more fundamentally than it will the reinvented state.

10

Conclusion
Whither the Third World?

LOUISE FAWCETT

As the end of the cold war becomes history, what long-term conclusions about its impact and importance for Third World countries can be drawn? To generalize about the impact across a wide range of countries of the momentous series of events which characterized the decade between 1985 and 1995 risks falling into the trap of clumsy oversimplification. The aim of this concluding chapter is to gather together some of the threads of the thematic and regional chapters and to identify some common ground as well as some obvious differences of opinion that have emerged. An attempt will be made to rethink the place of the Third World in the international system both from the inside out and the outside in. In other words, how have Third World countries come to perceive themselves and how are they perceived by the rest of the world? A final section will look at how mainstream theories of international relations and of development have fared in helping to explain and understand the progress of Third World countries 'beyond the cold war'.

To state that a Third World of sorts still exists appears relatively uncontroversial—at least to the contributors to this book. Despite the obvious problems involved in any such classification, the term remains in common use in both international relations and development studies literature, possibly more popular than competing ones like 'developing countries', 'less developed countries' or the 'South'.[1] For different reasons, to which I will return later, it remains attractive to scholars, academics, and policy-makers alike. But clinging to the term, admittedly partly out of habit, does not make it easier to identify and explain patterns of change.

Part of the problem, of course, is that the boundaries of the Third World, always fluid and shifting, have become arguably more porous with

The author is grateful to Ngaire Woods for her encouragement and helpful suggestions in preparing this chapter.

the completion of decolonization and the breakdown of the cold war system. Since its origins, the countries that came to comprise the Third World were endowed with very different territories and resources, and inhabited by very different peoples sharing different cultural and historical experiences. Despite its obvious poverty—identified by the Brandt Report of 1980 as a key characteristic of the 'South'[2]—the infant Third World otherwise presented a far from united picture. Yet decolonization and the cold war itself that helped to steer the emergence of the Third World did supply cohesion, providing a kind of straitjacket, partly self-, partly externally imposed, that came to guide and limit the Third World agenda. The absence or growing irrelevance of these factors had a liberating effect on states and peoples, leading to greater fragmentation and disunity than before. For some, the Third World has merely lost old colonial and cold war masters to find new ones, but it is hard to be satisfied with such externally driven explanations of the Third World's condition. The new force of globalization—if seen as merely a tool of the powerful—may indeed be seen as a form of slavery, promoting marginalization, turmoil, and greater inequality in the periphery. That view however, contrasts with the other face of globalization as a means of integrating developing countries into the world economy offering thereby ultimately richer vistas of greater equality and independence.[3]

Suggesting that the Third World has become more complex and diverse since the late 1980s does not mean that it has disappeared. However it does put paid to the 'plus ça change' thesis regarding the end of the cold war. Given, as Ian Clark reminds us, that the Third World was 'organically linked' to cold war processes,[4] how could the ending of the latter fail to have triggered 'organic' change? Few contributors to this volume have echoed Noam Chomsky's sentiment that the 'view from below' has changed but little.[5] Yet if we agree that change has been the victor over continuity we still need to consider its nature and degree, and here the highly differentiated picture the Third World presents is most striking. Indeed, if this book has demonstrated one thing it has been that states and regions have responded very differently to the new forces at work in the international system, making generalization even more difficult.

In Part I three themes were introduced as a means of charting change in the developing world. Different case studies considered these themes, giving weight to one or more as appropriate, as well as others of relevance to a particular region. How did the main issue areas fare? What findings were shared across cases?

DEMOCRATIZATION: THE POLITICAL LEVEL

Some degree of political liberalization has been attempted by virtually all developing countries, including such unlikely contenders as Saudi Arabia, but its motivation, extent, and permanence differ widely from country to country and region to region. Fully fledged or 'consolidated' democracies functioning in the 'five arenas' identified by Juan Linz and Alfred Stepan are still relatively hard to find.[6] Latin America and the Indian subcontinent provide some important exceptions, although in both regions established democracies existed long before the cold war ended. Nevertheless as Roland Dannreuther points out, an unmistakable trend towards greater democratization and a parallel challenge to authoritarianism can be identified—a trend which owes much to the 'contagion' effect of the former USSR and Eastern Europe.[7] But he guards against the domino theory by pointing out some notable exclusions from the 'Third Wave' as well as highlighting the limits of the democratic transition process in many areas. Africa provides a good example, and Keith Somerville has reviewed some of the continent's abortive democratic efforts, in a region in which the mere holding of multi-party elections cannot guarantee democratic consolidation, particularly where states and civil societies are chronically weak and local and international conditions are only intermittently favourable.

Clearly domino-effect democracy is likely to be more stable where other conditions favouring its establishment are also present. Here both timing and the level of preparedness of states are critical. For some states the end of the cold war had the effect of accelerating existing processes. For others it propelled the democratic agenda into relatively uncharted territory. Not surprisingly, as the relevant chapters of this volume have shown, the successes are to be found in the former group, which features, for example, Latin American states, the failures in the latter group, featuring for example African or Middle Eastern states, where 'stop-start' democracy or what Yezid Sayigh has called moderated authoritarianism has been tried (and often failed). Yet it would also be wrong to discount such liberalizing efforts even if they do falter: that a former dictator should agree to compete in relatively free and fair elections and surrender power if the ballot box so determines, or even to concede some modest measures in the direction of greater pluralism is no small achievement.

The great diversity of experience as regards political liberalization that this book has highlighted brings us to the problem of definition and measurement. Is only one type of democracy, or a set of democratic types familiar in the Western world, *genuine* democracy? How important *are* elections as a democratic yardstick? Should we be constructing alternative models that share certain characteristics with Western democracies but are also moulded on historical or cultural experiences unique to different regions? There is already a considerable literature on the possibility of an Asian or Islamic 'way' to accommodate democracy within existing cultures.[8] It is important however, to hold on to the idea, powerfully put forward by Norberto Bobbio and others, that democracy 'denotes one of many possible modes of government . . . in which power lies with everybody or the majority'.[9] The beliefs that majority might hold, or the conduits it might choose to secure representation of its power, will perforce be very different. Bobbio is, of course, concerned with achieving the fusion between democracy and liberalism, but just as 'a liberal state is not necessarily democratic . . . A democratic government does not necessarily issue in a liberal state.'[10] This latter point is particularly pertinent to our discussion. In the Third World and the emerging states of Eastern Europe and the former USSR, modes of democratic governance can and do differ widely from the familiar 'liberal democratic' norm of the West. Particularly worrying for some, but perhaps indicative of current and future trends, is how the phenomenon of what Fareed Zakaria has called 'illiberal democracy' seems to have taken hold.[11]

LIBERALIZATION: THE ECONOMIC LEVEL

If political change and moves towards greater pluralism have accompanied the ending of the cold war, what is their relationship to economic liberalization? More generally, to what extent have economic liberalization and globalization affected the development of the Third World in the post-cold war period?

Economic liberalization, like its political counterpart, responded positively to the stimulus provided by the end of the cold war. It was also, however, part of an ongoing process that had led to a major revision of economic strategies, incorporating a shake-up of existing orthodoxies on the best route for development for Third World countries. Indeed the fall-out from the US decision in 1979 to raise interest rates, in particular the debt crisis, made liberalization a necessity. As Gautam Sen's chapter and those of different contributors have revealed, it is not necessarily that the problems facing many developing countries have substantially changed— slow growth, depressed living standards, low diversification and lack of competitiveness to name a few—but the available options and remedies to overcome them have. The end of the cold war, combined with the pull of globalization, and the pressure of powerful countries and the institutions they dominate, have effectively reduced these options to variants on a single theme encompassed by the broad term 'liberalization'. The failure of the centrally planned economies in the former USSR, Eastern Europe, and elsewhere, and the poor record of the import substitution policies pursued by many developing countries, have only reinforced this. If revamped modernization theory lacks its initial lustre, the 'follow my leader' theme has considerable resonance in the economic climate of the millennium, as developing countries struggle to meet the conditions and deadlines of the International Monetary Fund or World Bank's stabilization or structural adjustment programmes.[12] 'Restructure or die' has become the post-cold war motto for the debt-ridden countries of the 1980s.

How have developing countries fared as the result of their attempts at liberalization and restructuring? The results of now more than a decade of restructuring have been at best mixed. To be sure, a number of developing countries had already broken with early orthodoxy by pursuing export-led policies and thus raising themselves to the ranks of the 'newly industrialized'. The Asian NICs (newly industrialized countries) were thus followed by the Latin American NICs, with Chile leading the way, as emerges so clearly in Jorge Heine's chapter. But as in the case of political liberalization, economic liberalization in some areas remains patchy and incomplete, and has distorted and exaggerated existing inequalities.[13] Arguably it has brought few real benefits to the peoples or economies of the countries in which it has been implemented. It has also contributed to severe financial crises in both Latin America and East and Southeast Asia.

Thus liberalization has not proved to be the panacea that many believed and anticipated it would be. In fact, just as the theories of dominance and dependence that shaped a generation of thinkers never worked for *all* the Third World (or at least suggested different conclusions for different countries), the results so far also suggest that the new liberalizing philosophy does not work for all. Where local and international conditions remain unfavourable, globalization and liberalization offer only marginalization for Third World countries—at least in the short term.

Political and economic liberalization—widely regarded as processes that have been promoted by the end of the cold war—are often portrayed as going hand in hand. Powerful states and institutions demand of developing states evidence of efforts to pursue parallel policies. Yet it is evident that the ends of economic liberalization may not be best achieved by a democratic state, particularly a democratizing one. Indeed, the successful economies in the Third World are precisely those where a strong and 'efficient' state has acted first as the motor for development while guiding closely the process of economic liberalization, and here again one can look to different parts of Asia and Latin America for examples.[14] For Taiwan, like other Asian NICs, a 'potent state' provides the key to understanding economic progress and development.[15] More recently, however, evidence from Russia and parts of Africa has shown the ugly face of economic liberalization in the absence of broad-based democratic institutions. If one believes in the ultimate triumph of the union between capitalism and liberal democracy—and many do not[16]—the problem is how the two may best be brought together.

DEMOCRATIZATION AND LIBERALIZATION: IMPLICATIONS FOR THE SECURITY LEVEL

In discussing the two themes above, liberalization and democratization were the words chosen to analyse post-cold war change in the Third World. What about security? Has the end of the cold war resulted in a more liberal set of security arrangements? What indeed would a liberal security regime for developing countries look like? If we take the example of Western Europe as providing a model—albeit far from perfect—of how a liberal security regime might look (high levels of security interdependence, common security agendas, successful interlocking institutions which encompass both regional and global security issues, and perhaps, most important, a common desire to achieve and preserve peaceful relations) it is evident that, with the possible exception of Central and parts of South America and Southeast Asia, no parallel immediately suggests itself among the clusters of different developing countries. Third World security has certainly been profoundly affected by the end of the cold war and the loosening of superpower overlay, but regime type, regional rivalries, and international pressures still heavily dominate local agendas and continue to work against countervailing pressures in the direction of a more liberal order.[17] The absence of any global security regime obviously feeds into the Third World security dilemma, but Third World insecurity in turn contributes to the difficulties of constructing such a regime.

Different contributors to this book have looked at how security agendas for developing countries have changed in the years since the cold war. The most obvious transformation, that of the ending of superpower–client relationships that characterized the cold war era, has obviously reduced one level of Third World insecurity, though not obliterated it altogether. Many developing countries still depend on great powers for arms and protection. If they can no longer gain leverage by playing off East against West (or vice versa) there is still room at the local level for bargaining, for example to promote regional security against the pretensions of rogue or pariah states. At other levels, which Amitav Acharya has considered in some detail, old insecurities remain and new insecurities have emerged, making it difficult to determine whether or not the overall incidence of conflict has decreased.

The scope and nature of local conflicts may have changed, but many remained unresolved by the end of the cold war. A number of new post-cold war conflicts have broken out. Where their origins are locally or regionally determined they fester on, only attracting the attention of the international community if the interests of major players are intimately affected. That these 'interests' have expanded to include issues like human rights, humanitarian aid, good government, refugees—the components of what some Western governments call a 'moral' foreign policy—has not made the Third World any more secure. Arguably greater security will only come with more extensive liberalization—both economic and political—and high levels of regional and global interdependence reflected in effective institutions. This is not the place to debate the rights and wrongs of democratic peace theory, but it is not difficult to see how regime type and a host of regional and domestic factors combine to make it unlikely that the Third World, or even certain parts of it, will be converted to a zone of peace in the short term. Certainly one effect of the end of the cold war has been the exposure of 'weak' states in the Third World, contributing to a serious crisis of legitimacy for some: Rwanda provides perhaps one of the best illustrations. Without the cold war shield, such sources of weakness have multiplied, such that one cannot talk merely of quasi-states but of 'failed states' or even 'statelessness'.[18] Where state viability is threatened, be it from above, by international agencies and governments, or from below, by ethnic, religious, or other sectarian groups, peace remains an unlikely outcome.

Not all the Third World of course is riven by sectarian strife, economically weak and marginalized and devoid of political accountability: a zone of 'turmoil', as some would have it.[19] Growing levels of economic, security, and even political cooperation have come to characterize clusters of developing countries and in these areas institutions have emerged to reflect these interdependencies. Regional arrangements in Latin America and Southeast Asia reflect common security themes and agendas, with the Association of South East Asian Nations (ASEAN), the Central American Common Market (CACM), and the South American Common Market (MERCOSUR)—pre- and post-cold war creations—leading the way. To say that regionalism had changed the security agenda in developing countries would be utopian and misleading, although there is certainly evidence of increased regional activity across a range of countries since the end of the cold war.[20] Barring Latin America, and there the evidence is contested,[21] there is very little sense in which a new liberal regionally based order might be said to be emerging.

Third World countries then throw up very different pictures when tested against the three themes. In general the end of the cold war has been the most effective motor of change in countries where conditions were already favourable; whether countries less favoured will follow suit remains an open question. Nevertheless all developing countries have had to adjust to new security, economic and political imperatives that relate in some ways to an agenda that is specific to the end of the cold war.

Other useful ways of understanding the end of the cold war include approaches along the lines of 'globalization versus fragmentation' suggested by writers like John Louis Gaddis or Ian Clark.[22] Globalization, it could be argued, incorporates many of the themes captured by 'liberalization', while fragmentation captures the ethnic, religious, and national turmoil, the 'challenges from below' that have been characteristic of many post-cold war states inside and outside the Third World. Both are somewhat problematic when applied only to developing countries. The concept of globalization in particular has proved to be fuzzy and imprecise. If it were taken to mean—as some argue—transnationalism rather than liberalization and interdependence, it would be rather less helpful in explaining Third World change.[23] Fragmentation affects some but by no means all Third World countries and societies. For many it is hardly a new issue, identifiable as much with the post-colonial as post-cold war era. Overall, while there is some overlap, the themes selected in this volume have proved robust in measuring the nature and degree of change across different regions, despite the wide variety of experience recorded.

THIRD WORLD IMAGES

With the preceding pages yet again stressing the theme of diversity, we must again return to the question: is there a Third World after the cold war? If we have been hard pressed to find common identifying characteristics in either the 'old' or 'new' Third Worlds, what is it then that holds these countries together as a category? Here it is useful to turn to external and internal images of the Third World, to see how identity and perception continue to shape a collective entity.

From the *inside out*, there is still a loyalty to the Third World idea and its shibboleths that seems stubbornly resistant to change. Why, for example, did Argentinians oppose the idea of their government's departure from the Non-Aligned Movement? Though admittedly the non-aligned agenda became less and less preoccupied with cold war issues over time, why one might ask does the Non-Aligned Movement continue to exist in a world where 'alignment' has lost most of its relevance? Here is the conundrum. Many Third World countries, albeit to different degrees, still see themselves as 'alienated' from the major powers and forces in the international system and by extension from the system itself. In some ways this sense of alienation, of being outside the main currents in the international system, has been reinforced by the end of the cold war. Talk of 'marginalization' was common: a fear exacerbated by the new competition for aid, markets, and resources from the newly emerging states of the former Soviet Union and Eastern Europe.

This sense of marginalization, of sharing a common plight, has helped to re-emphasize the commonalities that exist among Third World countries. Of course not all countries feel marginalized, and not on all fronts simultaneously. Though perhaps economically comfortable with the arrangements that characterize the New World Order, developing states, in East or Southeast Asia for example, often remain awkwardly outside mainstream political and security trends. Hence the argument for the Asian way, most strikingly practised in China, where economic and political liberalization do not go hand in hand. If there is to be a 'global' human rights regime many Islamic and/or Asian regimes do not wish to be part of it. The same applies to an environmental regime which asks of the South that which the North decades ago (and even today in some striking cases) was unwilling to concede.[24] Arms control, including nuclear proliferation, is another area where the Third World often sees things differently. This was amply borne out by developments in the Indian subcontinent in the spring of 1998. Without arms, the fragility and vulnerability of many developing countries would be all the more cruelly exposed.

So, in short, there is still a sense of identity which brings an otherwise disparate group of states together. If colonialism is a thing of the past, the neo-colonial spirit lives on. That Third World insitutions only weakly or intermittently reflect this sense of common purpose does not mean that such a sense does not exist. But Third World countries and institutions *have* recast their image as rebels, fighters for change. The emphasis now is on cooperation rather than conflict as the desired means of securing a better deal. But the desire to cooperate, partly imposed by circumstance rather than choice, does not undermine a continuing sense of common purpose. So the Non-Aligned Movement continues, with well over 100 members, even if its rhetoric, as the 1998 Durban summit showed, is less conflictual than before.

If the inside-out perspective provides some useful indicators as to the persistance of a Third World identity, the *outside-in* perspective is no less illuminating. For just as developing countries have a shared perception of their situation, so too do the developed countries hold a common set of beliefs about the Third World. Some of these beliefs are rooted in history: present images draw heavily on past analogies. The emergence of the Third World in a cold war climate ensured that a combination of colonialism, paternalism, protection, and competition coloured First World views. The balance of these changed as the Third World became more established and more assertive. In particular, as the cold war mellowed, the idea of the Third World as the major repository of the world's problems, and as a source of disorder and rebellion, grew. What had started as a rebellion against colonialism became a rebellion against the prevailing international order and its social, political, economic, and cultural mores. This rebellion was apparent in Third World action in United Nations' forums, in the Non-Aligned Movement, and more weakly in the indigenous institutions that emerged, mostly after the Second World War. The idea of the Third World as a source of disorder has not only survived the end of the cold war, and the more cooperative nature of regimes noted above, but also been reinforced by the dwindling of alternative sources of actual or potential conflict, the instability in the former Soviet bloc notwithstanding. This perception has been sharpened, as noted, by the way in which the absence of cold war restraints has helped bring to the surface and expose the weaknesses of Third World countries.

From this revised perception of the Third World after the cold war, two conflicting sets of conclusions and prescriptions emerged, both with important implications for developed and developing countries. The first, popular in the early 1990s was that the Third World and its attendant problems no longer 'mattered'.[25] Europe—the wider Europe, the 'common home' frequently referred to by Gorbachev—mattered,[26] so too did the successful states of Asia and a few other friendly states within the South. The rest no longer needed to be courted for their favours and could be simply ignored. This 'South as periphery thesis' fed powerful images from above and below of a Third World marginalized and commanding scant interest from the rest of the world.

A second set of conclusions contradicted the first, though in differing ways and degrees. Precisely because the Third World was a source of disorder, it could not be safely ignored. Put quite simply, it threatened the advanced industrialized countries and particularly their economic and security interests.[27] Hence Third World security was inseparable from First World security. If for no other reason, the destabilizing influence of the developing countries on the international system demanded that both the causes and symptoms of their instability be addressed. The kinds of intervention that characterized the cold war era may have largely become a thing of the past but new kinds of intervention soon replaced them. The US military operation in Haiti (albeit with UN Security Council sanction) provided a good example of how challenges to US security interests might be met in the post-cold war era.

For some of the 'Third World matters' school, action or intervention crafted around the idea of the Third World as a threat to international stability does not go far enough. On this reading, the advanced countries have a moral responsibility, an obligation to tackle the sources of Third World disorder. Making the world a safer place should not only reflect narrow self-interest but a desire to advance the broader interests of humanity, or in this case the developing countries. While in reality it is often hard to separate the two, the moral obligation school focuses on Third World disorder rather than First World security as the object of international security efforts. Hence the pressure to pursue humanitarian challenges, correct human rights abuses, promote good government practices, protect against environmental degradation, with peace and stability but also greater prosperity and equality as an ultimate goal. All this represents a belief in the possibility of progress and improvement absent from much traditional thinking about the Third World. Here the Third World is no longer portrayed as the enemy, but becomes a partner in a shared global mission.

Although these outside-in images of the developing countries yield very different policy prescriptions, they share a similar perception of the Third World's condition, again providing elements of unity to an otherwise diverse picture. In sum, whatever has changed, and few would doubt that much has, both internal and external images continue to give shape and form to that collectivity of countries known as the Third World.

IN SEARCH OF A THEORY

What place does theory have in this analysis? What, in particular, have past and current theories of international relations and development taught us about understanding the Third World? Have they helped us to understand the role of the Third World in international relations and its development process? Have they helped to chart a path for the future? While theory has not been a centrepiece of this book, a number of chapters have referred to the strengths and weaknesses of particular theoretical approaches inasmuch as they relate to change and development in the Third World. Here we can only briefly sketch some of the major theoretical positions taken up and speculate as to their utility.

From the outset, it might be observed that two of the most resilient paradigms of international relations and development studies emerged considerably shaken from the end of the cold war. I refer here, on the international relations side, to realism and its modern counterpart, neo-realism; and on the development side, to theories of dependence. To be sure, contending theories have fared little better, but these two dominant paradigms are of particular interest here. Realism's insistence on states as units in a self-help anarchical society has long been problematic for students of the Third World. For it condemns the Third World to perpetual subservience, as weak states in the world of the strong. Change is difficult if not impossible. Theories of dependence, for their part, also seem to condemn the Third World to subservience or worse: to a state of progressive impoverishment and dependence from which only prolonged struggle or revolutionary change provides an outlet.

It is evident to any observer that the capacity of many Third World states has changed radically in past decades and that the two key paradigms outlined above must therefore be deficient in certain ways. Some states, it is true, still conform to the image of the weak and dependent state that realism and dependency theory offered us. Clearly then, elements of those theories remain useful. But what about the states that have 'advanced' and embraced a neo-liberal agenda which now closely ties them to the major economic and/or political processes at work in the international system? How for example do the cases of Chile or the Far Eastern NICs square with traditional theories of dependence? Furthermore, as a number of chapters in this book have highlighted, realist understanding of the Third World is seriously compromised by its failure to open the sealed box that (for realists) represents the state, and take a closer look inside. To return to a point made in the Introduction, and alluded to repeatedly throughout the book, it is the nature of states and societies in the Third World that is critical to understanding performance. The external environment may help explain many things, but cannot explain everything. In this respect Mohammed Ayoob's concept of 'subaltern realism' represents an interesting departure from prevailing orthodoxy.[28]

It would be wrong to infer from the above that competing paradigms are less problematic. Neo-liberalism, still highly state-centred but giving greater weight to cooperation and interdependence, regimes and institutions, is also strangely irrelevant to the concerns of many developing countries. Given its West-centric focus, neo-liberalism, not surprisingly, can only partially help to explain the advance of the more successful developing countries. Is it then the case that, as one recent book has suggested, theories of international relations have never taken the Third World seriously and cannot therefore be relied on to provide either a guide to understanding the past or signposts for the future?[29] The effect of the end of the cold war has been to open up a space for the development of inventive new theories: a space that has yet to be filled. At the very least, a more multi-dimensional approach, incorporating the best of the old and the new, is called for, but also one which is intelligible to the Third World and relevant to its concerns.

Similarly on the development side while there is clearly an acceptance of the shortcomings of theories of dependence, not least their failure to antic-ipate events, there is considerable reluctance to surrender or replace them. Defenders of dependency theory point to how the so-called Washington consensus is no less flawed. Both ISI and export-led growth have proved to be problematic prescriptions when applied to different developing countries. Indeed, one significant contribution of recent debates has been precisely to challenge the idea that there can be any *one* model of the developmental state.[30]

If the shelves in the theoretical cupboard have proved rather bare in terms of providing explanations as to the progress of the Third World beyond the cold war, it is perhaps worth reminding ourselves that even on the 'big issues', notably the end of the cold war itself, international rela-tions theory has been tried and found wanting.[31] This does not mean that we should abandon the search—far from it. Theory matters: it is, in part, the absence of relevant concepts and paradigms that makes the task of understanding the role of the Third World in international relations so dif-ficult. An efficient set of theories would help both to explain why develop-ing countries have come to occupy the position they now do in the international system, and to identify which are the most important actors in the process.

Turning, by way of a final conclusion, to the characteristics of the Third World 'beyond the cold war', we come back to the differentiated picture that has been the hallmark of this study. That we have witnessed dramatic change since the late 1980s is not in doubt: democratization, liberaliza-tion, globalization, peace and war, have visited all developing countries and have left an indelible mark. But otherwise there is no common pattern here, beyond that of the resilience of the concept of the Third World, iden-tifiable to insiders and outsiders alike. It is perhaps unsurprising that exist-ing paradigms have failed adequately to explain change and development in that fluid, complex, and shifting group of countries. (One is reminded here of the array of explanations for the emergence of the Third World through the decolonization process.) For some the very existence of a Third World remains baffling. But to move *beyond the concept of a Third World* will require more time and far more effort and commitment at the local, regional, and international level than we have hitherto seen. That remains a challenge for the future.

NOTES

INTRODUCTION

Louise Fawcett is grateful to Andrew Hurrell, Robert O'Neill, and Adam Roberts for their helpful comments on an earlier version of this introduction.

1. For one attempt to champion a new 'cosmopolitan' model of democracy in the post-cold war order, see David Held, *Democracy and the Global Order: From the Modern State to Cosmopolitan Governance* (Cambridge: Polity Press, 1995), esp. ch. 12.
2. For a critical view of 'transformational' arguments regarding the post-cold war international order, see Adam Roberts, 'A New Age in International Relations?', *International Affairs*, 67/3 (1991), 509–25.
3. For an elaboration on this theme see Peter J. Katzenstein (ed.), *The Culture of National Security: Norms and Identity in World Politics* (New York: Columbia University Press, 1996). See in particular the editor's introduction: 'Alternative Perspectives on National Security', pp. 1–32.
4. See e.g. James Mayall, 'Intervention in International Society: Theory and Practice in Contemporary Perspective', in Barbara A. Roberson (ed.), *International Society and the Development of International Relations Theory* (London: Pinter, 1998); also James Mayall (ed.), *The New Interventionism 1991–1994* (Cambridge: Cambridge University Press, 1996); John Harriss (ed.), *The Politics of Humanitarian Intervention* (London: Pinter, 1995).
5. See e.g. Laurence Whitehead, 'Three International Dimensions of Democratization' in Laurence Whitehead (ed.), *The International Dimensions of Democratization: Europe and the Americas* (Oxford: Oxford University Press, 1996), pp. 3–4.
6. See J. L. Gaddis, *The United States and the End of the Cold War* (Oxford: Oxford University Press, 1992), 196–202; also Ian Clark, *Globalization and Fragmentation* (Oxford: Oxford University Press, 1997), pp. 1–2.
7. Since 1995 elected governments have tumbled in Burundi, Gambia, and Niger. See Michael Bratton, 'Deciphering Africa's Divergent Transitions', *Political Science Quarterly*, 112/1 (1997), 92.
8. Samuel P. Huntington, *The Clash of Civilisations and the Remaking of World Order* (New York: Simon and Schuster, 1996). On the limits of Westernization, see also Serge Latouche, *L'Occidentalisation du monde* (Paris: Editions la decouverte, 1989). In a thoughtful article Richard Falk argues that resistance to globalization needs to be understood in terms of the West's denial of a 'civilizational identity' to Third World countries. See Richard Falk, 'False Universalism and the Geopolitics of Exclusion: The Case of Islam', *Third World Quarterly*, 18/1 (1997), 7–23. The Huntington thesis is, of course, much contested. Some would argue that rather than confrontation, societies are moving towards a global culture. See e.g.

David Rieff, 'A Global Culture?', *World Policy Journal*, 9/4 (Fall/Winter 1992), 73–81.

9. Karl P. Magyar, 'Classifying the International Political Economy: A Third World Proto-theory', *Third World Quarterly*, 16/4 (Dec. 1995), 704.

10. John Lewis Gaddis, 'The Cold War, the Long Peace and the Future', in Michael J. Hogan *The End of the Cold War* (Cambridge: Cambridge University Press, 1992) 21–38.

11. In this book the terms 'Third World' and 'developing countries' are used interchangeably except where different contributors have expressed their own particular preference.

12. For one attempt to provide an answer to this question see Jean-Germain Gros, 'Failed States in the New World Order: Decaying Somalia, Liberia, Rwanda and Haiti', *Third World Quarterly*, 17/3 (1996), 455–72.

13. See his 'Introduction: Liberalisation, Regionalism and Statehood in the New Developmental Agenda', in *Third World Quarterly*, 17/4 (1996) Special issue 'The Developmental State? Democracy, Reform and Economic Prosperity in the Third World in the 1990s', eds. Barry Gills, George Philip, Christopher Clapham and Shahid Qadir, pp. 593–602.

14. See e.g. Susan George, *A Fate Worse than Debt* (London: Penguin, 1994 edn.).

15. See Andrew Hurrell and Ngaire Woods, 'Globalisation and Inequality', *Millennium*, 24/3 (1995), 447–70.

16. For one study of ethnic challenges, old and new, see Stephen Ryan, *Ethnic Conflict and International Relations* (Aldershot: Dartmouth Publishers, 1995). Also David A. Lake and Donald Rothchild (eds.), *The International Spread of Ethnic Conflict* (Princeton: Princeton University Press, 1998).

17. See Jeffrey Herbst, 'Responding to State Failure in Africa', *International Security*, 21/3 (Winter 1996/97), 120–44.

18. For this idea see Paul Harrison, *Inside the Third World* (London: Penguin, 1993); Zaki Laidi, *Power and Purpose after the Cold War* (Oxford: Berg Publishers, 1994).

19. Noam Chomsky, 'A View from Below', in Hogan, *End of the Cold War*, pp. 137–8.

20. For a useful definition of the 'old' Third World, see Christopher Clapham, *Third World Politics: An Introduction* (London: Routledge, 1985), 217–28; see also Guy Arnold, *Third World Handbook* (London: 1994), 30–1.

21. Hedley Bull, 'The Revolt against the West', in Hedley Bull and Adam Watson (eds.), *The Expansion of International Society* (Oxford: Clarendon Press, 1985), 217–28.

22. Arnold, *Third World Handbook*, 9.

23. See Robert Gilpin, *The Political Economy of International Relations* (Princeton: Princeton University Press, 1987), 304.

24. Mark T. Berger, 'The End of the "Third World"?', *Third World Quarterly*, 15/2 (1994), 257–75.

25. Some argue for an amplification of the term to include 'new' Third World countries from the former Soviet bloc. See Arnold, *Third World Handbook*, p. xii. Hans Henrik Holm and Georg Sorensen distinguish two basic societal structures in the post-cold war order: 'core-type, industrialised countries with consolidated liberal democracies . . . and periphery-type, semi- or nonindustrialized, authoritarian or semidemocratic areas'. See Holm and Sorensen (eds.), *Whose World Order?*

Uneven Globalization and the End of the Cold War (Boulder, Colo., and Oxford: Westview, 1995), 1.

26. See Srinivas R. Melkote and Allen H. Merriam, 'The Third World: Definitions and New Perspectives on Development', in Alfonso Gonzales and Jim Norwine, *The New Third World* (Boulder, Colo., and Oxford: Westview Press, 1998), 9–27.

27. See e.g. Mehran Kamrava, 'Conceptualizing Third World Politics: The State–Society See-saw', *Third World Quarterly*, 14/4 (1993), 703–16; and idem, 'Political Culture and a New Definition of the Third World', *Third World Quarterly*, 16/4 (December 1995), 691–701. For a useful exposition of the current problems in defining a Third World see also Heather Deegan, *Third Worlds* (London: Routledge, 1996), 219–21.

28. See also Robin Broad and Christina Melhorn Landi, 'Whither the North-South Gap?', *Third World Quarterly*, 17/1 (Mar. 1996), 7–17. At a minimum, they feel it is useful to examine the changes since the end of the cold war that compel us to rethink our terminology and definitions, even if their purpose is not to assert the actual existence of a Third World.

29. One example of such an institution might be the Islamic Conference Organisation (ICO), another the Malaysian-led initiative to form an East Asia Economic Caucus (EAEC).

30. Martin Hollis and Steve Smith, *Explaining and Understanding International Relations* (Oxford: Oxford University Press, 1990), 7–9.

31. The notion of 'security complexes' from Barry Buzan, *People, States and Fear: An Agenda for International Security Studies in the Post-Cold War Era* (Hemel Hempstead: Harvester Wheatsheaf, 1991).

CHAPTER 1

1. See, most notably, Immanuel Wallerstein, *The Modern World System*, i–iii (New York: Academic Press, 1974, 1980, 1989).

2. See Barry Buzan, 'Third World Regional Security in Structural and Historical Perspective', in Brian Job (ed.), *The Insecurity Dilemma: National Security of Third World States* (Boulder, Colo.: Lynne Reiner, 1992), 167.

3. In most cases, this is conscious. Kenneth Waltz, for example, in his model of international politics holds the ordering of the international system (anarchy) and the character of the units (states) constant, in order to explore the explanatory utility of one variable—the distribution of capability in the system. Kenneth Waltz, *Theory of International Politics* (New York: McGraw-Hill, 1979), *passim*.

4. Hedley Bull, *The Anarchical Society* (New York: Columbia, 1977), 96–7.

5. Since values are themselves social constructs and vary in different social contexts, security is itself a 'social construct'. On this point, see Myron Weiner, 'Security, Stability, and International Migration', *International Security*, 17/3 (Winter 1992–3), 103.

6. For an interesting discussion of the expanding agenda of security, see Clement Adibe, 'Weak States and the Emerging Taxonomy of Security in World Politics', *Futures*, 26/5 (1994), 490–505. On environmental security, see Jessica Tuchman Mathews, 'Redefining Security', *Foreign Affairs*, 68/4 (Fall 1989).

7. Barry Buzan, *People, States, and Fear* (Chapel Hill, NC: University of North Carolina Press, 1983), 67.

8. As John Ravenhill put it: 'The concept of the "Third World" is of growing irrelevance in an increasingly differentiated global economy.' John Ravenhill, 'The North-South Balance of Power', *International Affairs*, 66/4 (1990), 731.

9. See e.g. Mark Berger's analysis in 'The End of the "Third World"?', *Third World Quarterly*, 15/2 (1994), 257–5.

10. As with Ravenhill, 'North-South Balance', 731–48, although for Ravenhill the term and the juxtaposition appear to be a matter of convenience rather than substance. See also Bahgat Korany, 'End of History or its Continuation and Accentuation? The Global South and the "New Transformation" Literature', *Third World Quarterly*, 15/1 (1994), 7–14; and André Gunder Frank, 'Third World War: A Political Economy of the Gulf War and the New World Order', *Third World Quarterly*, 13/2 (1992), 267–82.

11. See James Goldgeier and Michael McFaul, 'A Tale of Two Worlds: Core and Periphery in the Post-Cold War Era', *International Organization*, 66/2 (Spring 1992), 467–91.

12. This chapter eschews use of this term for a number of reasons. The term 'developing states' presumes development. This is absent in many of the states and regions under consideration. There is also in it a taste of historicism à la W. W. Rostow that seems anomalous, given that so many of the countries covered in the study seem to be taking a direction quite different from that predicted by liberal development theory.

13. See e.g. André Gunder Frank, *Capitalism and Underdevelopment: Historical Studies of Chile and Brazil* (New York: Monthly Review Press, 1967); and his *Latin America: Underdevelopment or Revolution* (New York: Monthly Review Press, 1969); and Wallerstein, *Modern World System*.

14. Buzan, *People, States, Fear*, 65–9. Buzan does not himself employ the category 'Third World' in this section. It is noteworthy, however, that all of his examples of weak states (p. 66) are in regions of the Third World. See also Robert Jackson, *Quasi-States: Sovereignty, International Relations and the Third World* (Cambridge: Cambridge University Press, 1990); and Joel Migdal, *Strong Societies and Weak States: State–Society Relations and State Capabilities* (Princeton: Princeton University Press, 1988).

15. James Blight and Thomas Weiss, 'Must the Grass Still Suffer? Some Thoughts on Third World Conflict after the Cold War', *Third World Quarterly*, 13/2 (1992), 249.

16. See S. Neil MacFarlane, *Superpower Rivalry and Third World Radicalism: The Idea of National Liberation* (Baltimore, MD.: Johns Hopkins University Press, 1985), 7.

17. For an extensive argument along these lines with regard to the Middle East, see Edward Said, *Orientalism* (New York: Pantheon, 1978).

18. See e.g. Mohammed Ayoob, 'The Security Problematic of the Third World', *World Politics*, 42/2 (Jan. 1991), 264; and Blight and Weiss, 'Must the Grass', 235–6.

19. See the exchange in *Survival*, 22/3 (May–June 1990) between Douglas MacDonald ('Anti-Interventionism and the Study of American Politics in the Third World', 225–46); and Jerome Slater ('Reassessing Third World Interventionism: A Response to MacDonald', 247–59). Both recognize the tendency of the United States to support anti-democratic regimes during the cold war, although they differ on the desirability of such a policy.

20. This point is convincingly made by Ayoob, 'Security Problematic', 263.
21. See e.g. George Breslauer's analysis, 'Soviet Policy in the Middle East, 1967–72: Unalterable Antagonism or Collaborative Competition?', in Alexander George (ed.), *Managing US-Soviet Rivalry* (Boulder, Colo.: Westview, 1983), 65–106.
22. See Gerald Helman and Steven Ratner, 'Saving Failed States', *Foreign Policy*, 89 (Winter 1992–3), 4. See also Helen Desfosses-Cohn, *Soviet Policy Toward Black Africa: The Focus on National Integration* (New York: Praeger, 1972).
23. Kenneth Waltz noted in this context the inherently conservative quality of the superpowers in a bipolar world, and in the same analysis noted that in such a world, there are no peripheries. Kenneth Waltz, *Theory of International Politics* (New York: McGraw-Hill, 1979), 171, 174.
24. Blight and Weiss, 'Must the Grass', 249. See also S. Neil MacFarlane, 'Superpower Rivalry in the 1990s', *Third World Quarterly*, 12/1 (Jan. 1990), 1–25.
25. For a related point focusing on Third World alignment behaviour, see Steven David, 'Explaining Third World Alignment', *World Politics*, 63/2 (Jan. 1991), 233–56.
26. See e.g. S. Neil MacFarlane, 'The Superpowers and Third World Security', in Job, 225–8. This would also appear to be the inference of the conclusion to Blight and Weiss, 'Must the Grass', 249–51.
27. See also Bruce Russett and James Sutterlin, 'The U.N. in a New World Order', *Foreign Affairs*, 120/1 (1989–90), 82–3.
28. On this point, see Morton Halperin, 'Guaranteeing Democracy', *Foreign Policy*, 91 (Summer 1993), 117.
29. Carol Lancaster, 'Democracy in Africa', *Foreign Policy*, 85 (Winter 1991–2), 161.
30. Halperin, 'Guaranteeing Democracy', 119.
31. See Lancaster, 'Democracy in Africa', 152.
32. Charles Krauthammer, 'The Unipolar Moment', *Foreign Affairs*, 70/1 (Winter 1991), 23–33. Krauthammer's conclusions concerning the power-political aspect of American hegemony were paralleled by Francis Fukuyama's argument concerning the uncontested ideological hegemony of liberal political and economic values subsequent to the collapse of communism as an alternative system of ideas. See Francis Fukuyama, 'The End of History', *The National Interest*, 16 (Summer 1989), 1–18.
33. For examples of this thinking, see Michael Klare, 'The New Challenges to Global Security', *Current History*, 92/573 (Apr. 1993), 155–61; and Alvaro de Soto and Graciana del Castillo, 'Obstacles to Peacebuilding', *Foreign Policy*, 94 (Spring 1994), 69.
34. André Gunder Frank, 'Third World War: A Political Economy of the Gulf War and the New World Order', *Third World Quarterly*, 13/2 (1992), 267.
35. Ibid. 279.
36. Goldgeier and McFaul, 'Tale of Two Worlds', 487.
37. On this point, see again Frank, 'Third World War', 270.
38. See Korany, 'End of History', 11.
39. On this point, see de Soto and del Castillo, 'Obstacles', 69–83. See also James Boyce and Manuel Pastor, 'Aid for Peace: Can International Institutions Help Prevent Conflict?', *World Policy Journal*, 15/2 (Summer 1998), 43–4.
40. As noted already, it could be argued that the end of the cold war was a factor contributing to the Iraqi assault on Kuwait. To attribute a primary causal role to structural change in this instance would, however, be misleadingly simplistic, given the amplitude of local and regional factors impinging on the Iraqi decision.

41. T. R. Gurr, 'Peoples against States: Ethnopolitical Conflict and the Changing World System' (ISA Presidential Address, 1 Apr. 1994), as reprinted in *Commentary* (Canada), 50 (Nov. 1994), 3–4.
42. IISS, *The Military Balance*, 1987–8 and 1997–8 (London: IISS, 1987 and 1997).
43. David Malone and John Cockell, *1996 Jules Léger Seminar: The Security Council in the 1990s* (Ottawa: DFAIT, 1997), 5.
44. For a general analysis of this point, see Michael Mandelbaum, 'The Reluctance to Intervene', *Foreign Policy*, 95 (Summer 1994), 3–18.
45. See on this point Andrew Hurrell, 'Latin America in the New World Order: A Regional Bloc of the Americas?', *International Affairs*, 68/1 (1992), 128.
46. For a general analysis of this point, see Sean Lynn-Jones and Steven Miller, *Changing Dimensions of International Security* (Cambridge, Mass.: MIT Press, 1995).
47. See Myron Weiner, 'Security, Stability, and International Migration', *International Security*, 17/3 (Winter 1992/3).
48. On this question, see Thomas Weiss (ed.), *Beyond UN Subcontracting: Task-Sharing with Regional Security Arrangements and Service-Providing NGOs* (London: Macmillan, 1998).

CHAPTER 2

1. The literature is obviously vast on these two opposing paradigms. A good general summary can be found in Diana Hunt, *Economic Theories of Development: An Analysis of Competing Paradigms* (New York: Harvester Wheatsheaf, 1989). For a representative contrast between the two approaches, see Walt Rostow, *The Stages of Economic Growth: A Non-Communist Manifesto* (Cambridge: Cambridge University Press, 1960); and André Gunder Frank, *Capitalism and Underdevelopment in Latin America* (New York: Monthly Review Press, 1967).
2. Seymour Martin Lipset, 'Some Social Prerequisites for Democracy: Economic Development and Political Legitimacy', *American Political Science Review*, 53/1 (1959), 86.
3. The most influential book in this regard was Samuel P. Huntington, *Political Order in Changing Societies* (New Haven: Yale University Press, 1968), who argued that the earlier modernization writers had the 'same hopeful unreality which characterised much of the sympathetic Western writing about the Soviet Union in the 1920s and 1930s': cf. p. 35.
4. Daniel P. Moynihan, 'The American Experiment', *Public Interest* (Fall 1975), 7.
5. This was the title of Samuel P. Huntington, *The Third Wave: Democratisation in the Late Twentieth Century* (Norman and London: University of Oklahoma Press, 1991). For a review on the massive literature generated by this model, see Doh Chull Shin, 'On the Third Wave of Democratisation: A Synthesis and Evaluation of Recent Theory and Research', *World Politics*, 47 (Oct. 1994), 135–70.
6. See Carol Lancaster, 'Democratisation in Sub-Saharan Africa', *Survival*, 35/3 (1993), 38–50.
7. See in particular The World Bank, *Accelerated Development in Sub-Saharan Africa: An Agenda for Action* (Oxford: Oxford University Press, 1981).

8. But the reality of considerable state intervention is well illustrated in the studies of Alice Amsden, 'Taiwan's Economic History: A Case Study of Etatisme and a Challenge to Dependency Theory', *Modern China*, 5/3 (1979); and Robert Wade, 'East Asia's Economic Success: Conflicting Perspectives, Partial Insights, Shaky Evidence', *World Politics*, 44 (1992).

9. Jerry F. Hough, *The Struggle for the Third World: Soviet Debates and American Options* (Washington, DC: The Brookings Institution, 1986), 235–41.

10. See Karen L. Remmer, 'The Political Economy of Elections in Latin America', *American Political Science Review*, 87/2 (1993), 393–407.

11. For the case of the Middle East, see Robert Springborg, 'The Arab Bourgeoisie: A Revisionist Interpretation', *Arab Studies Quarterly*, 15/1 (1993), 13–39.

12. Most famously by Samuel P. Huntington, 'The Clash of Civilisations?', *Foreign Affairs*, 72/3 (1992), 22–49.

13. This is based on the famous analysis of democracy in Joseph Schumpeter, *Capitalism, Socialism and Democracy* (London: Routledge, 1994), 269.

14. John Locke, *Second Treatise of Government* (1689); and John Rawls, *A Theory of Justice* (Oxford: Clarendon Press, 1972).

15. J. Lonsdale, 'States and Social Processes in Africa: A Historiographical Survey', *African Studies Review*, 24 (1981), 139.

16. For a fuller analysis, see Peter R. Moody, Jr., *Political Opposition in Post-Confucian Society* (New York: Praeger, 1988).

17. To use Olson's analogy it is better to have a stationary bandit than roving bandits; see Mancur Olson, 'Dictatorship, Democracy and Development', *American Political Science Review*, 87/3 (1993), 567–73.

18. Roland Dannreuther, 'Creating States in Central Asia', *Adelphi Papers*, 288 (1994), 71–2.

19. The meaning of civil society is brilliantly analysed in Ernest Gellner, *Conditions of Liberty: Civil Society and its Rivals* (London: Hamish Hamilton, 1994). For a much more sceptical account, see Krishan Kumar, 'Civil Society: An Enquiry into the Usefulness of the Term', *British Journal of Sociology*, 44/3 (1993), 375–95.

20. Evelyne Huber, Dietrich Rueschmeyer, and John D. Stephens, 'The Impact of Economic Development on Democracy', *Journal of Economic Perspectives*, 7/3 (1993), 78–83. These authors also note the importance of an organized working class in promoting democracy.

21. Ghassan Salame (ed.), *Democracy without Democrats?: The Renewal of Politics in the Muslim World* (London: I. B. Tauris, 1994).

22. For a good basic survey, see Stephen Mulhall and Adam Swift, *Liberals and Communitarians* (Oxford: Blackwell, 1992); for a selection of writings, see Michael Sandel (ed.), *Liberalism and its Critics* (Oxford: Blackwell, 1984); and for a more entertaining Platonic-style dialogue on the liberal-communitarian debate, see Daniel Bell, *Communitarianism and its Critics* (Oxford: Clarendon Press, 1993).

23. For the distinctiveness of political Islam, see Ernest Gellner, *Islam, Post-Modernism and Reason* (London: Routledge, 1992); Patricia Crone, *Slaves on Horses: The Evolution of the Islamic Polity* (Cambridge: Cambridge University Press, 1980); and John A. Hall, *Powers and Liberties: The Causes and Consequences of the Rise of the West* (Harmondsworth: Penguin, 1985).

24. See Sami Zubaida, *Islam, the People and the State* (London: I. B. Tauris, 1993),

esp. ch. 6; and Yayha Sadowski, 'The New Orientalism and the Democracy Debate', *Merip* (July–Aug. 1993).

25. Graham Fuller, 'A Phased Introduction of Islamists', in Yehudah Mirsky and Matt Ahrens (eds.), *Democracy in the Middle East: Defining the Challenge* (Washington, DC: Washington Institute for Near East Policy, 1993).

26. John Waterbury, 'Democracy without Democrats?: The Potential for Political Liberalisation in the Middle East', in Salame, *Democracy without Democrats*, pp. 39–42.

27. Gilles Kepel, *The Prophet and the Pharaoh: Muslim Extremism in Egypt* (London: Al-Saqi, 1985).

28. Gilbert Rozman (ed.), *The East Asian Region: Confucian Heritage and its Modern Adaptation* (Princeton: Princeton University Press, 1991).

29. For a recent treatment of this question see Laurence Whitehead, 'Three International Dimensions of Democratization', in Laurence Whitehead (ed.), *The International Dimensions of Democratization: Europe and the Americas* (Oxford: Oxford University Press, 1996), 3–25.

30. Though some of the liberal aides to the Clinton administration recommended such an interventionist policy, see Morton H. Halperin, 'Guaranteeing Democracy', *Foreign Policy*, 91 (Summer 1993), 105–22.

31. Richard J. Bloomfield, 'Making the Western Hemisphere Safe for Democracy? The OAS Defence-of-Democracy Regime', *Washington Quarterly*, 17/2 (1994), 157–69.

32. Development Action Committee, *OECD Development Cooperation, 1993: Aid In Transition* (Paris: OECD, 1994), 52.

33. Francis Fukuyama, *The End of History and the Last of Man* (London: Penguin, 1992).

34. For an excellent historical survey of the contribution of the Scottish Enlightenment, see Laurence Whitehead, 'Introduction: Some Insights from Western Social Theory', *World Development*, 21/8 (1993), 1245–61.

35. Adam Ferguson, *Essay on the History of Civil Society* (1767) (Edinburgh: Edinburgh University Press, 1966), 387.

36. Karl Polanyi, *The Great Transformation: The Political and Economic Origins of our Time* (Boston: Beacon Press, 1957); Joseph A. Schumpeter, *Capitalism, Socialism and Democracy*; and Barrington Moore, Jr, *Social Origins of Dictatorship and Democracy* (London: Penguin, 1966).

CHAPTER 3

1. This is not true for all or even a majority of developing countries but it does encompass a large majority of the populations of developing countries taken in the aggregate. It is therefore wise to employ the inclusive term Third World with considerable caution and as a limited and subjective expression of a political nature.

2. In recent years a host of former radicals and liberals, including the German poet Hans Enzensberger and the former revolutionary Regis Debray, to name but two, have expressed exasperation with Third World politics. A number supported the bombing of Iraqi cities and the general population as means of punishing Saddam

Hussein's regime, while simultaneously expressing horror at his oppressive rule over the very same population.

3. It is necessary to bear in mind the widespread confusion between markets and privatization since they are not synonymous, especially where quasi-monopolistic utilities are concerned. But the espousal of pro-market policies and ideas are undoubtedly a historical turning-point because of the absence of rival intellectual concepts of economic organization for the first time in over a century. The attempt by some socialists to posit an alternative in the idea of democratic planning cannot be taken seriously. See Andrei Schleifer and Robert W. Vishny, 'The Politics of Market Socialism', *The Journal of Economic Perspectives*, 8/2 (Spring 1994); also comment by Pranab Bardhan and John E. Roemer in the same issue, pp. 165–81.

4. I shall be using the terms markets and capitalism interchangeably and propose to indicate variations specifically only when necessary, e.g. between private ownership and market and capitalist competition.

5. State involvement in the economy was extensive in a majority of authoritarian countries of this group of the political right.

6. Joan Nelson (ed.), *Economic Crisis and Policy Choice: The Political Economy of Adjustment in the Third World* (Princeton: Princeton University Press, 1980).

7. The weakening of a host of social, safety, and environmental legislation may also be regarded as microeconomic measures considered to allow freer play of market forces.

8. The revision of banking supervision in favour of the so-called looser touch may also be deemed an aspect of liberalization, but actually prompted by competitive deregulation to prevent the flight of financial activity to other less regulated centres. In this sense the debt crisis can be regarded as originating from the interplay of market forces.

9. Anne O. Krueger, 'The Political Economy of the Rent Seeking Society', *American Economic Review*, 64/3 (June 1974), 291–303.

10. See John Toye, *Dilemmas of Development* (Oxford: Blackwell, 1987).

11. Measured in terms of trade/GNP ratios and international capital flows, highlighting market opening, i.e., liberalization.

12. Some of the specific local problems were in fact similar in different developing countries and these comparable issues were, in some respects, connected to the underlying changes in the international political economy. See Barbara Stallings and Robert Kaufman (eds.), *Debt and Democracy in Latin America* (Boulder Colo.: Westview, 1988).

13. The importance of international agencies (i.e. IMF and the World Bank) derives not merely from the economic assistance which they provide, but their role in mediating a complete economic package involving private international lenders. See Lance Taylor, *Varieties of Stabilization Experience Towards Sensible Macroeconomics in the Third World* (Oxford: Clarendon, 1992); also Jeffrey Sachs (ed.), *Developing Country Debt and the World Economy*, (London: University of Chicago Press, 1989).

14. For an analysis of the new market conditions see Donald R. Lessard and John Williamson (eds.), *Capital Flight and Third World Debt* (Washington, DC: Institute for International Economics, 1987; also Peter B. Kenen, *Managing Exchange Rates*, RIIA (London: Routledge 1988).

15. The latter has distorted the debate on economic development by creating false

analogies (any country can copy irrespective of the stage of economic development) and misreading success as the exclusive product of appropriate pro-market
policies.

16. The Mexican economic crisis of late 1994 underlined these dangers and they also
threatened Southeast Asia as well during 1996, confirming the complications of a
high degree of dependence on international capital flows, especially short-term
capital. The IMF recognized the problem earlier in *International Capital Markets:
Developments, Prospects and Policy Issues* by David Folkerts-Landau and
Takatoshi Ito (Washington, DC, 1995), esp. pp. 11–16.

17. Several African countries are undergoing violent political turmoil and ethnic conflicts. The evident example of these is Rwanda which underwent complete chaos
with a collapse in economic activities and deterioration in infrastructure. Angola,
Liberia, Somalia, Sudan, Mali, Niger, Sierra Leone are experiencing costly civil
war both in terms of economic costs and human tragedies. Zaire, Togo Nigeria,
Kenya, Lesotho, Mozambique are suffering from political instability that
adversely affected investment and, in the case of Kenya, tourism. See UNIDO,
Industrial Development Global Report 1995 (Oxford: Oxford University Press,
1995), 80–6.

18. The emerging patterns of international specialization in East and Southeast Asia
are likely to accelerate in the context of the Uruguay round. The relocation of
manufacturing activity to the region from the advanced developed countries,
especially Japan, as well as between countries within the region has already been
occurring because of a new hierarchy of relative costs. Recent attempts to advance
the process of regional economic integration in the Asia Pacific should also serve
to reinforce the confidence of investors. Even the slumbering Indian giant
improved its growth performance after two decades of indifferent self-righteous
socialist economics.

19. See Rosemarie Forsyth, *The Political Economy of Oil in the Caucasus and Central
Asia*, Adeplhi Paper No. 300 (Oxford: OUP for the IISS, 1996).

20. For a lucid summary of the issues see 'Getting Out of a Fix', *The Economist* (13–20
Sept. 1997), 139. Also see Paul Krugman, 'What Happened in Asia' (Feb. 1998):
http://web.mit.edu/krugman/www.

21. See Sheila Page and Michael Davenport, *World Trade Reform: Do Developing
Countries Gain or Lose?* ODI Special Report (London: ODI, 1994); also Taylor,
Varieties.

22. See Taylor, *Varieties*; UNIDO, *Industrial Development*. Also Paul Mosley,
Conditionality as Bargaining Process: Structural-Adjustment Lending 1980–86
(Princeton: Princeton University Press, 1987).

23. Taylor, *Varieties*, 166.

24. See Toye, *Dilemmas of Development*. Also Mehdi Safaeddin, 'The Impact of
Trade Liberalisation on Export and GDP Growth in Least Developed Countries',
UNCTAD Review 1995 (Geneva: UN, 1995), 1–16.

25. The near-universal hostility towards such structural adjustment programmes,
which even unites the populace and governments which might otherwise lack
popular support, must signal political interference in the functioning of a
society.

26. There is empirical confirmation of this proposition in the growth of recent Latin
American trade interdependence. See *The Economist* (15 May 1993), 99–100.

27. See Pippa Malmgren, 'Economic Statecraft: United States Anti-Dumping and Countervailing Duty Policy', Department of International Relations, Ph.D. dissertation, LSE, 1989.

28. It is worth noting in passing that most economists are concerned to demonstrate the range of possibilities and conditions for the functioning of the market, but only venture in abstraction to point to the persistent actions of powerful agents in distorting the market—unless they happen to be weak Third World governments (e.g. rent-seeking). There is no mileage in highlighting the anti-market activities of the chief sponsors of market economics.

29. See Lakis Kaounides 'Looking into the Crystal Ball', *Business News* (Summer 1996), 17–21; also, by the same author, 'Advanced Materials: Corporate Strategies for Competitive Advantage', *Financial Times Newsletters and Management Reports* (Oct. 1995).

30. See Robert Wade, *Governing the Market* (Princeton: Princeton University Press, 1990).

31. World Bank, *East Asian Miracle* (Washington, DC, 1994).

32. Paul Krugman, 'The Myth of Asia's Miracle', *Foreign Affairs*, 73 (Nov.–Dec. 1994), 62–78; Alwyn Young, *The Tyranny of Numbers: Confronting the Statistical Realities of the East Asian Growth Experience*, NBER Working Paper Number 4680 (Mar. 1994).

33. See Kaounides, 'Crystal Ball'.

34. The ability to transact in the context of secure property rights was crucial in the four Asian cases and, significantly, weaker or absent where economic growth is lower, e.g. in India or in the stark instances of civil war in Africa. See Douglass C. North, *Structure and Change in Economic History* (New York: Norton, 1981). See more recently, Mancur Olson, 'Big Bills on the Sidewalk: Why Some Countries are Rich, and Others Poor', *The Journal of Economic Perspectives*, 10/2 (Spring 1996), 3–24.

35. See Toye, *Dilemmas of Development*.

36. For recent figures on the surge of fdi in developing countries see *The Economist* (10–16 Oct. 1994), 132, and UNCTAD, *World Investment Report* (New York: UN, 1997). The dominance of a small number of developing economies as host countries is noteworthy.

37. For recent contributions to the contrasting primacy of Europe see Robert Bartlett, *The Making of Europe* (London: Allen Lane, 1993) and Linda Colley, *Britons: Gorging the Nation 1707–1837* (London: Pimlico, 1992).

38. Of course this outcome is predicated, not only by the disappearance of ideological interpretations of conflict offering the possibility of amicable resolution in the future, however long-term, but also by the absence of any serious counterbalancing player to US dominance. If there is to be no eventual justice in a godless universe or reconciliation of disparate ethnicities in a classless world, all accounts must be settled in the here and now. Most ominously for adherents of the Enlightenment and notions of linearity in progress, the equanimity of major powers and their electorates, in the face of grave war crimes in the former Yugoslavia and elsewhere, is significant. Samuel Huntington elaborates the ideological justification to be deployed in such situations. See his 'The Clash of Civilizations?' *Foreign Affairs*, 72 (Summer 1993), 22–49.

39. The complicity of dominant powers over the Indonesian resort to genocide in East

Timor ought to have alerted the world to the degree of cynicism that was in store over Bosnia-Hercegovina.

40. A recent newspaper article by an anonymous Indian diplomat analyses the view from what is described as a South perspective. 'The Indo-Japan War of 1996', *The Asian Age*, 3/283–4 (28 and 29 Nov. 1996), consecutively, p. 9 (in two parts).

41. The high cost in unemployment to Argentina (up to a fifth of the workforce) of maintaining international confidence in its national currency by backing the entire currency issue with dollar reserves needs serious examination.

CHAPTER 4

1. In this chapter the term 'Third World' is used interchangeably with 'developing countries' and 'South'.

2. Evan Luard, *War in International Society* (London: I. B. Tauris, 1986), appendix 5. See also Kal Holsti, *The State, War, and the State of War* (Cambridge: Cambridge University Press, 1996); Mohammed Ayoob, *The Third World Security Predicament: State-Making, Regional Conflict and the International System* (Boulder, Colo.: Lynne Rienner, 1995); Amitav Acharya, 'The Periphery as the Core: The Third World and Security Studies', in Keith Krause and Michael Williams (eds.), *Critical Security Studies* (Minneapolis: University of Minnesota Press, 1997), 299–329.

3. Fred Halliday and Maxine Molyneux, 'Olof Palme and the Legacy of Bandung', in Kofi Buenor Hadjor (ed.), *New Perspectives on North-South Dialogue: Essays in Honour of Olof Palme* (London: I. B. Tauris, 1988), 159.

4. Hedley Bull, 'The Revolt Against the West', in Hedley Bull and Adam Watson (eds.), *The Expansion of International Society* (Oxford: Oxford University Press, 1984), 217–27.

5. Hedley Bull, 'The Third World and International Society', in George W. Keeton and George Schwarzenberger (eds.), *The Yearbook on International Affairs 1979* (London: Stevens and Sons, 1979), 18.

6. Mohammed Ayoob, 'The Third World in the System of States: Acute Schizophrenia or Growing Pains', *International Studies Quarterly*, 33 (1989), 67.

7. Robert L. Rothstein, 'Limits and Possibilities of Weak Theory: Interpreting North-South', *Journal of International Affairs*, 44/1 (Spring/Summer 1990), 170.

8. See Eli Kedourie, 'A New International Disorder', in Bull and Watson, *Expansion of International Society*, 347–55.

9. For an assessment of the role of the cold war in aggravating Third World conflict, see Amitav Acharya, *Third World Conflicts and International Order After the Cold War*, Working Paper no. 134 (Canberra: Australian National University, Peace Research Centre, 1993).

10. This scenario conforms to the neo-realist (Waltzian) argument that multipolar international systems are less stable that bipolar ones. Applying this perspective to post-cold war Europe, John Mearsheimer argues that 'a Europe without the superpowers . . . would probably be substantially more prone to violence than the past 45 years', despite the constraining impact of economic interdependence, political and functional institutions such as the CSCE and EC, and the pluralist domestic structure of European nations. 'Back to the Future: Instability in

Europe After the Cold War', *International Security*, 15/1 (Summer 1990), 54–5. Responses to Mearsheimer can be found in three subsequent issues of *International Security*. Although no forceful and predictive commentary about Third World security has yet been made, Mearsheimer's thesis appears to have found an echo in a number of recent scholarly writings on the subject.

11. Jose Thiago Cintra, 'Regional Conflicts: Trends in a Period of Transition', in *The Changing Strategic Landscape*, Adelphi Paper no. 237 (London: International Institute for Strategic Studies, 1989), 96–7.

12. Robert Jervis, 'The Future of World Politics: Will it Resemble the Past?', *International Security*, 16/3 (Winter 1991–2), 59.

13. Geoffrey Kemp, 'Regional Security, Arms Control, and the End of the Cold War', *Washington Quarterly*, 13/4 (Autumn 1990), 33.

14. William Pfaff, 'The World Reels in the Backwash of the Cold War', *International Herald Tribune* (9 Aug. 1993).

15. Christoph Carle, 'The Third World Will Do More of its Own Fighting', *International Herald Tribune* (15 Mar. 1989).

16. A number of surveys confirm this. One by Istvan Kende found that of the 120 wars during the 1945–76 period, 102 were internal wars (including anti-regime wars and tribal conflicts); while another study by Kirdon and Segal found that during the period 1973–86, there were 66 internal wars as opposed to 30 border wars. Cited in Caroline Thomas, 'New Directions in Thinking about Security in the Third World', in Ken Booth (ed.), *New Thinking about Strategy and International Security* (London: Harper Collins Academic, 1991), 269.

17. Barry Buzan, 'New Patterns of Global Security in the Twenty-First Century', *International Affairs*, 67/3 (1991), 441.

18. On the norms of territorial status in Africa see Robert H. Jackson and Carl G. Roseberg, 'Why Africa's Weak States Persist: The Empirical and the Juridical in Statehood', *World Politics*, 35/1 (Oct. 1982), 194–208.

19. 'The World's Wars: Tribalism Revisited', *The Economist* (21 Dec. 1991–31 Jan. 1992), 23–4.

20. It may be argued that at least some of the 'new' states of Eastern Europe and Central Asia may be considered part of the Third World, given that their security predicament bears considerable resemblance to that of the traditional Third World states. This includes low levels of socio-political cohesion and a strong element of state-nation dichotomy. If this criterion is applied, the Balkan states and the new states of Central Asia may be regarded as part of the Third World, since their security predicament is likely to centre on problems of internal stability and regime legitimation.

21. For a critical perspective on Africa's political and security challenges see Ken Booth and Peter Vale, 'Critical Security Studies and Regional Insecurity: The Case of Southern Africa', in Krause and Williams, *Critical Security Studies*, 329–58.

22. Oluyemi Adeniji, 'Regionalism in Africa', *Security Dialogue*, 24/2 (1993), 220.

23. For an interesting debate on the link between war and democracy in the context of the post-cold war era, see the response published in three subsequent issues of *International Security* to John Mearsheimer's article, 'Back to the Future'.

24. Barry Buzan, 'People, States and Fear', in Edward Azar and Chung-in Moon (eds.), *National Security in the Third World* (Aldershot: Edward Elgar, 1988), 32.

25. Kenneth N. Waltz, *Theory of International Politics* (Reading, Mass.: Addison-Wesley, 1979), 171.
26. See e.g. Zbigniew Brzezinski, 'Selective Global Commitment', *Foreign Affairs*, 70/4 (Fall 1991), 1–20. Testifying to the selectivity is the North's delayed and initially muted response to the unfolding humanitarian disasters in Rwanda and Somalia, which was pointed out by the UN Secretary-General himself (who contrasted the Northern response to African crises with its preoccupation with the Balkans conflict).
27. Mohammed Ayoob, 'Regional Security and the Third World', in Ayoob (ed.), *Regional Security in the Third World* (London: Croom Helm, 1986), 14.
28. Shahram Chubin, 'Third World Conflicts: Trends and Prospects', *International Social Science Journal*, 127 (Feb. 1991), 157.
29. Yezid Sayigh, *Confronting the 1990s: Security in the Developing Countries*, Adelphi Papers no. 251 (London: International Institute for Strategic Studies, 1990), 64.
30. Lawrence Freedman argues that the US victory over Iraq would discourage Third World regional powers from mounting a frontal assault on Western interests. 'The Gulf War and the New World Order', *Survival*, 33/3 (May–June 1991), 203.
31. Fred Halliday, *Cold War, Third World* (London: Hutchinson, 1994), 162.
32. On the sources of Third World conflict and insecurity, see Mohammed Ayoob, 'Security in the Third World: The Worm About to Turn', *International Affairs*, 60/1 (1984), 41–51; Udo Steinbach, 'Sources of Third World Conflict', in *Third World Conflict and International Security*, Adelphi Papers no. 166 (London: International Institute for Strategic Studies, 1981), 21–8; Soedjatmoko, 'Patterns of Armed Conflict in the Third World', *Alternatives*, 10/4 (1985), 477–93; Edward Azar and Chung-in Moon, 'Third World National Security: Towards a New Conceptual Framework', *International Interactions*, 11/2 (1984), 103–35; Buzan, 'People, States and Fear', 14–43; Sayigh, *Confronting the 1990s*; Mohammed Ayoob, 'The Security Predicament of the Third World State', in Brian L. Job (ed.), *The (In)Security Dilemma: The National Security of Third World States* (Boulder, Colo.: Lynne Rienner, 1992); Steven R. David, 'Explaining Third World Alignment', *World Politics*, 43/2 (Jan. 1991), 232–56.
33. Chubin, 'Third World Conflicts', 159.
34. George Bush, 'The Possibility of a New World Order', *Vital Speeches of the Day* (15 May 1991), 450–2.
35. Mitsuru Yamamoto, 'Redefining the North-South Problem', *Japan Review of International Affairs*, 7/2 (Fall 1993), 272.
36. Marc Williams, 'Re-articulating the Third World Coalition: The Role of the Environmental Agenda', *Third World Quarterly*, 14/1 (1993), 20–1.
37. Vandana Shiva, 'Why South Greens See Red', *The Sunday Times of India* (26 Apr. 1992), 10.
38. 'A Bargain Not a Whinge', *The Times* (1 June 1992), 15.
39. Cited in Patricia Adams, 'Third World Tactics in Rio: Soak the West', *Globe and Mail* (4 June 1992), A19.
40. Thomas Risse-Kappen, 'Between a New World Order and None: Explaining the Reemergence of the United Nations in World Politics', in Krause and Williams, *Critical Security Studies*, 244–99.
41. 'New World Order: An Interview with Zbigniew Brzezinski', *SAIS Review*, 11/2 (Summer–Fall 1991), 2.

42. The concept of humanitarian intervention, though by no means novel, was high-lighted in the wake of the US-led UN intervention in northern Iraq to protect the Kurds in 1991. In supporting the international community's 'right to intervene' in humanitarian cases, the then UN Secretary-General, Javier Perez de Cuellar, spoke of 'an irresistible shift in public attitudes towards the belief that the defense of the oppressed in the name of morality should prevail over frontiers and legal documents'. He added that the Universal Declaration of Human Rights does 'implicitly call into question this inviolable notion of sovereignty' and conse-quently a 'balance' has been established 'between the right of States, as confirmed by the Charter, and the rights of the individual, as confirmed by the Universal Declaration'. Cited in Richard N. Gardner, 'International Law and the Use of Force', in *Three Views on the Issue of Humanitarian Intervention* (Washington, DC: United States Institute of Peace, 1992), 2.

43. David J. Scheffer, 'Challenges Confronting Collective Security: Humanitarian Intervention', in *Three Views on the Issue of Humanitarian Intervention* (Washington, DC: United States Institute of Peace, 1992), 2.

44. Mohammed Ayoob, 'Squaring the Circle: Collective Security in a System of States', in Thomas G. Weiss (ed.), *Collective Security in a Changing World* (Boulder, Colo.: Lynne Rienner, 1993), 56–7.

45. Hedley Bull, 'Intervention in the Third World', in Hedley Bull (ed.), *Intervention in World Politics* (Oxford: Clarendon Press, 1984), 135–56.

46. Don Oberdorfer, 'U.S. Military Strategy Shifts to Large-Scale Mobile Forces: Plan Emphasizes Regional Threats', *International Herald Tribune* (20 May 1991), 1. For the origin and evolution of US rapid deployment forces, see Amitav Acharya, *U.S. Military Strategy in the Gulf: Origin and Evolution under the Carter and Reagan Administrations* (New York: Routledge, 1989).

47. K. Subrahmanyam, 'Regional Conflicts and their Linkage to Strategic Confrontation', in Joseph Rotblat and Sven Hellman (eds.), *Nuclear Strategy and World Security* (London: Macmillan, 1985), 322.

48. Shahram Chubin, 'The South and the New World Disorder', *Washington Quarterly* (Autumn 1993), 98.

49. K. Subrahmanyam, 'Export Controls and the North-South Controversy', *The Washington Quarterly* (Spring 1993), 135.

50. S. D. Muni, 'The Post-Cold War Third World: Uncertain Peace and Elusive Development', *Bulletin of Peace Proposals*, 23/1 (1992), 93–102.

51. Li Chien-pin, 'Fear, Greed, or Garage Sale: The Analysis of Military Expenditures in East Asia', *Pacific Review*, 10/2 (1997), 274–88; Desmond J. Ball, 'Arms and Affluence: Military Acquisitions in the Asia-Pacific Region', *International Security*, 18/3 (Winter 1993/94), 78–112; and Amitav Acharya, *An Arms Race in Post-Cold War Southeast Asia? Prospects for Control*, Pacific Strategic Papers no. 8 (Singapore: Institute of Southeast Asian Studies, 1994).

52. For discussion of these issues see Amitav Acharya, 'Beyond Anarchy: Third World Instability and International Order after the Cold War', in Stephanie Neuman (ed.), *International Relations Theory and the Third World* (London: Macmillan, 1998), 159–211.

53. FBIS-EAS-92-173-S, 4 September 1992, p. 25.

54. 'Take Pragmatic Line on Human Rights: Kan Seng', *The Straits Times* (17 June 1993), 1.

55. Jefferson R. Plantilla and Sebasti L. Raj (eds.), *Human Rights in Asian Cultures: Continuity and Change* (Osaka: Asia-Pacific Human Rights Information Center, 1997).

56. On the origins and role of NAM see: Peter Lyon, *Neutralism* (Leicester: Leicester University Press, 1963); A. W. Singham and S. Hume, *Non-Alignment in the Age of Alignments* (London: Zed Books, 1986); Peter Willetts, *The Non-Aligned Movement* (London: Frances Pinter, 1978); Satish Kumar, 'Non-Alignment: International Goals and National Interests', *Asian Survey*, 23/4 (Apr. 1983), 445–61; Fred Halliday, 'The Maturing of the Non-Aligned: Perspectives from New Delhi', *Third World Affairs* (London: Third World Foundation, 1985); Bojana Tadic, 'The Movement of the Non-Aligned and Its Dilemmas Today', *Review of International Affairs*, 32/756 (5 Oct. 1981), 19–24; A. W. Singham (ed.), *The Non-Aligned Movement in World Politics* (Westport, Conn.: Lawrence Hill, 1977).

57. Pervaiz Iqbal Cheema, 'NAM and Security', *Strategic Studies* (Islamabad), 14/3 (Spring 1991), 15.

58. Mohammed Ayoob, 'The Third World in the System of States: Acute Schizophrenia or Growing Pains', *International Studies Quarterly*, 33 (1989), 75.

59. Cheema, 'NAM and Security', 18.

60. Peter Lyon, 'Marginalization of the Third World', *Jerusalem Journal of International Relations*, 11/3 (Sept. 1989), 65.

61. 'Jakarta Wants NAM to Focus on Pressing Economic and Human Problems', *The Straits Times* (4 Aug. 1992), 17.

62. 'Goodbye Nehru, Hello Suharto', *The Economist* (19 Sept. 1992), 32.

63. 'Jakarta Wants NAM to Focus', *The Straits Times* (4 Aug. 1992), 17.

64. Timothy M. Shaw, 'The Non-Aligned Movement and the New International Division of Labour', in Hadjor, *New Perspectives*, 178.

65. On NIEO, see Ervin Laszlo *et al.* (eds.), *The Objective of the New International Economic Order* (New York: Pergamon Press for UNITAR, 1979); Craig Murphy, *The Emergence of the NIEO Ideology* (Boulder, Colo.: Westview Press, 1984); Jagdish Bhagwati, 'Ideology and North-South Relations', *World Development*, 14/6 (1986), 767–74; Robert W. Cox, 'Ideologies and the New International Economic Order: Reflections on Some Recent Literature', *International Organization*, 32/2 (Spring 1979), 257–302.

66. Helen O'Neill, 'The North-South Dialogue and the Concept of Mini-NIEO', in Kimmo Kiljunen (ed.), *Region-to-Region Cooperation Between Developed and Developing Countries* (Aldershot: Avebury, 1990), 4.

67. Halliday and Molyneux, 'Olof Palme', 158.

68. Michael W. Doyle, 'Stalemate in the North-South Debate: Strategies and the New International Economic Order', *World Politics*, 35/3 (Apr. 1983), 426–64; Roger D. Hansen, *Beyond the North-South Stalemate* (New York: McGraw-Hill, 1979).

69. Steven G. Livingstone, 'The Politics of International Agenda Setting: Reagan and North-South Relations', *International Studies Quarterly*, 36 (1992), 318–19.

70. John Ravenhill, 'The North-South Balance of Power', *International Affairs*, 66/4 (Oct. 1990), 738.

71. S. D. Muni, 'The Post-Cold War Third World: Uncertain Peace and Elusive Development', *Bulletin of Peace Proposals*, 23/1 (1992), 98.

72. François Mitterand, 'Let North and South Set a Global Contract', *International Herald Tribune* (2–3 July 1994), 4.

73. Fred Halliday, 'The Third World and the End of the Cold War', Paper presented to the Conference on the New International Context of Development, Madison, Wis., 24–6 Apr. 1992, p. 44.

74. Paul Lewis, 'Negotiators in Rio Agree to Increase Aid to Third World', *New York Times* (14 June 1992), 1.

75. Paul Lewis, 'Poor vs. Rich in Rio', *New York Times* (3 June 1992), A1.

76. See e.g. Louise Fawcett, 'Regionalism in Historical Perspective', in Louise Fawcett and Andrew Hurrell (eds.), *Regionalism in World Politics* (Oxford: Oxford University Press, 1995), 10–17.

77. Lincoln Gordon, 'Economic Regionalism Reconsidered', *World Politics*, 13 (1961), 245.

78. Charles A. Duffy and Werner J. Feld, 'Whither Regional Integration Theory', in Gavin Boyd and Werner Feld (eds.), *Comparative Regional Systems* (New York: Pergamon Press, 1980), 497.

79. Thomas Perry Thornton, 'Regional Organizations in Conflict-Management', *Annals of the American Academy of Political and Social Science*, 518 (Nov. 1991), 132–42; Fen Osler Hampson, 'Building a Stable Peace: Opportunities and Limits to Security Cooperation in Third World Regional Conflicts', *International Journal*, 45/2 (Spring 1990), 454–9.

80. Esperanza Duran, 'Pacification, Security and Democracy: Contadora's Role in Central America', in Peter Calvert (ed.), *The Central American Security System: North-South or East-West* (Cambridge: Cambridge University Press, 1988), 155–76; Kenneth Roberts, 'Bullying and Bargaining: The United States, Nicaragua, and Conflict-Resolution in Central America', *International Security*, 15 (Fall 1990), 67–102.

81. Gareth Evans, *Cooperating for Peace* (Sydney: Allen and Unwin, 1993), 31.

82. 'Liberia: Imposing Peace', *The Economist* (18 Aug. 1990), 35–6; 'Liberians Sign Truce, a First Step', *International Herald Tribune* (30 Nov. 1990), 2.

83. Amitav Acharya, *A New Regional Order in Southeast Asia: ASEAN in the Post-Cold War Era*, Adelphi Paper no. 279 (London: International Institute for Strategic Studies, 1993).

84. Samuel M. Makinda, *Seeking Peace From Chaos: Humanitarian Intervention in Somalia*, Occasional Paper Series, International Peace Academy (Boulder, Colo.: Lynne Riener, 1993), 84; Jeffery Clark, 'Debacle in Somalia', *Foreign Affairs*, 72/1 (America and the World 1992–3), 116.

85. Amitav Acharya, 'Regional Organizations and UN Peacekeeping', in Ramesh Thakur and Carlyle Thayer (eds.), *A Crisis of Expectations: UN Peacekeeping in the 1990s* (Boulder, Colo.: Westview Press, 1995).

86. For a discussion of the limitations of regional peace and security organizations, see Michael Barnett, 'Partners in Peace: The UN, Regional Organizations, and Peacekeeping', *Review of International Studies*, 21 (1995), 411–33.

87. Davidson Nicol, 'Introductory Studies', in Davidson Nicol, et al, *Regionalism and the New International Economic Order* (Oxford: Pergamon Press, 1981), p. xxv.

88. Sayigh, *Confronting the 1990s*, 66–7.

89. Hans Henrik-Holm, 'The End of the Third World', *Journal of Peace Research*, 27/1 (1990), 5; Bruce Moon, 'Political Economy and Political Change in the Evolution of North-South Relations', in Gavin Boyd and Gerald Hopple

(eds.), *Political Change and Foreign Policies* (London: Frances Pinter, 1987), 225–50.

90. 'NAFTA is Not Alone', *The Economist* (18 July 1994), 47.
91. Barry Buzan, *People, States and Fear: The National Security Problem in International Relations* (Brighton: Wheatsheaf Books, 1983), 141.
92. Olusegun Obasanjo, 'Africa in the 21st Century', *Security Dialogue*, 24/2 (1993), 201.
93. For a discussion of the debates about the Third World in IR theory, see Neuman, *International Relations of the Third World*.
94. The extent of North–South economic interdependence is evident from the fact that the Third World and the countries of the former Soviet bloc are the destination for 42% of America's exports, 20% of Western Europe's (47% if intra-European Union trade is excluded), and 48% of Japan's. On the import side, American imports of manufactured goods from the Third World rose from 5% of the value of US manufacturing output in 1978 to 11% in 1990. 'A Survey of the Global Economy', *The Economist* (1 Sept. 1994), 13 and 16.
95. Buzan, 'New Patterns of Global Security'.

CHAPTER 5

1. Robert Kaufman and Barbara Stallings (eds.), *Debt and Democracy in Latin America* (Boulder, Colo.: Westview, 1989).
2. The literature is enormous, but see e.g. Rosemary Thorp and Laurence Whitehead (eds.), *Latin American Debt and the Adjustment Crisis* (London: St Antony's/ Macmillan, 1987); Pedro-Pablo Kuczynski, *Latin American Debt* (Baltimore: Johns Hopkins University Press, 1988); Stephany Griffith-Jones and Osvaldo Sunkel, *Debt and Development Crises in Latin America* (Oxford: Clarendon Paperbacks, 1989).
3. In fact, the debt increased from US$ 379 billion in 1985 to US$ 443 billion in 1990. Unless otherwise indicated, all figures are from ECLAC.
4. On the thesis of marginalization see e.g. Jorge G. Castaneda, 'Latin America and the End of the Cold War', *World Policy Journal*, 7/3 (Summer, 1990), 469–92.
5. See e.g. Sebastian Edwards, *Crisis and Reform in Latin America. From Despair to Hope* (Oxford: Oxford University Press, 1995).
6. See e.g. Fareed Zakaria, 'The Rise of Illiberal Democracy', *Foreign Affairs* (Nov./Dec. 1998), 22–43.
7. Benn Ross Schneider, 'Democratic Consolidation: Some Broad Comparisons and Sweeping Arguments', *Latin American Research Review*, 30/2 (1995), 225.
8. Antoinette Handley, 'Lessons from Latin America', in Antoinette Handley and Greg Mills (eds.), *From Isolation to Integration? The South African Economy in the 1990s* (Johannesburg: South African Institute of International Affairs, 1996), 167–79.
9. Michael Camdessus 'Latin America and the Challenge of Globalization', *IMF Survey* (1 July 1996), 213, 219–20.
10. Andrés Bianchi, 'Winning Legitimacy for Central Bank was Chile's Priority', *Business Day* (Johannesburg, 13 Jan. 1995), 8.
11. The standard work on the politics of economic reform in Latin America is

Stephen Haggard and Robert Kaufman (eds.), *The Politics of Economic Adjustment* (Princeton: Princeton University Press, 1992). See also Luiz Carlos Bresser Pereira, José María Maravall, and Adam Przworski, *Economic Reform in New Democracies: A Social Democratic Approach* (Cambridge: Cambridge University Press, 1993).

12. Werner Baer and Melissa H. Birch (eds.) *Privatisation in Latin America: New Roles for the Public and Private Sectors* (Westport, Conn.: Praeger, 1994).

13. Larry Diamond and Marc F. Plattner (eds.), *Economic Reform and Democracy* (Baltimore: Johns Hopkins University Press, 1995).

14. On some of the lessons of the Mexican crisis, see Handley, 'Lessons', and Camdessus, 'Latin America'.

15. See Alejandro Foxley, 'The Neoconservative Economic Experiment in Chile', in J. Samuel and Arturo Valenzuela (eds.), *Military Rule in Chile: Dictatorship and Oppositions* (Baltimore: Johns Hopkins University Press, 1986), and Eduardo Silva, 'The Political Economy of Chile's Regime Transition: From Radical to Pragmatic Neo-Liberal Policies', in Paul W. Drake and Iván Jaksic (eds.), *The Struggle for Democracy in Chile 1982–1990* (Lincoln, Neb.: University of Nebraska Press, 1991).

16. See speech by Eduardo Aninat, Chile's Minister of Finance, 'Opening Address by the Chairman', 1996 Annual Meeting of the International Monetary Fund, and the World Bank group, 1 Oct. 1996 (mimeo).

17. See Jorge Heine, 'A UN Agenda for Development: Reflections on the Social Question in the South', in Ramesh Takur (ed.), *The United Nations at Fifty: Retrospect and Prospect* (Dunedin, New Zealand: University of Otago, 1995), 119–26.

18. On the efforts to eradicate poverty in Chile, see *La pobreza en Chile: Un desafío de equidad e integración social* (Santiago: Consejo Nacional para la Superación de la Pobreza, Aug. 1996).

19. Haggard and Kaufman, *Politics of Adjustment*, 25. Cited in Larry Diamond 'Consolidating Democracy in the Americas', *Annals of the American Academy of Political Science* (Mar. 1997), 27.

20. See Moises Naim, *Paper Tigers and Minotaurs: The Politics of Venezuela's Economic Reforms* (Washington: Carnegie Endowment for International Peace, 1993), 30.

21. On the challenges this has entailed, see Juan J. Linz and Alfred Stepan, *Problems of Democratic Transition and Consolidation: Southern Europe, South America and Post Communist Europe* (Baltimore: Johns Hopkins University Press, 1996).

22. Samuel P. Huntington, *The Third Wave: Democratization in the late Twentieth Century* (Norman: University of Oklahoma Press, 1991).

23. See the excellent essay by Guillermo O'Donnell, 'Transitions, Continuities, Paradoxes', in Scott Mainwaring, Guillermo O'Donnell, and J. Samuel Valenzuela (eds.), *Issues in Democratic Consolidation: The New South American Democracies in Comparative Perspective* (Notre Dame, Ind.: University of Notre Dame Press, 1992). See also the wide-ranging collection of essays in Laurence Whitehead (ed.), *The International Dimensions of Democratization: Europe and the Americas* (Oxford: Oxford University Press, 1996).

24. Diamond, 'Consolidating Democracy'.

25. J. Samuel Valenzuela, 'Democratic Consolidation in Post Transitional Settings', in Mainwaring, O'Donnell, and Valenzuela, *Issues*, and Larry Diamond and Marc Plattner (eds.) *Civil Military Relations and Democracy* (Baltimore: Johns Hopkins University Press, 1996).

26. O'Donnell, 'Transitions'.

27. Alicia Frohmann, 'Cooperación política e integración latinoamericana en los '90', Nueva Serie Flacso (Santiago: FLACSO, 1996), 6. For an earlier, book-length treatment of the subject by the same author, see *Puentes sobre la turbulencia: La concertación política latinoamericana en los 80* (Santiago: FLACSO, 1990). See also Luciano Tomassini (ed.), *Nuevas formas de concertación regional en América Latina* (Buenos Aires: Grupo Editor Latinamericano, 1990).

28. Carl Kaysen, Robert A. Pastor, and Laura W. Rood (eds.), *Collective Responses to Regional Problems: The Case of Latin America and the Caribbean* (Cambridge, Mass.: The American Academy of Arts and Sciences, 1994).

29. See e.g. Andrew Hurrell, 'Regionalism in the Americas', in Louise Fawcett and Andrew Hurrell (eds.), *Regionalism in World Politics* (Oxford: Oxford University Press: 1995), 250–82.

30. ECLAC, *Panorama de la Inserción Internacional de América Latina y el Caribe: Edición 1996* (Santiago: ECLAC, 1996), 30.

31. For a recent appraisal of the revival of regionalism in Latin America, see ECLAC, 'Desenvolvimiento de los procesos de Integración en América Latina y el Caribe', *LCIR*, 152–8 (Santiago, Chile, 16 May 1995); and ECLAC, 'Evolución y perspectivas del comercio y las inversiones intrarregionales', *LCIR*, 1623 (5 Feb. 1996). See also Jean Grugel, 'Latin America and the Remaking of the Americas', in Andrew Gamble and Anthony Payne (eds.), *Regionalism and World Order* (London: MacMillan, 1996), 131–68.

32. ECLAC, *Panorama*, 14. Part of my analysis draws on this excellent report.

33. Ibid.

34. For a recent assessment, see ECLAC. 'Evolución, análisis y perspectivas del Mercado Común del Sur', *LCIR* 1706 (24 Jan. 1997).

35. See my 'Open Regionalism in the South has Obvious Lessons', *Business Day* (10 Oct. 1996), 26.

36. The World Bank recently issued a highly critical report of MERCOSUR on those grounds. See 'Informe del Banco Mundial Critica Barreras Comerciales de MER-COSUR', *The Wall Street Journal Americas, El Mercurio* (23 Oct. 1996), B7.

37. Alvaro Ramos Trigo, 'Uruguay: Gateway to MERCOSUR', an address given at the South Africa Institute of International Affairs, Johannesburg, 16 September 1996 (mimeo).

38. Greg Mills, 'A Blueprint to Meet the Challenge of Africa's Regional Demands', *Business Day* (31 Oct. 1996), 16.

39. 'Chilean Deal Paves the Way for Regional Success', *Sunday Times* (Johannesburg, 14 July 1996), 8.

40. ECLAC, *Panorama*, 121–8.

41. Edwards, *Crisis and Reform in Latin America*, vii.

CHAPTER 6

1. Richard F. Donner and Gary Hawes, 'The Political Economy of Growth in Southeast and Northeast Asia', in Manocherhr Doraj (ed.), *The Changing Political Economy of the Third World* (Boulder, Colo.: Lynne Reinner, 1995), 146.
2. Ibid. 146.
3. Perhaps the most famous of these models is Chalmers Johnson's 'four-fold structural model of East Asian high-growth systems'. The model consists of the following elements: 'stable rule by a political-bureaucratic elite not acceding to political demands that would undermine economic growth; cooperation between public and private sectors under the overall guidance of a pilot planning agency; heavy and continuing investment in education for everyone, combined with policies to ensure the equitable distribution of the wealth created by high-speed growth; and a government that understands the need to use and respect methods of economic intervention based on the price mechanism.' Chalmers Johnson, 'Political Institutions and Economic Performance: the Government-Business Relationship in Japan, South Korea, and Taiwan', in Frederic C. Deyo (ed.), *The Political Economy of New Asian Industrialism* (Ithaca, NY: Cornell University Press, 1987), 145. See also Richard Stubbs, 'Asia-Pacific Regionalization and the Global Economy: A Third Form of Capitalism?', *Asian Survey*, 35/9 (Sept. 1995), 785–97.
4. Susunu Awanohara, ' "Look East": The Japan Model', *Asian-Pacific Economic Literature*, 1/1 (May 1987), 75–89.
5. Cal Clark and Steve Chan, 'The East Asian Development Model: Looking Beyond the Stereotypes', *International Studies Notes*, 15/1 (Winter 1990), 1.
6. See e.g. 'Asia's Competing Capitalisms', *The Economist* (24 June 1995), 20.
7. Stubbs, 'Third Form of Capitalism', 792.
8. Mark Mason, 'Foreign Direct Investment in East Asia: Trends and Critical Issues', *CFR Asia Project Working Paper* (1994), 6.
9. See *ASEAN-Japan Statistical Pocketbook 1995* (Tokyo: ASEAN Centre, 1995), iv–1.
10. *Far Eastern Economic Review* (12 Oct. 1995), 54–60.
11. 'The Formation of a Self-Supporting Cycle of Structural Transformation in East Asia', *Japan Review of International Affairs*, 9/3 (Summer 1995), 237.
12. Amitav Acharya, 'Arms Proliferation Issues in ASEAN: Towards a More "Conventional" Defence Posture?', *Contemporary Southeast Asia*, 10/3 (Dec. 1988), 242–68.
13. Fred Hiatt, 'Cheney's Message in Asia: U.S. Troops are Here to Stay', *International Herald Tribune* (24–5 Feb. 1990), 1.
14. 'Asian Conflicts "may Pose Post-Cold War Threats" ', *The Straits Times* (Singapore, 3 Jan. 1992), 13.
15. Testimony by Lieutenant General James Clapper to the Senate Armed Services Committee, 22 Jan. 1992, in *Regional Flashpoints Potential for Military Conflict* (Washington, DC: United States Information Service, 24 Dec. 1992), 6.
16. 'Singapore Leader Warns on Power Shift in Asia', *International Herald Tribune* (28 May 1990), 2.
17. *Asia-Pacific Defence Reporter* (Aug. 1991), 18.

268 *Notes to Pages 126–132*

18. Robert Scalapino, 'The United States and Asia: Future Propects', *Foreign Affairs*, 70 (Winter 1991/92), 19–40.
19. This section draws heavily from Amitav Acharya, *Human Rights in Southeast Asia: Dilemmas of Foreign Policy*, Eastern Asia Policy Papers no. 11 (Toronto: University of Toronto and York University Joint Centre for Asia Pacific Studies, 1995).
20. Cited in *New Straits Times* (Kuala Lumpur, 20 July 1991), 1.
21. 'Alatas: No Nation can Judge Others on Human Rights', *The Straits Times* (16 June 1993), 1.
22. 'KL will Continue to Speak Up: Foreign Minister', *The Straits Times* (22 June 1993), 8.
23. 'Take Pragmatic Line', *The Straits Times* (17 June 1993), 1.
24. *The Straits Times* (23 July 1991).
25. 'Take Pragmatic Line', *The Straits Times* (17 June 1993), 1.
26. Kishore Mahbubani, 'News Areas of Asean Reaction: Environment, Human Rights and Democracy', *Asean-ISIS Monitor*, 5 (Oct.–Dec. 1992), 13.
27. 'Alatas: No Nation can Judge', *The Straits Times* (16 June 1993), 1.
28. *The Straits Times* (23 July 1991).
29. 'Alatas: No Nation can Judge', *The Straits Times* (16 June 1993), 1.
30. Adam Malik, 'Regional Cooperation in International Politics', in *Regionalism in Southeast Asia* (Jakarta: Yayasan Proklamasi, Centre for Strategic and International Studies, 1975), 162–3.
31. Amitav Acharya, *A New Regional Order in Southeast Asia: ASEAN in the Post-Cold War Era*, Adelphi Paper no. 279 (London: International Institute of Strategic Studies, 1993).
32. 'Movement Still has Role to Play, says Dr M', *New Straits Times* (21 Oct. 1995), 2.
33. Nobutoshi Akao, 'Strategy for APEC: A Japanese View', *Japan Review of International Affairs*, 9/3 (Summer 1995), 170–1.
34. Richard Higgott and Richard Stubbs, 'Competing Conceptions of Economic Regionalism: APEC versus EAEC in the Asia Pacific', *Review of International Political Economy*, 2/3 (Summer 1995), 524.
35. See Amitav Acharya, 'ASEAN and Asia Pacific Multilateralism: Managing Regional Security', in Amitav Acharya and Richard Stubbs (eds.), *New Challenges for ASEAN: Emerging Policy Issues* (Vancouver: University of British Columbia Press, 1995), 182–202; and Acharya, 'Making Multilateralism Work: The ASEAN Regional Forum and Security in the Asia Pacific', Paper presented to the Pacific Symposium, Multilateral Activities in Southeast Asia, National Defense University, Honolulu, 22–3 Feb. 1995.
36. Amitav Acharya, 'Multilateralism: Is There an Asia Pacific Way?', Paper prepared for the Conference on National Strategies in the Asia-Pacific: The Effects of Interacting Trade, Industrial, and Defense Policies, organized by the National Bureau of Asian Research and the Center for Trade and Commercial Diplomacy, Monterey Institute of International Studies, 28–9 Mar. 1996, Monterey, Calif.
37. See Marianne H. Marchand, 'The Political Economy of North-South Relations', in Richard Stubbs and Geoffrey R. D. Underhill (eds.), *Political Economy and the Changing Global Order* (London: Macmillan, 1994), 297–8.

CHAPTER 7

1. 'New Winds of Change in Africa', BBC World Service, 21 Apr. 1991; see also Samuel Decalo, 'The Process, Prospects and Constraints of Democratisation in Africa', *African Affairs,* 91/362 (Jan. 1992), 35; Carol Lancaster, 'Democratisation in Sub-Saharan Africa', *Survival,* 35/3 (Autumn 1993), 3–43.
2. Leaders such as General Obasanjo, the former Nigerian head of state, were pessimistic about the likely outcomes of the moves towards democracy and of the sincerity of governments which were trying to manipulate the process: interview with the author, London, Feb. 1991.
3. Keith Somerville, *Foreign Military Intervention in Africa* (London: Pinter, 1990), 107–8.
4. Interview with the author, Harare, 11 Mar. 1991.
5. Barry Buzan, 'National Security in the Post-Cold War World', *Strategic Review for Southern Africa* (Institute of Strategic Studies, University of Pretoria), 16/1 (Mar. 1994), 9–11.
6. James Barber, 'The Search for International Order and Justice', *World Today,* 49/8–9 (Aug.–Sept. 1993), 154.
7. Colin Legum, 'The Coming of Africa's Second Independence', *Washington Quarterly,* 1 (Winter 1990), 129–40.
8. Lancaster, 'Democratisation', 3–43.
9. Interviews with the author, Feb.–Mar. 1992.
10. Keith Somerville, 'Africa Moves Towards Party Pluralism', *World Today,* 47/8–9 (Aug.–Sept. 1991), 152; Kaunda interview with the author, State House, Lusaka, 5 Mar. 1991.
11. Martin Plaut, 'Rwanda: Looking Beyond the Slaughter', *World Today,* 50/8–9 (Aug.–Sept. 1994), 149–50.
12. Ibid.
13. Stephen Riley, 'Africa's "New Wind of Change" ', *World Today,* 48/7 (July 1992), 118.
14. The World Bank, *Sub-Saharan Africa: From Crisis to Sustainable Growth* (Washington, DC: World Bank, 1989), 34.
15. Peter Anyang Nyong'o, 'Political Instability and Prospects for Democracy in Africa', *Africa Development,* 13 (1988), 72.
16. The views were put to the author in Mar. 1991 by the Tanzanian democracy campaigners Rev. Christopher Mtikila, James Mupalala, and Dr Ringo Tenga; in Zambia by Arthur Wina, Fred Chiluba, and Vernon Mwaanga of the MMD; and by General Olusegun Obasanjo in London.
17. Guy Arnold, 'Crippling Debt Problems', *New African* (Nov. 1993), 25.
18. Ibid.
19. Decalo, 'Process, Prospects and Constraints', 35.
20. Chester Crocker, *High Noon in Southern Africa: Making Peace in a Rough Neighbourhood* (New York: W. W. Norton, 1992), 488.
21. Simon Baynham, 'Regional Security in the Third World with Specific Reference to Southern Africa', *Strategic Review for Southern Africa,* 16/1 (Mar. 1994), 85.
22. Ambassador L. J. Legwaila, 'The Security Agenda for Africa: Role of the OAU', *ISSUP Bulletin* (Institute of Strategic Studies, University of Pretoria, 1994), p.2.

23. For a detailed elaboration of this, see Somerville, *Foreign Military Intervention.*
24. For a detailed examination of the different strands of Angolan nationalism, see David Birmingham, *Frontline Nationalism in Angola and Mozambique* (London: James Currey, 1992), 26–7; also Keith Somerville, 'The Failure of Democratic Reform in Angola and Zaire', *Survival*, 35/3 (Autumn 1993), 56–8.
25. Buzan, 'National Security', 11.
26. See Ioan Lewis and James Mayall, 'Somalia', in James Mayall (ed.), *The New Interventionism 1991–1994* (Cambridge: Cambridge University Press, 1996), 94–124.
27. Jakkie Cilliers, 'National and Regional Stability: Expectations versus Reality', in Minnie Venter (ed.) *Prospects for Progress: Critical Choices for Southern Africa* (Cape Town: Maskew Miller Longman, 1994), 43.
28. Thomas Ohlson and Stephen John Steadman, *The New is Not Yet Born: Conflict Resolution in Southern Africa* (Washington, DC, Brookings Institution, 1994), 272–94.
29. L. Nathan, unpublished submission to ANC strategic group on foreign affairs, Oct. 1993.
30. Peter Vale, 'Fashioning Choice in Southern Africa', in Venter (ed.), *Prospects.*
31. Cilliers, 'National and Regional Stability', 43 and 49.
32. Ohlson and Steadman, *New Not Yet Born*, 294.
33. For a fuller discussion of these and other themes relating to Africa's subordinate status in the international system, see Christopher Clapham, *Africa and the International System: The Politics of State Survival* (Cambridge: Cambridge University Press, 1996).
34. Cilliers, 'National and Regional Stability', 49.
35. Claude Ake, 'A View from Africa', in Hans-Henrik Holm and Georg Sorensen (eds.), *Whose World Order?* (Boulder, Colo.: Westview Press, 1995), 22–3.

CHAPTER 8

1. Afghanistan and Myanmar (erstwhile Burma) are often treated as part of the region As an Islamic state Pakistan sees Middle East as its natural bloc while Sri Lanka has been trying to join the economically prosperous Southeast Asia. In recent years India's strategic community has been articulating a 'southern Asia' that includes nuclear China. In this study the term South Asia is used to denote Bangladesh, Bhutan, India, Maldives, Nepal, Pakistan, and Sri Lanka.
2. On this theme, see Barry Buzan and Gowher Rizvi, *South Asian Insecurity and the Great Powers* (London: Macmillan, 1986).
3. This idea is developed in Gowher Rizvi, *South Asia in a Changing International Order* (New Delhi: Sage 1993).
4. On this point see e.g. J. Mohan Malik, 'World Politics and South Asia: The Beginning of an End?', *Journal of South Asian and Middle Eastern Studies* (Villanova) 19/3 (Spring 1996), 52.
5. On the eve of India's independence, Jawaharlal Nehru succinctly explained this position Speaking in the Asian Relations Conference in Mar. 1947 he remarked: 'For too long we of Asia have been petitioners in Western courts and chancelleries. That story must now belong to the past. We propose to stand on our feet

and to co-operate with all others who are prepared to co-operate with us. We do not intend to be the playthings of others.' *Asian Relations: Report of the Proceedings and Documentation of the First Asia Relations Conference, New Delhi, March–April 1947* (New Delhi: Asian Relations Organisation, 1948), 24.

6. During the freedom struggle, the Muslim League defined Hindus and Muslims of India as two separate nations and hence it argued that they were entitled to two separate states.

7. Both countries approached this arrangement differently. Washington was eager to enlist Pakistan as an important state on the southern frontiers of the Soviet Union. Islamabad however saw the military cooperation with Washington as a cornerstone of its security policy *vis-à-vis* India. Anees Jillani, 'Pakistan and CENTO: An Historical Analysis', *Journal of South Asian and Middle Eastern Studies*, 15/1 (Fall 1991), 40–53.

8. Rodney W. Jones, 'Old Quarrels and New Realities: Security in Southern Asia after the Cold War', *The Washington Quarterly*, 15/1 (Winter 1992), 107.

9. Marvi Memon, 'Reorientation of Pakistan's Foreign Policy after the Cold War', *Pakistan Horizon* (Karachi), 47/2 (Apr. 1994), 47.

10. For a recent and comprehensive study of Soviet policy during the Gorbachev era see Linda Racioppi, *Soviet Policy towards South Asia since 1970* (Cambridge: Cambridge University Press, 1994).

11. In his *Pakistan's Politics: The Zia Years* (New Delhi: Konark, 1991), noted Pakistani writer Mushahid Hussain presented a broad and somewhat disjointed assessment of Zia's tenure.

12. Critical and detailed appreciation could be found in Chintamani Mahapatra, 'US Approach to Nuclear Proliferation in Asia', in Jasjit Singh (ed.), *Asian Strategic Review, 1992–93* (New Delhi: IDSA, 1993), 167–204. See also P. R. Chari, *Indo-Pak Nuclear Standoff: The Role of the United States* (New Delhi: Manohar, 1995).

13. Robert G. Wirsing and James M. Roherty, 'The United States and Pakistan', *International Affairs* (London), 58/4 (Autumn 1982), 588–609; and Rodney W. Jones, 'Pakistan and the United States: Partners after Afghanistan', *The Washington Quarterly*, 12/3 (Summer 1989), 65–87.

14. Under Zia, Pakistan emerged as a major player in the international drug market and drug money is believed to play an important role in Pakistani politics. Sumita Kumar, 'Drug Trafficking in Pakistan', in Jasjit Singh (ed.), *Asian Strategic Review, 1994–95* (New Delhi: IDSA, 1995), 194–222.

15. For an interesting background to this relationship see P. R. Chari, 'Indo-Soviet Military Co-operation: A Review', *Asian Survey* (Berkeley, Calif.), 19/3 (Mar. 1979), 230–44. See also Jyotirmoy Banerjee, 'Moscow's Strategic Link with New Delhi: An Interim Assessment', *China Report* (New Delhi), 19/1 (Jan.–Feb. 1983), 7–20.

16. Its willingness to lease a Charlie class nuclear-powered submarine to India in the 1980s shows the depth of this relationship.

17. J. Mohan Malik, 'India Copes with the Kremlin Fall', *Orbis* (Philadelphia), 37/1 (Winter 1993), 69–87; and Amit Gupta, 'The Indian Arms Industry: A Lumbering Giant', *Asian Survey*, 30/9 (Sept. 1990), 846–61.

18. A corresponding military build-up based on Western inventories would have been prohibitive for India or would have demanded substantial and continued military aid and assistance from the US or other Western powers.

19. For critical evaluations see Chris Smith, *India's Adhoc Arsenal: Direction or Drift in Defence Policy?* (Oxford: Oxford University Press, 1994); and Eric Arnett, 'Military Technology: The Case of India', *SIPRI Yearbook 1994* (Oxford: Oxford University Press, 1994), 343–65.

20. The shortage was so alarming that the air force was forced to ground some key squadrons, to curtail training to 'save' erosion and 'mothball' aircraft and vehicles to preserve operational ability In certain cases, some units resorted to 'cannibalization' to ensure availability of spares. Among others see Shekhar Gupta *et al.*, 'A Middle-Aged Military Machine', *India Today* (international edn., New Delhi, 30 Apr. 1993), 22–30; Saritha Rai, 'Wanted: A Foreign Match', *India Today* (31 Jan. 1994), 35; *Indian Express* (New Delhi, 21 June 1991).

21. *Far Eastern Economic Review* (Hong Kong, 15 Oct. 1992), 16. Anita Inder Singh, 'India's relations with Russia and Central Asia', *International Affairs*, 71/1 (Jan. 1995), 75–6.

22. According to this arrangement India's debts to Moscow stood at Rs360 billion (slightly more than $12 billion at then existing prices), to be repaid in fourteen years at an annual rate of Rs.30 billion. C. Narendra Reddy, 'India and Russia on Common Path', *Financial Express* (New Delhi, 12 July 1994); Vidya Ranganathan, 'India's Russian Debt: Time for a Better Deal', *The Economic Times* (New Delhi, 25 Aug. 1994); and Commerce Minister Pranab Mukherjee's interview to *The Economic Times* (4 July 1994).

23. India's ability to renegotiate a more favourable repayment arrangement based on the realistic value of the rouble is likely to depend on two closely related economic developments. One, India should be able to procure its defence supplies from non-Russian sources; and two, it should succeed in replacing the existing Russian market for Indian exports with other destinations.

24. One cannot however discard the impediments to such a relationship. See P. R. Kumaraswamy, *India and Israel: Evolving Strategic Partnership* (Security and Policy Studies, 40; Ramat Gan, Israel, 1998).

25. For instance see M. Granger Morgan, K. Subrahmanyam, K. Sundarji, and Robert M. White, 'India and the United States', *The Washington Quarterly*, 18/2 (Spring 1995), 155–79. In the words of one analyst: 'Given India's tense relations with Pakistan and China, the withdrawal of Moscow's security umbrella, the need for economic aid and investment, the quest for sophisticated dual-use technology, *India has no option but to nurture close links with the West.*' Malik, 'India Copes', 71. Emphasis added.

26. After protracted negotiations and pressure in July 1993 Russia abandoned its plans to supply cryogenic technology to India. Shahid Alam, 'Some Implications of the Aborted Sale of Russian Cryogenic Rocket Engines to India', *Comparative Strategy* (New York), 13/3 (July–Sept. 1994), 287–300; Chari, *Indo-Pak Nuclear Standoff*, 63–71 and Brahma Chellaney, 'The Missile Technology Control Regime: Its Challenges and Rigours for India', in Francine R. Frankel (ed.), *Bridging the Non-Proliferation Divide: The United States and India* (New Delhi: Konark, 1995), 234–7. I am grateful to Pinak R. Chakravarty for bringing the last work to my attention.

27. Commenting on Indo-US relations following the Democratic victory in 1992, one leading Indian analyst remarked: 'The incremental advance in building mutual confidence in Indo-US relations carefully nurtured by the Reagan and Bush

Administrations appears to have been squandered by the Clinton Administration in its mechanical application of the slogans of human rights and non-proliferation in the Indian sub-continent.' C. Raja Mohan, 'Indo-US Co-operation in Arms Control', in Frankel, *Bridging the Non-Proliferation Divide*, 357.

28. In the words of US Assistant Secretary of State Robin Raphel, 'Pakistan has been a valuable friend and ally of the United States for nearly five decades . . . Pakistan is often seen as an alternative model to Iran in Central Asia'. Quoted in I. K. Gujral, 'Strains on Indian Security', *The Hindu* (New Delhi, 13 Oct. 1995).

29. Among others it arrested and extradited to the US Ramzi Ahmed Yousef, accused of masterminding the 1993 bombing of New York City's World Trade Centre. Strongly rejecting Indian pleas, the administration refused to place Pakistan on the terrorism watch list. In its view, such an action would imply siding with India and hence would undermine American interests and influence in South Asia.

30. Rahul Roy-Chaudhury, 'The Brown Amendment: Implications for the Indian Navy', *Strategic Analysis* (New Delhi), 18/11 (Feb. 1996), 1455. A noted Pakistan journalist argued that the importance of these supplies was exaggerated. N. Naqvi, 'Much Ado about Sale of "Junk" ', *The Times of India* (New Delhi, 29 Oct. 1995).

31. For the text of the White House fact sheet on Clinton's non-proliferation and export control policy see *PPNN Newsbrief* (Southampton), 23/3 (1993), 23–24. Emphasis added.

32. For instance two recent studies of SIPRI namely, Ian Anthony, *The Arms Trade and Medium Powers: Case Studies of India and Pakistan 1947–90* (Exeter: Harvester Wheatsheaf, 1992) and Smith, *India's Adhoc Arsenal*, treat India's arms build-up predominantly as an Indo-Pakistan phenomenon. One cannot however ignore the traditional reluctance of Indian leaders to articulate forthrightly the Chinese threat.

33. It is strongly argued that *Agni* had intensified and consolidated the Missile Technology Control Regime (MTCR), a Western cartel aimed at missile proliferation. For an Indian perspective towards MTCR see Ravinder Pal Singh, 'A Perspective of the Missile Technology Control Regime', in Jasjit Singh (ed.), *Asian Strategic Review 1991–92* (New Delhi: IDSA, 1992), 205–26. See also Brahma Chellaney, 'Non-Proliferation: An Indian Critique of US Export Controls', *Orbis*, 38/3 (Summer 1994), 439–56.

34. American indifference towards suspected Pakistani deployment of M-11 is understandable. Any formal acknowledgement of intelligence assessment to this effect would force the administration to impose MTCR sanctions against Pakistan as well as China. Such a drastic action would severely curtail American influence *vis-à-vis* these countries.

35. For a recent discussion see P. R. Kumaraswamy, 'Rationalising Narasimha Rao: India and Nuclear Non-Proliferation', *Asian Studies Review* (Clayton, Australia), 20/1 (July 1996), 135–50.

36. Interestingly this 'entry into force' clause was introduced in late June 1996 or shortly after the new United Front government took office and reiterated India's rejection of CTBT.

37. As in the case of NPT, Pakistan opted for a tactical stand and expressed its willingness to sign and ratify CTBT if New Delhi took a similar stand. In the event, the UN General Assembly approved the text of the CTBT by a vote of 158:3. Only

Bhutan and Libya joined India in rejecting it, a decision which arguably cost India the chance to fill one of the five non-permanent seats on the Security Council. See Ramesh Thakur, 'India in the World', *Foreign Affairs*, 76/4 (July/Aug.1997), 15.

38. Historical background to this problem can be found in Atul Kohli, *Democracy and Discontent: India's Growing Crisis of Governability* (Cambridge: Cambridge University Press, 1991) 339–77; and Paul R. Brass, *The Politics of India since Independence* (Cambridge: Cambridge University Press, 1994), 193–201.

39. For a detailed historical analysis see Ajit Bhattacharjea, *Kashmir: The Wounded Valley* (New Delhi: UBS, 1994). See also the Kashmir-special of *Contemporary South Asia*, 4/1 (Mar. 1995).

40. Even a sober and non-polemical leader like Narasimha Rao was uncompromising on Kashmir. Delivering his 1994 independence day address to the nation from the rampart of the Red Fort, the Indian Prime Minister declared: 'With you, without you, in spite of you, Kashmir shall remain an inseparable part of India.'

41. The decision by the Bush administration to place it on the terrorism watch list was largely due to Pakistani involvement in the ongoing violence in Kashmir. The Clinton administration however saw the violence as leverage to secure political concessions from India and managed to work out an understanding over the NPT extension.

42. See P. R. Kumaraswamy, 'India's Recognition of Israel, September 1950', *Middle Eastern Studies* (London), 31/1 (Jan. 1995), 124–38; 'India and Israel: Prelude to Normalisation', *Journal of South Asian and Middle Eastern Studies*, 19/2 (Winter 1995), 53–73.

43. Taiwan is believed to have secured India's support for its bid to join the World Trade Organization, International Monetary Fund, and other multilateral forums.

44. *The Jerusalem Post* (21 Nov. 1995). Before the May 1996 election of Benjamin Netanyahu as prime minister of Israel, Ms Bhutto indicated that progress in Israel-Syrian negotiations would enable her country to establish formal ties with Israel.

45. See P. R. Kumaraswamy, 'The Israeli Connections of Sri Lanka', *Strategic Analysis*, 10/11 (Feb. 1987), 1341–55; and G. P. V. Somaratne, 'Sri Lanka's Relations with Israel', in Shelton U. Kodikara, *External Compulsions of South Asian Politics* (New Delhi: Sage, 1993), 194–225.

46. Amal Jayawardane, 'Sri Lanka's Foreign Policy under J. R. Jayawardane and Ranasinghe Premadasa, 1977–1993', in Mahinda Werake and P. V. J. Jayasekera (ed.), *Security Dilemma of a Small State: Internal Crisis and External Intervention in Sri Lanka* (New Delhi: South Asian Publishers, 1995), 224–6.

47. Personal conversation with a senior Sri Lankan diplomat, Oct. 1995.

48. Interestingly Tehran's position as a champion of Islamic cause and vehement opponent of the peace process had not affected the newly emerging relations between India and Israel.

49. John Cherian, 'A new impetus: Indo-Iranian Ties, after Rafsanjani's Visit', *Frontline* (Madras, 19 May 1995), 4–12.

50. Syed Rifaat Hussain, 'Pakistan and Central Asia', in David O. Smith (ed.), *From Containment to Stability: Pakistan-United States Relations in the Post-Cold War Era* (Washington: National Defence University, 1993), 191–215.

51. G. Balachandran, 'Sovereignty at Bay: The Political and Military Utility of

Nuclear Weapons in the Post-Cold War Era', in Frankel, *Bridging the Non-Proliferation Divide*, 68–85.

52. Reflecting on this rivalry, one former Indian Foreign Secretary remarked: 'To some extent I would call it our naiveté of not objecting to Pakistan's joining the non-aligned movement [in 1979]. In fact, we gave Pakistan one more forum to bother us.' J. N. Dixit, *Anatomy of a Flawed Inheritance: Indo-Pak Relations, 1970–94* (New Delhi: Konark, 1995), 57.

53. The members are Algeria, Argentina, Brazil, Egypt, India, Indonesia, Jamaica, Malaysia, Mexico, Nigeria, Peru, Senegal, Venezuela, Yugoslavia and Zimbabwe.

54. The members are Australia, India, Indonesia, Kenya, Madagascar, Malaysia, Mauritius, Mozambique, Oman, Singapore, South Africa, Sri Lanka, Tanzania, and Yemen.

55. Juergen Rueland, 'India's New Interests in Southeast Asia', *Aussenpolitik*, 46/1 (1995), 94–9.

56. V. Jayanth, 'Winning Friends', *Frontline* (8 Sept. 1995), 47.

57. Jayawardane, 'Sri Lanka's Foreign Policy', 212–15.

58. Between 1988 and mid-1998 there were eight governments in India, six in Nepal, four in Pakistan, three each in Bangladesh and Sri Lanka, and two in the Maldives.

59. The issue has been studied in details in Rehman Sobhan, *Bangladesh: Problems of Governance* (New Delhi: Konark, 1993), 4–75.

60. Lok Raj Baral, *Nepal: Problems of Governance* (New Delhi: Konark, 1994), 67–101.

61. The American tendency to intervene in domestic politics appears to be continuing even after Pakistan moved towards democracy. Mushahid Hussain and Akmal Hussain, *Pakistan: Problems of Governance* (New Delhi: Konark, 1994), 29–41 and 110–14.

62. According to some Pakistani scholars the judiciary 'is viewed as a status quo institution which does not go against an incumbent government. The 1959 Supreme Court decision justifying Martial Law, the 1972 Supreme Court decision declaring Martial Law illegal and Yahya Khan as "usurper" (after he was out of office), the 1977 Supreme Court decision on the "Doctrine of Necessity", and the 1988 Supreme Court ruling against Zia's dissolution of the National Assembly after his death are cited as examples of the judiciary endorsing the executive's decisions. Circles close to Mr. Junejo, once privately remarked that the only reason the former Prime Minister did not go to court after his dismissal was his view that the judiciary would not go against General Zia in his lifetime.' Hussain and Hussain, *Pakistan*, 56.

63. For a discussion of the 'autocratic style' of Seshan see *Frontline* (11 Aug. 1995), 4–12. Some Pakistani leaders including former cricket star Imran Khan have demanded a similar non-governmental constitutional body to conduct and supervise elections.

64. Chief Justice Bishwanath Upadhyaya who headed the panel wrote: 'The dissolution of the House of Representatives by King Birendra at the recommendations of the Communist Part of Nepal (United Marxist Leninist) without considering possibilities of an alternative government by Opposition parties was unconstitutional and illegal.' Quoted in *Frontline* (22 Sept. 1995), 37.

65. Sobhan, *Bangladesh*, 58.

66. Responding to Gayoom's personal appeal Indian Prime Minister Rajiv Gandhi swiftly sent a military contingent and throttled the *coup*. See Shekhar Gupta, 'A Close Shave', *India Today* (30 Nov. 1988), 28–32; S. Bilveer, 'Operation Cactus: India's "Prompt-Action" in the Maldives', *Asian Defence Journal* (Kuala Lumpur, Feb. 1989), 30–3; and Maqsud ul Hasan Nuri, 'Maldives in the 1990s', *Regional Studies* (Islamabad), 10/2 (Spring 1992), 53–7.
67. See e.g. Edward Mansfield and Jack Snyder, 'Democratization and War', *Foreign Affairs*, 74/3 (May–June 1995), 79–97.
68. The devaluation proposal was favourably received in India. See S. Guhan, 'Breakthrough in Sri Lanka', *The Hindu* (8 Aug. 1995); Nikhil Chakravarty, 'Light from Sri Lanka', *The Hindu* (10 Aug. 1995): V. R. Krishna Iyer, 'The Tamils' Tryst with Destiny', *The Hindu* (6 and 7 Sept. 1995); and A. G. Noorani, 'Advance and Retreat: Constitutional Reform in Sri Lanka', *Frontline* (8 Sept. 1995), 111–14.
69. Among others MQM demands a greater share in economic and political power and proportional representation of *mohajirs* in national and provincial assemblies, federal and provincial services and armed forces. Farhat Haq, 'Rise of the MQM in Pakistan: Politics of Ethnic Mobilisation', *Asian Survey*, 35/11 (November 1995), 990–1004. See also Feroz Ahmed, 'Ethnicity and Politics: The Rise of *Muhajir* Separatism', *South Asia Bulletin* (Los Angeles), 8 (1988), 33–45; and Aabha Dixit, *Ethno-Nationalism in Pakistan, Delhi Papers 3* (New Delhi: IDSA, 1996), 56–97.
70. An internal note prepared by Indian Home Ministry recorded: 'According to the figures available (in 1987) with the Government of West Bengal, the total number of Bangladeshi infiltrants in that State was around 44 million. It should be near about five million today [Mar. 1992]. In Assam, the estimated figure of infiltrants today is about 2.2 million. Tripura and Bihar are also seriously affected by infiltration from Bangladesh. The infiltrants are now spreading to newer areas of Manipur and Nagaland.' Reproduced in Arun Shourie, *A Secular Agenda: For Saving our Country, for Welding it* (New Delhi: ASA Publications, 1993), 269–93.
71. Paramand and Saroj B. Khanna, 'Ethnicity in Bhutan: Causes and Effects', *Journal of South Asian and Middle Eastern Studies*, 17/1 (Fall 1993), 76–94; A. C. Sinha, 'Bhutan in 1994: Will the Ethnic Conflict be Resolved?' *Asian Survey*, 35/2 (Feb. 1995), 166–70; Michael Hutt, 'Bhutan in 1995: Weathering the Storm', *Asian Survey*, 36/2 (Feb. 1996), 204–8; and Ramesh Upadhyaya, 'Bhutan, a Nation "divided" ', *The Hindu* (10 Apr. 1996).
72. For a historical discussion see A. Sivarajah, 'Indo-Sri Lankan Relations and Sri Lanka's Ethnic Crisis: The Tamil Nadu Factor', in Shelton U. Kodikara (ed.), *South Asian Strategic Issues: Sri Lankan Perspective* (New Delhi: Sage, 1990), 135–59.
73. For a comprehensive study of the party see, Yogendra K. Malik and V. B. Singh, *Hindu Nationalists in India: The Rise of the Bharatiya Janata Party* (New Delhi: Vistaar, 1995).
74. Robert G. Wirsing and Debolina Mukherjee, 'The Saffron Surge in Indian Politics: Hindu Nationalism and the Future of Secularism', *Asian Affairs* (New York), 22/3 (Fall 1995), 181–206. In the 1996 elections the BJP won 160 out 535 seats and emerged as the largest single party and was duly invited to form a government. Prime Minister Atal Bihai Vajpayee however failed to master enough

support and resigned before the Lok Sabha was to vote on the confidence motion.

75. Reacting to a court ruling the clergy sought to amend the criminal law that would restrict the payment of alimony only to three months. Having initially opposed the move Rajiv Gandhi saw it as a means of winning back the Muslims who were moving away from Congress and endorsed their demand. Likewise secular India was the first country to ban *Satanic Verses* and yet worse riots over this controversy took place in Mumbai (Bombay). Critical, some might say adverse, evaluation of these two issues can be seen in Arun Shourie, *Indian Controversies: Essays on Religion in Politics* (New Delhi: ASA, 1993), 254–89 and 327–36.

76. Among others see K. R. Malkani, *The Politics of Ayodhya and Hindu-Muslim Relations* (New Delhi: Har-Anand, 1993). Various aspects of the controversy were discussed in *Asian Survey*, 33/7 (July 1993) and *South Asia* (Armidale, Australia), 17 (1994).

77. Sabbir Ahmad, 'SAPTA: A Preliminary Analysis', *Regional Studies*, 14/2 (Spring 1996), 17–21.

78. N. Chandra Mohan, 'Towards Regional Integration', *Business India* (Mumbai, 8–21 May 1995), 65–7.

79. In July 1992 as he was completing his tenure in New Delhi, Pakistan High Commissioner Abdus Sattar told Indian Foreign Secretary J. N. Dixit: 'We have known each other for nearly 20 years since 1971. I have spent nearly half my diplomatic career dealing with India. I do not think India and Pakistan can be friends or have normal relations in our lifetimes. Not perhaps for another two generations. One can keep on trying, but it seems pointless.' Dixit, *Anatomy of a Flawed Inheritance*, 1.

80. Some claim these fears have been overstated and that India's ability to exercise force in the region is severely circumscribed. See Gowher Rizvi, 'South Asia and the New World Order', in Holm and Sorensen, *Whose World Order?*, 74–6.

81. For a long list of Indian policies of 'hegemony' see Shaheen Akhtar, 'India in S. Asia: An Analysis of Hegemonial Relationship', *Regional Studies*, 11/3 (Summer 1993), 60–89.

82. Chaitanya Mishra, 'Indo-Nepal Relations: A View from Kathmandu', in Kodikara, *External Compulsions of South Asian Politics*, 179–93.

83. Jayawardane, 'Sri Lanka's Foreign Policy', 223–4.

84. Gambhir Bhatta and Thomas P. Chen, 'SAARC: Is Economic Integration Possible amid the Political Squabbles?', *American Asian Review* (New York), 12/3 (Fall 1994), 69–77.

85. The importance Rao attached to Singapore raised some veiled criticisms in India as well as in Southeast Asia. This approach proved successful when the city-state vigorously campaigned to upgrade India's position *vis-à-vis* ASEAN.

86. Under an agreement reached in Apr. 1995, India offered to extend tariff concessions to 106 items, followed by Pakistan (35 items), Sri Lanka (31 items), the Maldives (17 items), Nepal (14 items), Bangladesh (12 items), and Bhutan (7 items). They receive tariff concessions ranging from 10 to 100 %. At one point when there were doubts about Pakistan's ratification of SAPTA, President Kumaratunga suggested that India and Sri Lanka could go ahead and create a bilateral free trade area.

87. At Colombo deliberations in Mar. 1996 India offered to reduce tariff cover on 1,200 items and Sri Lanka, an active player in economic integration, favoured tariff cuts on 2,900 items.

88. For a broad yet critical review of the economic reforms of Rao-Singh duo see Amit Bhaduri and Deepak Nayyar, *The Intelligent Person's Guide to Liberalisation* (New Delhi: Penguin, 1996).

89. Shortly after a series of electoral setbacks suffered by the Congress party, Prakash Karat, a polit-bureau member of the Communist Party of India (Marxist) wrote: 'the central cause for the defeat is the Narasimha Rao-Manmohan Singh liberalisation policy. In a real sense these elections have been a referendum on the economic policies; the policies so beloved of big business, the affluent upper classes and the rural rich but the bane of the rural and urban poor.' *Frontline* (30 Dec. 1994), 20.

CHAPTER 9

1. To paraphrase an idea from Jan Aart Scholte, *International Relations of Social Change* (Buckingham and Philadelphia: Open University Press, 1993), 30–1.

2. For such criticism, see Ch. 1.

3. Speech to Arab Cooperation Council summit in Amman, 24 Feb. 1990. Also cited in Ofra Bengio, 'Iraq', *Middle East Contemporary Survey*, 14 (1990), 388–9.

4. Hearing of the House Foreign Affairs Committee, 4 Sept. 1990, *USIS*, p. 18.

5. Cited in Barry Rubin, 'The United States and the Middle East', *Middle East Contemporary Survey*, 15 (1991), 27.

6. The multilateral working groups dealt with arms control and regional security, economic development, water, environment, and refugees. For background and analysis of the groups, Joel Peters, *Pathways to Peace: The Multilateral Arab–Israeli Peace Talks* (London: Royal Institute of International Affairs, 1996).

7. Quote from Martin Indyk, then senior director for the Near East and South Asia at the US National Security Council, speaking in May 1993. Cited in Phebe Marr, 'The United States, Europe, and the Middle East: An Uneasy Triangle', *Middle East Journal*, 48/2 (Spring 1994), 217.

8. Donald Neff, ' "Dual containment" Goes on', *Middle East International*, 544 (21 Feb. 1997).

9. On US lethargy, Edward N. Krapels, 'The Commanding Heights: International Oil in a Changed World', *International Affairs*, 69/1 (Jan. 1993), 85–7.

10. On the US view of Soviet policy in the region, Richard K. Hermann, 'Russian Policy in the Middle East: Strategic Change and Tactical Contradictions', *Middle East Journal*, 48/3 (Summer 1994), 473.

11. e.g. the statement by Clinton in Feb. 1997. Cited in Donald Neff, 'Clinton Critical of Israel', *Middle East International*, 545 (7 Mar. 1997).

12. An alliance endorsed for this reason in the strategy paper prepared by the 'Study Group on a New Israeli Strategy Towards 2000'. *A Clean Break: A New Strategy for Securing the Realm* (Washington and Jerusalem: Institute for Advanced Strategic and Political Studies, June 1996).

13. Point made in Ibrahim Karawan, 'Arab Dilemmas in the 1990s: Breaking Taboos and Searching for Signposts', *Middle East Journal*, 48/3 (Summer 1994), 438.

14. The Sultanate of Oman, for one, argued in 1991 that regional security arrangements in the Gulf without Iran would be 'unthinkable'. In December 1993 it reiterated that the time for *rapprochement* with Iraq and Iran was overdue, and that the US policy of dual containment was detrimental to GCC interests. 'The Middle East', *Strategic Survey 1993–1994* (London: Brassey's for the IISS, 1994), 142. For criticism of US failure to promote 'constructive engagement' and 'critical dialogue' with Iran and opposition to Iranian candidature for membership in various organizations, Shahram Chubin, 'US Policy Towards Iran Should Change: But it Probably Won't', *Survival*, 38/4 (Winter 1996–7), 16–17. Significant US criticism has also come in articles by Brent Scowcroft and Zbigniew Brzezinski in *Foreign Affairs* (Spring 1997); and in Zbigniew Brzezinski and Brent Scowcroft (co-chairs), Richard W. Murphy (project director), *Differentiated Containment: U.S. Policy Toward Iran and Iraq*, Report of an Independent Task Force Sponsored by the Council on Foreign Relations, 1997.

15. Baker testimony to Senate Foreign Relations Committee on 7 Feb. 1991. Cited in R. K. Ramazani, 'Iran's Foreign Policy: Both North and South', *Middle East Journal*, 46/3 (Summer 1992), 403.

16. Shahram Chubin, *Iran's National Security Policy: Capabilities, Intentions and Impact* (Washington, DC: The Carnegie Endowment for International Peace, 1994), 5.

17. The notion of an 'insurance premium' is confirmed by GCC officials cited in Jeffrey McCausland, *The Gulf Conflict: A Military Analysis* (London: Brassey's for the IISS, Adelphi Paper no. 282, Nov. 1993), 75.

18. Figures from *The Military Balance, 1996/7* (Oxford: Oxford University Press for the International Institute for Strategic Studies, 1996).

19. For a brief summary of European thinking, Tim Niblock, 'Towards a Conference on Security and Cooperation in the Mediterranean and the Middle East (CSCM)', in Gerd Nonneman (ed.), *The Middle East and Europe: The Search for Stability and Integration* (London: Federal Trust for Education and Research, 1993; 2nd edn.), 251–5.

20. On US opposition, Yezid Sayigh, 'The Multilateral Middle East Peace Talks: Reorganizing for Regional Security', in Steven L. Spiegel and David J. Pervin (eds.), *Practical Peacemaking in the Middle East* (New York and London: Garland Publishing, 1995), 209 and 214. More generally on the multilateral working groups and the potential for a CSCME, Peters, *Pathways to Peace*, 73–4.

21. Mohamed A. El-Erian, 'Middle East Economies' External Environment: What Lies Ahead?', *Middle East Policy*, 4/3 (Mar. 1996), 143–4.

22. Ghassan Salamé, 'Torn between the Atlantic and the Mediterranean: Europe and the Middle East in the Post-Cold War Era', *Middle East Journal*, 48/2 (Spring 1994), 226–7.

23. Hermann, 'Russian Policy', 473.

24. Robert O. Freedman, 'Israel and the Successor States of the Soviet Union', in Robert O. Freedman (ed.), *Israel under Rabin* (Boulder, Colo.: Westview Press, 1995), 47.

25. Gerges, 'Washington's Misguided', 7.

26. Jonathan Rynhold, 'China's Cautious New Pragmatism in the Middle East', *Survival*, 38/3 (Autumn 1996).

27. Rodney Wilson, 'The Economic Relations of the Middle East: Towards Europe or Within the Region?', *Middle East Journal*, 48/2 (Spring 1994), 269 and 270.

28. Ibid. 268.

29. On impact of oil, Roger Owen, 'The Arab Oil Economy: Present Structure and Future Prospects', in Samih K. Farsoun (ed.), *Arab Society: Continuity and Change* (London: Croom Helm, 1985), 18–19. On increased dependency, James A. Bill and Robert Springborg, *Politics in the Middle East* (New York: Harper-Collins, 1994; 4th edn.), 421.

30. Erian, 'Middle East Economies', 139.

31. On polarization, Gerd Nonneman, 'Problems Facing Cooperation and Integration Attempts in the Middle East', in Nonneman, *Middle East and Europe*, p. 43.

32. Bill and Springborg, *Politics*, 420.

33. Michael Barnett, 'Identity and Alliances in the Middle East', in Peter J. Katzenstein (ed.), *The Culture of National Security: Norms and Identity in World Politics* (New York: Columbia University Press, 1996), 422–32.

34. Wilson, 'Economic Relations', 285–6.

35. Erian, 'Middle East Economies', 140–1.

36. Ibid. 144.

37. Fred Lawson, 'Domestic Transformations and Foreign Steadfastness in Contemporary Syria', *Middle East Journal*, 48/1 (Winter 1994), 48.

38. Relative gains thinking in the North African states effectively doomed the AMU to failure. Roger Owen, 'Arab Integration in Historical Perspective: Are There Any Lessons?', *Arab Affairs*, 8 (Spring 1988), 48.

39. Point made in Karawan, 'Arab Dilemmas', p. 452.

40. This is the argument of Charles Dunbar, 'The Unification of Yemen: Process, Politics, and Prospects', *Middle East Journal*, 46/3 (Summer 1992).

41. Laurie Brand, *Jordan's Inter-Arab Relations: The Political Economy of Alliance Making* (New York: Columbia University Press, 1994), 283–4.

42. On Israel-EU association, Lynn Welchman, 'Flaws in the EU-Israel Association Agreement', *Middle East International*, 544 (21 Feb. 1997), 17–18.

43. For arguments questioning the impact of peace on regional complementarity, see Hisham Awartani and Ephraim Klieman, 'Economic Interactions Among Participants in the Middle East Peace Process', *Middle East Journal*, 51/2 (Spring 1997); and Steven Yetiv, 'Peace Interdependence and the Middle East', *Political Studies Quarterly* (Spring 1997).

44. Ziya Oniş, 'Turkey in the Post-Cold War Era: In Search of Identity', *Middle East Journal*, 49/1 (Winter 1995), 61; and Philip Robins, 'Between Sentiment and Self-Interest: Turkey's Policy toward Azerbaijan and the Central Asian States', *Middle East Journal*, 47/4 (Autumn 1993), 610.

45. Ramazani, 'Iran's Foreign Policy', 403.

46. This is the argument of Oniş, 'Turkey', 54.

47. Robins, 'Between Sentiment and Self-Interest', 610.

48. Ramazani, 'Iran's Foreign Policy', 393.

49. This is the argument of Adam Tarock, 'Iran and Russia in "Strategic Alliance" ', *Third World Quarterly*, 18/2 (1997), 220–1.

50. The argument here runs counter to that e.g. of Robert Jervis, who predicts more conflict, rather than less, in the Third World after the end of the cold war. 'The Future of World Politics: Will It Resemble the Past?', *International Security*, 16/3 (Winter 1991/92), 58–61. The possibility of joint Arab and Israeli membership in regional bodies was approved in the draft charter proposed by the League of Arab States in early 1996. Details in *al-Hayat* (4 Feb. 1996).

51. Point made in Charles Tripp, 'Regional Organizations in the Middle East', in Louise Fawcett and Andrew Hurrell (eds.), *Regionalism in World Politics: Regional Organization and International Order* (Oxford: Oxford University Press, 1995), 306.

52. To borrow a phrase from Richard Ned Lebow, 'The Long Peace, the End of the Cold War, and the Failure of Realism', in Richard Ned Lebow and Thomas Risse-Kappen (eds.), *International Relations Theory and the End of the Cold War* (New York: Columbia University Press, 1995), 49.

53. A second attempt to pass a modified charter also failed. Details in *al-Hayat* (4 Feb. 1996).

54. Tripp, 'Regional Organizations in the Arab Middle East', 285–6.

55. Claire Spencer, 'The Mahgreb in the 1990's' (London: Brassey's for the 1155. Adelphi paper no 274, 1993), 47.

56. On Egyptian competition with Iraq, Ann Mosley Lesch, 'Contrasting Reactions to the Persian Gulf Crisis: Egypt, Syria, Jordan, and the Palestinians', *Middle East Journal*, 45/1 (Winter 1991), 34–5.

57. On Arab fears of Israeli economic domination, Eliyahu Kanovsky, *The Middle East Economies: The Impact of Domestic and International Politics*, Ramat Gan: BESA, Security and Policy Studies no. 31 (1997), 26. On Egyptian distrust of Israel, Fawaz Gerges, 'Egyptian-Israeli Relations Turn Sour', *Foreign Affairs* (May/June 1995), 71. On Saudi opposition to forming new regional agencies with Israel, e.g. statement by Saudi minister of trade dismissing the US-sponsored proposal for a Regional Cooperation and Development Bank for the Middle East and North Africa, *al-Hayat* (30 Oct. 1995).

58. Examples of Egyptian concerns regarding possible Israeli domination in regional organizations and on the NPT issue are Taha'Abd-al-Halim, *The Middle East Market in the Equation of Arab-Israeli Peace* (Arab.), Strategic Papers 33 (Cairo: al-Ahram Centre for Political and Strategic Studies, 1995); and Mahmoud Karem, *The 1995 NPT Review and Extension Conference: A Third World Perspective*, a paper submitted to Institut Français des Relations Internationals, June 1995.

59. For a definition of accommodational, international, and restructural strategies, Michael Barnett, 'High Politics is Low Politics: The Domestic and Systemic Sources of Israeli Security policy, 1967–1977', *World Politics*, 42/4 (July 1990), 452–3.

60. Ishac Diwan and Lyn Squire, 'Private Assets and Public Debts: External Finance in a Peaceful Middle East', *Middle East Journal*, 49/1 (Winter 1995), 69.

61. Ibid. 70.

62. Report issued by the Arab Investment Corporation, based on UNCTAD statistics, cited in *al-Hayat* (7 Apr. 1997).

63. The developing world is taken here to include the newly industrializing countries and emerging markets. Statistics from UNCTAD report cited in *al-Hayat* (16 Dec. 1995). Other sources estimate that the Middle East attracts only 2% of total

flows of private equity, bond, and fdi to the developing countries. Erian, 'Middle East Economies', 141.

64. Noted e.g. by Eberhard Kienle, 'Syria, the Kuwait War, and the New World Order', in Tareq Y. Ismael and Jacqueline S. Ismael (eds.), *The Gulf War and the New World Order: International Relations of the Middle East* (Gainesville Fla.: University of Florida Press, 1994), 394. Higher estimate cited by the president of the Union of Arab Exchanges and Egyptian Banks, in *al-Hayat* (27 June 1995).

65. Jamal al-Saghir, 'Privatization of Infrastructure Facilities in the Middle East and North Africa Region' (Arab.), *al-Hayat* (4 June 1997).

66. Detail on stock market capitalization in Henry Azzam, 'Implications of Economic Reforms and Structural Adjustment in the Arab States' (Arab.), *al-Hayat* (7 May 1997).

67. Kiren Aziz Chaudhry, 'Economic Liberalization in Oil-Exporting Countries: Iraq and Saudi Arabia', in Iliya Harik and Denis J. Sullivan (eds.), *Privatization and Liberalization in the Middle East* (Bloomington and Indiana: Indiana University Press, 1992), 157.

68. Iliya Harik, 'Privatization and Development in Tunisia', in Harik and Sullivan, *Privatization and Liberalization*, 215.

69. Bill and Springborg, *Politics*, 429.

70. On these and other aspects of private-public dynamics, John Waterbury, *Exposed to Innumerable Delusions: Public Enterprise and State Power in Egypt, India, Mexico, and Turkey* (Cambridge: Cambridge University Press, 1993), 212–34.

71. On Egyptian *infitah*, Bill and Springborg, *Politics*, 428.

72. Wilson, 'Economic Relations of the Middle East', 238.

73. On this phenomenon in North Africa, Dirk Vandewalle, 'Breaking with Socialism: Economic Liberalization in Algeria', in Harik and Sullivan, *Privatization and Liberalization*, 204; and C. Spencer, Mahgreb 47.

74. For example in Syria. Volker Perthes, 'The Syrian Economy in the 1980s', *Middle East Journal*, 46/1 (Winter 1992), 49–50.

75. Iliya Harik, 'Privatization: The Issue, the Prospects, and the Fears', in Harik and Sullivan, *Privatization and Liberalization*, 13.

76. Alan Richards, 'Economic Imperatives and Political Systems', *Middle East Journal*, 47/2 (Spring 1993), 223–5.

77. Lawson, 'Domestic Transformations', 51–2.

78. Raymond Hinnebusch, 'Asad's Syria and the New World Order', *Middle East Policy*, 2/1 (1993), 10.

79. Lawson, 'Divergent Modes of Economic Liberalization', 129.

80. On triangle, Vandewalle, 'Breaking with Socialism', 200.

81. Lawson, 'Domestic Transformations', 56–8.

82. Emma Murphy, 'Structural Inhibitions to Economic Liberalization in Israel', *Middle East Journal*, 48/1 (Winter 1994), 74.

83. Onis, 'Turkey in the Post-Cold War Era', 64–5.

84. Raymond Hinnebusch, 'The Politics of Economic Reform in Egypt', *Third World Quarterly*, 14/1 (1993), 166–7.

85. Bill and Springborg, *Politics*, 450; and Cassandra, 'The Impending Crisis in Egypt', *Middle East Journal*, 49/1 (Winter 1995), 23.

86. The revival of the hopes of 'aid addicts' by the Arab–Israeli peace process is noted in Brand, *Jordan's Inter-Arab Relations*, 3.

87. Noted e.g. in relation to Jordan by Laurie Brand, 'Economic and Political Liberalization in a Rentier Economy: The Case of the Hashemite Kingdom of Jordan', in Harik and Sullivan, *Privatization and Liberalization*, 171. And in relation to Syria (and Egypt) by Steven Heydeman, 'Taxation without Representation: Authoritarianism and Economic Liberalization in Syria', in Ellis Goldberg, Resat Kasaba, and Joel Migdal (eds.), *Rules and Rights in the Middle East: Democracy, Law, and Society* (Seattle and London: University of Washington Press, 1993), 98.

88. Gary Sick, 'The Coming Crisis in the Persian Gulf', *Washington Quarterly* (Spring 1988), 204–5.

89. Denis J. Sullivan, 'Extra-State Actors and Privatization in Egypt', in Harik and Sullivan, *Privatization and Liberalization*, 28–9.

90. As in the case of Iraq, Chaudhry, 'Economic Liberalization in Oil-Exporting Countries', 158.

91. Hinnebusch, 'Politics of Economic Reform', 164.

92. Jahangir Amuzegar, 'The Iranian Economy before and after the Revolution', *Middle East Journal*, 46/3 (Summer 1992), 425.

93. Waterbury, *Exposed to Innumerable Delusions*, 28–9.

94. Vandewalle, 'Breaking with Socialism', 205–6. Build-Own-Operate-Transfer (BOOT) involves arrangements in which foreign companies construct major enterprises and operate them commercially as privately owned ventures for an agreed period, after which ownership is transferred to the state.

95. Harik, 'Privatization and Development', 215 and 221.

96. Dirk Vandewalle, 'Qadhafi's "*Perestroika*": Economic and Political Liberalization in Libya', *Middle East Journal*, 45/2 (Spring 1991), 225.

97. Statistics from Philippe Fargues, 'Demographic Explosion or Social Upheaval?', in Ghassan Salamé (ed.), *Democracy without Democrats? The Renewal of Politics in the Muslim World* (London: I. B. Tauris, 1994), 161.

98. An example of growing interest in regional ties is investment banking, *The Economist* (7 June 1997).

99. Richards, 'Economic Imperatives', 221.

100. Sick, 'The Coming Crisis', 203.

101. Jan Aart Scholte, 'Global Capitalism and the State', *International Affairs*, 73/3 (July 1997), 431–2.

102. Abdelbaki Hermassi, 'Socio-Economic Change and Political Implications: The Maghreb', in Salamé, *Democracy without Democrats*, p. 240.

103. On bifurcation and its possible consequences, Lawson, 'Domestic Transformations', 59–60.

104. C. H. Moore, 'Money and Power: The Dilemma of the Egyptian Infitah', *Middle East Journal*, 40/4 (Autumn 1986), 637.

105. Adrian Leftwich, 'Governance, Democracy and Development in the Third World', *Third World Quarterly*, 14/3 (1993), 607.

106. Chaudhry, 'Economic Liberalization in Oil-Exporting Countries', 163.

107. John L. Esposito and James P. Piscatori, 'Democratization and Islam', *Middle East Journal*, 45/3 (Summer 1991), 427 and 440.

108. On challenge to patriarchy, Fargues, 'Demographic Explosion', 175 and 177.

109. Salamé, 'Introduction: Where are the Democrats?', in Salamé, *Democracy without Democrats*, 14.

110. Point made in Vandewalle, 'Breaking with Socialism', 204.
111. Augustus Richard Norton, 'The Future of Civil Society in the Middle East', *Middle East Journal*, 47/2 (Spring 1993), 211.
112. On ethos, Karawan, 'Arab Dilemmas', 439.
113. James Mayall, 'Nationalism and International Security after the Cold War', *Survival* (Spring 1992), 30–1.
114. Cassandra, 'The Impending Crisis in Egypt', 17. On closure, Roger Owen, 'Socio-Economic Change and Political Liberalization: The Case of Egypt', in Salamé, *Democracy without Democrats*, 194–5.
115. Hermassi, 'Socio-Economic Change', 241; and Hinnebusch, 'Politics of Reform in Egypt', 168.
116. John Waterbury, 'Democracy without Democrats?: The Potential for Political Liberalization in the Middle East', in Salamé, *Democracy without Democrats*, 23 and 27; and Raymond Hinnebusch, 'State and Civil Society in Syria', *Middle East Journal*, 47/2 (Spring 1993), 253.
117. Luciani, 'The Oil Rent, the Fiscal Crisis of the State and Democratization', in Salamé, *Democracy without Democrats*, 135.
118. Lisa Anderson, cited in Waterbury, 'Democracy without Democrats?', 28.
119. Jill Crystal, *Oil and Politics in the Gulf: Rulers and Merchants in Kuwait and Qatar* (Cambridge: Cambridge University Press, 1990), 47–8.
120. Eberhard Kienle, 'More Than a Response to Islamism: The Political Deliberalization of Egypt in the 1990s', *Middle East Journal*, 52/2 (Spring 1998), 221.
121. Simon Bromley, *Rethinking Middle East Politics* (Cambridge: Polity Press, 1994), 165.
122. Hinnebusch, 'State and Civil Society in Syria', 254; and idem, 'Asad's Syria', 12–14.
123. Salamé, 'Introduction', 2.
124. Hinnebusch, 'State and Civil Society in Syria', 251.
125. Norton, 'The Future of Civil Society in the Middle East', 211 and 214–15. Also Peter Evans, 'The Eclipse of the State? Reflections on Stateness in an Era of Globalization', *World Politics*, 50 (Oct. 1997), 79.
126. Salamé, 'Introduction', 15.
127. Mehran Kamrava, 'Political Culture and a New Definition of the Third World', *Third World Quarterly*, 16/4 (Dec. 1995).
128. Hermassi, 'Socio-Economic Change', 239.
129. Cassandra, 'The Impending Crisis in Egypt', 16.
130. Salamé, 'Introduction', 10.
131. Olivier Roy, 'Patronage and Solidarity Groups: Survival or Reformation?', in Salamé, *Democracy without Democrats*, 274.
132. See e.g. Simon Bromley and Ray Bush, 'Ajustment in Egypt? The Political Economy of Reform', *Review of African Political Economy*, 60 (1994), 210.
133. Hermassi, 'Socio-Economic Change', 241; and Hinnebusch, 'Asad's Syria', 14.
134. Michael Hudson, 'After the Gulf War: Prospects for Democratization in the Arab World', *Middle East Journal*, 45/3 (Summer 1991), 424–5; and Bill and Springborg, *Politics*, 437.
135. The notion of low-intensity democracy is discussed in Barry Gills and Joel Rocamora, 'Low Intensity Democracy', *Third World Quarterly*, 13/3 (1992).

Also referred to as 'two-track politics' in Atul Kohli, 'Democracy Amid Economic Orthodoxy: Trends in Developing Countries', *Third World Quarterly*, 14/4 (Nov. 1993), 683. On reform being put on hold, Hinnebusch, 'Politics of Economic Reform in Egypt', 169.

136. Vandewalle, 'Breaking with Socialism', 202; and Hinnebusch, 'Politics of Economic Reform in Egypt', 170.

137. Larbi Sadiki, 'Towards Arab Liberal Governance: from the Democracy of Bread to the Democracy of the Vote', *Third World Quarterly*, 18/1 (1997).

138. Discussed in Yezid Sayigh, *Confronting the 1990s: Security in the Developing Countries*, Adelphi Papers no. 251 (London: Brassey's for the International Institute of Strategic Studies, 1990); and Mayall, 'Nationalism and International Security', 30–1.

139. On power as key asset, Nelson Kasfir, 'Popular Sovereignty and Popular Participation: Mixed Constitutional Democracy in the Third World', *Third World Quarterly*, 13/4 (1992), 596.

140. Gianfranco Poggi, *The State: Its Nature, Development and Prospects* (Cambridge: Polity Press, 1990), 100–1.

141. Argument adapted from Leftwich, 'Governance, Democracy and Development', 615.

142. Hinnebusch, 'Asad's Syria', 14.

143. Quote from John Brohman, 'Economism and Critical Silences in Development Studies: A Theoretical Critique of Neoliberalism', *Third World Quarterly*, 16/2 (June 1995), 301.

144. L. Carl Brown, *International Politics and the Middle East: Old Rules, Dangerous Game* (London: I. B. Tauris, 1984), 4. On theoretical contraposition, Fred Halliday, 'The Middle East and the Great Powers', in Yezid Sayigh and Avi Shlaim (eds.), *The Cold War and the Middle East* (Oxford: Clarendon Press, 1997), 19.

145. Scholte, *International Relations*, 31 and 117.

146. Ian Clark, *Globalization and Fragmentation: International Relations in the Twentieth Century* (Oxford: Oxford University Press, 1997), 31.

CHAPTER 10

1. See e.g. Srinivas R. Melkote and Allen H. Merriam, 'The Third World: Definitions and New Perspectives on Development', in Alfonso Gonzalez and Jim Norwine (eds.), *The New Third World* (Westview: Oxford, 1998), 9–12.

2. Willy Brandt (ed.), *North-South: A Programme for Survival* (London: Pan Books, 1980), 30–2.

3. For the two sides of the globalization debate, see Max Singer and Aaron Wildavsky, *The Real World Order: Zones of Peace/Zones of Turmoil* (Chatham, NJ: Chatham House Publishers, 1993); Stephan Haggard, *Developing Nations and the Politics of Global Integration* (Washington: Brookings, 1995); and Andrew Hurrell and Ngaire Woods, 'Globalization and Inequality', *Millennium*, 24/3 (1995), 447–70.

4. Ian Clark, *Globalization and Fragmentation* (Cambridge: Cambridge University Press, 1997), 144.

5. See Noam Chomsky, 'A View from Below', in Michael Hogan (ed.), *The End of the Cold War* (Cambridge: Cambridge University Press, 1992), 137–50.
6. Juan J. Linz and Alfred Stepan, *Problems of Democratic Transition and Consolidation* (London: Johns Hopkins University Press, 1996), 7.
7. For the idea of 'contagion', see Laurence Whitehead, 'Three International Dimensions of Democratization', in Laurence Whitehead (ed.), *The International Dimensions of Democratization: Europe and the Americas* (Oxford: Oxford University Press, 1996), 5–8.
8. See e.g. Michael Freeman, 'Human Rights, Democracy and "Asian Values"', *Pacific Review*, 9/3 (1996); Ghassan Salamé, 'Introduction: Where are the Democrats?', in Ghassan Salamé (ed.), *Democracy Without Democrats* (London: I. B. Tauris, 1994), 1–9.
9. Norberto Bobbio, *Liberalism and Democracy* (London: Verso, 1990), 1.
10. Ibid.
11. Fareed Zakaria, 'The Rise of Illiberal Democracy', *Foreign Affairs* (Nov./Dec. 1997), 22–43.
12. For a discussion of the link between modernization theory and the present neo-liberal agenda, see Anna K. Dickson, *Development and International Relations* (Oxford: Polity Press, 1997), 34–6 and 141–2. On the politics and effects of stabilization and adjustment, see Devesh Kapur, John Lewis, and Richard Webb, *The World Bank: It's First Half Century* (Washington: Brookings, 1997).
13. See Albert Berry and Frances Stewart, 'Globalization, Liberalization and Inequality: Expectations and Experience', in Andrew Hurrell and Ngaire Woods (eds.), *Inequality, Globalization and World Politics* (Oxford: Oxford University Press, 1999).
14. John A. Hall and G. John Ikenberry, *The State* (Milton Keynes, Open University Press, 1989), 69–74.
15. Alice H. Amsden, 'The State and Taiwan's Economic Development' in Peter R. Evans *et al.*, *Bringing the State Back In* (Cambridge: Cambridge University Press, 1985), 78.
16. For one critique see Paul Cammack, *Capitalism and Democracy in the Third World: The Doctrine for Political Development* (London: Leicester University Press, 1997).
17. For a comprehensive treatment of post-cold war security issues and how they related to Third World countries, see Mohammed Ayoob, *The Third World Security Predicament* (London: Lynne Rienner Publishers, 1995), esp. chs. 7 and 8, pp. 139–88.
18. For the notion of the quasi-state, see Robert Jackson, *Quasi States: Sovereignty, International Relations and the Third World* (Cambridge: Cambridge University Press, 1990); on failed states and statelessness see respectively, J. G. Gross, 'Failed States in the New World Order', *Third World Quarterly*, 17/3 (1996), 455–7; Christopher Clapham, *Africa and the International System: The Politics of State Survival* (Cambridge: Cambridge University Press, 1996), 274.
19. Singer and Wildavsky, *The Real World Order*.
20. See Louise Fawcett 'Regionalism in Historical Perspective', in Louise Fawcett and Andrew Hurrell (eds.), *Regionalism in World Politics* (Oxford: Oxford University Press, 1995), 9–36.

21. See e.g. Andrew Hurrell, 'An Emerging Security Community in South America?', in Emanuel Adler and Michael Barnett (eds.), *Governing Anarchy: Security Communities in Theory and History and Comparison* (Cambridge: Cambridge University Press, 1998).

22. See J. L. Gaddis, *The United States and the End of the Cold War* (Oxford: Oxford University Press, 1992) and Clark, *Globalization and Fragmentation*.

23. Jan Aart Scholte, 'Global Capitalism and the State', *International Affairs*, 73/3 (1997), 427–52.

24. See e.g. Henry Jacoby *et al.*, 'Kyoto's Unfinished Business', *Foreign Affairs* (July/Aug. 1998), 54–66.

25. Stephen Van Evera, 'Why Europe Matters, Why the Third World Doesn't: American Grand Strategy After the Cold War', *The Journal of Strategic Studies*, 13/2 (1990), 1–59.

26. M. S. Gorbachev, *Perestroika: New Thinking for Our Country and the World* (London: Collings, 1987), 194–5.

27. See Stephen R. David, 'Why the Third World Still Matters', *International Security*, 17/3 (Winter 1992/3), 127–59.

28. See Mohammed Ayoob, 'Subaltern Realism: International Relations Theory Meets the Third World', in Stephanie G. Neuman, *International Relations Theory and the Third World* (London: Macmillan, 1998), 31–54.

29. This argument is developed by Stephanie G. Neuman, 'International Relations Theory and the Third World: An Oxymoron?', in Neuman, *International Relations Theory*, 1–29.

30. See Barry Gills and George Philip, 'Towards a Convergence in Development Policy: Challenging the Washington Consensus and Restoring the Historicity of Divergent Development Trajectories', *Third World Quarterly*, 17/4 (1996), 585–91.

31. See John Louis Gaddis, 'International Relations Theory and the End of the Cold War', *International Security*, 17/3 (Winter 1992/3), 5–58.

INDEX

Note: **Emboldened** numbers indicate chapters